Living Like the Future Matters

The Evolution of a Soil to Soul Entrepreneur

DONNA MALTZ
www.DonnaMaltz.com

"**Full of relatable life and business lessons,** Donna reminds us we are more powerful than we think. She shows us how we can change our world by changing our perception of business and wealth, and turn complacency into compassion and action."

~ Dr. Alvita Soleil, OMD., LAc., NCCAOM

I dedicate this book to the Wonders of Nature.
To my dear husband, Kevin, our gracious son, Jazz,
my courageous granddaughter Freya, and precious mother earth.

Cover Illustration Copyright © 2019 Artist: Kirsten English
Front cover photo: Kevin Maltz
Back cover photo: Lisa Haug
All Nature Photography by Donna Maltz (unless she is in the photo)
Soil to Soul Illustration © 2015 Amanda Brannon
Editors: James Mattie, Evan Boyer, Landry Fuller, Julie Clayton,
Sharon Reese, Carla Orellana, Meg Schadee
Printed in the United States of America: First Printing, 2020
Soil to Soul Solutions Productions

Proceeds from this book will go toward making the
world a better place for future generations.

Contents

Foreword

Dr. Alvita Soleil OMD., LAc., NCCAOM
Founder of Aloha Health Clinic and Hawaii Healing Arts Academy

Many of us are familiar with the Native American saying, "Heal yourself and heal Mother Earth and all our relations." Our ancestors had a deep understanding of the Earth and our relationship to it that modern science is only now just able to validate. For centuries, many teachers have been saying that one of our greatest services to humanity is the development of our own consciousness. In order to transform our self, our life, to change what we do, we first need to change the way we think, and release the mental beliefs that have grown outdated to allow new positive beliefs to emerge. *Living Like the Future Matters* is achieving this goal.

In writing this book Donna Maltz has one purpose in mind; to empower us in making conscious choices that lead to a thriving life, success and love at the end of the rainbow. She brings a liberating and empowering sense of encouragement in owning the power of who we are and to live like the future matters. She invites us to rethink our relationship to our body, to the world, and the way we have been conditioned to solve fundamental issues.

If we truly value our planet, we need to look closely at our personal lifestyle choices and our public policies. We need to realign with nature and start caring for our bodies and souls with the same divine love that Mother Earth offers us. When we realize that we are not separate from the environmental issues, from the Earth, from each other, and invariably from ourselves, we may then acknowledge that our ailing planetary consciousness is a reflection of our ailing humanity. Mother Earth is the sustaining womb for the evolution of humanity. Caring for her is a necessity for our enfolding journey.

Donna, "Mama Donna" for some, is the real deal. She deeply cares for the Earth and for life-kind. Charged with a passion for life, her determination and wisdom inspires us toward taking the steps toward a full co-creative participation in building a healthier body and a better world. She shares an honest and factual journey of her evolution, weaving her struggle with dyslexia, her compulsive work and a food addiction as well as her great business ventures. With concrete research, a good blend of spirituality, and creative "soulutions," she inspires us to grasp the inseparability between soul, spirit, matter and nature.

Living Like the Future Matters is a virtual treasure map that offers both practical and inspirational resources from an innovative, entrepreneurial, and compassionate caring heart. I encourage you to read this valuable book.

Welcome Beautiful Souls

Since the Ice Age, nothing has changed the world faster than
business. It is ethical businesses, led by morally courageous people,
that can rapidly transform our world for the better.

Aloha,

My name is Donna Maltz, but many know me as Mama Donna. I will
be 62 when this book is published, and I live by these words, "Why retire
when I can inspire."

Throughout my career as a Soil to Soul Entrepreneur, I've established many
successful Eco-businesses. Now, a Business and Life Mentor, I enjoy helping
others define what success means to them and help them to succeed. For
me, Nature photography and writing have become enlightening mediums to
serve humanity and the world. But best of all, I'm a mother, a grandmother,
and a happy wife.

Inside this memoir of sorts, you will discover relatable life and business lessons and learn how everything relates to Nature. I invite you to seek a better world for yourself, for humanity, and our precious Mother Earth. I write to inspire us to be better humans.

Living in harmony with Nature, we help make our world a better place now, and for future generations.

The revelation that turned me on to write this book came in the winter of 2002 while swimming in the deep blue sea. I was in recovery mode after several years of self-inflicted emotional abuse. It was a hot winter's day in Hawaii. The calm, clear, Pacific Ocean spread out before me, adding to the clarity of my thoughts and easing my aching body. How had things gotten so screwed up in my life and the world? And what I was going to do about it? My emotions were raw, so I opened myself to receive guidance. Nature spoke to me, and I listened. From that day forward, my life evolved into something more beautiful than I could ever have imagined.

For me, this book was not only a channel through which to heal myself but also an opportunity to help awaken people of all generations to the value of living like the future matters. I offer you a different perspective on life, wealth, and business, as well as guidance to help you succeed, all while taking part in healing the world. You are encouraged to expand upon your purposeful why in life, to branch out and reach your full potential. Avoid the pitfalls and landmines that I endured on my journey. Energy vampires and inner demons suck!

If you're stuck in old patterns, you may decide to "compost" unfulfilling old scripts and learn to nourish what serves you. You might get pissed off by some facts in this book and then, hopefully, be inspired to hear about the solutions, or more accurately, the Soul-utions. Soulutions go beyond the simple Band Aid-nature of solutions by approaching issues soulfully and with love.

At the time of writing this book, the coronavirus, COVID-19, hadn't infected the world, but we were infected with other kinds of viruses and didn't realize it. Corporate greed, political agendas, environmental sabotage and other deadly virus have been infecting the world for years. The deadly COVID-19 finally showed up to get our attention. It is an atrocity that so many people had to die for us to wake up. Let's hope their sacrifice was not in vain.

This book is for you if:

• You are ready to embrace the wisdom of Nature, learn the truth about the unsustainable "American Dream," and understand how ethical businesses can change our world.

• If you are an aspiring Eco-Entrepreneur, you'll learn what it takes to start a successful Eco-business while staying healthy and truthful to your values.

• If you have Eco-business experience, I encourage you to mentor up-and-coming entrepreneurs. Why retire when you can inspire?

• For anyone else who is yearning to live like the future matters, this book will hearten your journey.

Before I go any further, let me answer the main question that budding Eco-Entrepreneurs ask: "Can I make money while being ecologically conscious?" My story says YES, you can.

My journey began back in the radical 60s and 70s. I was born and raised as a Jewish American Princess in a suburban middle-class town in New Jersey, sheltered from the rest of the world. There were 67 million baby boomers born during these wonder years. The ethos of the time shaped our attitudes toward consumption and entitlement. My alternative college years changed my perspective on life, and I rebelled from my past. I took my degree as a sign of freedom and evolved into an Eco-Bohemian.

In 1980, I started a small organic farm and a bakery business in Olympia, Washington. In 1982, a road trip to Alaska gave me the pioneering idea to start the first natural foods bakery in the state. In 1984, surrounded by the beauty of Alaska, I hired the man who would become my husband, my partner, my soulmate, and the father of our terrific Eco-Bohemian son. I then started a successful national food brand, AH!LASKA, and launched the first organic hot cocoa and chocolate syrup in the nation. Numerous other small businesses followed. Who would have thought this would be my destiny or was even possible for a former Jewish American Princess — a suburban babe?

Along with all the highs of being a Soil to Soul Entrepreneur, there was a crushing low in 2001. I fell into the trap of negativity and became a compulsive workaholic and foodaholic: Coming face to face with addiction. At 5-feet 2¾ inches and 205 pounds, the physical and mental pain left me utterly defeated, and I got lost in a sea of doubt. The moral agony was distasteful!

Why had I let the negative sides of life eat away the best of me? My defeat came because I did not have the tools to cope with difficult times. My good intentions drowned as I strived to help repair the state of affairs in our rapidly changing world. It took conviction and determination to recover and regenerate. Recovery came slowly with more hurdles and lessons, but it made me a better person.

Now, I am the happiest person I know. I live on the beautiful Big Island of Hawaii with my wonderful husband and a bevy of darling animals. Our open-hearted community feels like family. Here, I can truly focus on being a lover of Nature and life. Most of my words are inspired and written while immersed in the multiple facets of Nature's genius. I am awakened when connected to the sacred Hawaiian shorelines, where I spend most of my time these days, or in Alaska, influenced by its rugged, raw, and rare beauty.

Like a tree that buds, blooms, fruits, and reseeds, our lives evolve with deep roots and complexities. From head to toe, treetop to roots, the whole of our being should be taken into consideration. What goes on beneath the soil's surface — or internally, in our souls — if undervalued, gets depleted. Future generations suffer from malnourished consequences.

It took me an immense amount of time to do the research, rehash my past, and learn to write. The truth is, like many other successful entrepreneurs, I am dyslexic and have a touch of ADD. I approach things differently, with an out-of-the-box mindset. I have always done my best to avoid getting boxed into a stifling social construct. To go out on a limb is my style. It can, at times, be challenging to focus and stay on task. Maybe that's why it took me so many years to finish this book! Still, over my career, I have managed to start and run all these successful businesses and live a prosperous life. I have done this by having an open mind and digging deep within for answers. Early on in life, a wise teacher made a profound statement that has stuck with me: "Living on the surface is shallow."

You see, I sense many humans have become narrow-minded, i.e., they are mono-thinkers. Republican or Democrat, black or white; where have all the shades gone? Society is marginalized when it is homogenized; uniformity siphons human potential. Mono-thinking diminishes the value of diversity. A diversified forest is much healthier than a Christmas tree farm. Everything gets compromised when we do not interconnect the cause and effect of our actions: Our integrity, our health, the environment, political, and educational systems. A business book that does not address all these issues is not a book worth my time to read or write.

In my blessed life, I've witnessed massive atrocities and many wonders. I got tired of hearing people tell me that this is the worst time in history. I dug deeper for answers in history and interviewed people born in the Great Depression and World War II. Some had lived through the Holocaust and saw lynchings by the Ku Klux Klan. I asked these elders lots of questions:

"Is this the worst time in history?" "How did we get to this place?" "What do you think we need to do?" The answers I got were compelling and reinforced my desire to finish this book so that I might share them with you.

I get it — living in a sexist, capitalist, patriarchal, and white-supremacist society is hard to digest. We live in a misled world driven by a fossil fuel economy, and one that is saturated with fillers, fake news, and artificial "intelligence." Many people are starving while some live in a synthetic bubble of opulence. That's a lot to accept without getting angry and thinking that this is the worst time in history. It's easy to get seduced by the unsustainable way of life birthed from colonialism. The idea of the American Dream convinced many people to adopt an attitude of entitlement and achieving financial success at any cost. Meanwhile, others settled for rejection and deprivation and accepted the cruel reality of this unattainable dream. Neither of these attitudes offers the Soulutions we need.

As people get further divided into various social strata, tensions grow. The overwhelming influx of information and changes in uncertain times results in a web of chaos rather than a web of life. Many people end up addicted to something as they attempt to mask the pain of unfilled dreams. I get it! Negativity, 'poor me' victimization, and 'what the fuck am I doing with my life' attitudes are real. The challenges we face can blind and stifle us, making it difficult to see and act upon the opportunities.

The challenges made more sense once I observed how the human condition gets influenced by the times, then I came to terms with how the times changed me. I learned that an open-minded person could entertain a thought without judgment and that we also do not have to accept something that is not right.

Early in my life, I witnessed how business can be a powerful force for change; for better or worse, which motivated me to be an Eco-warrior businesswoman. Business plays an intricate part of everyday life. It is in our schools, our government, and our congregations. After all, it's your business what you do with your life; how you spend your money and time, and how you treat yourself and others, and how you walk on the Earth.

The Peacemaker taught us about the Seven Generations. He said, when you sit in council for the welfare of the people, you must not think of yourself or of your family, not even of your generation. He said, make your decisions on behalf of the seven generations coming, so that they may enjoy what you have today.

~ Oren Lyons (Seneca) Faithkeeper, Onondaga Nation

To elevate any society, we must reintegrate the natural web of life. With current events, the costs of living in harmony with Nature are explicit; the first necessary step is to imagine something better and to live like the future matters. We must make it our business to be part of implementing humanitarian and environmental Soulutions into our life and the way we do business. Just as our parents and grandparents dreamed of a better life, so must we—in harmony with the systems and cycles of Nature.

I encourage you to live a wholesome and prosperous life, embrace your hopes and dreams, and to share your wisdom to enrich and cultivate the life energy and the love-light in others. And also, to see the agony of despair as a powerful gift of life. Despair can feel enough like death to send us humbly into the arms of the love that heals us.

With all life's complexities, when we focus on the good, it will grow. Each of us can be part of the regenerative process to heal ourselves and our world. We have the power and choice to change. There is no reason we can't earn a living and be true to your values at the same time. When we are part of the Soulution and not the pollution, we are living like the future matters.

Love yields the highest return. It keeps us joyful, vibrant, and prosperous.

Success comes when we know:
who we are,
and what we love to do
and our purposeful 'why.'

The Soil to Soul Principles

I've cultivated these guiding principles throughout my life. They inspire me to live like the future matters and have provided the foundation for this book, my career, and my life. Together they form a general blueprint of values that can help regenerate people, and the planet itself.

Be Part of the Soulution: *With reverence, cultivate a life that prioritizes restoring the Earth and caring for one's self and others. Support endeavors that are focused on regenerative Soulutions. Be a mindful, active citizen — a soulful light in the world. Give more, take less. What we appreciate, appreciates.*

Health is Your Greatest Wealth: *A healthy body fosters a healthy mind, which lays the groundwork for a more vibrant world. Nourish everything, from the soil to your soul. Respect. Replenish. Rejuvenate.*

Live in Harmony with Nature: *The Earth is our home. Honor and integrate the wisdom of the systems and cycles of Nature into your life. Nature-based Soulutions hold the keys to humanity's most challenging problems. A restored connection to the Earth is essential for our survival.*

Know Your Truth: *Know who you are, and know what you love to do, with a purposeful why. Celebrate life from the depths of your soul and rejoice with others. Manifest your dreams and embody your highest potential. Love and accept yourself. What we focus on, grows.*

Mentors are Essential: *At any age, have mentors and mentor others. The benefits received from intergenerational support are priceless. Knowledge fertilizes the mind to think and create. Wisdom comes when we apply what we have learned. Be a mindful lifetime learner and teacher.*

The Past ~ History is No Mystery: *Reference the past to improve the future. Connect with your roots. Then, compost what does not serve you and nurture what does. Forgiveness allows you to live in the present and to look forward to the future.*

The Present ~ A Gift, Receive It in the Now: *Invest your time and energy into a purposeful passion. Cultivate love and compassion with gratitude. Gratitude changes our attitude. Time is our most valuable currency; spend it wisely.*

The Future ~ Live Like the Future Matters: *In shifting our focus from the good of mankind to the good of life-kind, we can create an evolving paradigm and improve the quality of life for all. Resilient, we can adapt to the unknown.*

Connection Is Sacred: *Support and take part in creating a vibrant community and local economy. Cultivate unity and reverence for all life in your community. United, we bring value, balance, and diversity to our world. Our sacred yet vulnerable web of life connects us all and we depend on it. Together, we can strive to live like the future matters.*

Get the Most from this Book

There are six Evolutions and 13 Cycles. I call them Cycles rather than chapters to honor the life Cycles of the trees in relationship to our own Cycles of life. I interweave stories with heartfelt wisdom, business nuggets, and the nine Soil to Soul Principles. Each Evolution encapsulates a period in my life.

At the end of each Evolution is a *Digging Deeper* section. Here you will find additional history and insights that impacted my life and the world. Perhaps you will relate. I'll also guide you toward Soulutionists and change-makers fighting for social and environmental justice. May these valuable resources spark your inner desires and guide you on your priceless path.

 You will see this icon when facts and ideas are mentioned to support the stories.

 You will see this icon to represent the relevant history.

 You will see this icon when there are Soulutions and relatable resources to the Cycle. You will also find more at the end of the book.

All the citations and sources referenced in this body of work can be found at the back of the book. They are organized by Cycle.

Here are some definitions I use throughout the book and in my life to give more clarity to the Soil to Soul Philosophy and Living Like The Future Matters.

→ **Soulution:** There are many ways to solve problems. When approached soulfully, with the intention to better the world for the long term, through understanding and love, it is a Soulution. We do not find Soulutions.

→ **Soulutionist:** Are people actively engaged in building a more harmonious society and living like the future matters. They adhere to the Soil to Soul Principles and are stewards of the Earth.

→ **Eco-Bohemian:** Are a cross between a naturalist, a transcendentalist, and a modern-day flower child. They are free-thinkers who work to regenerate humanity and the Earth. As a voice for Nature, they take into consideration everything from the soil to the soul to guide their choices and actions.

→ **Soil To Soul Entrepreneurs:** Are forward-thinking entrepreneurs who create businesses that are based on Soulutions. They earn a living while being true to their values and themselves. They do not measure success, wealth, or happiness by money or possessions.

→ **Aloha:** In Hawaii, we often say "Aloha" to one another in greeting or departure, and to express peace and love. As a relative newcomer to Hawaii, the spirit of this beautiful word warmed and welcomed me. A deeper meaning of Aloha: "Alo" means "sharing" and "in the present," and "ha" means "life energy" or "the breath of life."

The heart of this book is in the spirit of Aloha. May my journey take you on an adventure to further explore your inner truth and inspire you to branch out and root into your purpose. It offers guidelines to live in concert with the belief, "What's good for the Earth is good for us. We are connected from the soil to our souls."

Just like trees add more oxygen to the air, let's strive to add more positivity to this world! Remember, it's never too late to change; your dreams do not have an expiration date. There are as many ways to improve the world as there are people on Earth. Soulutions to the world's most challenging problems are already within our reach. We need only to greet them with wisdom, clarity, and Aloha, while we live like the future matters.

I bid you Aloha and welcome you to accompany me on my journey.

Big Love, Mama Donna

From our crowns to our roots,
heads to toes, over time we evolved
into ourselves, at liberty
to cultivate our visions.

EVOLUTION 1

The Beginning

A mother is always the beginning. She is how things begin.
- Amy Tan

The Principles that influenced my life in this Evolution:

- History is no mystery.
- Act as a citizen, not a consumer.
- Reference the past to improve the future.
- Nourish everything from the soil to your soul.
- Every action and choice has a cause and effect.
- Health is your greatest wealth, take care of yourself.
- Compost what does not serve you and nurture what does.

Seed to Sprout

Seeds of change are inevitable.

A seed is an embryonic plant enclosed in a protective outer covering — as we are in our mothers' wombs before we *sprout*. Like a seed, our environment shapes us. Vulnerable, we require maximum nurturing to root and to survive. We also need the proper ratio of light, temperature, oxygen, and water to germinate and transform into the next cycle of life. Our early development is formed by our genetic makeups, as well as the ways in which we are raised. How we evolve depends on our individual choices; it's your business.

My sprouting years took place in a nice Jewish family, post-WWII, in a suburb outside New York City. Optimism was high and development unstoppable. From fields to subdivisions, *The Flintstones* to *The Jetsons*, consumerism to excessive consumerism, need to greed, my starter years coincided with the blossoming of the American Dream. It seemed there was no end to the Earth's riches. Unbridled economic growth encouraged and accompanied this naïve mindset. There was little awareness of, or accountability for, humanity's mounting impact on the Earth and on our health.

Seeds of Change

Mother's milk can never be replaced;
the sweet taste and connection are second to none.

One of my first memories is waking to the sound of a hysterically screaming baby — my newborn brother. It was 1962, and I was five years old. It was late August, and still hot in the darkness of the wee morning hours. I was now the middle child. My bedroom, located close to the stairs, led down to our modern kitchen. Concerned and curious, I tiptoed down the stairs, and like a goose, wrapped my head around the doorway for a better view. There was my beautiful mother hovering over the stove, clad in the new pink bathrobe my father had bought for her to wear home from the hospital. I remember my mother's breasts looking big in that robe, and I remember the stress on her face as she tried to comfort my wailing baby brother. She was impatiently waiting for the water to heat his formula. After she pushed the artificial nipple into his mouth, he calmed down. Like a church mouse, I tiptoed back up to my room, flopped down on my bed, curled up in the fetal position, and wondered what my first day on this planet was like.

When I had my first child, I questioned why my mother hadn't breast fed me. Many of my friends and peers had the same question for their mothers. When I asked my mom why she had not breastfed me, she said that her doctors had told her that breast milk was too thin and unsuitable for feeding a baby, and that formula milk would provide the best nutrition. Besides, it was not socially acceptable to breastfeed. This pissed me off! What kind of solutions were artificial nipples and synthetic nourishment?

The World Health Organization has warned that "a lack of breast-feeding — and especially lack of exclusive breastfeeding during the first half-year of life — are important risk factors for infant and childhood morbidity and mortality."

Forgiving my mother was easy. Overlooking the corrupt system was not! How could an act as pure as breastfeeding your child be frowned upon, painted with shame, and replaced by a profit-making endeavor? I can't think of any action that takes us further away from living in harmony with Nature than disrespecting and belittling a mother's choice to breastfeed. Man's attempt to master Nature was on a dismal trajectory. The choice to breastfeed or bottle-feed continues to get muddled in a war between medical science and basic nutrition vs. corporate greed in our growing fast-food culture.

The overall popularity of infant formula skyrocketed in a social climate that viewed breastfeeding as "dirty" and "unclean." For many families, buying formula was a financial burden. This pure act reflected an impoverished economic status and deficient caregiving. Women who used such formulas were seen as superior because they could provide what was perceived as best for their children. What an outrage!

The Starter Years: Yearning to Belong

*A "starter," sometimes called "the mother," is a microbiological culture
used to assist the fermentation process in preparation of sourdough
bread and fermented beverages. A microbiological culture also
lives in the soil, in your gut, and metaphorically in your soul.*

On May 12, 1957, at New York Hospital, in the heart of Manhattan, I was born into the baby boomer generation. My mom, Bonnie Brown, married at eighteen. She gave birth to my older brother when she was twenty-one and had me at twenty-three. A few days after my birth, my parents brought me to their new suburban home right outside of Manhattan, in New Jersey, the Garden State.

My dad, Jerome Goodman, took advantage of the low-cost housing movement and the GI Bill and bought a house in the quaint town of Closter. In 1950 the average new home cost $8,450, and by 1959 was $12,400. This is about $88,000-$130,000, adjusted for inflation rates in 2019. It was cheaper to buy a house in the suburbs than to rent an apartment in the city! The suburbs were seen as a safer and more wholesome location in which to raise a family and offered a lower cost of living. The commute was just twenty minutes to Manhattan from our comfy home. Tract homes and larger, economy-built houses, with all the modern "necessities," became the preferred way of life. The city continued to bustle as the major point of entry to the "land of the free and the home of the brave." New York, New York, the Big Apple, the City that Never Sleeps, was a melting pot of multiple nationalities and cultures which bred following generations.

Car manufacturers got into the consumerism game and picked up on the trends by manufacturing vehicles that reflected the times. Cars, vans, and trucks were designed to bring out the personality and status of the driver. Since the price of a gallon of gasoline was around thirty cents, people could drive vehicles of many sizes, shapes, and colors cheaply.

As my dad prospered in his dental practice, he bought my mom a classy gold Cadillac and himself a sporty Buick, both gas-guzzling hogs. This meant adding another garage to house both cars. I missed our family station wagon. There was enough room for our bikes and the overflow of stuff. Everything including extra Tupperware, slot cars, train sets, skateboards, lava lamps, go-go boots, sports equipment, and cases of seltzer and soda bottles got stuffed inside of that garage! Superficial affluence created the belief that excessive comforts made us happier. Our desire for more stuff came with a need for more space to store it. Earth's precious resources turned into STUFF that started overflowing into storage units.

The storage unit business would become a multi-billion-dollar industry. SquareFoot.com states that nearly 10 percent of the population rents from one of the estimated 50,000 self-storage facilities. These units take up about 2.3 billion square feet of the Earth just to store stuff that many people forget about! The average annual cost for a self-storage unit is $1000 a year.

Act as a citizen, not a consumer.

The Unsettling Sound of the Bulldozer

I'd choose soiled and dirty over bruised and bloody, any day.

 Pine Hill Road in Closter, New Jersey, was where I lived until I was seventeen. During my early years, it was like living in the country, complete with a hardwood forest across the street where I played with my older brother and my friends. We would build elaborate forts from branches and cushion the floors with piles of leaves. We played hide-and-seek amidst the tall trees, coming home most days dirty from head to toe, with soiled clothes and shoes, tracking in trails of mud across plush carpets. I loved to explore the woods with the squirrels searching for acorns. I made whistles from the tops of the acorns while the squirrels collected nuts for the cold winter. My favorite critters of the woods were the majestic Red-headed Woodpeckers. I'd whistle to them as they pecked away.

My grandmother was fascinated by Nature, especially the birds. Although my grandparents lived most of their time in Manhattan, they also had a lake house in upstate New York. It was delightful to spend time in the pristine countryside, learning about the natural world from my kind grandparents. My grandfather spent much of his time in his wood shop building birdhouses while my grandmother fed and observed the birds.

Grandma loved to read to me, and I remember her quoting William Shakespeare, "One touch of nature makes the whole world kin." When I was in the woods, I got lost in my thoughts among Nature's rich web of life. Imaginary friends were okay, as was talking to myself and the squirrels — we were kin.

One spring morning, instead of waking to the songs of the birds, I awoke to the disturbing sounds of bulldozers. I watched, mournfully, as my entire wooded wonderland was clear-cut for development. Tears rolled down my cheeks, though I stifled my cries, so as not to appear wimpy around my older brother and my father. Within only a few weeks, the magical

7

beauty and fragrance of the enchanted forest were gone. The developers had destroyed the habitat that housed my animal friends, and provided me with the perfect playground, which fed my soul, from the topsoil to the treetops. The woodpeckers flew off to find new places to live. I missed them dearly.

The Food and Agriculture Organization of the United Nations informs us, "Deforestation is the second-leading cause of climate change - after the burning fossil fuels - and accounts for almost 20% of all greenhouse gas emissions."

Soon, larger houses appeared up and down the street where my forts once stood. Lawns replaced the forest floors. The scarred Earth was speckled with a variety of imported trees and an assortment of ornamental plants. As the years passed, and the houses filled up with families, new friends eased the loss of my forts and the forest. The asphalt streets became the new playground for my buddies and me to play soccer and spud, to ride skateboards and bikes in the summer, and to sled in the winter. Now I would come home bruised and bloody instead of soiled, dirty, and in touch with Nature!

When I was old enough to ride my Schwinn bike outside the neighborhood, I went in search of my beloved woods and woodpeckers. Each time I was successful in finding a pocket of Nature, its existence was short-lived. Each beautiful forest was quickly consumed by suburban sprawl. I would later come to understand that real progress is the sound of Nature, not the sound of the bulldozer.

Imagine this: In 1950, the average home was less than 1,000 square feet and the average family had more children than today. According to first quarter 2018 data from the Census Quarterly Starts and Completions by Purpose and Design and NAHB analysis, median single-family square feet floor area increased to 2,436 square feet.

The Garbage Men

Our society has been built on transforming Nature into trash.

The baby boomers created a demand for bigger houses. This shift in preferences required more building material and more stuff to fill each nook and cranny of the oversized dwellings. People were led to believe that these superfluous goods would "make their house a home." This also meant more maintenance to upkeep the houses, and more energy to heat and cool them. Consumption was in fashion, and everyone got caught up in the consumption cyclone, including my family and me. We judged the richness of our lives by our possessions. In doing so, an addicted society was sown and cultivated.

Access to unhealthy choices came easily. The modern lifestyle, based on quick fixes and instant gratification, created more trash. No one talked about where the garbage would end up when people tired of the latest fad. We never considered where all this stuff came from and where it would all go. We merely tossed things out and replaced them with something that was perceived as *better.* This mindset hasn't really changed, has it?

Once or twice a week, the *garbage men* came to pick up our trash. I remember them having a different skin color from mine, and often speaking a different language. They had to be strong to chuck the mounds of rubbish into the back of the gigantic, smelly garbage trucks. I wondered, "Where does the trash go?" It disappeared like magic, gobbled right up. Even in my young soul, I felt something was wrong with the way the monstrous garbage truck ate my trash and everyone else's.

There was no such thing as recycling. No one I knew was composting. We did not even have trash bags. Heaps of stinky trash, often maggot-infested, were mingled together and mindlessly thrown into a metal can, and placed curbside for the garbage men. It was not until the late 1960s that the Union Carbide Company developed the first plastic garbage bag for household use. They were called *Glad Bags*! We had plenty of waste, and so did all our neighbors. Dumps and landfills became big business. While our new suburban town prohibited the burning of trash, in many parts of America, rubbish was burned, producing toxic air pollution. Sadly, this practice still goes on in parts of our country and around the world.

It wasn't until I went to college that I began to learn just how trashy and unsustainable our lifestyle had become. Today, it is politically correct to call the garbage man a sanitation worker. But this *better* term for the worker creates more distance from the reality of the garbage we produce.

Each generation is known forever by the tracks it leaves behind.

Priceless resources of the Earth continue to get robbed and raped to make a lot of crap we don't need. Imagine this: If everyone around the globe consumed resources at the rate we do in the United States, we'd need five planets to keep up — this is a sure sign of addiction to a toxic lifestyle. According to an Environmental Protection Agency, the average American generated 4.4 pounds of trash every day. That means every person in the country, on average, produces over 1,600 pounds of garbage per year! Damn, that's a lot of shit! Nearly a ton!

The Tiny Home and Minimalist Mindset Movements are two examples of Soulutions. They are helping to build a more practical economy, based on a future that matters. Nature-based Soulutions can also be found in innovative eco-villages around the world.

Growing up with The Flintstones
and The Jetsons

Build, therefore, your own world.
~ Ralph Waldo Emerson

The 1960s marked the tail end of the baby boomers, and the steady rise of the self-contradictory, consumer-driven American Dream. I was a Jewish American Princess and I lived that dream. This was a time of rapid changes and conflicting ideologies. These were the *wonder years*. I loved to play hopscotch, jump rope, use my hula hoop, shoot hoops, and play ball with the boys when they let me. On rainy days, my favorite pastime was playing with jacks, pick-up sticks, Barrel of Monkeys, and playing card games such as Go Fish, Old Maid, and Crazy Eights. The milkman delivered fresh milk to our doorstep in returnable glass jugs. Many houses built in the early '50s, including ours, came with an underground bomb shelter. My brothers, neighborhood friends, and Yvonne (who you will learn about in the coming pages) helped me turn this *safe zone* into a clubhouse. We hosted make-believe Beatles concerts and played charades *down under*.

Let's face it: I grew up in the wonder years. Disneyland was the "happiest place on earth." My favorite ride was It's A Small World After All. The song and colorful moving figures, dressed in unique festive cultural fashion, offered me the naïve perspective of our imperfect world. As I got older, I wondered why life was not so wonderful for everyone.

Our phones were connected to the wall, and there were just three TV networks: ABC, NBC, and CBS. Birthdays, going to the circus, the mall, and when the carnival came to town were the primary forms of entertainment where dreams came true! This must sound like the Stone Age to the younger readers, but this era was short-lived as the Jetsons' lifestyle became more appealing to the masses and replaced the era of the Flintstones.

The Flintstones and The Jetsons, two favorite family TV shows, painted contrasting views. I watched them both. Like any curious child I tried to decipher what made more sense: The Flintstones, who lived in a world powered by prehistoric birds and dinosaurs, or the Jetsons, who lived in a futuristic utopia devoid of Nature. Elaborate robotic contraptions and whimsical inventions made life look fun and easy. One idea from the Jetsons that came true was the ability to fix meals within seconds! It was like the writers foresaw the microwave oven being popularized in everyone's household. Before we knew it, TV dinners got replaced by microwavable meals. Happily, we indulged.

Society shifted from a Stone Age way of thinking to a futuristic Jetsons mentality as the use of fossil fuels made inroads across every sector of life and business. The extremes were symbolic for that era's state of flux as a new social fabric replaced the stone-age slowness with new-age jettisoning; leaving the Flintstone's lifestyle in the dust. In both shows, the woman's place was in the home. TV programs like "Father Knows Best" glorified the male-dominant patriarchal construct.

The consumer-driven era had a new, ingenious delivery system. TV became the primary place to advertise. Savvy marketers made everything look fantastic! Colorful billboards and persuasive radio ads were inescapable. Propaganda played on our emotions, psychological needs, and desires. My friends and I bought into the hype. We believed that we needed all this stuff to be happy. Grocery and box stores grew in size and numbers, and the shelves filled up with cheap, inferior products, each likewise coated in plastic. As a result, many small family farms and businesses disappeared as the quality shrank — and like dinosaurs, became extinct.

We ate Flintstone vitamins and rode in trendy vehicles fueled by petrified plants, animals and dinosaurs. I witnessed almost everything made of wood, metal, copper, and steel transition to plastic. Leather seats in cars and couches turned to vinyl. Cotton clothing got replaced by unbreathable polyester. Yo-Yos once made from wood and sold in a wooden barrel, were made of plastic and wrapped in plastic. Products were less expensive but lacked in quality. Like everything, they manufactured these plastic products using fossil fuel energy: coal, gas, and oil. Plastic replacements and new synthetic creations grew as fast as they could pump the *black gold* from the deepest cavities of the Earth.

It's hard to believe that we once lived without cell phones, computers, and single-use plastic bottles and bags. Salesmen came to our front door selling the latest and *greatest* products: vacuum cleaners, kitchen gadgets, bibles and encyclopedias. We took for granted the conveniences of this modern society and accepted them as the norm.

Our instinct as children is to conform to societal standards and adopt our family values. Yet, this shallow way of life created inherent problems. It's ironic that a sign of freedom was to have more stuff, however, having all this stuff resulted in less freedom and less family time. Like most adults, my parents worked more hours to make more money to acquire and maintain all their stuff! This mindset made more dollars than sense. Something valuable got lost in the generational transition, but I didn't notice that until later in life. Understanding my family roots, I gained a greater acceptance of how scarcity and short-sightedness caused us to embrace the mirage of the *good life*. Hard-working parents wanted to show their children that the American Dream was attainable. This was love in action.

The growing sentiments of entitlement and the desire for material goods and wealth weakened our connection to Nature. It also weakened our connections with each other. Many of the new inventions and technology diluted the value of Nature and our human nature. Capital gains became more important than the proposed definition of the American Dream. I believe that if my parents' generation had known of the consequences, they would have made some different choices. In retrospect, it's understandable how we lost connection to the truth of what was meaningful. The fake reality was admittedly pleasing. The slick picture of a Jetsons-like future had transcended and dulled our basic instincts.

 *The American Dream was publicly defined in 1931 in James Truslow Adams' book,* The Epic of America. *Adams states, "It is not a dream of motor cars and high wages merely, but a dream of social order in which each man and each woman shall be able to attain to the fullest stature of which they are innately capable, and be recognized by others for what they are, regardless of the fortuitous circumstances of birth or position." Unfortunately, sometimes dreams turn into nightmares or move beyond the grasp of the hard-working middle class.*

This comment stated in 1953, attributed to a member of President Eisenhower's Council of Economic Advisers, sums up the mentality that changed the good intentions of a well-intended dream: "The economy's ultimate purpose is to produce more consumer goods."

History Is No Mystery

The American Dream is that dream of a land in which life should be better and richer and fuller for everyone, with opportunity for each according to ability or achievement.
~ James Truslow Adams

As I got older, I asked myself, "HOW did we get to where we are today and WHY?" Through extensive reflection and many years of research, I offer you a summary of some of the factors, as examples, to show how our current lifestyle emerged.

America has been steeped in capitalism since the takeover of colonialism. The primary goal of colonialism was to gain profits from the colonies at any cost. This led to the violation and genocide of the indigenous people and to slavery. The flow of money and greed defined our economy and also reshaped the priceless natural resources. The rights of Nature were dismantled.

It was the Progressive Era that ignited a period of social activism and political reform in the United States. This transformative time flourished from the 1890s to the 1920s and fostered rapid business growth. By the end of the nineteenth century, considerable changes occurred that shaped the country, enabling new industries to flourish.

This was when the fossil fuel industry and the banking systems capitalized on our government. The citizens were left in the dark with the lights on.

John D. Rockefeller, one of the most renowned and successful entrepreneurs, tapped into the oil we depend upon. He invested his capital in oil wells and refineries, which developed into the Standard Oil Company. Flora and fauna from millions of years ago, subjected to immense pressure and heat deep within the Earth's core, was the *black gold* that turned into a perceived savior for humanity. Rockefeller took his oil business to a whole other standard. Fossil fuels morphed the American Dream and sculpted our society. He wasn't alone in his business savvy and innovation. Cornelius Vanderbilt became king of the railroad industry, and Andrew Carnegie ruled the steel industry. These self-made men rose from obscurity and used their creativity to invent and manufacture things that would become household staples, which profoundly transformed the way we live. They turned America into a global superpower. Among his 1,093 patents, Thomas Edison's development of the phonograph has to be one of my favorites. I never imagined I'd be downloading and listening to music on a cell phone. Imagine what Alexander Graham Bell, the inventor of the telephone, would think about that. When Henry Ford perfected the assembly line and gave birth to the fossil fuel-driven automobile industry, a light bulb of opportunities spread nationwide. I am grateful for many of these inventions, yet they ushered in our dependence on electricity and a multitude of gadgets reliant on fossil fuels.

During the Bank Panic of 1907, Wall Street turned to banker J.P. Morgan to steer the country through the economic crisis. An American financier, he dominated corporate finance and industrial consolidation in the era. His savvy business mentality made it possible for major corporations to explode while building his empire. This act came at the expense of the people as it eroded the government's power. The mysterious and controversial *Federal Reserve,* an independent entity established by the Federal Reserve Act, came about in 1913. This act changed our government, and captains of industry like Morgan helped turn our country into a leading industrial power. Their creations became the fuel for the engine of capitalism, as they transformed everything they touched into necessities for the ordinary person. Although they made it possible for the middle class to grow and entrepreneurship to bloom, their innovations have come at a high cost to our environment and to those of other nations.

The rapid growth of the industrial complex created the demand to strengthen the labor unions. Power for the working-class people was demonstrated by the multiple strikes demanding fair pay and safe working conditions. United these brave people sacrificed to make things better for all of us today. It was a time when the government listened to the people — *well, sort of.*

As the post-World War II economy boomed, it brought an increase in wages and opportunities for new businesses. The surge in the variety of consumer goods made life even more comfortable — and citizens complacent. Americans were eager to have children because they were led to believe the future held nothing but peace and prosperity after the war. This mindset led to the Baby Boomer era, which began in 1946 and lasted until 1964. Four million babies were born each year in the United States during those years. My brother and I were two of them. My younger brother was born when the boom tapered off in 1962. Over 76 million Boomers added to the three billion people already on the planet and made up 40 percent of the U.S. population. The times they were a-changin'. Lots of us in the Boomer generation grew up with no real concept of the hardships experienced by our parents and our grandparents. Holding onto a vision for a better future, many of our parents hid the burdens of their past from their innocent children. Clueless and spoiled, we expected to have everything we wanted.

On June 29, 1956, a year before I was born, President Dwight Eisenhower signed the Federal-Aid Highway Act of 1956. The law and the construction of an elaborate expressway system was presumed to be "essential to the national interest." History.com states, "The bill created a 41,000-mile 'National System of Interstate and Defense Highways' that would, according to Eisenhower, eliminate unsafe roads, inefficient routes, traffic jams and all of the other things that got in the way of 'speedy, safe transcontinental travel.'" At the same time, highway advocates argued, "In case of atomic attack on our key cities, the road net [would] permit quick evacuation of target areas."

Meanwhile, a corrosive economy catapulted, built upon the dirty fossil fuel conglomerate. Everything about the transportation industry - from the asphalt to the tires, to the gas and oil needed to run the transportation industry - is tied into the black gold extracted from our Mother Earth's womb. The entire highway system is dependent on the arteries of the Earth's resources. Fast-food, strip-malls, and unsightly billboards litter the landscape demanding consumers to buy - buy - buy into a system that provides temporary pleasure at the expanse of our future. The climate crises, pollution, deforestation, road kills, and tragic accidents are results of such a system. We know the technology is available to rapidly integrate regenerative systems. It's up to consumers and voters, to demand better for the next seven generations. Transition time might feel uncomfortable. Change takes getting use to newness.

No one was thinking or talking about the side effects of population growth or reckless consumerism until Paul Ehrlich came out with his controversial book, *The Population Bomb*, in 1968.

If everyone demanded peace instead of another television set, then there'd be peace.
~ John Lennon

CYCLE
2

Seedling

The oak sleeps in the acorn; the bird waits in the egg; and in the highest vision of the soul a waking angel stirs. Dreams are the seedlings of realities.
~ James Allen

The Hawaiian word *keiki* is used to describe both child and seedling. A young seedling, like a child, requires the right elements to develop and survive. It is a fragile and receptive time. A keiki is reliant on Nature's delicate balance. After sprouting and shooting, a seedling eagerly grows as it develops. Branching out, the seedling roots deeper and takes on a unique shape. Leaves form and through the process of photosynthesis, oxygen is generated and promotes growth. Sensitive and in tune with the sun, rain, wind, and seasons, the seedlings progress proportionately.

It is likewise an impressionable stage for a child. Immature and vulnerable, we were reliant on what others fed us and how they cared for us. We grew accordingly. Life experiences fortified or stunted our constitutions. Resistance was part of the development that strengthened our cores. Prepared, we could endure the unexpected storms and surprises.

From our *crowns to our roots*, heads to toes, over time we evolved into ourselves, at liberty to cultivate our visions.

I seeded and sprouted in a somewhat normal household in a likewise relatively stable point in history. While not without tears and surprises, my youth was raw and innocent, sweet and bitter — complete with a richness experienced with the liberties of childhood. I ingested it all. Like a *good girl* I did my best to present or display the persona expected of me by my family and society. Internally, my true character was evolving.

Digging into My Family Roots

If you want to understand your parents more, get them to talk about their own childhood; and if you listen with compassion, you will learn where their fears and rigid patterns come from. Those people who 'did all that stuff to you' were just as frightened and scared as you are.
~ Louise L. Hay

My dad was born in 1928 into a Jewish family and grew up in Brooklyn, New York. When the stock market crashed one year later, his parents and most of the new immigrants watched helplessly as their dreams of a prosperous life were destroyed. Those grim times met with struggle and sacrifice that bred stoic determination.

My grandpa was a dental entrepreneur. He owned and operated a dental lab in Manhattan. He invented a bridge system contrary to what was taught in school. The innovative system made bridgework affordable and helped many people. Hard work and perseverance enabled this innovative man to avoid bankruptcy and sustain his laboratory throughout the Great Depression.

When my dad was a young boy, he worked hard to help his struggling parents. Determined that his children learn this discipline, he made sure we knew how to work. He expected his kids to pass on the family values. Regardless of the hardships he endured, my dad kept his vibrant spirit. He routinely reminded me, "Be somebody worth being, do something worth doing." He wanted me to have it better and to be the best person I could be. I learned from observing him make tough decisions just how important it was to support and protect one's family.

Dad was a self-made man with strict, often unpredictable patterns. Like many men of his generation, my dad was a workaholic and a foodaholic. He loved his daily 5 p.m. cocktails and smoked a pipe with sweet-scented tobacco all day, in between cigarettes and an occasional cigar. My father's passion for music, art, travel, golf, and eating was clear by his zest for life. He excelled in business and was a savvy investor. He was a great provider for our family, and a fun-loving daddy, most of the time. I adored him. But like most parent-child relationships, we endured conflicts and disagreements. Some of his contrary opinions and mannerisms rubbed me the wrong way. His eating, drinking, and a medley of other compulsive behaviors that suited his palette and pleasure points, were to me, excessive and problematic. Yet, my dad's tenacious — aholic personality infiltrated my being.

He never held back from telling me to "go on a diet," "study harder," "try harder," or "get off your ass." When I hung around kids he did not approve of, he did not hesitate to say, "Hang out with those kids and you're grounded." When I decided I was not college material, he sternly replied, "You are going to college!" And I did. He often said, "Each action has a cause and effect, be mindful Donna." These were tough-love lessons, mixed with a healthy dose of fear. Looking back, I realize my dad said all those things because he cared. While he was brash at times, I am eternally grateful for his honesty.

As I got older, I rebelled against his country club lifestyle. We disagreed on politics and investments. Plus, he expected me to follow in his footsteps, to which I responded, "I don't think so!" Both of us were bull-headed, which created expectations and disapproval on both sides. We had many open, heartfelt, and yes, some heated debates, yet we acknowledged and learned to respect our differences, since love conquers all.

My beloved father instilled in me meaningful values; to have a passion for whatever I do, to be dedicated and compassionate, and to have a strong work ethic. Later in life, I realized that these qualities helped me to succeed in business, and to live a prosperous life.

Business 101

Do not train a child to learn by force or harshness; but direct them
to it by what amuses their minds, so that you may be better able to
discover with accuracy the peculiar bent of the genius of each.
- Plato

I was exposed to the world of business by my ambitious father, which left a positive impression on me. His career was all about helping people, so they could eat and smile with confidence. Like his father, my dad was a dental entrepreneur making changes in conventional dentistry, in a conventional era. He started his dental practice in New York City in 1954.

His office was a twenty-minute commute from our comfortable home that sat on a half-acre of manicured, emerald green grass, sprinkled with an array of ornamental plants and a token apple tree. Even though we lived in the Garden State, it was more important to display a beautiful lawn to our neighbors than to boast a bounty of healthy vegetables. I never saw one vegetable garden in my neighborhood nor in any of my friends', until I planted one.

New York was a major hub for business growth and the suburbs sprawled as the city evolved. Dealing with traffic became an accepted evil. After years of commuting, my entrepreneurial father had the foresight to remodel our overbuilt three-story house and convert part of the basement into his dental practice. To work from one's home was a new concept. Giving up his NY office made financial sense. He saved money on gasoline and gained more free time without his former need to commute. He got a tax deduction on our house since one-third of the home was used for business. The biggest bonus was that we had more family time.

Many of his New York patients faithfully continued to see him even if it meant taking a taxi to the New Jersey office. With the surge of processed sugary foods infiltrating the marketplace, tooth decay escalated, and my dad's practice grew proportionately. When his patients could not afford to pay, Dad never denied them. He would discount the cost or set up a payment plan. New York had a lot of talented, starving artists. Most of the artwork in our home Dad traded for crowns and bridges. The barter system worked, just as it had before the money system took over. Now, several of the lovely paintings grace our home in Hawaii. These works of art remind me of my dad's generosity and his admiration for other people's gifts. I have passed these lessons of compassion on to my son and eventually will pass on the paintings.

Once my dad established his practice, he partnered with my grandfather. For years, father and son, worked together and continued to develop and promote my grandfathers' bridge system invention. After my grandfather died, my dad leveraged the company. He crafted patented tools to advance the technology. He wrote a book and a training guide on how to use the system. He then developed a certification program and trained dentists and laboratories around the world.

My father created a sustainable business habitat meant to last, doing what he loved as he diversified and expanded his unconventional enterprise. He later passed the business on to his oldest son. My brother continues to run the lab with his personal touch.

My dad was smart with his savings and took advantage of the systems of the times. He leveraged his income by diversifying his portfolio and invested in the stock market and real estate. Even though some of his investments were not what I would have chosen, they were useful skills to learn. I cultivated entrepreneurial consciousness at an early age by observing my amusing father. He mentored me without even trying. His actions nourished the peculiar bent of my genius. It sank in that laziness was not an option, and that diversification was a key factor for success. It was an impressionable time.

Dare to Be the Queen Bee

Behind every good man is a fabulous woman.

———————

My mom was a classic housewife in many respects but, being California-raised, she was a bit of a liberal. Born in 1934, amid the ravaged era of the Great Depression, her family avoided much of the devastation. They were in the grocery business, which was thriving pre-Depression. During those tumultuous times, they never went hungry or wanted for much.

I know little about my mother's roots. Being Jewish left holes in our lineage. Both sets of my grandparents survived two World Wars, the Depression, and skirted the horrific Holocaust. I do know that growing up around her multitasking, and entrepreneurial parents brought positive dynamics to our home. I observed her help my workaholic dad in his dental practice, manage the household, pay the bills, do the grocery shopping, and take care of her and my dad's active social schedule. She did all this with three spoiled kids.

My mom liked to stay current on fads and trends. She was driven to "keep up with the Joneses." Advertisements showed the typical lady clad in a shirtwaist apron, wearing high heels and stockings. Smiling, underpaid actresses addressed a growing audience with the latest "must-have" products — everything from kitchen gadgets to the newest fashion statement. Food, alcohol, and cigarette ads programmed our minds.

The popular TV shows exemplified the ideal modern lifestyle. My family would often gather around the *boob tube* after dinner and watch several programs. Little did I know I was being programmed. *Leave it to Beaver, I Love Lucy, The Beverly Hillbillies, Bewitched, The Dick Van Dyke Show, Gilligan's Island, I Dream of Jeannie, Bonanza,* and *The Andy Griffith Show* were some of our favorites. Role model women were few and far between except in fantasy Disney films or beauty pageants. Saturday morning cartoons were my favorite after a fun sleepover with my best buddies.

The stereotypical homemakers and working moms were looking for faster and more convenient ways to feed their families — and they got it. Ready-to-eat foods became all the rage. It delighted most housewives to save time. Women were busy keeping a clean home and embracing the role of being a good wife and mother — the persona of perfection. They were expected to give up their freedom and personal preferences to take care of everyone else and everything around the house or if they could afford it, hire a maid. Most of my friends' moms were homemakers. If they worked outside of the home, they were school teachers, nurses, assistants, or secretaries.

With the onset of persuasive advertisements and advances in media, things transformed fast. My mom branched out of the homemaker role, grew her hair, wore slacks, and became a travel agent. Since Dad often traveled to lecture and Mom went with him, my savvy mother figured, why not enjoy the perks of the travel industry. The discounts and tax breaks from being able to write off their trips enabled them to take nice side vacations.

First and foremost, my mom was an awesome mother: An ordinary woman, who in my eyes did extraordinary things. She was a role model, gracefully juggling many tasks and always offering words of wisdom. When I struggled in school or needed something, she was there for me. Mom was my ride everywhere: the mall, softball practice, ballet classes, and girlfriends' houses. She always welcomed my brothers' friends and mine to our house, which included a home-cooked meal or a TV dinner. My mother showed me the value of being in a meaningful marriage, often reminding me, "Behind every great man is a fabulous woman." Leaning toward being a feminist, my mom impressed upon me the need to be strong, courageous, and to stand up for myself. She taught me that health was my greatest wealth. We spent memorable times laughing — the best medicine. Her actions instilled in me how to be a loving and attentive parent. My mom's genuine gifts have amplified throughout my life. What more could one ask from a mother?

What Was In?

Beauty is health, yet it is said to be in the eyes of the beholder.

It was hard for women to maintain their Marilyn Monroe hourglass figures, 36-24-36, the desired ideal in my mother's generation. It was more fashionable to be skinny than to be a brilliant woman. The famous fashion model Twiggy and other skeleton-thin models and actresses were the trendsetters. In their search for glamour and attention, many women were obsessed with having the perfect body type. Shiny images were plastered on billboards and magazine racks planting these standards in their minds.

The decision to eat or not to eat was a constant battle. Eating disorders including anorexia, bulimia, and binge-eating were common, but not talked about. Weight-loss products took off like rockets into space as the weight-loss industry boomed. Miracle diets targeted those longing to be trophy wives and promised to help them shed those unwanted, unsightly pounds. My mother, like so many other women, was a guinea pig of the weight-loss industry. She was always on the latest fad diet, attended Weight Watchers, and had her fair share of Jenny Craig meals. Fresh and fermented foods such as essential bacteria-rich brined pickles, sauerkraut, homemade yogurt, and fruits and veggies had nearly disappeared from the American diet. Processed foods left the gut flora compromised, which made it even harder to lose weight. Persuaded to eat food products with more chemicals than nutrients, she still struggled to lose weight. Since I was chubby, I fell into the same trap.

An article from Eating Disorder Hope, published on March 1, 2017, says: "It's no surprise that eating disorders are on the rise throughout the world. With the rise of global Westernization, technology advances, and cultural shifts, a rise of the idea of an ideal body shape and size has affected most all parts of the world. According to the National Eating Disorder Association, up to 70 million people (both male and female) suffer from eating disorders."

Fake Food Was In!

Our cupboards were filled with diet pudding mixes, Jell-O in every color and artificial flavor, fat-free salad dressings, and reduced calorie wafers with fillers that tasted like cardboard. My mom kept us kids happy by supplementing our somewhat healthy diet with entertaining boxes of cereal, crackers, crunchy chips, cookies, and ice creams. These refined groceries became our fillers. The longer the list of ingredients the better they tasted. Products laced with sugar, salt, trans fats, and loaded with preservatives, were the yummiest!

Food chemists had figured out how to make junk food that tempted us to want more! Poor-quality products became cheaper to buy and were marketed to be more appealing than real food. That was the trend. The industrial food giants were thrilled with my choices, as well as those of the millions of others who grew addicted. The masses were brainwashed, while only a few profited. These harmful products were making people sick, although we didn't realize it then. Nobody talked about diet and disease in the same conversation.

Some of the most popular tantalizing and chemically processed foods of my youth were Swanson TV dinners, Cheez Whiz, Tang, Hunt's canned Franks and Beans, Oreo cookies, Devil Dogs, Twinkies, Lucky Charms, and Kellogg's Frosted Flakes whose motto, "They're GRRREAT!" still rings in my ears! Then there was Diet Rite, the first diet soft drink. I'm disgusted to admit that I had my share of it all. It was preferable to have a perfect-looking tomato rather than a vine-ripe delicious one. Addiction to unhealthy foodstuffs turned into the norm.

Halloween was one of my favorite holidays, second only to Thanksgiving. I loved eating my way through the festivities of *Hana-Mas* — a name our family coined to celebrate both Hanukkah and Christmas. My idea of a good time was a sleepover with my buddies, pigging out on mint-chocolate-chip ice cream smothered in chocolate syrup while watching the comedy, *Get Smart*, on TV. Food had a way of making everything better. It was ridiculous, but we even got a lollypop if we were good at the doctor's office!

In 1951, the average family income was only $3,700. The average family spent 22 percent, or about $814, of its disposable income on food. According to an article from NPR, published on March 2, 2015, people now spend proportionally less money on quality food than their grandparents did. The Department of Agriculture reported that about one-third of people's money gets spent while dining out at food service establishments.

Artificial Beauty Was In!

Religiously, my mom went to the beauty parlor every week to get her hair and nails done. I would often accompany her. It was a fun day since it included a shopping binge at the mall and then going out to lunch. While her head was under the heavy-duty dryer, she would have her nails shaped and painted with pretty shades of toxins. I read Archie comics, colored, or did homework and anticipated the shopping binge. The folks at the salon were super busy yet friendly. They treated my mother like a queen and offered me candy and soda for being a good girl. Eventually, false silicon nails got glued to my mom's fingers, and I got more homework done since the process of installing fake nails took even longer.

Daily, Mom applied hairspray to her stylish hairdo. I remember the smell and the sound of the chemicals invading her ears, nose, and throat, and mine too since I loved to hang out with her. This era marked the start of the consumer use of chlorofluorocarbon (CFC), an organic compound produced as a volatile derivative of methane and ethane that affects the ozone layer of our Earth. These applications of toxins kept Mom's hair in place until her next appointment. The CFCs from the new aerosol sprays undoubtedly contributed to my sweet mama's subsequent poor health. But she didn't stop using hairspray until she went bald from chemotherapy. The United States banned Chlorofluorocarbons in 1978.

Because of my youthful innocence, I saw the beauty parlor as a great place. I now see it as a business that was killing natural beauty. The friendly characters running the shop never intended it to be that way, but they too became caught up in the latest products. They were, no doubt, nice folks but misled as we all were into believing the products were harmless.

As *supermarket* chains expanded in size and numbers, they were filled with more and more unhealthy groceries. Pharmaceutical giants grew as the quality of food shrank. Many of the drugs concocted and marketed were misleading and presented as remedies that masked the side effects of the corporate junk foods sold in the same store!

As I grew up, I wondered why humans had strayed so far from the understanding of food as medicine, and why there were Big Pharma pharmacies in our food markets. I learned that what I put in and on my body mattered! I came to realize that most of what I purchased or used had negative consequences for people and the planet. This was an affront to my soul. My anger rose as developers leveled forests, paved paradise, put in parking lots, box stores, and shopping malls in the name of progress. My appetite for change would become ravenous. I would come to appreciate that food is sacred, not a commodity, that life is a blessing, not a chore — and that the Earth is My Home, not a resource! People in my generation and in those to come, are paying for this shortsightedness of "What Was In."

Today, farm-to-table restaurants, farmers' markets, and grocery stores with healthier choices give us healthier options. There are also watchdog organizations to help us identify the good, the bad, and the dangerous products. You can find more of them in the Soulution section at the back of the book.

The Alchemy of Turning Lemons into Lemonade

Love sets the table to nourish us and others. It enables soulful alchemy to occur, a seemingly selfless magical process of transformation.

One of my fondest memories of my mom comes from when I was six, when she encouraged me to start my first business; a lemonade and cookie stand. We would shop for the lemons, sugar, and the ingredients to make chocolate chip cookies. Then my patient mother helped me set up for production and crank out the goods. Turning lemons into lemonade was alchemy; a magical process of transformation and creation that Mom and I shared.

Our corner lot on Pine Hill Road was the ideal spot for my enterprise. It was where I learned my first valuable business lesson: Location! Location! Location! Our homemade cookies and the thirst-quenching elixir of lemonade were a hit among the neighbors. It was a fun place for us kids to hang out, with plenty of places for bicycles to park — a colorful Norman Rockwell scene. While I waited for patrons, I kept busy turning succulent dandelion stems into jewelry, which I shared freely with my customers. Business and profits were excellent. I had no overhead, rent, utilities, or advertising costs, and Mom never billed me for the ingredients! Of course, my family and I ate and drank our share.

The next summer, Mom was not willing to invest so much of her time in the kitchen, given the appeal of modern conveniences. Kool-Aid, a new, sugary drink mix made with artificial flavors and dyes, replaced our homemade lemonade. Nestlé or Pillsbury's refrigerated cookie dough replaced the made-from-scratch chocolate chip cookies. Voilà — in just minutes, instant cookies and Kool-Aid! Profits were still healthy, and customers did not seem to care. When inventory got low, I resorted to selling Oreo and Chips Ahoy cookies. I believed I had an excellent business. However, in retrospect, I realized that I was pushing artificial alchemy!

The time spent with my sweet mama in the kitchen, turning lemons into lemonade and licking the bowl of homemade cookie dough, are some of my sweetest memories. The allure of creating something so yummy from scratch produced a lasting impression that stirred up my career path. Turning lemons into lemonade, we leveraged love.

Soul Food from the Inside Out

Darkness cannot drive out darkness; only light can do that.
Hate cannot drive out hate; only love can do that.
~ Martin Luther King, Jr.

Do you have someone in your life who has entered your soul so deeply you can't even describe it? In 1962, Ruby, forever known as Mother Dear, came into my life as our live-in homemaker. I was five years old. My brother was seven, and Mom was pregnant with my younger brother. Mom had complications with her pregnancy, so her doctor ordered bed rest. Mother Dear came to the rescue.

Mother Dear was a woman of color, full of stories and magic from the Deep South. She was my Mary Poppins, except she was real, my first soulful mentor. She was barely five feet tall, a petite woman with a huge smile and a bold personality. Mother Dear was not only a housekeeper, nurse, and carpooler, she was also the governess of our household. She brought balance and harmony to our family business, and she and my mom were the best of friends.

Mother Dear had moved from her Southern roots to the North during the thick of the civil rights movement in the 60s. At twenty-seven years old, she left her three children with her parents in Georgia to make enough money to support them. Every year she ventured to Georgia to visit her daughters. It was cultural bliss for me when her girls came to visit us in the summer. I learned about soul and soul music, how to dance the Mashed Potato and the Jerk, and did some twisting and shouting. The Temptations, The Supremes, and James Brown were my favorites.

When Mother Dear arrived, I used the word hate a lot to describe something or someone I did not like. I'd say things such as: "I hate liver. I hate Beth Ann, she is mean." That did not go over well with Mother Dear. I learned that hate was not only a four-letter word, but you never, ever hate, and if you did, you would get a spanking, or worse, a mouth full of soapy water. Soap in the mouth is nothing like a spoonful of sugar. She only popped me in the butt once, and that was enough for me to turn hate into love real fast. She would look me straight in the eye and say sternly, in a thick Georgia accent, "Child, you may not like someone, but you have gotta love 'em. There is so much hatred in this world there's no room for no more." I cannot even begin to describe how the feeling behind those words, coming from a woman with Southern roots, hit me. It was like I was born again with new inner guidance. Not only had I absorbed Mother Dear's tenacity, but I have ever since been trying to share peace and compassion, making room for love to blossom in all I do.

I loved going to church with Mother Dear. The church members declared me the sweetest *inside-out Oreo*: White on the outside, a woman of color on the inside. My spirited side shined in the small Baptist Church as we sang to Jesus. Reminded by the preacher, "Jesus was a Jew, so sing, girl, sing!" I sang, and I hugged a lot, and ate a lot of soul food, which filled my belly, but not as much as it filled my soul!

To support the church, the members had many rummage sales. My parents, and other well-to-do folks, who employed many of the church members, donated plenty of stuff. Good stuff, and useless stuff, ridiculously priced. I would see the same handbag that sold at Saks Fifth Avenue for $50 sell for $1 at the rummage sales. I have since become a lifetime garage, rummage, and thrift store shopper, saving money and repurposing stuff. A rummage sale was my first reality check with distorted economics.

I'm sure you're familiar with the expression, "When the cat's away, the mice will play." Well, when my folks left on their business trips/vacations, we got some excellent *Southern cookin'*. I learned to enjoy soul food like pig knuckles and okra, collard greens, cornbread, and black-eyed peas stewed with a ham hock. However, my favorite was Mother Dears fried chicken made with tender love from her grandmother's recipe! I can taste it now! Crispy, a bit greasy, yet so yummy. Love and the connection to the spirit world were the additional essential ingredients. I never thought twice about going back for seconds. Friends were always welcome to enjoy the evening. Mother Dear was not shy about teaching a bunch of upper-middle-class Jersey kids how to eat soul food and to be soulful. She blessed us with some significant life-changing lessons that have helped guide us through our lives — filling us with finger-licking-good feelings all around. I wasn't too crazy about collard greens, but that did not stop me from wanting to learn all I could from this wise and loving woman.

The time is always right to do what's right. - Martin Luther King, Jr.

On April 4, 1968, I was down in the laundry room hanging out with Mother Dear as she enthusiastically ironed my dad's shirts while dancing the Mashed Potato (which looks just like it sounds). She always had her transistor radio tuned to a rhythm and blues soul music station playing dance tunes. We boogied together. The radio crackled, and then an abrupt message interrupted the broadcast: "Martin Luther King Jr., American clergyman, and civil rights leader, has been assassinated at the Lorraine Motel in Memphis, Tennessee."

Her life, my life, and the world changed forever. I watched this twenty-nine-year-old African American woman — who had left her home in the South to get away from segregation, prejudice, and poverty — drop to the floor and sob uncontrollably. I remember feeling helpless and was overwhelmed by her grief, as her sadness shook the core of my being — a gut-wrenching memory! I was ten years old and oblivious to the racial tensions in America. This was when the South met the North in my life.

I did not understand at the time that Martin Luther King Jr. was a savior, leading a new revolution. He fought for social equality without violence. After centuries of repression, injustice, and abuse, he, a preacher, stood proudly and shared a dream: Equal rights for all human beings. He was a brilliant, righteous leader assassinated at thirty-nine, who reminds us, "Our lives begin to end the day we become silent about things that matter."

Mother Dear mourned the tragic loss, as did so many others around the world. This remarkable man was buried a few days later, but the wound never closed. That same year, Mother Dear's youngest daughter, came to live with us. Yvonne was five and had become deathly ill in Georgia. My parents opened their hearts and invited Yvonne to move into our home. They made sure she had the best medical care. An integral part of our family, Yvonne enriched our lives. To this day, she is my soul sister.

Over the years, Mother Dear taught me by example, that racism is a disease of the mind and that there is only one race — the human race. She taught me that race was a man-made concept. She made it clear that striving for racial equality is an expression of our humanity. She would say, "The soul has no race, no color, and no bias." She showed me by example, how to treat and honor others as I wished to be treated: With respect, regardless of cultural or religious differences.

Mother Dear also taught me to cultivate peace, love, and compassion, and to live my life like the future mattered. I learned from her to feel and listen to my gut and to share my truth. She would say to me, "Love is the most meaningful motivator for everything — the power of its magic is gigantic." She explained to me why compassion should be the driving force behind actions, and that when there is love, there is hope and trust. Mother Dear helped me to understand that love opens doors and fear closes them, that love will always conquer fear and the more we love, the stronger we will become. Her wisdom is beyond words.

As I ventured out into the world, I saw how segregation weakened society — and that division is a product of fear. I also learned to forgive, to differentiate between right and wrong, and to understand that you cannot always be right. Living my truth sometimes came with having to be defiant and standing up for what was right.

Thank you, Mother Dear, for being my first soulful mentor. From a seedling to a mature adult, I have been blessed by your wisdom.

Mother Dear

*Mother Dear was part of our family household until 2006 and then moved
back to her Georgia roots, where I would visit her twice a year. On July 27,
2018, she journeyed to heaven to be with her Lord, her loving husband, and
all those waiting for her sweet embrace, including my mom and dad. My
grief was profound, yet her spirit is embedded even deeper into my soul.*

"You might not like
someone, but you
gotta love 'em."
— Mother Dear

Animalizing

You cannot share your life with a dog or any animal and not know that they have personalities and minds and feelings.

After years of begging for a dog, we finally got one. I was seven when our new furry darling arrived. One requirement was that my older brother and I take care of him. My mom got to pick out the puppy. To no one's surprise, it was a fashionable, miniature gray French poodle that made his way into our home and our hearts. Dad's favorite drink was brandy, so that was the name he chose for our new family member.

Brandy and I had an immediate affection for one another. My favorite time of day was walking and talking to him. I routinely leashed the frisky puppy and off we went for a stroll around the block twice a day: Nothing like a one-sided conversation, when there's so much to say. Somehow Brandy understood everything better than my family or friends, and I felt safe sharing my deepest childhood thoughts with him. Walk time got me outside and gave me a break from chores or homework. Rain or shine, I enjoyed communing with what was left of Nature's beauty in the developing neighborhood. It was especially lovely when the ornamental wild cherry trees were in bloom.

My four-legged best friend had an excellent sixth sense, and when we encountered others, he greeted them with either a wag or a growl. Instinctively, Brandy picked up on my feelings. He treated me accordingly, whether it was a lick or a look of "let's go." He would jump in my lap when I was sad. My first animalizing mentor, a sophisticated poodle, awakened this *sixth sense* intuition in me. I loved to nurture and observe him grow and develop into a mature, happy dog. *He was my living doll.*

As a child, I was not aware of all the benefits of having a dog. Dog owners usually have lower cholesterol, lower blood pressure, and are better able to manage what stress they have. That adds up to fewer heart attacks! To top it off, I was even burning calories and bumping up serotonin levels without even being aware.

Our darling poodle was the being of my love of dogs. I have since always had one, or two, or three dogs at any given time. All my animals have been great teachers of unconditional love and made excellent companions on my life's journey. These playful animals continue to bring out my inner child, calm my mind, and boost my mood. They also have instilled in me the virtue of being in a routine. Reflecting on the gifts they have brought me, I realized that all my pets taught me to "animalize" more, rather than to over "analyze"— to dig deeper into my primal roots.

Get Animalized

Why is it that most people analyze things to death without considering their instincts? Animals always live in the present – neither the past nor the future consumes them. They depend on their senses and trust their instincts. I have found that the essential characteristics of an entrepreneur are, intuition, instinct, and taking calculated risks before the gut reaction becomes diluted. Trust me, procrastination is a killer!

Some consider animalizing as a cruel act that lacks human qualities. What's up with that? Animals are not cruel, and humans are animals too — specifically, mammals. Why do many humans put themselves at the top of the pyramid of importance and alienate themselves from other species? This self-determined hierarchy has allowed us to believe humans are smarter and more important than all other creatures. But, if we disappeared from the Earth tomorrow, Nature would begin to re-balance, and all other species would thrive.

They have used dogs for years with tremendous success in the treatment of the aged and the terminally ill. Now, animal-assisted therapy is benefiting people living with post-traumatic stress disorder (PTSD).

Creepy Crawlers

*If all mankind were to disappear, the world would regenerate back
to the rich state of equilibrium that existed ten thousand years ago. If
insects were to vanish, the environment would collapse into chaos.*
~ E. O. Wilson

One grueling task as a child was to weed the gardens where the ornamental
plants grew in the dirt. I did not have a problem with getting dirty; my
quandary was the worms! They grossed me out! I was not sure what was
worse, the slimy texture, or the way they squirmed — yuck! When I came
across a worm, I nearly had a panic attack. New Jersey, the Garden State,
had great topsoil and produced long, fat, enormous worms!

When I was seven, my dad bought a sporty boat. His idea of a good time
and enjoying the family was fishing on the Hudson River. Dad called the
thirty-six-foot cruiser The Bonnie G, hoping the name would entice his
beloved wife to love the boating lifestyle as much as he did. My mom,
Bonnie G, saw her namesake as too much work.

For our fishing adventures, Dad asked the absolute worst task of me:
collect worms for bait. Growing up in the Depression and doing his time
in the Navy, my dad got used to doing chores he did not enjoy. He had
"zippo tolerance for wimpy behavior." So, I sucked it up, dug them up,
and collected my allowance for weeding and worm-fetching. Reluctantly, I
gathered dozens of the squirming, slimy critters, dropped them into a glass
jar, and prudently delivered them to my father.

Once our family was out on our boat, it got worse: Dad asked me to bait the hook! That was the straw that broke this young girl's back. One day I flat out refused! My outright defiance to bait the hook relieved me of having to deal with removing panicky fish from the line. AMEN!

Not baiting the hook meant I washed the deck or polished the chrome: a blessing in disguise! I was left on my own, clad in a bulky orange life jacket, under my mother's watchful eyes. Taking a stand for what I wanted was my first taste of rebellion and independence. Until then, my dad was the captain of his ship. From that time forward, I took control of my decisions and accepted their consequences.

As we toured around trolling for the evening's dinner, I did my chores, sang and talked to myself and make-believe friends. There were dramatic skyscrapers to my right and the stunning New Jersey cliffs to my left, a contrasting scene. The hum of the boat's engine was in harmony with the breeze and the waves slapping against the ship. I ended up enjoying these tasks and got rewarded with a swim in the river. The trips down the Hudson River were wondrous experiences.

Sadly, once the river became too polluted to swim in, Dad sold our boat, and he joined the nearby country club. Here, my family and I thought we were on a wholesome outing, only to find that toxins were contaminating us. The pollution came from the industries that carelessly dumped their waste into the once clean waters! The thought disgusts me to no end. To think there are millions of people suffering from disease due to negligence from corporate greed! Not to mention, the disregard and spoiling of the natural environment and beauty!

According to River Keeper, "Between 1947 and 1977, General Electric (GE) dumped an estimated 1.3 million pounds of polychlorinated biphenyls (PCBs) into the Hudson River," turning a 197-mile stretch of the river into the nation's largest Superfund site. Even today, GE's PCBs are found in the sediment, water, and wildlife throughout the Hudson River ecosystem. They are also found in people!

By having this *soil to soul* experience as a child, it began to sink in that everything is somehow interconnected. The worms that I harvested traveled from the soil, then got cast out into the river, then were snagged by a fish, and ended up in my stomach - *that is, if I ate the fish.* Ambrose Bierce puts it this way in *The Devil's Dictionary*: "Good to eat, and wholesome to digest, as a worm to a toad, a toad to a snake, a snake to a pig, a pig to a man, and a man to a worm." I did not particularly like the taste of flounder and catfish, but when Mother Dear deep-fried them, Southern-style, I ate it. She cooked them with love and served up the worm-eating catch of the day in a way that made me feel like I was eating real soul food.

Little did I know how the soil, worms, and all the other critters of the Earth are crucial to our survival, and that the earthworm is the greatest tiller of the soil. Charles Darwin referred to earthworms as nature's ploughs. As ecosystem engineers, they aerate and cultivate. Now, whenever I shop, prepare, and eat, I give thanks to the land, the sea, and all it provides for me. As I weed my vegetable gardens and encounter earthworms, I have endearing respect and admiration for them. These miraculous creepy crawlers are more than extraordinary — as are all the creatures that populate our planet. Everything works together to create this miracle we wake up to every day: life.

All life matters, from the smallest organism to the biggest mammal to the tallest trees.

Boxing Yourself in is for Wimps

A gender line...helps to keep women not on a pedestal, but in a cage.
~ Ruth Bader Ginsburg

When I was growing up, Chatty Cathy and Barbie dolls set a standard for Baby Boomer girls to strive to be, something they couldn't become. Frankly, Chatty Cathy, the first talking doll on the market, bored me with her nonsense one-liners. I must admit; I loved my stocky, furry headed, good luck Troll Doll collection. I had my share of Barbies, including Ken and Skipper. These fashion figures, made from new hard plastic, were launched in 1959. Since I popped out in 1957, I was just in time to catch this trend. From their inception, these dolls impacted little girls' psyches and body images, just as the G.I. Joe action figures affected little boys' behavior. Was I supposed to grow up and look like Barbie and have the vocabulary of Chatty Cathy? Were little boys groomed to go to war and to be fearless and brutal in action?

Short, strong, and stocky, I used my stature to my advantage, kicking ass in sports and keeping up with the guys. Thanks to my stamina, I managed to avoid falling prey to traditional patriarchal gender roles. As a result, I was a "he-she-girl," a tomboy who developed the shrewdness and courage to take part in a man's business world. Resisting the many stereotypes, I forged ahead.

One of the social constructs funneled into my generation was that a woman's place was still in the home, and the man "brought home the bacon." Of course, this meant that men made most of the household income and were "deservedly" paid more than women for whatever job they did. While the boys played with Tonka Trucks and Erector Sets, most girls were having a tea party or baking something in their Easy-Bake Oven. Girls were groomed to be doomed in the workplace.

Being a girl or woman in the '50s and '60s and even today is a challenge. Have we come a long way? According to the American Association of

University Women (AAUW), the pay gap has barely budged in the last decade and grows with age. From schoolteachers to professors, researchers, and computer programmers, women are typically paid less than men. Stephanie Holland, the founder of SheEconomy.org, states, "Women account for 85% of all consumer purchases including everything from autos to health care." Doesn't it make sense to pay women more? Wouldn't this stimulate the economy?

In the latter part of the 1800s, the women's rights and anti-slavery activist, Susan B. Anthony, who played a pivotal role in the women's suffrage movement, preached, "Join the union, girls, and together say Equal Pay for Equal Work." That was nearly 150 years ago! Praises to her, and the countless others who devoted their lives to fight for and defend women's rights. Women can vote and become CEOs of major corporations, run for and win positions of political power, and do a "man's" job in almost any field, and often even better!

We must never take our freedoms and human rights for granted. It was not until August 26, 1920, with the passage of the 19th Amendment, that the right to vote was "bestowed" upon American women. It's time for all of humanity to stop boxing us in and to respect the magnificence and ability of women. It's also the time to honor and draw out the feminine side of men. There are plenty of "gentle-men" fighting for equality. To be able to appreciate the deep healing that comes with the sensitivity and gentleness of the feminine energy, for all genders, is ginormous.

The reproductive female births the next generation, yet she cannot without a male. But, let's face it, the hens lay eggs, and they only need one cock. Regardless, let us proceed peacefully and stop the judgment and discrimination. We can and must do this to advance as a society. Balance and diversity make the world go around.

Dumb is no Fun — It can be Overcome

Children must be taught how to think, not what to think.
~ Margaret Mead

Adding to the plethora of my childhood memories was my struggle with schoolwork. In third grade, I received a D in language arts. Worse than the D, my self-esteem plummeted. When I had to read out loud in front of the class, my palms got sweaty as I stumbled over the words. The conditions and rules at school, and sometimes at home, did not work for me. Schoolwork accentuated my shortcomings rather than focusing on my strengths. My mom was super supportive and helped as best she could, but she finally gave up and got me a tutor.

No one realized I was dyslexic until after I failed several spelling tests. Back in those days, they did not understand dyslexia as they do today. It was my tutor that figured out I had been copying the spelling words off the blackboard incorrectly. If tested on what I copied and studied, I would have gotten 100 percent. My nice teacher moved me to the front row, which helped, and she made sure I wrote the words correctly. My brother teased me about that D, and I felt dumb for a good part of my childhood. "D for Dumb Donna." I wished D simply stood for dyslexia. Sports and faithful friends made up for the hurt and humiliation.

When I was in college, I researched dyslexia, and found that I had been blessed with some of the overlooked gifts and strengths of having a learning disability. One study I read by Sally Shaywitz, co-director of the Yale Center for Dyslexia and Creativity, found numerous beneficial characteristics in people with dyslexia: "Curiosity, great imagination, ability to figure things out, eagerness to embrace new ideas, getting the gist of things, a good understanding of new concepts, surprising maturity, a large vocabulary, enjoyment in solving puzzles, and excellent comprehension of stories when being read to."

It was comforting to learn that many of the wealthiest and most prominent people in the world, including successful business leaders, have been dyslexic. Some also have Attention Deficit Disorder (ADD), or Attention Deficit Hyperactivity Disorder (ADHD) or a combination of them. I have lived with two "learning disorders," a touch of (ADD) and dyslexia, and having a labeled "learning disability" — a disorder, can be an exceptional asset.

Regardless of my shortcomings, the ability to make intuitive decisions, which is like a sixth sense, has enabled me to flourish. Common sense is an underrated skill set, as are animalizing and not wimping out. Here I am five decades later, writing a book — actually two at one time! Trust me, it hasn't been easy, and it has taken me the better part of a decade to learn how to write. Still, I didn't wimp out. Perseverance is also an essential ingredient of an entrepreneur.

It wasn't just dyslexia that characterized me as someone who danced to the beat of a different drummer. In the fourth grade, our teacher asked all the children what they wanted to be when they grew up. The answers sounded similar, with the boys shouting, "firefighter, construction worker, pilot, soldier, doctor," and the girls saying "nurse, teacher, mother, fashion designer." And me? I wanted to be a rock-and-roll singer! Labeled tone-deaf by my fifth-grade choir teacher, my dreams of being on stage were crushed. I still struggle to sing in public. However, the burning desire to do so remains on my bucket list.

As a child, I was told I was different. And that there was something wrong with that. It was up to me to compost any harmful scripts that no longer served me, and to nourish the soulful lessons that did. I grew to accept that growth comes with complex challenges. And when I counted my blessings, my happiness multiplied — this is the equation that made real sense. What good is an education that stifles potential and puts us in labeled boxes — and worse, is complicit with drugs as a means of "managing" our so-called learning or attention disorders? If children were taught how to love the learning process and provided nourishing food, there would be little need for medication or boxes. I'm grateful to have escaped the Ritalin rage that exploded in 1991.

For thousands of years before our current-day educational systems, learning was hands-on. We learned by experience and out of necessity in a communal environment, like all other species in Nature. We animalized more and analyzed less, used our hands, bodies, hearts, and minds. What happened?

I learned about finances by observing my entrepreneurial father and playing the game of Monopoly. Dad would say, "What you focus on will grow." I learned how countries get conquered and how wars destroy from playing the games of *Risk* and *Battleship*. Antiquated textbooks filled in the gaps. My upbringing and education had attempted to box me into a life of excessive comforts and false realities. A rebellion was on my horizon.

> *The word "education" is derived from the Latin word educere, which means to bring up, to nourish, to lead forth, and to draw out.*

Knowledge fertilizes the mind, experiences cultivate the imagination, and proper nutrition boosts our wellbeing. Bright minds brighten the future. For thousands of years before our current-day educational systems, learning was hands-on. We learned by experience and out of necessity in a communal environment, like all other species in Nature. We animalized more and analyzed less, used our hands, bodies, hearts, and minds. What happened?

How might our world be different if our public educational system:

- Emphasized how to live happily and be healthy mentally and physically.
- Respected individual learning styles.
- Brought out the unique talents and abilities in each child and nurtured the child's authenticity.
- Inspired children to be creative, curious, benevolent, and altruistic thinkers, and to be humanitarian and philanthropic.
- Provided a creative environment that instills a reverence for Nature and human potential.
- Incorporated non-violence and ecology into all subjects.
- Taught us to consume less and conserve more.
- Inspired active citizenship and Soulution-driven leadership.
- Included family and community engagement as vital parts of the school system.

More families are choosing to homeschool, and there are more alternative education choices available. According to CNS News and the National Home Education Research Institute, homeschooling increased by over 61 percent between 2003 and 2012, and continues to grow in popularity. Waldorf and Montessori-inspired schools have risen exponentially, encouraging children to master what they naturally excel in and preparing them for meaningful careers and lives.

CYCLE
3

Sapling

Roots grow deeper, bark thickens, and the core strengthens.

∘⊙◉⊙◎⊙◉⊙∘

A sapling — a young tree — is nearing maturity and yet is still susceptible to its surroundings. It often struggles to grow and find its way, especially in a crowded forest competing with others for the same elements needed to mature.

As children move into adolescence, like a sapling, they experience uncertain challenges and changes. As a young tree matures, it requires different support and sunlight for its unpredictable growth. Metaphorically, we humans are nourished by the sunshine of good times and hardened by the storms of troubling times.

We evolved as we branched out in search of life's diverse ingredients. Newfound nourishment prepares us to bud, bloom, and fruit. Adapting to the challenges and changes of the storms, in turn, helps us to become resilient. With resilience, we can foster independence and growth. Confronted with raging hormones and social pressures, and faced with hypocrisy and reality, the sapling time is when inner and outer strength becomes apparent. This cycle brings about growth spurts that sometimes require us to grow up faster than our years. Transformation, both physically and emotionally, can be shocking if you're not prepared.

The sapling cycle brought turbulent changes and unexpected developments as I connected with my soul's identity. I questioned everything as I branched out into adolescence. My sheltered life dissipated as I came face-to-face with religion, cancer, high school drama, the workforce, cultural differences, and the temptations of drugs and sex. But as I waded through the mood swings and confusion, my family and friends were there for me, being the roots that grounded me.

Growing Up and Out

It takes courage to grow up and become who you really are.
~ e. e. cummings

I was ten years old in 1967, when my mom declared herself an atheist in the temple parking lot. My family had been celebrating Rosh Hashanah, the Jewish New Year, when my mother slipped out of the service. When I went in search of her, I found my beautiful mother crying, leaning against her new white Lincoln Continental. Why would she be crying? New car, new year, and our family was all together. She was not expecting me to see her in this emotional state. I hugged her and asked, "Mommy, why are you crying?" She replied, "I think God forgot about me." Unbeknownst to me, my loving mother had just been diagnosed with breast cancer and was scheduled to have a radical mastectomy. My mother hadn't told me or anyone else that she was ill to avoid being judged or pitied.

In the United States, 19.7 percent of all breast cancers occur in women under 50 years old. My mom was 32.

It wasn't until a couple of years later that I understood my mom had cancer. I was snooping through Mom's dresser drawers in search of a bra to support my newly formed breasts, when I stumbled upon her padded bras and round silicone boob tucked neatly away. I was baffled. Mother Dear caught me in the act, and I was in trouble, but not for long. Mom and I had *the cancer talk* soon after. From that day forward, our kinship strengthened and I became a pillar of strength for my mom. She no longer hid from me the side effects of her chemotherapy treatments. Mother Dear, and my mom and I were now tighter than ever. I embraced a sense of responsibility I had never known. Life was no longer all about me! This revelation strengthened both my inner and outer core as I grew into my sapling years. It was time for me to grow up and help my mom get well.

My mother saw numerous doctors and received the same directive many times: "Bonnie, your time is limited; it's time to get your things in order."

Each time she heard these discouraging words, she fought harder. Basically, she told the doctors to "Fuck off!" She had better things to do with her life. My father was her greatest advocate. Together, they found other doctors offering better prognoses.

As I witnessed my glamorous, courageous mother go through years of experimental treatments, I felt every imaginable emotion. Watching her vomit repeatedly into a toilet bowl sucked. Sad and frustrated, I felt helpless. Chemotherapy and radiation caused horrific side effects, including the loss of her magnificent mane of thick black hair. I was pissed and needed to blame something or someone! I wanted it all to go away and never come back!

My mother's struggle with this chronic disease was horrid, yet she was heroic through the entire ordeal. Her attitude around her illness blows me away. Her closet filled up with stylish wigs and clothing that hid any sign of deformity. When she felt good, she entertained, somehow ignored the evil and focused on the good. Betty Ford once said, "I believe we are all here to help each other and that our individual lives have patterns and purposes." Mom embodied Betty's words in her behavior toward others. When she was feeling well, I watched her support other cancer victims. Whenever possible, she celebrated life from the depth of her soul. She'd say to me, "Donna, time is your most valuable currency, so spend it wisely." She knew her time was limited. My mother was a light in the world. She cultivated peace, love, and compassion in our family and with all who knew her.

My mom battled her beastly cancer with tenacity and determination for 18 years, before it took her life at 50. I cherished the wonderful times in between the hard times. The dignity that she showed me as she fought for her life left a lasting impression on me. She taught me that it was my choice to make the most of my life, even in the worst of times. She demonstrated to me the meaning of being present — with oneself and with others. With her as a respected role model, I learned to be courageous, to never give up, and to live life with an attitude of gratitude. I honor my sweet mama for knowing her truth and sharing her weaknesses and strengths. For all of these life-lasting gifts, I am forever grateful.

Even as a young girl, I wondered what caused my mother's illness. Could it have been her lifestyle, chasing "what was in?" Could it have been what she put in and on her body? Or was it the high-dose estrogen birth control pills?

Birth control pills came on the market in 1960. With the advice of her doctor, my mother took the pills prescribed. Years later, I remember my mother questioning her decision to ingest the modern contraceptive and warning me of the possible dangers. Because of this, I never went on the pill. Since that time, studies have linked breast cancer to hormonal contraceptives.

It was First Lady Betty Ford, who helped shape the breast cancer movement after she was diagnosed with breast cancer in 1974. She spoke about it openly, breaking the unspoken vow of silence, which helped other survivors open-up about their experiences. Still, it took over ten years before the FDA acknowledged the link between those early contraceptives and breast cancer. Once that link was established, the chemical composition of contraceptives was modified. Many women suffered severe side effects, disease, and even death, during those years.

The New England Journal of Medicine states, "The risk of breast cancer was higher among women who currently or recently used contemporary hormonal contraceptives than among women who had never used hormonal contraceptives, and this risk increased with longer durations of use." The growth of the Standard American Diet (SAD), and industrial farming practices, both dependent on chemicals, were not publicly linked to health problems or the rise in cancer diagnosis. According to numerous recent studies, however, breast cancer is less common in countries where the diet is typically plant-based and low in total fat (polyunsaturated fat and saturated fat). Reports support that diet is responsible for 30–40 percent of all cancers.

Sadly, people were then, and still are, more concerned with counting calories than with the toxic chemicals in our diets. Cancer became common and turned into a big business for the medical industries. "Mammogram" became a household word.

Let's Do Lunch

I want every child in America to eat a nutritious, delicious,
sustainably-sourced school lunch for free.
~ Alice Waters

During the wonder years of my youth, I was fortunate my parents fed us real food — well, most of the time. They bought Angus beef from the local butcher, fish from the fish market (when we did not catch it ourselves), and seasonal vegetables from the oasis farm stand in our community. On our occasional visits to New York City, we would indulge in ethnic foods from Chinatown, Little Italy, or other cultural hubs. In Jersey we ate at family-style diners, Jewish delis, and pizzerias. The food from these diverse eateries stood in stark contrast to the greasy fare of the fast-food outlets which rapidly replaced them in my youth. As we became accustomed to the addictive flavors and textures of the franchise food, we started to lose interest in homemade meals and a homey atmosphere. With spare change, we would hop on our bicycles and ride to a fast food joint. Then we would down an artificial milkshake and a burger without our parents even knowing. We preferred burger meat smothered with Hamburger Helper and salty fries cooked in trans fats. We looked forward to happy meals at Burger King and McDonald's. I loved it all! *Food, glorious food!*

Public school did not equip me with the essential tools to decipher how the foods I ate affected my health or that of our planet. Throughout grade school and high school, when I did not partake in the marginal school lunch program, my mom put together a *compromised* lunch box. The main course was a baloney sandwich with a slice of processed American cheese between two slices of Pepperidge Farm or Wonder Bread, dressed in French's yellow mustard and Hellmann's mayo. It was tucked into a waxed baggie. For variety, she rotated with tuna, PBJ, or ham and Swiss sandwiches. Included in my metal lunch box was a processed dill pickle, token piece of fruit, and a wax baggie full of Pringles or Fritos corn chips, or my favorite, *Wise* potato chips. The best part about lunch was the dessert, a Hostess sweet treat in crinkly packaging: Twinkies, Devil Dogs, or Ding Dongs. I was envious when my friends got to eat a Marshmallow Fluff sandwich. Lots of trading happened in the lunchroom. For a drink we got the choice of artificially flavored milk from the cafeteria — chocolate, vanilla, or strawberry. At least the meals got prepared by a lunch lady in the school cafeteria. Friday was pizza day, and my brother and I indulged, while mom got a break from lunch duty.

> *What we feed our children is a reflection of what we see in our society and environment.*

Today, most school lunches get delivered frozen, packaged, or in a can. Every day, fast-food outlets infiltrate the school foodservice programs. They sell greasy junk food in the places that should be devoted to the care and nurturing of young minds. Over 4,500 US schools today serve Taco Bell products! According to researchers at the Institute for Social Research at the University of Michigan, whose study was published in JAMA Pediatrics, 10 percent of elementary schools and 30 percent of high school cafeterias serve branded fast food weekly, 19 percent of high schools served them daily.

According to the Center for Disease Control and Prevention, the last 50 years has been especially devastating to our health, as processed foods have increasingly taken the place of real food. The percentage of obese children has skyrocketed to more than double what it was in the '70s and '80s. Go figure.

One in six children are obese today. Dang... that's ridiculous. Children with obesity are more likely to have high blood pressure and high cholesterol, joint problems, impaired glucose intolerance, breathing problems, and heartburn. Also, psychological and social issues such as bullying and low self-esteem, anxiety, and depression have ramped up in our society. And what is our government doing about it?

If we all know well-nourished children benefit from healthy physical development and make better rational choices, why is this happening? Considering that over 31 million children in the United States consume most of their daily calories at school, five days a week, 180 days a year, you would think (or hope) that the food provided in school would be five-star, balanced and wholesome. Right?

About 23.5 million people live in food deserts, which are areas with limited healthy food choices. Grocery stores do not exist in food deserts, or they are too far away for low-income people to reach. The unacceptable options are either buying groceries at convenience stores or settling for cheap meals from fast-food restaurants. A high-calorie diet with little nutrition is a formula for failure. The crime rate is higher where there are food deserts.

> *Food is medicine, it is nourishment – an agricultural and an ecological act. Quality food is a human right, not something we should have to fight for – but we DO.*

The good news is that urban farming is taking off in food desert areas. Rooftop gardens and vacant lots are being cultivated. Abandoned buildings are turning into greenhouses. The rock stars of urban farming are spreading the word and their skills around the country. There is plenty of room for more growers and entrepreneurs to help solve the food crisis. Thankfully there are people and organizations we can depend on. Increasing numbers of educators, entrepreneurs, activists, and parents are challenging the public school system to wise up and rise up! We must also join them. From the Internet to farm schools, educational opportunities are limitless - as far-reaching as our minds - at any age. The children are the future. Check out what some incredible change makers are doing in the schools in the Soulution section at the end of the book.

Branching Out into the Workforce

*The first job experience sets the tone for the next. Learning
how to be of service is important for the youth to know.*

———————⸰⸰◉◎ ◎◉ ◎◉⸰⸰———————

At thirteen, I got my first real job as a corn shucker at the only farm stand
in town. The farmers grew the best corn I have ever eaten, along with plump
orange pumpkins, squash, gourds of every shape and size, and by far the
yummiest Jersey beefsteak tomatoes. I loved working there and the perks
that came with the job. The following summer, I worked my way up from
corn shucker to cashier. My mom's cancer was in remission, and she took
great pleasure in driving me back and forth to work.

For years, I watched this little farm stand expand and diversify into a bigger
business. Over time, the owners created value-added products: homemade
fudge, candied apples, and popcorn. I ingested it all, along with the perks
of business wisdom. They even added a little handmade donut shop,
which was *the bomb*. These items extended the business season and upped
the owners' earnings. The stand's colorful roadside harvest displays with
scarecrows, bales of hay, and mounds of pumpkins and gourds were eye-
catching. The abundance and diversity attracted clients from far and wide.

The vibrant products, friendly customer service, and playful ambiance enticed customers to come often and buy more.

The whole experience was an excellent business model for a young budding entrepreneur like me. You'd think the Garden State would have these roadside farm markets everywhere. However, that was not the case. Instead, fast-food franchises were planted.

The demand for bedroom communities grew as people's desire to live near NYC expanded. The population of our small, provincial town of Closter grew, as did the value of its real estate. The farmer's land was so valuable that he eventually gave in to the pressure of some developers and sold the land, which became part of the encroaching suburban sprawl. Energy-sucking large houses soon devoured the fertile fields and the quaint farm stand. Many of these large homes, ostentatious and lacking in architectural integrity, would later be referred to as *McMansions*. That local farm stand and the farmland of my youth are forgotten treasures for the community. For me, the farm stand remains a fond memory as well as an excellent first-job experience.

During my junior and senior years of high school, I worked part-time as a salesperson at a hip retail clothing store. We sold bell-bottoms and corduroy pants, Levi button-up jeans, colorful T-shirts, miniskirts, paisley bandannas, wide belts with big buckles, and bulky leather handbags to go with the groovy fashions of the early 70s. As an employee, I received a 20 percent discount, which helped me to stay in style. I saved my hard-earned money to buy a 10-speed bicycle, which I rode five miles to work on the weekends, and five miles each way to high school most days.

Taking personal responsibility and entering the workforce at an early age was an essential part of my growing up and declaration of my independence. I enjoyed what I was doing, so it was easy to be joyful in the workplace. Both sales experiences enhanced the work ethic my father had instilled in me and helped me realize what I enjoyed doing. My bosses and many customers let me know I was a damn good salesperson, building my confidence for what was yet to come.

Throughout high school, I also helped my dad in his practice. As his dental assistant, I learned a lot about my big-hearted father. I also learned that the dental business was not for me.

The High School Experience

*An educational system isn't worth a great deal if it teaches young people
how to make a living but doesn't teach them how to make a life.*
~ David Suzuki

The baby boomer student population and the size of the classes were large, often 30 kids lined up in rows. We were not free-range kids; instead, we were trained to be obedient in the public-school uncreative environment. You spoke when spoken to. Taking part in competitive sports and having good grades was expected. Homogenized federal standards measured test scores that summed up our intelligence. These ridiculous tests left many students, including me, feeling inadequate. It was no fun being humiliated and subjected to judgment for not fitting into the ideal student mold. Needless to say, the academic side of high school was *a drag*, and not supportive or tolerant of my learning style.

Often, it was not the subject that was the problem, it was how it was presented. In math, for instance, how come teachers never gave us problems that would help us learn to budget, or balance a checkbook, or inspire us to become entrepreneurs? How come in science class our teachers did not make us aware of the human impact on the environment? They never talked about the value of conserving energy and resources. Home Economics taught us how to incorporate processed foods in with our vegetables to make them more palatable. The system educated us to be unhealthy consumers rather than to know where our food came from and how our meals got to our tables. Ecology and art classes were the only subjects that rocked my world. Meanwhile, I struggled to pass courses I had no interest in and wouldn't use in real life.

On the other hand, the social scene in my teens was *far out*. My close friends called me "Goodie." Most who remember me would say I was popular, a dancing fool, well-rounded, crazy about the outdoor life, and a bit radical. I hung out with a tight group of *cool kids*, who grew up and became journalists, Hollywood writers, and art teachers, while others joined the corporate world. My tightest classmates remain my dear friends, and the fond memories of us together have crystallized.

In my freshman year of high school, my cousin Kenny from Los Angeles, moved in with us for a year. His family was going through tough times, and my folks opened our home once again. California was a hub for growing marijuana, and my cousin was the one to *turn on* our high school. He and I formed a lasting kinship. That year our home was jamming with five kids, lots of smoke and ash, and rock-and-roll. Our house was a party house, a place where friends could smoke a joint and raid the refrigerator. Yes, these were the wonder years.

The most responsible toking happened when my open-minded mother found out from another cancer patient that a few puffs of cannabis helped with nausea during chemotherapy. In those days, this was pretty much unheard of. My cousin kept her in good supply from reputable sources. Some of my fondest memories are the times I hung out with my precious mom and watched classic movies on her comfy king-size bed and shared a few puffs of illegality. It was a relief to see Mom relax and *chill out*.

Besides tearing up a few neighborhoods on Halloween with eggs, toilet paper, and shaving cream, or *hocking* (stealing) a few things from the five-and-dime store — I stayed out of big trouble. I must admit, weekends brought out the party animal in me, and I did my share of toking, beer-drinking, and barfing.

Mother Dear's words of wisdom, "You might not like someone, but you gotta love 'em," was always in my consciousness. It *bummed me out* when kids were mean to each other. When someone was being bullied, I'd step in with conviction, even if it meant getting bullied myself. I learned some hard lessons. Standing up for what was right ultimately built my character.

> Standing up for
> what was right
> ultimately built
> my character.

My idea of a good time was to take long hikes with Brutus, a purebred Siberian husky who joined our family after Brandy went to poodle heaven. For *Hana-Mas* that year my parents got me exactly what I wanted: A pair of clunky hiking boots with thick soles. They made those boots to last a lifetime. Right on the box it said, "If the shoe fits repair it." My new animalizing mentor and I would take off to the dramatic, historical Jersey Cliffs to trek the trails. Fall was my favorite time of year, when the leaves peaked out in shades of golden orange and red. Rustling through fallen dried leaves, I would imagine what it was like during the early stages of the American Revolution, when George Washington and British Military Commander Lord Cornwallis first came upon the Hudson River and saw the steep Palisades and dramatic rock formations.

In the winter months, Brutus and I explored the golf course at the country club that my folks belonged to. I loved when it snowed, and there were no signs of any golfers; just trees, white covered hillsides, and meadows. Our footsteps imprinted in the snow-dust. I would lie on my back and make angels in the fresh snowfall and capture large fluffy flakes on my tongue. Cloud watching was another highlight, as I witnessed the fluffy clouds transform from dinosaurs to birds. I learned more about life and myself on these hikes than in school. Spending time in Nature brought me clarity and a new perspective.

Other than hanging out with good friends, my most meaningful high school experience was during my senior year. We were given the option to do an internship for which we received school credit. I worked at a Nature center as a naturalist, taking kids on hikes to learn about flora and fauna. It was a natural fit. Teaching proved to be a good way for me to learn and retain information.

Europe, Another Planet

An everlasting vision is always in sight.

In the summer of 1973, after I had spent seven summers at an all-girls sleep-away camp, my folks answered my prayers and sent me off to explore Europe on my bicycle. Ten lively and naive middle-class teenagers, and one eccentric bohemian tour leader, Katrina, set forth on a two-month journey of a lifetime. Katrine was 5'8", had frizzy black hair, and hairy legs and armpits. She smelled like an incense shop when she was not all sweaty, and wore dangly earrings and bracelets on both arms. My parents had eight-weeks to indulge in relaxed socialite time, and I had a life-changing experience.

Traveling through France, Italy, and Switzerland, I experienced things that created a profound impression on my body and soul. Summer camp prepared me for the outdoor adventure parts, but not the rest. We rode our ten-speed bikes through the enchanting countryside, slept under the stars, and enjoyed fresh food and cultural bliss. My tent-mate ended up being a cute boy from Scarsdale, New York. This cultural learning curve was outstanding, as was French kissing and cuddling in a steamy tent.

The alien European lifestyle was like being on a different planet. We started the trip addicted to a privileged way of life and the Standard American Diet (Ahh, the irony of the acronym – SAD). After the food withdrawals and cravings passed, we immersed ourselves in the unique cuisine and culture of each region.

We rode our bikes through Paris and charming, quaint villages on scenic roads with rolling hills lined with hardwood trees and vineyards. Sometimes we had to wait for a herd of sheep to cross the country roads. Towns sprinkled with small businesses focused on regional foods and handcrafts rocked my world. There were plenty of handcrafted cheese shops, bakeries, bistros, butchers, tailors, and watchmakers — you get the picture. It was clear the cottage industries throughout all the counties we traveled were prosperous and added value to the communities. The bustling open-air markets, small farms, gardens filled with vibrant fragrant flowers, and edibles, graced the landscapes.

Only occasionally did we see an overweight person. The Europeans we met had not gotten Americanized yet — not a fast-food franchise, shopping mall, or big box store to be found. After all, Italy is where the Slow Food Movement began. Later in life, I learned it started in 1986, after a bold demonstration on the intended site of a McDonald's on the Spanish steps of Rome. It became more apparent how my lifestyle and food choices affected more than just me. Out of my comfort zone, a different *active culture* fermented my life.

The folks we encountered were warm and genuine. My limited high school Spanish did not cut it in France, Italy, or Switzerland. The language barriers, however, enhanced communications. Curiosity and wonder opened doors for non-verbal connections. Most Europeans smoked. I caved into peer and social pressure and partook of some robust foreign tobacco. Music also brought us together in cultural bliss around the evening campfires. Katrina spoke to us about peace and love and explained what that meant to her. It all made sense. Why would we not strive for anything less?

Before I left for Europe, I got turned onto Carole King's Tapestry album. Her alluring voice and relatable lyrics penetrated my soul. At a museum in France, assembled centuries before my generation, I had the privilege to be in the presence of wondrous woven magic tapestries with vibrant colors in bits of blue and gold. As I soaked in the earthly images on the walls of the historic buildings in ancient cities, I'd hum my version of her Tapestry song; an everlasting vision of the ever-changing world. I realized that my life had been a tapestry, and it was unraveling.

Katrina made sure we got a good mix of cultural and bohemian adventures and that we left our summer experience with a global appreciation. Before we separated, she brought us all together in a circle and reminded us that

"United, we bring value, balance, and diversity to our world." On this unexpected quest, I turned one of the most prominent corners of my life.

Highlights were listening to the colorful street musicians and the happenings at sweet-smelling cafés. I returned home healthy and looked like a *million bucks*. Exposed to the outside world, I absorbed the different foreign nutrients. My inner world took root. I woke up to the beauty and benefits of the diversity that humanity offers. Humbled, I became motivated to protect and preserve different cultures and lands. With a different direction and more confidence, I was ready to evolve, extremely grateful that I had gotten to experience *another planet*. I was *freakin' blown away*!

From that year forward, whenever I hiked, biked, or walked in Nature, I discovered more of myself. This is when the *Soil-to-Soul* principles sprouted in me.

Alliance Work partners reports that "Americans use their bicycles for less than one percent of all urban trips. Europeans bike in cities a lot more often — in Italy, 5 percent of all trips are on a bicycle, 30 percent in the Netherlands, and seven out of eight Dutch people over age 15 have a bike." The environmental benefits of riding a bike are numerous, including that bikes use no fuel, bikes require a lot less energy to manufacture than a car, and bikes don't require toxic batteries or motor oil.

United, we bring
value, balance,
and diversity
to our world.

Soil to Soul Music

High vibrational music opens our souls to the universe-moving body and mind, and raises them to new heights. Rhythm stirs imagination- bringing the beat of our heart to the surface.

The language of music is one of the most effective ways to communicate a message to millions regardless of faith, race, or economic position. It stirs up all kinds of emotions, bridges gaps, shapes cultures, and helps get us past the divisions we have created amongst ourselves. Music brings us closer together.

The music of the 60s and 70s — the Woodstock generation — is loaded with masterfully crafted and socially relevant lyrics. Music played a vital role in shaping my life and generation. To this day, the songs still rock my world. Some iconic revolutionary musical artists that influenced my attitude and beliefs are: Woody & Arlo Guthrie, Pete Seeger, Joan Baez, Bob Dylan, Cat Stevens, Joni Mitchell, Carol King, James Taylor, Willy Nelson, Elton John, The Beatles, Crosby Stills and Nash, Neil Young, Simon and Garfunkel, Jimi Hendrix, Janice Joplin, The Rolling Stones, and Bob Marley. Many of them are having a resurgence of popularity and impact with their music as new generations grapple with establishing social and environmental justice.

There is a growing movement for modern-day musical mavericks for the environment and social justice. Some favorites of mine include Jack Johnson,

Nako, Mike Love, Tubby Love and Amber Lily, Kaahele, Paul Izak, Prince Ea, Trevor Hall, Xavier Rudd, Rising Appalachia, and MindfulXpansion.

Music is a powerful tool. Like anything, a tool can be used for good or bad. Some mainstream music is negative, low vibration, and does not uplift or soothe our soul. But tuning in to positive tunes is the motivational medicine that makes us feel good and raises our personal vibration. Musicians, please take responsibility for the lyrics and energy you put out into the world. Creating and supporting conscious music helps make a better world.

In an NPR article titled, The Real Story Behind Britain's Rock 'N' Roll Pirates, it states, "In 1967 the British government made it a crime to supply music, commentary, fuel, food and water — and, most significantly, advertising — to any unlicensed offshore broadcaster. The law sounded the official death knell for most of the pirate stations."

Tuning in to positive tunes is the motivational medicine that makes us feel good and raises our personal vibration.

Culture Shock

Experiencing other cultures opens our minds to what is lacking in our culture. It can be shocking to realize how you have been living is not fulfilling your deep desires.

When I returned from Europe, my parents had to deal with my unruly teenage behavior. I did not expect the magnitude of culture shock. My European experiences fueled a passion for doing something, for being somebody, and to make a difference in the world. But how?

I craved a more meaningful way of life, not junk food or shopping at the mall. Desperate to hold on to what I had gained, I refused to take off the Alcatraz Prison skirt I bought years ago, on a family vacation to San Francisco. I would not leave my bedroom until my parents agreed to let me camp in the backyard. The discomfort of being so comfortable in my queen-size bed was unbearable. The Earth called, and I listened. My reluctant parents finally relented, and I set up camp in our backyard with our dog, Brutus. So, there I was, communing with Nature, camped under a weeping willow tree on our manicured lawn until the first snowfall.

The final condition I put forth to my parents was to allow me to put in a vegetable garden in a section of our perfectly coiffed lawn. Reluctantly, they agreed. The following spring, I planted the first edible garden on Pine Hill Road. Mindfully, I nurtured the growth of cucumbers, zucchini, tomatoes, peppers, lettuce, and herbs. My backyard bounty was plentiful, and I was full of pride! When my dear friend Judd and I delivered a load of manure from a nearby horse stable, my parents nearly had a cow! Judd ended up taking me to the Senior prom that year.

The return on investment from planting seeds in our backyard blew my mind. More profoundly, as I tilled the soil, I grew. My bond with Brutus deepened as we animalized under the stars, and my relationship with my parents cultivated. This new suburban approach was a mighty fine recipe, while it lasted.

As the temptations of the American Dream and peer pressure crowded in, any enlightenment I had gained, dimmed. I eventually caved in, settled for Burger King and trips to the mall with the notion that this would be short-lived. I continued to question, "How was this dream, full of artificial choices and comforts, impacting the rest of the world?" The ultimate challenge was to live a life interconnected to the systems and cycles of Nature — to cut ties with the temptations of this addictive, unsustainable lifestyle.

When it came time to get my driver's permit, I flat-out refused. How could this tree-hugging radical drive a gas-guzzling, polluting car? My European bike tour shaped me for the road less traveled, and I experienced it on only two wheels. Mentally and physically, I benefited from riding my bike to school and work. Mom and Dad eventually persuaded me to get my license saying things like, "What if someone gets hurt and you cannot drive to the hospital?" Jewish guilt sucks.

I failed the driver's test the first time. *Go figure.* I never wanted to drive in the first place. Being dyslexic is not an advantage when taking a written or road test. Parallel parking and backing up were the hardest to learn, yet with persistence, I got it. I continued on my quest to make a difference, driving only when necessary and on the roads less traveled.

High School in Retrospect

*Don't let the wonder years pass you by, and never
let good memories die.*

High school would have been more productive if it had actually prepared me for the real world. It would have been wonderful if my schooling emphasized the value of compassion, love, inclusion, creativity, tolerance, humility, humanity, communication, and Nature. To be kind and forthright.

In the 70s, divorce was not fashionable. Domestic violence was not talked about, and child services were not as up to date as they should have been. Smoking and drinking alcohol were trends that led to family and health issues. Values were compromised by consumption and kids acted out. That was part of my education that I learned outside of school.

College was perceived as the gateway to a better future. This was understandable since many parents had lived through the grueling Great Depression and World War II. In my parents' eyes, a good education was the way to get ahead, not something to be taken for granted. Parents of every socioeconomic class dreamt of a better life for their children. In the 70s, we had more options than our parents, which enabled us to reshape our futures. It was up to us to create our own paths and break away from the visions of our parents.

The message I got from my mom and dad was, "Go to college, pick a major and stick with it, get a good job in that field, and have a lifetime career." Then, "Get married, have kids, and move back to your hometown, preferably in the same neighborhood." The social stigma for boys to be successful men was to attend and graduate from medical or law school, preferably Ivy League. For girls, society looked for them to become teachers, nurses, secretaries, or stay at home moms and homemakers. But behind the facade, imperfection brewed in the patriarchal culture. My parents would learn to accept my choices to defy the odds. It wasn't always easy, but it was worth it.

While still considered a child by my parents, I did my absolute best to muddle through the countless options available to me. Between Career Day, and military and college recruiters, the possibilities were limitless. Those days were fun at school, going from booth to booth and coming home with stacks of pamphlets that gave you every reason why you should apply. I could hardly imagine what would become of my life if I were accepted to any one of these opportunities. Ultimately, I did what my parents wanted and applied to several colleges. I took for granted that I was one of the lucky kids, whose parents could afford to pay her way to a perceived better future.

Although college was the preferred option, it was not affordable for many families. Enlisting in the military was not just a cheaper option, but a paid one. After 33 years (1940-1973), the military draft, that had persisted in times of war and times of peace, ended. Ever since then, the United States has boasted an all-volunteer military. When the recruiters came to our school, dressed in uniform, and told us, "The military is a good career option and a way to pay for college later." I knew kids who took them up on their offer. Within months after graduation, they were enlisted in the armed forces: Air force, Army, Coast Guard, Marine Corps, or Navy.

The war in Vietnam ended in 1975, the year I graduated. The corruption revealed about this 20-year drawn-out tragic conflict, left a bad impression on my generation. The military provided an option that many regretted. Considering the outcome of Vietnam, which my peers and I viewed through the TV screen, most of us decided that wars were evil and wrong. Some older kids I knew fled to Canada, a relatively safe place for draft dodgers.

Vocational and trade schools or community colleges were also affordable options. Unfortunately, these options boxed kids in. You were perceived to be in a different class than the prepsters, or the smart kids and star athletes that got a full-ride scholarship. This never sat right with me. What if we were taught that we were all worthy, regardless of our socioeconomic status? What if the color of our skin, our gender, and our religion didn't affect the way we were treated?

It bothered me that kids were labeled as snobs, sluts, jocks, losers, or nerds. I found myself doing this, and it never felt right. There were some stuck up kids who exuded an aura of patronizing superiority. This amplified the separation and added tension to the social scene. I witnessed condescending attitudes amongst my peers and saw how biased judgment hurt people and created prejudice in school. I saw how this could scar a child. I have so much more compassion now when reflecting on the situations of my former classmates who came to class hungover, disheveled, bruised and confused. They were often the ones who endured additional punishment at school: Victims of detention or expulsion.

What if critical thinking and hands-on learning were emphasized, and we were taught to live like the future matters? Why were we groomed to be goal-oriented and college-bound — expected to either get a good-paying job and work for a corporation, or be a loser? Everybody's story was different as we set off into our new realities. Many of us were confused and conflicted with our choices. All of us were unaware of what lay ahead.

In retrospect, I saw how the school rules, for both students and teachers, could stifle one's potential. I'm grateful for the excellent teachers I had. Especially the ones who thought out of the school walls and helped us make sense of the outside world. I had earned the name "Goodie" from both my peers and teachers. Sometimes, I met with my more progressive and empathetic teachers after school. They listened to my concerns around bullying and answered questions about some of the mundane curriculum. These are the teachers I remember.

Yes, those were the wonder years all right — wondering what the hell we would do with our lives. Wondering who would marry whom, and what we would become. All the same, my youth was genuinely wonderful, and the sincere friendships I made are everlasting. We never worried about being gunned down in the classroom!

As an impressionable teen, the contradictory environment of the time confused me. It paired the awe of science that enabled humans to set foot on the moon, mingled with violence, with a counterculture that emerged embracing peace and love. By the time I graduated high school in 1975, there were four billion people on the planet. Humanity was disconnecting from the systems and cycles of Nature, connecting instead with man-made systems. How was I to sort it all out?

Why does the public-school system continue to stress compartmentalization? Why is it that the memorization of mundane information remains more important than an individual's true potential? Why must the glorification of standardized testing overtake the praise of one's true abilities?

Digging Deeper 1

The people in power control the power — the energy and the fuel we use.
The less we use, the more power we have.

I grew up during some very uncertain times and took for granted the conveniences of the new modern society. I enjoyed the wonder years. Playing in the woods, going to summer camps, and swimming and boating on the Hudson River were the highlights of my youth. At the same time, events occurred that shaped our future. People had not been living like the future mattered. Such behavior has and continues to reflect our unsustainable future.

The booming demand for unnecessary consumables escalated after World War II. Everything from margarine to menthol cigarettes, from miniskirts to Mustangs became part of the new way of life. There was an unprecedented air of affluence as the United States became a world leader in innovation. Unfortunately, some innovations were taken to the extreme. For several generations, people have become complacent about the cause and effect of overconsumption. The subliminal message, "Everyone needs this to be happy," turned citizens into compulsive consumers.

Caught up in material prosperity, we were sold on the corporate ideal of the American Dream. The pressure to conform in this competitive culture became a way of life. To have more was the primary goal, and for some, it would be bought at any cost. The unbalanced, rapid growth showed signs of spiraling out of control. Most people were unaware of the monumental consequences of human impact on the Earth. Nature's beauty and bounty were under attack. The Earth was being raped!

America began to go down the dark path of hoarding during this era, using over twenty-five percent of the world's fossil fuel resources while having only five percent of its population. In 2016, the United States was responsible for 17% of the world's total primary energy consumption. The world's economy became fertile soil for reaping benefits for American consumers at the expense of the rest of the world. The image of the American middle class set the standard for other nations. In actuality, however, the "economics of happiness" was under attack. Personal and family values became marginalized. Even though the postwar standard of living skyrocketed, the average American was less happy than before television and all this stuff!

Between 1945 and 1960, during the postwar economy, the gross national product (GNP) more than doubled, growing from $200 billion to more than $500 billion. Resources got gobbled up at an unprecedented rate.

As society shifted, species of every size and shape, as well as priceless indigenous cultures disappeared from their native landscapes. Pipelines intruded on sacred lands, and zoos and museums became big businesses. Science even enabled humans to set foot on the moon. Meanwhile, however, poverty, war, and violence also made the headlines. Conversely, there was the emerging counterculture that passionately suggested peace and love as the answer.

Dissatisfied with corporate-driven ethos and senseless wars, and driven by other social and political upheavals, the young people of the late '60s and early '70s developed a rebellious counterculture. When four young lads from Liverpool, known as the Beatles, hit the music scene in the 60s, they opened the doors for a flood of free expression to become popularized in music, literature, and poetry. Allen Ginsberg, Lawrence Ferlinghetti, and Jack Kerouac are well known to those who sought to be outside the norm. The Summer of Love in 1967, which started in Haight-Ashbury, continued to revolutionize the movement for peace and love. The power of this countercultural movement for change is possibly expressed best in the revolutionary music of the times. Woodstock, the iconic 1969 music festival, demonstrated the division of our nation and became for many a potent symbol representing a movement toward radical change. I was only twelve, but I wished I could have been there.

Beneath the facade of this booming, glamorous era, there was disillusionment. Substance abuse escalated. Everything from alcohol to tobacco, junk food to LSD, was easily obtainable. These substances were used as an escape, a release from the pain of our disconnection to reality. Most addictive substances were acceptable and expected at social gatherings. Addictive medicines such as tranquilizers, amphetamines, barbiturates, and opioids (synthesized opium products), became more common. These drugs robbed the lives of many, including Vietnam veterans and iconic rock and movie stars. Large corporations prospered, as they capitalized on creating the next generation of addicted and unhealthy citizens.

The use of synthetic fertilizers exploded after World War II when strategic developments enabled nitrogen fertilizer to be made cheaply, and on a grand scale. Nitrogen is one of the primary ingredients in explosives. Throughout the 1930s, the U.S. government had spent countless dollars in building production factories and research facilities. What were they going to do with all this capital after the nitrogen was no longer needed for bombs? The answer was to use the nitrogen-rich ammonia to fertilize the country's crops. This explosion of technology enabled the industrial food complex to flourish at the expense of both the environment and the quality of our food.

In her article, "*The Dark Side of Nitrogen*," Stephanie Ogburn explains the unsettling outcome of the millions of metric tons of nitrogen fertilizer that gets applied to our soils, and how these toxins make their way into our watersheds. The EPA states, "Nutrient pollution is one of America's most widespread, costly and challenging environmental problems, and is caused by excess nitrogen and phosphorus in the air and water... Too much nitrogen and phosphorus in the water causes algae to grow faster than ecosystems can handle."

The multiple, high-profile assassinations of President John F. Kennedy, his brother, Robert Kennedy, Dr. Martin Luther King, Jr, and the shootings at Kent State University in Ohio tried to silence the people and deter changemakers from positions of power. Meanwhile, an upwelling era of underground activism helped maintain some sense of balance in society.

Boomers are now grandparents, and many realize what their children and grandchildren have inherited. I must remind myself that this unsustainable way of life was the norm when I was a child; it was the way I was raised. I'm forever grateful for the outstanding breakthroughs and creations created over the years, many of which have saved lives and made our lives more comfortable. If we focus on the positive, we can move forward with grace and dignity. It is possible to learn from the past, work in the present, and finally, evolve into the future. I can only wonder what the younger generation thinks about my generation. What will happen in the next century? What part will each of us play? The renowned Pop artist, Andy Warhol, said, "They say time changes things, but you actually have to change them yourself." Yes, the times, they were a changin', and I was ready!

The definition of the American Dream continues to morph into unsustainable territory. The environment suffers in the name of progress. Destructive industries continue to bellow toxic smoke and waste into the atmosphere, the water, and the land. The health of our planet declines as Nature's fragile systems are exploited for the sake of new, man-made systems. Wars continue to be fought over the resources of the Earth. People suffer from greed. We must all dream up Soulutions to these problems and live as if the future matters. We must do this for our children.

We are taught to consume. And that's what we do. But if we realized that there really is no reason to consume, that it's just a mindset, that it's just an addiction, then we wouldn't be out there stepping on people's hands climbing the corporate ladder of success.
~ River Phoenix

EVOLUTION II

Branching Out

Principles that influenced my life in this Evolution:

- Mentors are essential.
- Be a mindful, lifetime learner.
- Learn, think, and take action.
- Thoughtful endeavors build a resilient future.
- Share and rejoice in inter-generational wisdom.
- Nature-based Soulutions and sound ecology hold
  the vital keys to humanity's most challenging problems.
- Knowledge fertilizes the mind to think and form our beliefs.
- Wholeheartedly invest energy and attentionin to a
  purposeful passion.

Out on a Limb

*Those who contemplate the beauty of the Earth find reserves of
strength that will endure as long as life lasts. There is something
infinitely healing in the repeated refrains of nature — the assurance
that dawn comes after night, and spring after winter.*
~ Rachel Carson

A limb is one of the main branches growing from the trunk of a tree
that bears foliage. At every cycle, new limbs can grow, take on a new
shape, and break. Limbs can either strengthen or weaken a tree. They also
provide room for other forms of life to visit and inhabit. Limbs add shape
to the core of a tree and, by going in different directions, add character. As
they strengthen, the limbs can divide, and branchlets and twigs will grow.

Our limbs are unique to our experiences and are only as strong as we are. *What
we focus on grows.* As I branched out, I would go out on a limb and find myself
in a different ecosystem than my roots were accustomed to. This experience
would open up my world and expand my reach beyond my imagination.

The Education of an Eco-Bohemian

An education is what you make of it.

I honored my parents' wishes and with a leap of faith, applied to several colleges. There were few alternative choices in 1975 but determined in my search, I found them. My parents were nervous about sending me off to some liberal college and worried about who I might become under its influence. But what else could they do with their child who was obsessed with bucking the system? My high school guidance counselor naturally directed me toward careers for women. As I was definitely not secretarial or nursing material, she led me to the field of social work. Apprehensively, off I went to explore higher education.

My biggest fear was losing the friendships I had built. It was emotional to say goodbye knowing we were going different directions and not knowing when our paths might cross. The thought of making new friends was as daunting as the thought of being back in school. How was I to make new ones and keep the old?

It took me six years to get a diploma, which my father would endearingly call a *sheepskin*. I attended three liberal colleges and changed my major multiple times. The schools that accepted me attracted New Age thinkers and eccentrics. I'd fit right in while absorbing newfound knowledge like a dry sponge. My education would inspire me to *learn, think, and take action like a Soulutionist.*

The first school I attended was Antioch College in Yellow Springs, Ohio. It was the most progressive school I could find that would accept me for who I was: A challenged learner with a tenacious personality and an optimistic attitude. The inspiring professors and intriguing subjects presented students with new ideas to help save humankind and our planet. There was so much to unlearn, and so much more to learn. The counterculture environment rocked my world.

Roommates were assigned, and we were expected to stick with whom we got. That meant moving into a room, smaller than my bedroom at home, with a total stranger! My *roomy* came to Antioch because it had an excellent social work program, and she was looking for a BIG life change. Boy, did she get it! Up to this point, Mary had been a straight-A student, attending an all-girls Catholic high school. She was a virgin, pimply-faced, and nearly six feet tall — pretty much a geek. When I first met her, I had a bad feeling in the pit of my stomach. How could I live with this girl?! As it turned out, after a few heartfelt talks, we became best friends.

Mary and I had a symbiotic relationship. She helped me write all my school papers, and I turned her onto rock 'n' roll, got her high for the first time, and taught her about boys and sex. I also helped her to clean up her eating habits and pimples. We shopped at the thrift store for a new wardrobe, and Mary took on a more confident disposition. My teachers thought I was pretty dang smart, and Mary fell in love with a tall, dark, and handsome man. Yes, I too fell in love with a beautiful man who brought me flowers and wrote me poems. New friendships made the college years extra special, and accelerated my emotional intelligence.

Life was more meaningful when I shared my truth, and cultivated peace, love, compassion, and respect for others.

My first semester classes were mostly in social work. I also took an ecology class because it was my favorite subject in high school. My professor, Walt, was a right on conservationist. He planted and cultivated into our minds that Nature-based solutions and sound ecology hold the keys to humanity's most challenging problems.

Walt assigned our class to read Rachel Carson's book, *Silent Spring*, and write an opinion essay on the text. This controversial book, published in 1962, documents the detrimental effects on bird habitats from the indiscriminate use of pesticides, which weakened eggshells so much that many birds were never born. Carson accused the chemical industry of harming the environment, and public officials for accepting the chemical industry's claims. The public was misinformed and put in harm's way. This was the first time anyone, let alone a woman, stood up to big chemical companies and held them accountable.

Affected so profoundly by even the thought of a silent spring, I changed my major to environmental studies. Carson's writing about the strength and resilience of natural systems opened my soul to the beauty of the Earth. It gave me more significant reasons to find "reserves of strength," and to do my part.

As I continued to dig deeper, I saw firsthand how the modern industrial agricultural system was responsible for most of the escalating environmental degradation. I found answers about how the food system became so fucked up, and how my diet and privileged lifestyle affected all life. My findings appalled me. I learned you are what you eat. My quest was to heal myself, my mother, and Mother Earth.

Studying ecology meant I got to spend more time in the woods. As I observed the behavior of wildlife in each diverse ecosystem, it became clear that everything is interconnected: Adaptation, seasons and cycles, balance and diversity, made perfect sense for Nature. I questioned how humans strayed so far from Nature's wisdom. I learned the constellations in the night sky, and got in tune with the cycles of the moon and my menstrual cycle.

My favorite classes were on ornithology and botany. I loved to learn about the vast diversity of Midwestern birds and plants. My desire to understand Nature's systems and cycles heightened my senses. The bird songs and the dance of the leaves fluttering in the wind were a symphony, and my feet rustling on Nature's paths were part of the orchestra.

Being mindful cleared my mind of negativity.

Determined to help save my mom's life, I pursued different modalities of healing: Homeopathy, herbalism, and nutrition. I took yoga classes that integrated visualization and meditation. Being mindful cleared my mind of negative thoughts and helped me to digest the academic download. There were no naturopaths in Yellow Springs. It was still not a common practice. But then there was Herman, an uncertified holistic health practitioner, who became my naturopath and first healing mentor. Herman was a wise older man who lived in an off-the-grid, hippie community. The colorful back-to-the-land characters in this commune grew most of their food, made their clothes, and crafted their herbal remedies.

Herman made me aware that *knowledge fertilizes the mind to think and form our beliefs*. He turned me onto several herbal remedies which I experimented on myself and my classmates. Convinced by the results, I shared the alternative approaches with my mom. I'd bring home a bevy of cancer-fighting herbs and tinctures, meditation techniques, and yoga asanas (poses). My mom lived an additional eighteen years after her diagnosis. In my heart, I know my love and efforts helped to extend her life.

The back-to-the-land movement motivated property owners to grow food on small-scale farms for themselves and others. Planting gardens in public places and private residences became a necessity to offset food rations in the United States, United Kingdom, Canada, Australia, and Germany during World War I and World War II. They called these victory gardens, war gardens, and food gardens for defense. The movement was resurgent in the '60s and '70s, as rural areas in the U.S. became hotbeds for disillusioned city dwellers. The sustainable movement of today brings hope that the values of raising our food and living in balance with Nature are viable.

Learn, think, and take action.

Alternative Living

*Education must be not only a transmission of culture, but also a provider of
alternative views of the world and a strengthener of the will to explore them.*
~ Jerome Bruner

Campus life at Antioch provided students with alternative options and
freedom to learn which naturally cultivated counterculture views. I lived in
a communal, co-ed dorm that usually smelled like patchouli oil or freshly
baked bread. We did a lot of bed-hopping. We burned handmade beeswax
candles and incense and often smoked dope while indulging in deep
conversations well into the wee hours of the night. Together, we prepared
and ate whole foods made from scratch, mostly vegetarian. To keep costs
down and have access to healthy foods, we joined a natural food buying
club. I was the bread baker in the dorm and wore thin my copy of *The
Tassajara Bread Book*. Author Edward Brown helped shepherd vegetarian
cooking from hippie to mainstream in the '70s. The revolutionary book
was dubbed "the bible for bread baking." I related to every recipe and
philosophical idea. His approach turned my generation onto the Zen of
baking. As I digested these healthy alternative ways to eat, shop, and live,
it gave me hope for a better world.

Immersed in this newfound wisdom, I searched for mentors and more resources. I read all the Rodale Press publications I could get my hands on. *Organic Gardening* magazine, *Mother Earth News*, and the *Utne Reader* reinforced what I learned in class. The professors at Antioch *blew my mind,* as did the words written by Arne Naess, E. F. Schumacher, John Muir, Wendell Berry, Henry David Thoreau, Aldo Leopold, Ralph Waldo Emerson, and other transcendentalists, environmentalists and social justice activists. On this path immersed in *deep ecology*, it felt more natural to learn from these spiritual thought leaders than it did to study purely scientific and material logic. I learned from these visionaries that *thoughtful endeavors build a resilient future and that mentors are essential.*

The Foundation for Deep Ecology "supports efforts to protect wilderness and wildlife, promote ecological agriculture, and oppose destructive mega-technologies that are accelerating the extinction crisis." The "deep ecology" movement recognizes the value of all living things, and considers their importance in the shaping of environmental policy. Arne Næss, the Norwegian philosopher who coined this term, was an inspirational figure within the environmental movement of the late twentieth century. Næss cited Rachel Carson's 1962 book, Silent Spring, as a key inspiration in his vision of deep ecology.

One day during a botany class, I met my new best friend. Out on the lawn of the beautiful old campus, surrounded by towering deciduous trees in full, fall colors, a small, handsome Irish setter mutt wandered into my life. Nearly starved, he sat by me and put his head in my lap. It was love at first sight. I named the stray dog Redbud (Red), after my favorite Midwestern tree. Having a dog at Antioch was acceptable, and my housemates were cool with it and helped me nourish him back to health. Fun-loving, playful, and affectionate, Red and I spent time in the wooded glen across the street from the campus. For the next several years, we explored forests, meadows, fields, and mountains, and always lived in the country. Having him in my life helped to shape my destiny.

The best part about Antioch was the work-study program. Every other semester, students got hands-on experience as interns doing something that interested them. A counselor at the school guided us through a library of possibilities. The program was a win-win-win: The recipient got free labor, the student got experience, and Antioch got paid.

My first internship was as a naturalist and head counselor for inner-city, middle school children. Twenty kids at a time, from a poor section of

Boston, ventured to New Hampshire for a week-long immersion in Nature on a 400-acre homestead. My dwelling for three months was a traditional tipi set in a meadow next to a hardwood forest teeming with wildlife. Red, my sensitive, animalizing friend, made his way into the hearts of the children. Most of the children had never built a fire, hiked in the woods, or even seen an owl or a deer, let alone gone camping or eaten a wild leek. Dealing with discipline issues was a challenge. But by the end of the week, the rebellious city dwellers calmed down as they absorbed the remedies from Nature. The positive changes in the kids were profound.

Sharing the stars and natural gifts was a blessing for all of us as we connected our hands, hearts, and heads with the Earth.

Engaged in the experiential work-study program and doing things that interested me, it became clear to me what courses to take next semester. What a concept — hands-on education proved to be the best way for me to learn, which is true for many, especially those of us with dyslexia. Antioch professors gave no grades or final exams, instead they evaluated us on our performance. If you were enthusiastic, motivated, and determined, this type of education was excellent. We were encouraged to think outside of the box and inspired by new ideas that fostered leaders and entrepreneurs: *To love, to learn, to think, and to take action.* My life had indeed taken a much more twisted direction than those of my high school classmates. I was high on alternative education. The culture at Antioch cultivated a new dream within me — one where I could flourish and evolve into my own.

Off-Grid

A time of evolution and profound wisdom can change everything.

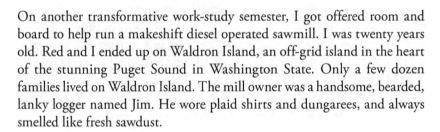

On another transformative work-study semester, I got offered room and board to help run a makeshift diesel operated sawmill. I was twenty years old. Red and I ended up on Waldron Island, an off-grid island in the heart of the stunning Puget Sound in Washington State. Only a few dozen families lived on Waldron Island. The mill owner was a handsome, bearded, lanky logger named Jim. He wore plaid shirts and dungarees, and always smelled like fresh sawdust.

I ended up doing less milling and more cooking and being a full-time nanny for Macy, Jim's eight-year-old daughter, who adored Red. Taking care of a child and the chores of an off-grid lifestyle was more rewarding than I expected. There was an old, one-room schoolhouse, the size of a two-car garage, where I volunteered and enjoyed hanging out with the children. We all played and explored as we gathered edible mushrooms and berries. Our adventures stirred up fond childhood memories of my time in the woods at Pine Hill Road.

Besides learning how to mill, I also learned homesteading skills from Jim. We did just about everything together. I learned to tan hides, sew on leather, and to plant a survival garden. Soon after arriving, Jim and I became lovers, and I felt myself drifting away from everything familiar.

We took baths in a wooden barrel in water heated over an open fire pit. The only mirror, at the mudroom entrance in the drafty cabin, was cracked. But there was no time for vanity. To keep the stove hot for cooking was a chore until I understood the difference between green wood and dry wood. Being the chameleon I had become, I grew accustomed to the lifestyle. I adapted to my new environment with the rhythm of the sun. I learned to appreciate the smell of my sweat after a hard day's work and found comfort each night in our mattress made from straw, and God knows what else.

Without a grocery store, our resources on the island were limited. We had chickens, so we ate lots of eggs and occasionally a tough rooster. Freshly killed wild rabbits were a special feast. On a worn, rickety bookshelf was a copy of *Laurel's Kitchen*, a vegetarian cookbook that Jim's sister gave him for his thirty-fourth birthday. With limited ingredients, I crafted many of the delicious recipes. Sometimes I added rabbit meat to the vegan stew and incorporated wild nettles, sorrel, and fiddlehead ferns. Also, on the shelf was the thought-provoking *Whole Earth Catalog* first published in 1968 and *The Foxfire Books* which became my lifestyle bibles — the ultimate homesteaders guide for dummies. The book series provides valuable information to live with less while gaining more from life. It was a revolutionary time for me. Content with less stuff, I felt more alive. This suburban, twenty-year-old girl had gone rogue.

A mail boat was the only public transportation back and forth between Waldron and the more developed Orcas Island, about an hour away. On one of our grocery trips to Orcas Island, I called my parents from a payphone at the Grange, the community center where I first met Jim. I had been unaware that my mother had taken a turn for the worse. My father summoned me back to New Jersey to help, and thus, my Waldron Island chapter ended. However, that island experience became a significant turning point in my life: A time of evolution, resilience, and profound wisdom. To this day, moonlit baths in the wooden barrel are some of my fondest memories.

The people of Waldron Island still sustain an off-grid, unincorporated style of living, away from the comforts most people depend on for happiness.

Peace on the Peace River

When the last tree has been cut down, the last fish caught, the last
river poisoned, only then will we realize that one cannot eat money.
~ Native American saying

I returned to New Jersey brokenhearted. It was bewildering to go back to my roots after four months of living off-grid. Even turning on a lamp felt unnatural. I had every intention of returning to Waldron to live out my days with the rugged logger and his daughter. Because it was 1977 — no cell phones or the Internet, communication was limited, and considering our age difference Jim and I naturally drifted apart. AH, young love. As the weeks passed, I began to indulge in the modern world again. My perfect fantasy of making Waldron Island my home, dimmed.

Instead, I supported and took plenty of time to love my sweet mama. Once her health stabilized, I did what my parents considered the *right thing* to do and returned to Antioch. I heard my father loud and clear: "Get the DAMN SHEEPSKIN, and then go back to the woods."

Antioch happened to be the perfect place for me to regain and regenerate my idealistic mindset. Campus life was an education in itself — never a dull moment. I took classes that interested me, and partied and debated with the students and the professors. It was an insightful period in my life.

While half of the time, students were off-campus on a work-study exchange program, there was also an opportunity to go on an Environmental Field Program — known as an EFP. I was fortunate to have been selected for an EFP in southwest Florida. It was a camping-canoe excursion that took us down the Peace River and was led by two Antioch seniors. Prior to that, I'd only been to Boca Raton, in the southeastern part of the state: An affluent area scattered with condominiums, large homes, shopping malls, and beautiful beaches. My parents owned one of those condominiums, as did many snowbirds who fled south for the winter.

Our instructors, Jim and Lucy, chose ten physically fit students interested in ecology. I was proud and excited to have gotten selected from a group of a hundred applicants. Jim and Lucy had grown up in southwest Florida near the Peace River. They had a deep love and respect for their homeland and were very knowledgeable. The fearless couple had witnessed a decline in the fragile environment because of human impact and led the trip as activists — voices for Nature. Our group's mission was to collect data that would substantiate all the reasons to clean up the river.

For three months, we lived in tents and out of duffel bags. We learned to view the landscape through a lens of environmental and social justice. The courses we took included: The Effects of Industry on the Ecology, Ornithology, Botany, The Psychology of Dreams, Nutrition, and Vegetarian Cooking. We cooked all our meals over a campfire.

I never expected to see so much wildlife and pristine landscapes in Florida. Each day during the EFP, we peacefully canoed down the Peace River. We saw manatees, alligators, ospreys, snakes, and a plethora of subtropical birds. It was mind-boggling to see bird rookeries with thousands of prehistoric-looking frigate birds. Although the snakes freaked me out, the diverse wildlife and the feeling of living in harmony with Nature mitigated my concerns!

One of the most memorable moments on the river was when it opened to the salt waters of the Gulf of Mexico, and the river turned brackish. Several crocodiles, nearly the size of our canoes, greeted us with wide-open mouths. At first, I was fearful for my life. Then I learned that these giant, toothy reptiles open their mouths to cool themselves because they don't have sweat glands. This defining moment helped conquer any fear of wild animals and inspired me to learn as much as I could about the other remarkable species that inhabit our planet.

Earth and sky, woods and fields, lakes and rivers, the
mountain and the sea, are excellent schoolmasters, and teach
some of us more than we can ever learn from books.
~ John Lubbock

We took day trips during our time canoeing down the Peace River and into the Everglades. I witnessed the industries responsible for economic growth and subsequent pollution in Florida. Agriculture, ranching, phosphate mining, and tourism were the main culprits.

Our first visit was to a phosphate plant. The size of the massive equipment moving the Earth *blew me away*. I never imagined that phosphate was in my toothpaste and laundry detergent. I questioned why we were destroying so much land for phosphate!

We visited a huge industrial dairy farm with more cows than I had ever seen in my life. We got there in time for the evening milking. The deafening sounds of the milking machines' suction, intermingled with the discomforted moos of discontented cows suffering from irritated teats, disturbed me greatly. Seeing these animals trapped in cramped quarters sapped away at my heart. The stench emanating from the mounds of manure haunts me to this day. It shattered my fond memories of the milkman who delivered our milk to Pine Hill Road.

Endless acres of citrus groves, and sugar cane and vegetable fields sprawled across the landscape for miles. Up to this point, I was clueless where my frozen orange juice originated from and what it took to get it into my glass. Industrial farmers plowed chemicals in the ground while fertilizers from aerial spraying permeated the air. The sugar cane processing plant was the worst! It was so bad that I stopped eating sugar for a year. Dairy and meat animals were scattered across the landscape. The runoff from the manure into the Peace River caused algae to bloom, which suffocated the river.

Each time we came to land, we got confronted by a swarm of tourists. Campgrounds were packed with huge, gas-guzzling motorhomes — the litter was unsightly and representative of human negligence. It was hard to witness what these industries were doing to the fragile, subtropical, sea-level ecosystems. The environmental impact was unacceptable, especially on a watershed that provides drinking water for residents.

At mealtimes, we discussed Sigmund Freud and Carl Jung's theories on dreams and the subconscious mind. Thanks to these discussions, my dreams made sense for the first time. The nightmares of being lost in a concrete jungle were particularly distasteful to me, and I hoped that they would never come true. I dreamed of living on Waldron Island and reflected on how my life would have been different had I stayed there. Had I made a mistake trying to sort out all this adult stuff in the *mad lands* of America? Conversations and debates around the campfire got heated as we indulged in bowls of vegetarian chili, cornbread baked in coffee cans, or other plant-based delights. We covered everything from irresponsible consumption and the mismanagement of resources to the causes of pollution and erosion and the inhumanity of humanity. The best part came when we got down to the boy-girl stuff!

Aldo Leopold was right when he said, "We abuse land because we regard it as a commodity belonging to us." For a sheltered suburban Jewish American Princess, seeing the Earth get raped shook me to my core. I questioned; How did the human race get to this place? Neglecting the priceless resources that sustain all life on the planet was no longer an option for me. The entire trip was a rude awakening — it opened the doors of knowledge.

Nature herself became my most influential mentor. The systems and cycles that managed the ecosystems became role models for what is possible. I was more determined than ever to figure out a way to make a difference, but how? Foremost, I would make the change within. My mindset shifted from "I have got to make a change" to "I will change." I was ready to be a Voice for Nature.

Dropout

Just because you drop out of something doesn't mean you're a dropout.

After the Peace River experience, I could not wrap my head around my studies. It was time to clear my mind and find a different flow — to flee from everything familiar. I was more than ready to gather new life ingredients that supported my independence and understanding of the natural world. Challenged, in-between two worlds, and unsure where I belonged, I branched out on a limb to satisfy my heart's desires and dropped out of school.

I ended up moving to the second largest state in the union: Oil country! Marcia, a woman I had befriended paddling down the Peace River, was driving back to her home in Austin, Texas and invited me to be her passenger and housemate. We were both ripe and righteous, ready to be part of the Soulution and not the pollution. It was time to educate our hearts and get more hands-on experience.

On the drive from Yellow Springs to Austin, Marcia and I took turns driving and reading aloud from the first edition of *Our Bodies Ourselves* — the classic book from the Boston Women's Health Book Collective. The groundbreaking book covered all aspects of women's health. It brought to attention ways we could achieve political and cultural changes that would improve women's lives. The stories took our minds off the atrocities going on in the world. We giggled and swapped our promiscuous tales as we got an in-depth look at women's sexuality. The book's progressive willingness to explore the otherwise universally, societally taboo topic fired us up! It was a far cry from what we had learned in sex education class.

Once we arrived in Austin, I found a part-time, minimum-wage job as a naturalist instructor for school children during the week. On the weekends, I took a second job at a health food store, working for an impatient older man who made his money pushing supplements. As I stocked the shelves with bottles, I wondered why people spent their hard-earned money popping pills when all they had to do was eat and live right. I could relate to the herbs and homeopathic remedies, but the rest seemed senseless. The grumpy owner had no time for my questions, so I kept my mouth shut and stocked.

One night a week, I was a model for a life-drawing class at a community college. My body was in tip-top shape from all the canoeing, so being naked in front of a bunch of art students felt natural. The pay was double that of my other jobs, and all I had to do was pose and be mindful. The art teacher complimented me on my curvy, well-toned body. Having identified myself as short and stocky all my life, that was a boost to my ego and self-image.

Four months later, having settled into my routine, my dad called to inform me my mom wasn't doing well. Although he was proud of me for fending for myself in the *real* world, he was insistent that I come home. I'm glad I did. I bid farewell to my new friends in Texas, and headed for New Jersey once again to help take care of my mom.

Upon my return, my mom became more receptive to my newfound knowledge, and our relationship further blossomed in those few months. I mentored my younger brother, then fifteen, who was struggling in the public-school system and wanted to drop out. Antioch had shown me there was a better way to educate. With determination, I found him a more suitable educational environment. Alternative schools in the late '70s were few and far between, but we found one called The Center. It was a progressive school that encouraged kids to be themselves. My brother excelled at The Center. He also became centered within himself.

Once my mom's health stabilized, my dad bugged me once again, "Get your damn sheepskin!" He called my diploma a sheepskin as his way to come to terms with the agrarian, naturalist path I had chosen. The nickname motivated me to continue with my studies.

I was ready
to be a voice
for Nature.

Social Ecology

Until society can be reclaimed by an undivided humanity that will use its collective wisdom, cultural achievements, technological innovations, scientific knowledge, and innate creativity for its own benefit and for that of the natural world, all ecological problems will have their roots in social problems.
~ Murray Bookchin

Of all the epic experiences during my time at Antioch, my passion for food rose above the rest! Everything about it from learning how and where it grew, to eating it and sharing it with others brought me joy. To indulge my interest, I searched out schools that would help me on my path. Goddard College, a progressive, liberal arts school in Plainfield, Vermont, offered an Organic Farm Program, and I jumped at the opportunity to learn.

The program was held at Cate Farm, an educational farm down the road from the Goddard campus. New England hardwood trees, maple, oak, hickory, and chestnut, surrounded acres of vegetable and herb gardens. The forest understory was carpeted with dwarf dogwoods, elderberries, and wildflowers and added to the grace of the landscape. The colors, textures, and fragrances of the diverse forest were the perfect setting in which to learn. A few classes were held in an old barn. Surrounded by beauty, we helped resurrect an old windmill and a worn-out greenhouse.

The ideology behind the program was to live a Utopian life. To do so, we learned what it took to live in harmony with Nature. The teachers encouraged us to implement social ethics in a culture where people collaborate rather than compete. I felt positive about the future while I was co-creating in Nature with others at Cate Farm.

I learned several methods on how to grow food, including biodynamic farming, a practice rooted in the work of scientist and philosopher Dr. Rudolf Steiner. In the early 1920s, he shared a new way to integrate scientific understanding with recognition of the spirit of Nature. I learned how ecological farming leads to better nutrition of the soil and human health. Growing and eating food became spiritual acts.

My interest in Native American studies heightened as I learned about nomadic lifestyles and the wisdom it took to hunt and gather food. The tribes who stayed in one place had sensible agricultural practices. The Iroquois tribe has a theory called the Three Sisters, which refers to their three staple crops: corn, beans, and squash. This symbiotic relationship makes for higher yields. The corn becomes the stake for the beans to climb. Together, the beans and corn shade the squash below. The squash, for its part, blankets the soil, holds moisture, and keeps the weeds away. What perfect synergy! We held bold and lively conversations as we planted seeds of change in the Earth and our minds.

The most thought-provoking course I took was in political science. Our teacher, Murray Bookchin, was an anarchist and an activist who coined the term *social ecology*. He was a robust professor and the mastermind behind the Farm Program. This quote from his 1982 book, *The Ecology of Freedom*, offers insight into the program: "Social ecology envisions a moral economy that moves toward a world that re-harmonizes human communities with the natural world while celebrating diversity, creativity, and freedom."

One of our required books was *The Communist Manifesto* by Karl Marx and Friedrich Engels. Needless to say, a lot of what I learned conflicted with my upbringing. A residue of the Joe McCarthy era lingered among conservatives who saw a non-conformist thinker as a threat. Some people in my generation feared that if they voiced counterculture thoughts, they would be labeled a communist, which stifled their will to take action.

Some of what Marx said made sense, including the vital connection he drew between humanity and the environment. It the chapter "Estranged Labour," in his *Economic and Philosophical Manuscripts* of 1844, Marx wrote, "Man lives on nature — means that nature is his body, with which he must remain in continuous interchange if he is not to die. That man's physical and spiritual life is linked to nature simply means that nature is linked to itself, for man is a part of nature." (No, I am not a Communist, I am a Soulutionist.)

More traditional colleges taught their students to conform to society. Many of my classmates from high school studied to become nuclear scientists, chemical engineers, or pharmacists to get a job. Goddard and a handful of progressive schools attracted students in search of a different path. I took the road less traveled. By returning to school, I appeased my parents, even if it was not the route they had expected or hoped for me to take.

Max, a brilliant student from Burlington, Vermont, who came from a right-wing, wealthy family, was always up to date on current affairs. He kept us students (those who would listen) plugged into the turmoil in the world from his newly righteous left-wing perspective. Max made us aware that he was NOT like his parents. Between Max's sermons and the information from class, learning about the destructive power of the industrial food complex could be a real downer. Cancer became a household word, climate change was in the air, and nuclear power plants leaked toxic radioactive waste across the country.

Max was obsessed with shutting down a nearby nuclear plant and convinced most of the students to get involved. A group of us got prepared for a protest. A local activist group called the Clamshell Alliance prepped us to stop Seabrook New Hampshire nuclear power plant site. We first got trained in non-violence and civil disobedience. As a collective, we decided who would stay and manage the farm and who would go to protest. On May 1, 1977, several Goddard students headed to the site to protest. They camped out for days until they were arrested and jailed for several days. Those of us who stayed back at the farm picked up the slack. We relentlessly called representatives, wrote letters to the White House, and collected thousands of signatures on a petition to stop them from building the plant. Because of the Clamshell Alliance, which inspired continual efforts, the Seabrook plant didn't go Online until 1990, and it was half the originally planned size.

I felt hopeful and was thankful to join forces with others committed to environmental and social justice.

Every day, students gathered to feast on food we prepared from the gardens. We talked about the revolutionary changes in the world and contemplated how we could bring about world peace. The aftermath of the corrosive Vietnam War weighed heavy on our hearts. Many students had older siblings who had endured the horrific, tragic war.

The professors encouraged us to *invest our energy and attention wholeheartedly into a purposeful passion.* This support helped to affirm my convictions to become the best version of myself. We collaborated on projects in small groups, inspired by a saying attributed to anthropologist Margaret Mead: "Never believe that a few caring people can't change the world." United and ignited, we believed we could be part of that change. Understanding that the whole is greater than the sum of all its parts was a practical revelation. Being aligned with like-minded people made us more productive. A sense of admiration for each other's strengths brought out the best in each of us. I never felt this way when competing just to win. My experiences affirmed that this way of thinking and being could make a ubiquitous difference. For me, it was a time of growth, frustration, and empowerment.

I now understood that we don't all belong in the same row, nor do we grow in the same way. And that is OK. We have a choice of what to plant, and where to sow the seeds. We can choose when, where, and how to branch out. We can also strengthen each other's good intentions as we grow. The mainstream is not for everyone.

Once the program was over and our tight-knit group disbanded, it was up to me to decide how I would evolve. A move back to the suburbs or metropolitan area wasn't an option, nor was going back to college. I was getting good at dropping out and branching out. As I muddled through the hypocrisy of the *real* world, I chose my friends wisely, weeded out the energy vampires, and continued searching for a deeper meaning to life.

I took my education into my own hands and created a fertile mindset that cultivated my imagination. I was now open and prepared for all the possibilities.

The Farm Program was shut down the next year, probably for being too radical. I was fortunate enough to have been there during its third and final year.

Life on a Bio-Diversified Farm

*You know, farming looks mighty easy when your plow is a
pencil and you're a thousand miles from the cornfield.*
~ Dwight D. Eisenhower

Like many college towns, the quaint village of Plainfield took on the
personality of the school. Vermont offered beauty, Nature, and an
opportunity for me to work on a small farm. Goddard attracted liberal,
educated characters who made up a significant portion of the townspeople.
It would be the perfect place for me to settle in for a while.

Homeless and school-less, out on a limb, yet hungry for growth, I jumped
on an opportunity to be a farmhand on the Lights' bio-diversified farm.
Bob and Lee Light had been city dwellers. Tired of the rat race, they left
their bustling, hectic lifestyle to raise their family and live more in harmony
with Nature.

*The Center for Biodiversity explains: "Greater biodiversity in ecosystems,
species, and individuals leads to greater stability. For example, species with
high genetic diversity and many populations that are adapted to a wide variety
of conditions are more likely to be able to weather disturbances, disease, and
climate change. Greater biodiversity also enriches us with more varieties of foods
and medicines."*

In awe of the Lights' work ethic, tenacity, and moral commitment to make
their farm work, I was willing to do just about anything to gain their
knowledge. They ran their farm with high standards and earned a modest

yet wholesome living. They were lean on money, yet BIG on LIFE. I spent the next five months working twelve hours a day and slept in a tent down by the peaceful river on the Lights' property. Red was welcome on their farm, and he shadowed me all day. The experience was like the WWOOF program today.

World Wide Opportunities on Organic Farms (WWOOF) is a loose network of national and international organizations that facilitate placement of volunteers on organic farms.

The only other farmhands who shared the endless chores were the Lights' two children. Sarah and James were ten and twelve. The farm was home to fifty Jersey cows, a couple of breeding pigs with a dozen adorable black-and-white piglets, fifty meat-bird chickens, productive laying hens, and three darling dogs. The stunning landscape held space for three acres of organic strawberries, a large organic vegetable garden, and acres of grazing land. When not occupied with chores, we made cheese, butter, and the best strawberry ice cream I've ever eaten. I did whatever else was needed to take care of the many tasks on a small, bio-diversified farm.

Some days, when I woke at 4 a.m., I felt like a brick house had fallen on me. But I put a smile on my face and headed for the barn where the beautiful, smiling Jersey girls greeted me, anxiously waiting to have their udders relieved. This breed of cow is known for producing the best tasting, creamiest milk because of its high butterfat content. Each cow had a name displayed on a hand-painted sign above her stall. I felt right at home with the cream-and-milk-chocolate-colored Jersey girls. After all, growing up in New Jersey made me a Jersey girl too! I got to drink warm milk right from the teat (along with the cats), and even assisted with the birth of several calves — amazing! In gratitude for my hard work, the Lights named a cow after me, *Donna Ann*.

The barn was so clean you could eat off the floor and guess who got to clean it sometimes! It wasn't my favorite job, but I learned humility, and that served me well. I remember often singing Carole King's song, *"Beautiful."* The lyrics got me through morning chores. I got up every morning, with a smile on my face to show the world I had love in my heart. I still remember the sweet scent of the barn — a far cry from the industrial dairy in Florida.

Bob aged the manure in a big pile behind the barn all winter. In the spring, he mixed it with other organic soil amendments and water in an enormous vat to brew compost tea. Bob rigged up a rudimentary spraying system and sprayed the strawberry fields with nitrogen-rich, potent tea. It was a full-cycle, zero-waste system that worked. This process saved the Lights money on fertilizer, spared the soils and the environment from chemicals, and produced the most abundant strawberry patch in all the land.

One of my many jobs was to care for the calves. The sweet, lanky babies were taken from their mothers just a few days after being born. Through their big brown eyes, I sensed the sadness in both the babies and their mothers, which profoundly affected me. The mama cows adjusted once they saw I was taking excellent care of their babies. This first mothering experience, other than my dolls and dogs, awakened my curiosity.

Bob explained to me that the milk from the cows was the profit for the farmer. I also saw the benefit for the farmers came at the expense of the mama cows, separated from their young and unable to nurse them. I grasped the concept of cash flow from the flow of the milk, and adjusted, not fully accepting the outcome for the animals.

We always saved enough milk to bottle-feed the calves. I was the nursemaid and fed the babies twice a day. At first, I had to force the artificial nipple into their hungry mouths until they got used to me. I recognized that it was a marginal substitute for the natural teats of their mothers, but it seemed to satisfy them. It shocked me to feel the determination of these week-old calves. Their strength nearly knocked me over as they eagerly thrust back-and-forth. My favorite part of working on the farm was the connection I had with these adorable beings. I fell in love with them! The milk not needed for the calves went through a mechanized system and was bottled in old traditional glass jugs for retail at local stores. The community got well-nourished from the raw, Jersey girls' milk.

At night, huddled in my tent, I read from E. F. Schumacher's 1973 book, *Small Is Beautiful: Economics as if People Mattered*. Schumacher's revolutionary work is carried on by the Schumacher Center for a New Economics. The work speaks to the urgent need to transform our economic, social, and cultural systems in ways that support both the Earth and its citizens. My desire to dream a new dream was again reinforced by this ideology.

Meet your Meat before you Eat

The greatness of a nation and its moral progress can
be judged by the way animals are treated.
~ Mahatma Gandhi

The reality of giving *a life for a life* came after months of caring for the sweet calves that depended on me. One day, a big, unfamiliar truck appeared in front of the barn pulling an empty livestock trailer. A gruff-looking man popped out of the cab and asked me to find Bob. I found him behind the barn, sweaty from pitching hay out in the field. Bob yelled out in his husky voice, "Hey, Chuck, you're early!" I had no idea why Chuck was there. Bob hollered, "Donna, get Veal, Ribeye, Shank, and Stew from the calf pen — leave Lily and Daisy alone." Those were the names Lee gave the calves. One by one, reluctantly I roped up the boys and brought them out to the gruff-looking man. Chuck was there to pick up the calves on a wagon bound for market. Nonchalantly, he waited for me leaning against the trailer while smoking a cigarette.

For the first time, I saw fear in the eyes of these young *wannabe* bulls. Ribeye was my favorite calf; one I had helped Bob birth at 3 a.m. one morning. I can still remember to this day, the mournful look in his eyes before the trailer door shut tight. The calves were terrified, and I was traumatized. As Bob took the payment for the calves, I held back tears and watched as the frightened boys turned around to look at me for the last time.

That night for dinner, veal was on the menu with freshly dug potatoes, salad, and homemade strawberry ice cream. I excused myself from the table, sick to my stomach and heartbroken. I went to bed hungry and bewildered and cried like a baby for hours until I finally fell asleep. It was the hard truth that a male calf had no place on a dairy farm.

Another task was taking care of the pigs raised for customers who pre-ordered, so that they could feast on them throughout the year. Twice daily,

I delivered the slop from our food scraps and excess high-fat whey from the cows, which made the Lights' pigs more tender and desirable. I feared for the cute piglets I nurtured, as I knew their fate. I also reluctantly helped kill, pluck, and butcher fifty chickens in a single day. This arduous task was grueling. My fingers were raw, and my desire to eat fowl disappeared for quite some time.

In the Lights' care, the animals were humanely treated. Livestock was an intricate part of the whole system's approach to their bio-diversified farm. All of this life for a life stuff left me confused about my food choices and my upbringing. Never had I realized the impact of taking a life to feed another. Why was this topic absent from family discussions? Why didn't grade school teach us about where our food comes from? I questioned, "How much meat do I need to eat? Am I willing to be the one to kill the animal?" I knew the meat I ingested was once a living creature with a spirit. I even wondered about the vegetables and fruits. Did they feel too?

I contemplated being a strict vegetarian. I have since practiced the vegetarian lifestyle — off and on. I decided that if I continued to eat animals, I would need to *meet my meat before I eat*. I concluded that food was life; food was sacred. Being mindful and grateful for what I ate became part of my consciousness. Even so, I did not fully understand the consequences, nor the depth of such complex reasons for my choices. At the time, I was too busy doing what needed to be done on the diversified farm to absorb the magnitude of my feelings and actions.

At each meal,
I give thanks from
the depth of my
soul to the plants
and animals who
gave up their life
for another life.

Strawberry Fields

No one ever told you that life would be easy, and if they did, they were lying.
~ Lee Light

The Lights' farm had the most fertile earth around. Besides the manure and compost tea, a narrow river lined with sturdy hardwood trees ran through the property. The rich nutrients of the river nourished the surrounding soil. Lee and Bob took care of these valuable assets as they knew this was essential for their ecological, agricultural farming system.

Through the food I ate, which grew in the soil I toiled in with my hands, I absorbed the *Mycobacterium vaccae*. Little did I know these tiny microbes that live in the soil triggered the release of serotonin in my brain! I love serotonin, the happy chemical, a natural antidepressant that strengthens the immune system. I learned so much about the soil — underestimated, undervalued, an overachiever — a carbon-sequestering hero where the trees and plants root and mingle with billions of vital organisms. Ahh, the soil, the fertile rich provider, the skin of Mother Earth; the breeding ground that provides the medium for healthy offspring of all species, far and wide. I love the soil — the smell, the fertile darkness, its taste, and feel! How is it that many people don't know about the life that lives beneath our feet? Some say a handful of soil has more living organisms than there are people on Earth. After my experience at the Lights', I never called soil *dirt* again!

After I did my morning chores, ate breakfast, and cleaned the milk bottling room, Lee sent me to the garden to weed, mulch, and harvest, or out to the strawberry field to deadhead. To deadhead meant to pick off all the pretty white flowers from the first year's crop so more energy could go into its roots and strengthen the plants. The following year, the strawberries would be more productive. The bigger the yields, the higher the profits — a growth management strategy, and a vital lesson in economics.

A few days after the calves left, Lee sent me to deadhead the strawberry plants. I was feeling sorry for myself after losing my calves. I had been working consecutive twelve-hour days, and sleeping in a tent, rain or shine, and was probably on my period. I was worn thin! Lee came out to the field to check on me and to let me know lunch would be ready in an hour. Lee was a tough lady. She seemed so old at the time, but in retrospect, she was only in her late thirties. All things considered, I was doing my best, but that never seemed to be good enough for Lee. If she were at all sensitive, she would have seen I had been crying from my puffy red eyes and a drippy nose.

All Lee seemed to notice was that I had missed some of the flowers. "Donna," she belted out, "how do you expect me to pay the bills if you can't get those deadheaded?" I could not handle her badgering anymore and burst into tears. Lee looked at me as if I were pathetic and pierced my soul with these words: "Donna, no one ever told you that life would be easy, and if they did, they were lying!" She walked away, hands on her hips, in a red-and-black plaid shirt and blue jeans rolled up at the ankles, with a jet-black ponytail and zero swagger in her step. Red sensed my vulnerable emotional state and did not leave my side for a minute.

I cried and cried some more, deadheading every last flower I could see through a flood of salty tears. Mother Dear's words, "You might not like someone, but you gotta love 'em," comforted me. I promised myself I'd never treat anyone like that. I came to understand that life wasn't easy for the Lights, and perhaps that's why Lee was so rough around the edges. It would have been so easy for me to quit right then and there, but I carried out my commitment to the Lights, and to myself, to learn all I could.

The systematic crop rotation on the Lights' strawberry patch made for productive yields. They broke the field down into three sections; one acre was covered with a nitrogen-fixing cover crop, like buckwheat or alfalfa to amend the soil, the second acre was full of young strawberry plants we

102

deadheaded, and the third had the older, fruiting plants that folks picked on the weekends.

The *u-pick day* at the farm was my favorite day of the week. People would travel from miles away on the gorgeous country roads to indulge in the delicate, yet voluptuous, sweet, juicy berries. The scenery through the rolling, pastoral hills scattered with cows, horses, and sheep, as well as mountains in the distance and canopies of New England hardwood trees, put everyone in a great mood. It refreshed me and allowed me an opportunity to talk to someone other than the Lights, the pigs, and the calves.

The business model made economic sense. The Lights made a good portion of their income from their well-managed u-pick strawberry operation. They didn't have to hire anyone to pick, sort, package, or distribute the berries. People didn't mind paying a premium for this fun family experience — a win-win.

I loved dinner on the farm after the strawberry pickers left. The meal included garden salad, veggies, potatoes, free-range chicken (which I reluctantly picked at), a glass of raw milk, and homemade bread smothered with churned butter. Dessert was always fresh strawberry shortcake with hand-made strawberry ice cream. Of course, we topped it off with extra berries and real whipped cream. I was grateful for the strawberry patch and the Jersey girls!

Ahh, the soil, the fertile rich provider, the skin of Mother Earth; the breeding ground that provides the medium for healthy offspring of all species, far and wide.

Biodiversity makes Economic Sense

Biodiversity starts in the distant past and it points toward the future.
~ Frans Lanting

The Lights referred to the cash they brought in from the strawberries as bonus money: a supplement to the dairy business. They allocated this money to buy new clothes and household items they could not make or grow, including toilet paper, pencils, tools, and occasional junk food. The money earned from the sale of the pigs and meat birds was their emergency fund. Every asset on the farm got calculated — including the revered manure. A good year meant the Lights could take a vacation to visit family.

The Lights' lifestyle made total sense, even to a girl raised in a suburban jungle. Their meager income was not the reason the Lights kept doing the work; it was the lifestyle that kept them rooted. As blunt as Bob and Lee could be, they appeared to be the wealthiest people around.

After five months on the Lights' diversified farm, I gained a greater understanding of business and the environment than I had in college. I was twenty-one and had reaped some of my most influential life and business lessons. I learned how bio-diversified farming makes sense — and dollars and cents — and that diversity is essential to sustain life. I found out how much skill and work it takes to get food from the soil to our tables. I learned how to produce sellable products, manage cash flow, budget, leverage assets, and supply and demand. I also learned what it meant to cut losses and still make a profit. We valued and used everything, including the manure!

I gained enormous respect for the farmers who used natural farming practices. I experienced first-hand that the farmer feeds the world, and that vibrant soil makes that possible. It was a privilege to be part of a farm that applied these natural systems. It was a *whole system* designed after the principles of Nature and a way for humans to live more harmoniously. If the emphasis on healthy soil and biodiversity has persisted for centuries and has proven sustainable, I questioned why we weren't required to raise all food this way? When diversified and in balance, we have quality water to drink and food to eat. The pollinators — the birds and the bees are busy. Fertility is everywhere. The nutrient cycles are stable, the systems and cycles of nature, go around and around.

> *The law says if you poison the water, you'll die. The law says that if you poison the air, you'll suffer. The law says if you degrade where you live, you'll suffer... If you don't learn that, you can only suffer. There's no discussion with this law.*
> ~ Oren Lyon

It was a bonus to discover how to manage my life better and to harness and sustain my energy for a long workday. I gained practical life lessons, such as life is not as easy as you might think, and when you sow more than you reap you get a greater harvest. Most importantly, I gained the confidence to do whatever I put my mind too. Being famished from an honest, hard day's work felt good. Enjoying a meal that I helped prepare from the bounty of the harvest, made my tasks worth it. My pay for this work, which began before dawn and ended after dark, was three square meals a day, a place to pitch my tent, and a pile of wisdom I could never have dreamed possible. There was no turning back now that I understood these straightforward yet complex ideologies of sowing and reaping.

The New England autumn colors at the farm were breathtaking, and the garden harvests were abundant. On crisp fall days we canned, pickled, and made berry jams and syrups in Lee's outfitted country kitchen. I often stared out the big, bay kitchen window. The leaves danced in the air like feathers, and I envisioned what my life could be like if I had my own farm one day. I questioned how I would make money to buy land. Could I gain the additional skills to master my trade and the confidence to proceed?

The visible signs of winter, including a constant chill in the air, told me it was time to move out of my tent, find a place to rent, and earn money. As a rogue Jersey girl, I left cultured, ripe, and ready for what was ahead.

"The farm consolidation that has taken place has grave consequences for the environment and for climate change as well. The newly passed Farm Bill barely touches the structural and fairness issues that led to this on-going disaster for family-scale farms and the food security of this country." - Elizabeth Henderson, Independent Science.

Earth Artisan

Trust is the glue, a fundamental principle for success.

Although my parents wanted me back in school, they supported my decision to take time to make money and gather more life skills. Their support was contingent on my promise to get a degree. With a small loan from my patient parents, I rented my first little cabin not too far from town. I bought myself a 1969 Datsun pickup truck, which faithfully got Red and me to work on time — even in a blizzard.

Earth Artisan, a hip, little health food store in Plainfield, close to the Goddard campus, was looking for full-time help. I went for an interview and got hired on the spot. The owners figured if I worked on the Lights' farm, I knew how to work! The minimum wage was $3 an hour. Plainfield had only a few hundred residents and a handful of shops. I was psyched to get a job; the best part was that the owners were fine with Red being at the store.

The 1000-square-foot store had an earthy feel. Complete with wooden bulk bins for beans and grains, it offered more real food than the pill shop in Austin. Supplements, packaged foods, and books filled the shelves, and there was minimal refrigeration for fresh goods. Back then, carob was the rage, and dark chocolate had not yet hit the scene. Tofu was trendy, and much of what we sold was not very tasty.

We did not stock Pepperidge Farm products, cold cuts, or French's mustard — everyday items that showed up in my household during childhood. There weren't any Flintstones vitamins either. Health food stores were viewed as almost cult-like and frequented by the counterculture population back then — granola-crunching hippies who voted with their dollars. The Lights did not shop at the health food store since they grew most of their food and settled for traditional, cheap supermarket grocery items for the rest. This was all a small-time farmer could afford.

After a month on the job, the owners, Harris and Ellie, liked and trusted me enough to bump up my wage 25 cents, and put me in a management role. It thrilled them and me too! They had run the shop for ten years, had two young children, and were ready to hand over some responsibilities. The opportunity flattered me, yet it was a big commitment. I embraced the challenge and learned the business from the inside out. My duties included: Inventory control, ordering, stocking, merchandising, customer service, deposits, bathroom duty, snow shoveling, and anything else necessary before I locked the door.

Earth Artisan was the only health food store for miles. Still, it was often quiet at the store, especially in the peak of winter. The silence of the typical Vermont snowstorms brought welcome customers and conversations. I had plenty of time to read and learn about the newest health food products.

The health food industry was in its infancy. Natural food companies were challenged to pierce conventional food prices without a strategic marketing plan. With cancer on the rise, competitive brands promoted their herbal or vitamin formulas to help cure and prevent the disease, or at least reduce the pain. A lot of the information was propaganda. I eventually turned my mom on to some products I researched and vetted for quality. It astonished me to decipher what most of this new stuff was, let alone how it earned the classification as a health food. The book section in the store was chock-full of reference and recipe books that quenched my thirst for knowledge for the time being.

Bread, milk, and egg sales were never better — we always sold out. To guarantee sales and freshness, I let customers know when the deliveries for these perishables were to arrive. The best things we sold were the Lights' raw milk, local eggs, and fresh sourdough bread. The big profit was not in these items. They were the *loss leaders* (a product sold with a small profit or at a loss to attract customers) that drove people to the store, where they picked up more profitable items. When you bought milk, you paid a 15-cent bottle deposit, another way to get folks to return to the shop. Once customers were at the store, I enticed them to buy high-margin items.

One benefit of my job was sampling the products. Many of the health food options cost twice as much as conventional foods. To convey the value of the products I liked and thought a customer might enjoy, was important. I paid close attention to customer purchasing habits. The more educated I became, the more the customers trusted my recommendations. It was never about selling; it was about trust and educating.

I learned how fun customer service was from my previous experiences. I applied lessons learned from Mother Dear and my gracious father to my salesmanship (sales-womanship). I greeted people with an open heart, radiant smile, and often by name. I was thrilled to be of service. Customers loved sweet-natured Red and would often stop by just to visit and get some puppy love. The job was fun and rewarding when I shared knowledge. To top that off, the *ka-ching* of the cash register was music to my ears!

Trust was the glue, the fundamental principle that helped grow the business. For the first time in my life, I made enough money to provide for myself. I paid my parents back, which was empowering. My time at Earth Artisan instilled in me the confidence to start an enterprise of my own someday — part of the Evolution of a Soil to Soul Entrepreneur. Again, I learned to trust that a healthy business model is like a thriving ecosystem and a healthy body: All depend on nourishment and diversity. You could say *I got paid to go to business school.*

The more educated you are, the more the customers trust your recommendations. It's never about selling; it's about trust and educating.

The Staff of Life

How can a nation be called great if its bread tastes like Kleenex?
~ Julia Child

My favorite product in the whole store was the freshly baked sourdough bread. Helen and Jules Rabin were the bakers, but the art of bread making was their side occupation. Jules was the anthropology teacher at Goddard College and Helen, an artist. The elderly, eccentric couple stood out in the community as wise, enterprising, and humble.

They called their successful business, Upland Bakery. The couple baked eighty loaves of fermented sourdough bread three times a week in a wood-fired oven. The bakery, located on the same property where the Rabins lived, was a few miles away from town. On one of my first days on the job, Jules delivered some warm, rustic, sourdough bread. Recognizing I was a newbie, he randomly bellowed out, "How can a nation be called great if its bread tastes like Kleenex?" Apparently, that was something Julia Child was known for saying. That broke the ice, and we shared in-depth conversations that revealed his political activism and stirred mine up.

Jules knew he had a guaranteed sale before he even walked in the store, as I'd always snatch up the best-looking caraway rye bread. I displayed the rest of the loaves in an attractive woven basket on the counter near the cash register — the whole shop filled with an earthy aroma. My lunch ritual on delivery days consisted of a chunk of Vermont cheddar cheese and half a loaf of the *staff of life*. When customers saw me doing this, they followed suit. As each loaf sold, I repositioned the rest of the loaves, so they looked their best for the next lucky customer. The more organized the shop was, the better the sales. Merchandising became an artistic outlet. Life was good, and I did not miss dead-heading strawberry plants one bit.

When I visited the Rabins' home, it struck me how beautifully it fit Helen and Jules's personas. Their gardens, crafted to be productive and convenient, were within feet of their front door. The house was designed to be energy-efficient for cold Vermont winters. Their business was only a fifty-yard commute. It was a fine example of how to live a simple, practical lifestyle. The day I visited, Helen took sick, so I offered to assist. They were thrilled to have my help!

The couple had not let anyone help in the bakery until that day. To protect their proprietary secrets, they made me promise to keep everything they did confidential. I assured them I had no plans to open a bakery in Vermont — my first experience with a confidentiality agreement, even if it was just a handshake. Helen came into the bakery to teach me the art and the heart of bread kneading and shaping. Within an hour, I had it down.

While I kneaded and shaped, Jules tended the fire and mixed several batches of dough to perfection. It was cold outside, but the heat of the hearth and the sound of crackling wood warmed me as it performed its alchemy transforming dough into bread. The aroma was intoxicating.

The Rabins built the stone hearth oven with seventy tons of fieldstones hauled from nearby fields. This impressive masterpiece was a replica of a nineteenth-century peasant oven. The stones covered an igloo-shaped, brick-baking chamber that was five-and-a-half feet in diameter. Alongside the mixer was a grain mill. The noisy machine turned the plump organic wheat and rye berries into a warm, aromatic flour. No one talked about gluten sensitivity or intolerance back then; hence, there was no demand for gluten-free.

Gluten intolerance is a physical condition in your gut, not a food allergy. It is caused by undigested gluten proteins found in wheat and other grains. These proteins hang out in your intestines, and your body responds to them like a foreign invader irritating your gut. Symptoms of malabsorption include chronic fatigue, neurological disorders, nutrient deficiencies, anemia, nausea, skin rashes, depression, and more. Studies have determined that 70% of our immune system is found in the gastrointestinal system. According to the American Academy of Allergy Asthma and Immunology, "Awareness of celiac disease and concerns over reactions to gluten products have contributed to a 2.6-billion-dollar market for gluten free products."

Celiac disease is about four times more prevalent now than it was in the 1950s. "Just a decade ago, gluten-intolerance levels were at 1 in 2500 worldwide. Today, it's 1 in 133." What's going on? Modern wheat is not the same plant it used to be — it is genetically and biologically different.

It was an honor to spend the day with the Rabins, to help and share stories. *Mentors are essential.* I gained conscious business wisdom and learned how to earn a living while living my life. The Rabins' lifestyle made dollars and sense; they were Soulutionists. Jules instilled in me the understanding that the best revenge for hypocrisy was to live courageously and to be creative and honest. He helped shape my views, dreams, career, and many loaves of bread. The mystic sourdough experience changed my life. I fermented intellectually as healthy bacteria grew in my gut.

The Rabins gifted me with some priceless sourdough starter. I also received the gifts of their wisdom, enabling me to rise to almost any occasion. At twenty-two, I was financially and emotionally secure. To live independently was no longer scary.

As I reshaped my life, little did I know that over the years I would teach hundreds of others this same handcrafted technique and bake thousands of loaves — but not in Vermont!

Kris Gunners, CEO and Founder of Authority Nutrition, states that, "From 1843 until about 1960, the nutrients in wheat didn't change much... Modern wheat was introduced around 1960. It was developed via crossbreeding and crude genetic manipulation, which altered the nutrient and protein composition of the plant." Humans had been eating wheat with no problems for thousands of years. Our industrial agricultural system is responsible for the health crisis.

In the "old days" the wheat grains got prepared by soaking, sprouting, and fermenting. Bread was baked using slow-rise yeast — sourdough. These techniques led to many beneficial health effects. Today, they bleach the flour, and the bread is baked with quick-rise yeast.

In the late nineteenth century, new technologies "made it possible to create massive amounts of refined wheat" at a fraction of the cost. The process separates the "nutritious components of the grain (the bran and germ) from the endosperm, where most of the starchy carbs are contained." This has led to an obvious reduction in nutrient density. Refined grains spike blood sugar faster than unrefined grains.

Transition Time

*The business of procuring the necessities of life has been
shifted from the woodlot, the garden, the kitchen, and the
family to the factory and the large-scale enterprise.*
~ Helen Nearing

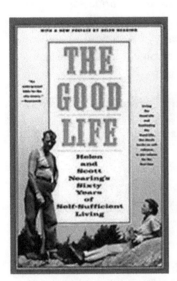

Barbara, a friend who had attended the Goddard farm program, came by Earth Artisans for a visit. She was eager to share an opportunity to help get an organic farm off the ground in Barre, a nearby town. The position offered room and board for labor. I was ready to get my hands back in the soil, and for the next adventure.

For generations, the farm had been a conventional vegetable business. Hard economic times and corporate farm policies caused the family to abandon their dream. Many small farms were left with a heartbreaking choice: Either get eaten by a bigger farm or sell to real estate developers. The oldest son, Alan, refused to let either happen. He worked out a deal with his parents and moved back into the old farmhouse where he was born. He was a hard-working, quirky guy, not much older than Barbara and me, and determined to turn his homeland into an organic vegetable farm. We committed to join his mission.

Alan worked tirelessly with no support from his family. Instead, they ridiculed their son for going organic and collected his monthly payment to stay on the land. To transition to organic meant stewarding the land with no chemicals for three years. It required additional manual labor and paperwork. Barbara and I were the extra labor. Little did I know what I was getting into when I gave up my comfy cabin and job!

The disorderly, worn out farmhouse, constructed in the early 1900s, made for chilly nights after the wood stove burned out. Barbara stayed warm and cozy because she ended up sleeping with the farmer, while I froze my ass off. Layered in long underwear and every available blanket, I snuggled with Red. We listened to the sounds of the lovers in the next room through uninsulated drafty walls.

Soon after, Barbara and Alan married. The wedding took place on the farm, overlooking the potato patch Barbara and I had planted bare-breasted in the spring, as we belted out tunes from the '70s. Surrounded by hardwood trees showing off their spectacular autumn colors, love was in the air the day of their union. A few of us gathered to celebrate the simple celebration. John, one of the guests, would be my soul mate for the next four years. He played his flute during the service and our eyes connected. That night, we slept out in a pasture under the stars. We awoke to dozens of cows hovering over us — an animalizing experience. It eased my fear when John reminded me that cows are vegetarians.

John had been in New England farm-hopping, gathering hands-on skills, and fixing cars and tractors. He was a jack-of-all-trades. His talents landed him winter work as a farmhand at the Wilson dairy, an hour away from Plainfield. The job came with meager pay, and room and board. After a few weeks of courtship, he asked me to go with him. I left the drafty farmhouse for love and a new adventure. Red had accepted John and we were golden.

An older couple ran the Wilson dairy, which had been in the family for several generations. Their kids wanted nothing to do with the farm, and I could understand why. The rundown, dark dingy house was miles away from town. The barn did not have a sweet-smelling manure scent blended with fresh hay for bedding like the Lights' barn. There were just as many cows, but not one of them were happy, clean, or clear-eyed. The cows were black-and-white Holsteins, bred to produce more milk, but lacking the rich butterfat and creamy flavor of Jersey cows. The calf pen replicated the conditions of the rest of the farm, boasting a downright disturbing stench which drove me far away from the troubled barn. The vet often came to administer needles full of antibiotics, which cost the couple more money than they had.

John did his best to improve the circumstances, but things had gone too far. The aging couple never diversified their farm and relied solely on the income from the milk to pay the bills. The price of milk plummeted as industrial factory farms grew with help from government subsidies, leaving small dairy farmers at a loss.

In the 1970s the cost of food in most parts of the country was very low. Conventional milk ran at about $1.71 a gallon. A dozen eggs were about 59 *cents, and pork chops cost 75 cents a pound. Imagine this: You could get either a pound of ground beef or ten pounds of potatoes for just under a dollar. The low price of oil to produce the fossil-fuel-driven agricultural industry impacted the small farmers, our food and political systems.*

John worked daily with Mr. Wilson. I did my best to help out the stressed couple in their home. When I wasn't working, I found refuge in the woods, sometimes tramping through deep snowfall. The snow-covered, droopy branches were not a sign of branching out in the right direction. It saddened me to see the Wilsons struggle to keep their multi-generational family farm. The uncertainty of their fate was hard on their relationship, and John and I wondered where we would end up at their age.

To get away from the daily situation, and to make money, I responded to an ad in the newspaper that read, "School Bus Drivers Wanted. We pay to train and guarantee work." Rural communities in northern Vermont did not offer many jobs, so I jumped on the opportunity. The wage was good enough, and I was willing and able — or so I thought.

I learned to drive a seventy-two-passenger bus. Maneuvering the beastly thing was a bear! It relieved me when the bus company put me on their substitute list instead of as a primary driver. A week later, in the early morning, before the rooster crowed, I got a call to come to work. I looked out the window at the snow swirling in the twilight, panicked, and called the bus company back. With a fake sniffle and a sneeze, I bowed out. "I'm so sorry, but I'm too sick to come in," I told them. What was I thinking? I didn't even like to drive. John and I agreed it was best not to take on this burden. He supported us while I took the homemaker role, which included making lots of sourdough bread and pancakes, as well as baked holiday clay ornaments. Baking warmed our drafty cabin and our hearts.

That same winter, on December 8, 1980, John Lennon was murdered. His lyrics struck a chord in the hearts of musical artists, pacifists, political activists, and the rest of humanity. The tragic loss of the forty-year-old legendary human-being left our spirits crushed. It was a hard winter.

John and I found comfort as we read out loud to one another from the book, *Living the Good Life,* by Helen and Scott Nearing. Published in 1977, their inspiring stories lifted our spirits. The book and our new love got us through the cold winter. We vowed that we would live *the good life* together like our mentors, the Lights, Rabins, and Nearings, and learn how NOT to live from our current situation.

Like two peas in a pod, we grew excited about all the possible ways to blossom our lives into a back-to-the-land experience. That same year, Norman Cousins, an American political journalist, and world peace advocate, stated, "The significance of Apollo was not so much that man set foot on the moon but that he set eye on the Earth."

John and I had our sights on each other and on caring for the Earth. The more we planned for our future, the more distant we became from our pasts.

Getting Greener

*Not having the best situation but seeing the best in
your situation is the key to happiness.*
~ Marie Forleo

From a check-in call to my parents, my dad sensed I was not too happy at
the Wilson Farm. He reeled me back into his reality and pressured me to
get my "damn sheepskin!" His persistence hung around my neck like a dead
chicken. This time, I was ready for a change and some direction, but on my
own terms. I spent hours at the library near the Wilson's farm and combed
through an enormous book of college listings. I came upon a farm program
at Evergreen State College in Olympia, Washington. The courses offered

were right up my alley. Like Antioch and Goddard, they gave students evaluations, not grades, freedom of choice rather than requirements, and the opportunity to shape your major. With some reluctance, I applied and was accepted into the 1980 spring semester. Evergreen accepted my atypical college credits that no traditional schools would even consider.

It relieved my father to know his daughter would be back in school, even if I was studying how to raise goats and grow carrots, rather than how to be a traditional homemaker or career woman. It excited me to go back to the Pacific Northwest. John was supportive and got ready to make the cross-country trek to Olympia with Red and me. He fixed up his old Chevy pickup truck with all the gear for a safe and comfortable journey. We packed up our minimal belongings, including the Rabins' precious sourdough starter and several loaves to munch on. At the first sign of spring, we hit the road on a cold day in March and began our transition. First were the stops along the way for a meet-and-greet with each other's families: New Jersey to see mine, and upstate New York to meet John's. Both visits went off without a hitch, and westward we ventured with parental blessings.

Most nights we camped out in the drafty truck. While crossing the Rockies the sourdough starter froze. It was a chilling moment when I discovered our once active culture was lifeless! From a smoky, crowded country cafe, we found a payphone, and I called the Rabins. Jules picked up the phone. Anxious and nearly in tears, I said, "Jules, the sourdough froze, what do we do?" In his thick, East Coast accent, he responded, "Donna, settle down! Boil some potatoes and feed the starter with the warm potato water and enough flour to thicken, then whip it like cake batter one hundred times, cover with a plate or cheesecloth, and then leave it alone until it sours. And, the last thing — ya might as well eat the potatoes." "Really, that's it?" I said with a sigh of relief. "Donna do what I say. Call me when you make it to Olympia. Safe travels. Oh, and one more thing, keep that culture from freezing!"

I followed the baker's orders. That night John and I boiled potatoes at our campsite and revitalized the liquid gold with this quick and easy fix. We had mashed potatoes and gravy for dinner. In a few days, the starter had rejuvenated. From that day onward, we protected the invaluable leavening, just as the Alaskan miners, who depended on its vitality for nourishment, had done. I also learned that in the most desperate of cases, you could make your own starter. And it might even taste better than the hundred-year-old sourdough that came with lots of great stories and bragging rights.

Fantasy Farm

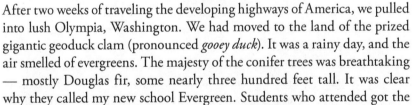

I'm glad that my parents drilled into my head,
action speaks louder than words.

⸺•ೲ☺☺☺☺☺☺ೲ•⸺

After two weeks of traveling the developing highways of America, we pulled into lush Olympia, Washington. We had moved to the land of the prized gigantic geoduck clam (pronounced *gooey duck*). It was a rainy day, and the air smelled of evergreens. The majesty of the conifer trees was breathtaking — mostly Douglas fir, some nearly three hundred feet tall. It was clear why they called my new school Evergreen. Students who attended got the distinguished name Geoduck or Greener. When called upon, I took both the nicknames as compliments.

A few miles from campus we scored a rental with acreage including a three-bedroom farmhouse, chicken coop, and a rustic barn. John and I rented out the other two bedrooms to fellow Greeners interested in organic farming who would help with the many chores. Here, John and I ran our diversified farm and turned it into a business while I took the final courses to get my damn sheepskin. Our operation was not even close to the magnitude of the Lights' farm, but it was a good starting point for budding Soil-to-Soul Entrepreneurs.

118

We called our three acres, Fantasy Farm, and approached the opportunity with bold enthusiasm. A nearby farmer offered to till two acres in trade for sourdough bread. He brought us a copy of *The Old Farmer's Almanac* as a gesture meant to welcome us to the farming world. For weeks, John and I pulled out weeds and stones and referred to the helpful Almanac. We prepared the rows for planting, amended the soil with organic materials, made compost tea with the Lights' recipe, and mulched the garden beds and paths to keep weeds out. When our seeds arrived in mid-April, it was like *Hana-Mas!* We planted everything from arugula to zucchini, including an array of flowers, some to deter pests and others to sell. We also incorporated the Iroquois three sisters' method: Corn, beans, and squash. Along with all this planting, we also gutted the barn and repaired the chicken house. We were living the good life.

Our scenic, colorful barnyard with two dairy goats, twenty laying hens, and six talkative Muscovy ducks, kept us busy and entertained. The goats gave us milk, and the chickens and ducks produced fresh eggs. What we did not eat we sold. We ate the birds that stopped laying. Nothing went to waste, including the poop, which made an excellent soil amendment. Our active three-bin compost system cranked! Soil management was crucial for reducing pests and weeds. Another acre of land had a thicket of blackberries and an orchard with plum and apple trees. There was plenty of pastureland for the goats and friendly ducks that followed their four-legged friends.

I hand-painted a rustic sign, which proudly identified our Fantasy Farm. John hung it from our mailbox on the road for all to see. We were eager to share our farm with anyone interested. There were other farms in the area, so folks in search of fresh produce and eggs knew this was where to shop and barter. Our model farm became a class trip for the Evergreen Farm students.

On occasional trips to the grocery store, we observed most people's carts piled high with packaged goods. John and I only shopped for cooking oil, toilet paper, dog food, and chocolate bars. We ate like royalty and practiced Soil-to-Soul living.

Soil to Dough

We must not be afraid to push boundaries; instead, we should leverage our science and our technology, together with our creativity and our curiosity, to solve the world's problems.
~ Jason Silva

Our farmstead was close to school, so I rode my bike to campus several days a week, even in the pouring Northwestern rain. I cherished the twenty-minute ride on the country road with the towering coniferous trees. It gave me time to clear my mind and tap into my intuitive side. As my blood pumped, it reminded me of all the systems in the miraculous human body and the systems necessary to run a diversified farm business, as well as the extraordinary systems that make up our natural world. They are all interconnected. I always seemed to be questioning, "How did we end up in a world where mono-crop agriculture was the way, and un-whole food was fashionable? Why did humans become so disconnected?" I pedaled hard, hoping if I pedaled hard enough, I'd find answers to all the problems. I was not willing to run or bike away from them.

The organic farm program attracted confident professors devoted to training natural farmers. We dove deep into the politics and history of food, soil science, ecology, and nutrition. And we were taught how to use farm tools and equipment to ease the strain on our bodies. Besides being trained on how to be a damn good organic farmer, I learned that as a civilization, we needed to build up our soils if we want to inhabit a vibrant planet. It surprised me to learn that soil sequesters' toxic carbons, as do plants growing in gardens, orchards, and forests. Why did they not emphasize this in grade school, in everyday life? Why was the rainforest being destroyed?

WorldWildlife.org states: "Half of the topsoil on the planet has been lost in the last 150 years. In addition to erosion, soil quality is affected by other aspects of agriculture. These impacts include compaction, loss of soil structure, nutrient degradation, and soil salinity. These are very real and at times severe issues." The steep decline in soil has occurred while the world's demand for food is skyrocketing. It is estimated the world will need to grow 50 percent more food by 2050 to feed an expected population of nine billion people.

Most profoundly, I learned that when the environment is strong and healthy, it is sustainable; the same goes for an economy. We can only reap more than we sow for so long before the system weakens. When a forest is not managed like the future matters—when it is clear-cut—it is exposed and depleted, and the land is prone to erosion. The next generation of trees suffers, as does the forest floor and its offspring. The more time I spent in gardens and forests, the more the answers became evident.

Improving our diet and refining our lifestyle, we contribute to a better world.

Of all the thought-provoking literature that my professors assigned me, one of my favorite required readings was *The One-Straw Revolution* by Masanobu Fukuoka. The book, published in 1975, chronicles his life, philosophy, and discovery of natural farming techniques. By applying these practices, Fukuoka produced yields that equaled or surpassed the most productive farms in Japan.

My main project to earn school credit was to document our farming techniques and their results. My experiences on the Lights' farm and at the Goddard Farm School opened me up to what was possible. Now I got to incorporate all that I had learned with the new knowledge, on my own farm. Convinced these natural systems of agriculture were *the way* I became a better student and farmer. It opened my mind to all the possibilities of the different sustainable farming method.

Available data proves that organic and sustainable farming practices can feed the world and save the planet. According to journalist, Bob Cooper: "Bio-intensive farms use 50-75 percent less land, 50-100 percent less fertilizer, 67-88 percent less water and 94-99 percent less energy to produce a given amount of food than does conventional farming. Perhaps most intriguing, bio-intensive methods 'grow' farmable soil — at a rate 60 times faster than occurs in nature — while traditional modern farming methods tend to deplete farmable soil through wind and water erosion." Why are world hunger and malnourishment at an all-time high? The Worldwatch Institute states, "A fair number of agribusiness executives, agricultural and ecological scientists, and international agriculture experts believe a large-scale shift to organic farming would not only increase the world's food supply but might be the only way to eradicate hunger."

Responsibility for all the decisions demanded keen observation and study. Unfortunately, there was not much business taught in the program, which is what most small farmers needed. It was my time to show up as an owner and own up to the tasks at hand.

Our yields were higher than expected. Once the crops were ready, we sold the bounty at the Olympia Farmers Market. Sales were good. To supplement our income, we geared up production of our sourdough bread and took some shapely loaves to market. We also made hard-crusted rolls and smothered them with garlic and herb butter. We displayed them front and center on the table. Our mouth-watering presentation got people's attention: Handcrafted baked goods, dozens of eggs, and baskets of colorful bunches of organic radishes, beets, carrots, and the rest of the vegetable kingdom. Vases of freshly cut flowers and aromatic herbs accented the fresh-smelling display. It was a recipe for profits and pride.

We offered a variety of two-pound sourdough breads and a specialty loaf of the week, such as rosemary-olive or oatmeal-raisin. Customers often bought two loaves and added a buttered roll or two. When they bought the baked goods, folks also loaded up on vegetables. The bursting-with-flavor rolls were our best sellers with the highest profit margin, the value-added bread and butter of our business. The herbs required the least amount of effort to grow, and the rolls sold for a premium. Since we ran out every week, customers came early to assure they got their rolls. We needed a fast solution to keep up with demand.

Our tiny farmhouse kitchen was not big or warm enough to raise enough dough, which takes around fourteen hours to reach peak fermentation. John had the genius idea to convert the cold frame that he had built for our vegetable starts into our dough-rising area. The makeshift cold frame was like a miniature greenhouse, just large enough to hold seven five-gallon buckets of dough, or about 150 pounds, equivalent to sixty loaves and forty rolls. We sold the loaves for $2.50 and the rolls for $1. (In 2019 dollars with inflation, bread sales would equal $491.33, and the rolls $131.02 that totals $622.35) In just baked sales in 1980, our total would have been $190.00. Add that to our healthy produce sales and we were rolling in dough — but not without a whole lot of work.

On a cloudy spring day in Olympia, the dough took longer to rise — meaning we had to work into the night. After the first rise, John and I hand-shaped loaves and rolls, followed by a second rise and then the big bake. We had limited oven space, which made the process even longer. In the wee hours of the morning, we prepared the garlic-buttered herb rolls and loaded the truck with everything necessary to set up the booth, including the produce we grew, harvested, and washed. All these preparations were essential, so we could get to the Saturday market in time to set up before the crowds arrived at 7 a.m. We were grateful for our housemates who were eager to help, and we shared the bounty.

As profits rolled in, we purchased a small, used, four-burner stovetop oven for $50, which cut the baking time in half. This minimal investment enabled us to maximize our efforts and gave us extra hours of priceless sleep. The propane oven would travel with us on our next venture to Alaska and earn its weight in gold.

One day at the market, the owner of a fancy French restaurant approached us to buy our specialty vegetables, herbs, and flowers for his white-tablecloth eatery. The Frenchman was very businesslike. He made me nervous at first, but I soon won him over. I had learned a bit of French on my trip to Europe. My earnest attempts to use it broke the ice. The restaurateur expected us to deliver every Monday and Friday promptly at 2 p.m., with only our best produce, preferably in miniature size. He had the only farm-to-table restaurant in Olympia back in 1980, which made sense since he was European and new to America. He had not yet been brainwashed by the Standard American Diet. He respected what John and I were doing and shared the sentiment that *the farmer feeds the world*.

I questioned why most of our food was raised and processed by underpaid migrant workers who lived in poor conditions. Why would people pay so much money for a fancy cocktail and complain about the price of asparagus? How did our priorities get so screwed up?

From the soil to my soul, at Fantasy Farm I gained an even greater appreciation of how the land, farmers, animals, and plants provide for us. We diversified and leveraged our knowledge, integrated the best of what we knew, and most importantly, included mindfulness in our daily lives. We provided a service and created a sustainable business that contributed to the collective well-being of our community, and we earned enough money to pay our bills. From the way we ate to how we lived and ran our business reflected our ethics. John and I were evolving into Soil to Soul Entrepreneurs. In just a few months, we created a sustainable, bio-diversified farming system. We were happy and full of gratitude.

In recent years the natural farming movement has grown. But is it growing fast enough? Consider that the average age of a farmer today is fifty-eight, according to the U.S. Department of Agriculture. Now we desperately need younger, wiser farmers devoted to interweaving the cycles of Nature into their practices, and consumers who demand produce that is grown for the health of the people and the planet. The time is now!

School Gardens

Inch by inch, row by row, we made a garden grow.

My other project for school credit was starting and maintaining one of the first organic school gardens in the country. Two other Evergreen students joined me on the project at Garfield Elementary. I wrote the curriculum for teachers to use in the classroom. The lesson plans addressed the origin of food, nutrition, ecology, and ecosystems, with some economics and politics sprinkled in that a child could relate to. My colleagues and I shared ideas with the children about staying healthy and eating real food.

We asked the students if they knew about the life that lives beneath their feet. They had no idea that it could take thousands of years to make fertile topsoil. They never thought of soil as a nonrenewable resource. The kids agreed we need to take care of soil now and stop calling it DIRT! It fascinated the children to learn that soil, with all its billions of microbes, works to break down the biomass. We showed them how we depend on the vital, fertile soil for survival. We explained to them how soil is the medium for the food we eat, the timber used to build our homes, and the fabric for our clothes.

My favorite lesson plan focused on geography. We had a gigantic map of the world in the classroom, and on it, we pinpointed where the variety of foods we ate originated. It blew the children and teachers away to learn how far most food travels to get to our tables! How did that orange get here from Florida, or that cocoa from Africa? These lessons helped the kids learn about the impact of our carbon footprint on the Earth.

The carbon footprint signifies the amount of carbon dioxide and other carbon compounds emitted by one person from his or her consumption of fossil fuels and its derived products. NOAA reported that in 1980 the CO2 levels were 336 parts per million, today they are well over 400 ppm. Carbon dioxide levels today are higher than at any point in at least the past 800,000 years.

What if all children and adults understood that without the resources of the Earth, there is no education, there is nothing? What if our educational system taught us to value the economics of happiness rather than material things? It all starts with education!

We had a question-and-answer session about how most schoolyards have room for a garden, and why it was such a good idea for all schools to grow food and to have a teaching garden. The children and teachers became aware that the less connected we are to the sources of our food, the more we take it for granted.

Together with the children and their teachers, we planted nineteen raised garden beds in the schoolyard. We followed Alan Chadwick's biodynamic French Intensive Method. This method works with Nature to foster vibrant plants in small spaces. The kids weeded, harvested, and ate from the garden. We even had a manure pile, a three-bin compost system, and a little greenhouse that we had built with a grant we received. I brought one of my goats to school one day, and some of our chickens another day. But the best visit was from a pair of our personality-packed Muscovy ducks. The kids connected with their new feathered friends as they all waddled around the garden, nibbled on greens and quacked with joy.

The garden left an impression of beauty and delight and was a highlight of the school year. It was therapeutic for the teachers, the children, and me. It was an honor to teach love and respect for the land. The school garden project was so well received that the teachers adopted it into their curriculum. Future Greeners continued to cultivate young minds in the garden for years. When our son was 18, he attended Evergreen, and we discovered that the Garfield garden was still growing.

The less connected
we are to the sources
of our food, the
more we take
it for granted.

The Psychedelic Sheep

When the student is ready, the teacher will appear.
~ Buddha

Six years after starting college, I finally earned my degree. I had the damn sheepskin! I was twenty-four, pleased with myself, and I had pleased my parents. Hallelujah! I am forever grateful to them for not giving up on me, for paying my tuition, and for allowing me freedom in my college choices. I did not let my college time impede my education. Instead, I sculpted my new knowledge to fit my learning style and my interests. It was fun, and the experiences changed my life. I was turned on to every spectrum of the rainbow, which opened my mind to the colorful, arching potentials.

I grew to appreciate that education is a vital part of the fabric of society and that it should be more relevant, accessible, and affordable at any age. What we are taught and who taught us influences the design and pattern of our lives. Everybody has a stake in what we teach in school, but the most valuable disciplines are self-knowledge and self-actualization.

The wisdom gained from my Eco-Bohemian education fertilized my mind and cultivated many of the dreams that later sprang forth in my life and career. With a strong foundation, I would be unstoppable. Even if my accomplishments weren't what my parents envisioned, they would make them proud all the same.

Digging Deeper 11

If you are planning for a year, sow rice; if you are planning for a decade, plant trees; if you are planning for a lifetime, educate people.
~ Chinese Proverb

College education has changed so much since I got my sheepskin in 1982. Thankfully, today we have more options to expand our minds and manifest our realities. However, the cost of education has surged over 500 percent since I graduated. Tuition fees continue to rise, as does student debt. These are not promising statistics. Zack Friedan, a senior contributor of *Forbes Magazine*, states, "Student loan debt is now the second highest consumer debt category — behind only mortgage debt — and higher than both credit cards and auto loans." Student loan debt is over 1.5 trillion dollars. Why would someone go into debt for something they might not use?

Corporate scholarships have become an integral part of recruitment for students with potential, but they can come with strings and consequences. Companies aim to encourage the next generation of employees and executives, prepping students to help lead their businesses to greater success. The companies, through generous scholarships, also benefit from the exposure of *philanthropic giving*. The free money offer means they expect you to climb the corporate ladder, which could come at a steep price. Some of my classmates got snookered into opportunities which distracted them from their desired career paths. Personal life goals got diluted while struggling to find happiness in someone else's dream. There were no such scholarships or free-rides available for prospective eco-entrepreneurs, organic farmers, or social or political justice leaders.

Today, scholarships and grants continue to play a large role in young students' abilities to seek higher education. "The National Center for Education Statistics says that 59.1 percent of undergraduate students received scholarships and grants to attend college." Special interest funds draw people away from vocational education options. As people were increasingly drawn to new things, old, valuable trades continued to wane. It is hard to find someone who can fix a toaster, blender, lawnmower, or mend our clothing. The trade careers were stigmatized, and the availability of inexpensive and inferior products added to the consumer craze.

The mainstream educational system failed my generation by not emphasizing the vital role that ecological systems play in our lives. There was little to no talk about how our lifestyles were affecting the planet. Instead, ignorance thrived in the name of progress. In college I learned that Nature-based solutions and regenerative agricultural systems could help restore our malnourished food systems, the environment, and the economy. Why isn't this common knowledge? Why isn't this taught as part of the core curriculum for students in kindergarten through higher education?

For example, the wisdom of ecology, if integrated into every subject, could teach students about everything from the toxicity of certain art materials to the math needed for calculating the costs of a fossil-fuel driven economy. Perhaps if people understood the real costs — in every respect — they might be more conservative and make better choices. Many of the problems are easy to fix. We can learn if we are taught!

Industrial agriculture and mono-crop farming became big business post-World War II. Unlike permaculture and agroecology, this single-crop system is not a sustainable method. When the same crop gets planted in the same soil each year, nutrients are depleted, and the soil is left weak and unable to support healthy plant growth. Since mono-crop farming also causes plant and soil diseases, the crops become dependent on chemicals to be productive. The use of petrochemicals in fertilizers and pesticides has skyrocketed, affecting communities, human health, and the environment; this sounds like a lose-lose situation to me!

Corn-fed cattle pumped with hormones and antibiotics became the norm. Feedlots grew as the demand for meat production rose to fill the swelling orders from fast-food franchises — all served in Styrofoam. As the industrial food complex grew to unprecedented heights, so did the number of food and agricultural specialists. Product and packaging engineers were in high demand. They challenged scientists and chemists to figure out how to get more food from less land, as well as how to make addictive food products at a perceived lower cost — the mainstream educational system adjusted to train people to fill the voids.

Food-Packaging and Money: For Thought

The mounting complexities from the industrial food complex went far beyond food. Packaging material — made from the resources of the Earth — were engineered for the growing processed packaged food movement. The fact that large amounts of wild and fertile land get abused to produce the resources for packaging is often overlooked, as is the money we spend to buy the goods. The land is deforested, mined, and drilled to make cardboard from forests, tin and aluminum from the minerals of the Earth, and toxic plastics from petroleum oil fields. It is unimaginable how many inferior products get bought, used, and consumed while wrapped in wasteful, single-use packaging.

Our economic system revolves around the Earth's resources. Pennies, nickels, dimes, and quarters are made from metals, while dollar bills are made from cotton fiber and credit cards from plastic. The capital interests attached to these resources, have devalued their origins and their value to the systems and cycles of Nature that we all depend on. What's in your purse or wallet? How will you spend it?

Fossil Fuels and Plastic: For Thought

We live in a wasteful society driven by fossil fuels, and ignited by mass consumption of unnecessary goods. The throwaway culture created wealth for a few at the expense of others and the Earth.

As the oil industry continued to diversify the black gold, plastics took on a life of their own and were introduced in nearly every sector of business. In a few years, during the latter part of the '70s, plastic bottles and bags started to replace glass bottles and paper bags. Before that though, they were nonexistent. How did we live without plastic bags and water bottles? Don't get me started on plastic straws! Regardless of the limited recycling program initiatives, most plastic did not get recycled. Mounds of so-called recyclables ended up mingled in with the rest of human consumer waste. The rest littered streets, streams, and beaches. Plastics started to suffocate and flood the ocean, deplete the fisheries, and threaten all underwater life. Did anyone notice or care?

According to Ban the Bottle, making bottles to meet America's demand for bottled water uses over 17 million barrels of oil annually. Bottled water now holds the second largest share of the beverage market in the U.S, ahead of milk and beer. It's hard to believe we once drank New Jersey tap water. We now find unsightly gigantic gyres — garbage patches floating out at sea. Single-use plastics are the most substantial part of the problem.

The times brought opportunities and obstacles.

Influential events happening in the '70s were hard to escape. The warning signs were there in the baby boomer era, but greed and power snuffed out the shouts from activists, concerned citizens, and environmental groups. Activists became known as hippies, radicals, stoners, whistleblowers, or worse. Environmentalists were labeled tree huggers — a title I was proud to embody.

A minority, determined to create a more natural organic persona, challenged the events that were shaping mainstream society. Remnants of peace and love from the '60s were still in the air. Most baby boomers are still around, and some have not lost sight of the Earth Day mindset. The increased interest in organic and non-GMO products has been derived, in large part, from the principles of remaining baby boomers, which valued health and clean living above speed and convenience. These pioneers, some of whom are now grandparents and great-grandparents, have laid the foundation for the health movement of tomorrow.

The energy crisis played a vital role in the economic downturn of the 1970s. President Jimmy Carter, an early adopter of solar solutions, became a political champion for conservation. Among his many environmentally conscious initiatives, on February 2, 1977, Carter asked consumers to reduce fuel consumption. Businesses and environmental advocates joined Carter in issuing advice on cutting back and fostering the design of new products. For the first time, gas prices rose to over one dollar a gallon because of decreased oil output in the wake of the Iranian Revolution. His calls for conservation did not work for a generation that expected creature comforts with no strings attached. Stung by the oil cartel, sadly, many remember Carter for the long gas lines during the oil crisis. I remember him as a great President, and founder of Habitat for Humanity.

The lack of popular support for Carter became apparent with the surge of support for the Reagan administration, which dismantled much of Carter's environmental protections. Reagan's decision to lift regulations on domestic production and consumption of oil and petroleum products was very popular with the general public. Under Reagan's eight-year term, larger, gas-guzzling vehicles hit the road, conservation efforts diminished, and solar panels disappeared from the White House property. International politics became increasingly mired in oil and war. Almost every hotbed of conflict today and the focus of trillions of defense budget dollars are in the now war-torn oil countries of the Middle East. The deficit of our government reflects the dwindling natural resources.

As I continue to branch out, I search for answers. One thing I know for sure is that we must learn from the wisdom of Nature. The Earth has been around for over four billion years, and industrialization started in earnest only in the 1800s. Many species have gone extinct in these brief 200 years. Are we next? Our dependence on fossil fuels has turned into an addiction. We have much to learn from our mistakes.

Media

How absurd that we have gotten to where the media
and entertainment trumps education?

The blockbuster movie, *Star Wars*, which gave Hollywood a facelift in 1977, transported viewers to outer space. We could be part of the virtual reality, helping to free the galaxy from the claws of the evil Empire. Fantasy became one of the many distractions from what was happening on Earth.

You could sit and be entertained, while you ate from a medley of artificial candy: Whoppers, Junior Mints, Milk Duds, Goobers, Raisinets, and Good & Plenty. Yes, the list of candy choices was as endless as the galaxy. All the sugar bombs played well with the hard to avoid, seductive trans fat-infested popcorn. The aroma filled the air, and the crunch was so satisfying. For a couple of hours, you believed good would conquer evil — for a $2.25 admission fee.

The growing trend of comic relief TV sitcoms in the '70s made it easier to escape from reality. And it was free. The phrase *couch potato* was coined in the '70s. You could make Jiffy Pop at home and eat more candy for half the price on your comfy couch and enjoy endless entertainment. *All in The Family*, staring the loudmouthed, uneducated bigot Archie Bunker, captured viewers' attention and fueled political controversy. Bunker's character became so controversial that it received attention from the left and right wing. The stories provided an ongoing social and political discourse that stereotyped inter-generational and racial conflicts. The relatable content amplified gaps in society, which continued to grow wider. TV junkies relied on the scripts that other people wrote to guide their lives. I, on the other hand, loved to watch the program *Wild Kingdom* that featured wildlife and Nature. I never imagined some of these fantastic creatures would disappear from our planet. Nor did I realize that comic relief was a Band-Aid to the problems I would soon encounter as an adult.

Then there was the iconic comedy, *M.A.S.H.* which made war palatable and even funny with well-crafted comic relief. Its mixture of truth and darkness, good and evil, captured the widespread attention of millions of viewers. I and others tried to make sense of war, social and political injustice, and the multitude of fast-moving parts happening in the world. The news was not entertaining enough. *Monty Python* broke all the rules about comedy and entertainment, while *Mister Rogers' Neighborhood* and *Sesame Street* entered children's hearts and captivated their imaginations. Parents had more reasons to sit their kids in front of the boob tube than to send them outside to play. TVs were now in full color and found in more than one room in the house, splitting families apart and keeping us indoors.

As mainstream media and technology have continued to advance, there are more avenues to escape to, and endless amounts of programs and news outlets available to program our minds. Sports, alcohol, shopping, drugs, and TV — almost everything that entertains us — creates distractions that keep us from witnessing the devastating destruction of our home, our Mother Earth. However, all those distractions cannot prevent us from feeling the pain, even if our minds fail to recognize it. The media has also become harder for me to trust, considering that in 1983, 90% of American media was owned by 50 companies. Now, in 2011, the same 90% is owned by 6.

Microsoft did not come into existence until 1975, and Apple was founded in 1976. The personal computer did not enter the market until 1977 and did not become common until the '90s. As we typed term papers into a typewriter, few of us had any notion of the electronic revolution about to explode, and how it would affect our lives. We were content with the mounds of books on our clunky desks and searching the library card catalog for our references.

Elvis Presley, the King of Rock-and-Roll and one of the most significant cultural icons of the 20th century, left the world mourning when he died from overworking and overdosing in 1977. Hard rock and punk music became a rebellious expression of the frustrating times in the '80s. AIDS became a mainstream medical diagnosis in the U.S. killing thousands and marking the beginning of an aggressive groundswell in the gay rights movement.

Margaret Thatcher was elected as the first female prime minister of Britain in 1979, but her conservative policies did little to advance women's rights. In 1972 the Equal Rights Amendment to the U.S. Constitution was passed, but it still has not been ratified.

The backlash against women's rights frustrated many, not just the feminists. We were on the cusp of radical change, but we knew that it would be a hard-fought war, with many lost battles. There was freedom of speech, as long as you didn't say too much, or the wrong things. All in all, it was a time of near progress with a looming shadow of past regrets, and old power keeping us from truly realizing our next steps.

My newfound Eco-Bohemian education gave me a fighting edge to pursue a more palatable, heart-centered reality in these complex times. I was ready for the growth and development offered by my next journey and evolution. I was ready to tune out the news and tune into my truth. Ah, yes, the times they were a changin'. I was about to enter a man's business world, and I was determined to be heard.

EVOLUTION III

Growth & Development

Principles that influenced my life in this Evolution:

- Mentors are essential.
- Gratitude changes our attitude.
- What we appreciate, appreciates.
- Cultivate unity and reverence for all life.
- Celebrate life from the depth of your soul.
- Strive to bridge the gap between the economic,
  social, and environmental needs with love, respect,
  and compassion. This is how we build a better future.
- Support and take part in creating a resilient, robust community.

CYCLE 5

Transplanted Eco-Bohemian: Getting Grounded

The journey of a thousand miles begins with one step.
~ Lao Tzu

When a young tree gets transplanted into the right environment, it will adapt and mature. It can thrive! But conditions are not always optimum. Unexpected storms and diseases can disturb, or worse; kill the immature trees.

Like anything, we are more resilient when there is a strong foundation. If we settle into a place that suits our desires, wanderlust dissipates, and our newly shaped roots can find a home. It is sometimes necessary to leave a world dense with memories so that our souls can fully cultivate and evolve. Even if the ecosystem is not optimal, when rituals of nourishment are followed, we can still grow, develop, and adapt to our new environment. Strong roots yield resilient fruits. It is important to choose where you settle wisely.

Transplant Recipe:

- *Dig deep for reasons why instead of why NOT. Take the time to prepare. Make sure the new environment is compatible.*
- *Like a plant, when your roots are gently loosened, transplantation is more successful. Take care of loose ends and carefully remove yourself from the old environment.*
- *Be patient as you get established in the new fertile ground. Allow yourself time to settle. Accept that change can shock us — this too will pass.*
- *Compost old scripts that do not help you root, bud, bloom, fruit, and re-seed. Be present and focused on your intentions.*
- *Nurture yourself and others. Your new ecosystem will feel like home as you grow into yourself and the surroundings.*

While uncertain what was next, John and I agreed that *"living the good life"* was still for us. We were unsure what it meant to be a Bohemian, let alone a Soil to Soul Entrepreneur. With sheer determination and luck (or perhaps destiny), we persevered and followed our instincts.

Childhood and my counterculture young adult experiences fortified me for our unforeseen adventures. My sincere and abiding love for Nature guided my adventurous spirit. With an innate instinct for business and a desire to serve others, I would take root in Alaska — the 49th state in the Union. I was ready to get transplanted. But was John?

It is sometimes necessary to leave a world dense with memories so that our souls can fully cultivate and evolve.

Journey to the Land of the Midnight Sun

We need to pay exquisite attention to our responses to things —
noticing what makes our flame glow brighter. If we pay attention
to those things, we'll be able to catch the flame and feed it.
~ Nina Simons

One overcast day at Fantasy Farm, while transplanting broccoli, John and I formulated a plan. The idea came from our admiration for our mentors — the Nearings, the Rabins, the Lights, and the professors who inspired me. Our plan was to teach homesteading skills in a rural setting for inner-city children who would visit our future homestead. Our combined experiences gave us confidence. We felt ready to share how we learned to be more self-reliant. Stewardship of the land, natural farming, animal husbandry, and how to cook over a fire and bake using a wood-fired oven were all practical life skills, yet challenging to come by.

We decided Maine would be a good choice. The land was affordable, relatively close to our families, yet far enough away from the big-city life. Both sets of parents were happy about the prospects of us being back on the East Coast.

Meg, a fellow Greener and a friend, had spent a semester in Homer, Alaska, with a remarkable homesteader. She inspired us to take a side adventure to Alaska before leaping into our Maine vision. The journey north would change our lives. There, we would befriend Yule Kilcher, a native Swiss who was one of the few homesteaders that had arrived in the 1930s and was still living the lifestyle.

Yule had produced a documentary film about homesteading with his family. He went on annual lecture tours with his movie, sharing his back-to-the-land lifestyle and a wealth of practical knowledge. Passing through Olympia on one of his trips, he stopped to visit Meg. She brought Yule by to meet us. Impressed with our farmstead lifestyle, he invited us to stay with him in Alaska. It felt comforting to have a friend and a destination.

Yule was a psychedelic sheep and a Soulutionist!

 *The National Park Service states that "The Homestead Act of 1862 had an amazingly long life compared to most American land laws. It became effective on January 1, 1863 and was in effect until 1986. Over these 123 years, some two million individuals used the Homestead Act to attempt to earn the patent to a piece of land. Along the way, they settled approximately 270-285 million acres-around eight percent of all the land in the United States."*

Before we left Olympia, John and I had an unofficial hippie wedding in our barn, attended by friends and barnyard animals. We made room for a bluegrass band and danced the night away. We feasted on an old goat we butchered and enjoyed garden delights and a homemade wedding cake garnished with our prize dahlias. We broke the news of our union to our families and let them know we were venturing to Alaska before moving to Maine. John and I had been partners for three years. We were young and idealistic. That was the way we rolled. Our parents were not too happy about any of this. We, on the other hand, were stoked and prepared to shift gears.

Alaska is referred to as the Land of the Midnight Sun, or the Last Frontier. Our desire to travel there was greater than the amount of money we had. The first challenge was to figure out a way to finance the trip. Our profitable sourdough bread business at Fantasy Farm was the ticket. We reasoned that everyone needs to eat, so we would create a soup-and-bread mobile cafe, nowadays called a food truck. We would set up at all the hippie and country fairs we could find and peddle our sourdough for *money dough*. The small, reliable propane oven that leveraged our farmers market bread business in Olympia would hit the road with us.

We bought a 1972 laundry van that John resurrected. He decked it out to be our home and business. The kneading bench John built into the van doubled as our dining room table. He fashioned cabinets for our tight quarters with multipurpose functions. The whole rig was totally efficient, set up like a transformer: Camper by night, bakery by day.

We painted the old van kelly green and named her The Sourdough Express. The mobile bakery on wheels was ready to roll after we mounted the trusty oven and supplies into a small custom-built trailer John made. We loaded up with dried fruits, canned vegetables from our farm, and staples including flour, beans, rice, a forty-pound block of cheddar cheese, and our priceless sourdough starter. There was no room for extra baggage or emotional junk. Letting go was liberating. Our new business model was born. We would bake our way to Alaska in our outfitted old laundry van while experiencing the scenic and wild frontier via our mobile soup-and-bread kitchen. How cool was that for two budding entrepreneurs?

> *With both feet in, we took the first step, and*
> *with wheels on, the journey began.*

Kindness: Pay It Forward

When you plant kindness, you harvest kindness.
~ Jack London

⋅∘⊚◉⊚◉⊚⊚◉∘⋅

It was mid-April 1982, and John, Red, and I were ready to hit the road less traveled. We were full of tenacity, piss, and vinegar, which some might call *chutzpah* — or *guts*. We heard the journey was rough and were advised by several people to take a ferry out of Prince Rupert, Canada, which let passengers off in Haines, Alaska. Doing so would eliminate several hundred miles of rugged, unmaintained roads from our long, adventurous journey. We pre-bought our ferry tickets at the off-season rate. Beginning May 1, the prices would double which left us two weeks to make the ferry.

It might have been spring in the rest of the country, but storms and snow prevailed as we traveled north. Gas prices soared the farther we got away from the American border, and the road deteriorated as we headed through the barren lands of Canada. At least we were still on schedule to meet the much-anticipated ferry.

Just outside the quaint town of Smithers, British Columbia, we encountered our first obstacle. The van decided it'd had enough of the rugged road. A burly bearded man wearing wide suspender overalls came to our rescue with his old-style tow truck. Our savior, Frank, diagnosed the problem as a cracked radiator and leaky water hoses. With a kind smile, he took our payment for the tow and assured us we would be in good hands at Hanks Auto Shop. Hank informed us that a dated vehicle in a rural community meant delays for days.

Cold, low on funds, and with nowhere to go, we were pretty bummed. Not for long though. Next door to the mechanic's shop was a classic diner that served hot cocoa and the best sourdough pancakes. John and I hung out for hours to stay warm while we figured out what to do next. A middle-aged couple came in for lunch and sat at the booth next to us. They overheard us ruminating about our journey and van troubles. Curious about our bakery on wheels, they introduced themselves and struck up a conversation.

The compassionate couple sympathized with our situation and invited us to stay at their home until our van got repaired. Bob and Betty owned the general store in town and lived in a modest home where they had raised their three children. Now empty nesters, they let us know how welcomed we would feel. We eagerly took them up on their kind offer. Betty loved to bake and had always wanted to learn how to make sourdough bread. She invited us to bake in her kitchen and sell bread at their store to help pay for the repairs. We loaded up their jeep with our baking supplies and headed to their house. We could hardly believe it! Rather than bum out, we baked for days and sold our hearty-crusted, fermented bread to the warm-hearted locals, referred to as *Smithereens*.

We taught Bob and Betty how to make the mystic bread and fed them homemade soup and sourdough bread for days while we nourished each other's souls. When it came time to say our goodbyes, our hearts were filled with a mix of sorrow and gratitude. We left some of our priceless sourdough starter as a parting gift. Distant from everything familiar and farther from home than either of our young souls had ever been, we were ready to continue fermenting our budding lives. The Smithereens taught us to plant and harvest kindness no matter where we were, an integral lesson that has stuck with me to this day.

Alaska or Bust — North to the Future

*The biggest regrets in life will not be the things you tried and failed at,
but the things you never tried at all.*

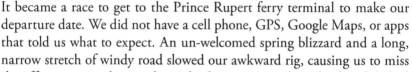

It became a race to get to the Prince Rupert ferry terminal to make our departure date. We did not have a cell phone, GPS, Google Maps, or apps that told us what to expect. An un-welcomed spring blizzard and a long, narrow stretch of windy road slowed our awkward rig, causing us to miss the off-season rates by one day! A husky woman at the ticket booth belted out, "If you want to get on this boat, you gotta pay an additional $125, or I'll give ya a refund!"

John and I scavenged through all our possessions and dug deep into our pockets with no luck. We were down to our last 50 bucks. We shared our grueling story and even bribed the battle-ax with loaves of fresh bread, only to hear a stern, "There's no way!" She slammed our refunded cash on the counter and shouted, "Next!" Granted we looked rough around the edges, but she still could have given us a break! She must have been having a bad day. Bewildered and pissed off, we carried on.

It was up to us to shift our attitudes and go with the flow. We would not let some battle-ax stop us from pursuing our dreams. Failure was not an option. Besides, there was no room in our mobile bakery for energy vampires or bitterness. In the ferry terminal parking lot, so that the burly woman could see us, we finger painted on the van's dusty body, "Alaska or Bust." We shouted out, "Cassiar Highway, here we come!" We then turned around and headed northwest to Alaska with lots of adrenalin.

With only $175 and many miles left to go, we would need to bake and sell enough bread for gas money to get to the Last Frontier. We adapted to our situation and drove down the narrow winding roads. With the right attitude, the detours would be fun and exciting yet challenging. John Muir's words fueled our curious souls as we journeyed through miles of majestic beauty: "To the lover of wilderness, Alaska is one of the most wonderful countries in the world." Our willingness to shift brought us the most rewarding lessons on this memorable adventure to the Land of the Midnight Sun.

For days we baked, sold, drove, and slept. The state's motto, "North to the Future" became our mantra. We encountered cold weather, blizzards, bears, moose, and herds of caribou. Wolves and coyotes howled into the night, which caused us restless sleep. The rugged backcountry personalities, high gas prices, and roads not fit for an old laundry/ bakery van were unexpected. John and I learned to slow down as we took in a new dose of reality. We had lots of time to talk and fantasize about our future. We also met extraordinary people and marveled at the beauty we encountered. To offset the high cost of gas, we traded bread for breakfast at remote cafes. To this day, a greasy-spoon scrambled egg has never tasted so good.

The population of Alaska was 488,000 in 1982. We arrived in the underwhelming city of Anchorage, Alaska, home to just over 200,000 people. We had traveled 2,500 miles from Olympia. It was my twenty-fifth birthday, May 12, 1982. With our last $25, John bought the business license permitting us to operate while on the road and at the country fairs — a mighty fine birthday gift. That evening we ended up in Bird Creek, a tiny township, twenty-seven miles south of Anchorage. There was a bar, a few backwoods residents, and a primitive campground. Here we would do our final bake before driving south to Homer.

Here I am again, 37 years later

After we set up camp, we baked thirty-six loaves of bread in our trusty propane oven. The aroma coming from our mobile bakery attracted other campers to our site. That night everyone gathered to celebrate my birthday. They sang "Happy Birthday" and we cut into a loaf of hot caraway rye bread that John presented with a beeswax candle and a bowl of butter. It had been a grand journey, and we were due for a celebration. The fellow campers enthusiastically supported us and bought some fresh bread. That birthday remains one of the top five in my life.

The next morning, we drove to Turnagain Arm Pass and parked our rig at the outhouse rest station. There were still about 150 miles of rough, curvy scenic road to venture through, and quite a bit of fresh bread to sell. We sold every loaf, nearly $100 worth (with inflation that equates to $251 today), which left us with enough gas money to get to Homer and a small margin of survival cash. It was now "Homer or Bust!" At that time, I had no idea that I was off to the place I would call home and start a new career.

Home Sweet Homer

*Each experience is a journey to behold. Always
be on the lookout to better the world.*

———————————————·❀◎◎◎◎◎◎❀·———————————————

Soaring bald eagles greeted us at the lookout at the top of the Bay Crest Hill that leads down into Homer. The spectacular vista of Kachemak Bay, with distant glaciers woven into the jagged snow-covered Chugach Mountain range, was magical. The glistening water had a mysterious, expansive reach, and the grandiose raw beauty of it all left us breathless. What might this wild place have in store for us? As the crisp, clean air seeped in through the cracks of our trusty Sourdough Express van, I felt warm inside. I turned to John and said, "We're home."

We arrived in Homer on May 13, 1982 with $43 and no place to live. John didn't even have a college degree, and mine was unfashionable, to say the least. What we did have was courage, grand ideas, and tenacious determination. My desire to save priceless wilderness ran deep. I felt I had a chance to be heard and to be taken seriously in Homer, Alaska.

While we took a calculated risk to move five thousand miles away from family and friends, I knew that to remain in a tight bud was no longer an option. I believed we were in the right place at the right time, ready to move forward and release the past. What I wanted was more important than the fear of failure and the unknown! I also sensed there was a business opportunity here. I was going to go for it!

Alaska offered everything for a budding Eco-Entrepreneur like me. There were more moose than people and fewer people per square mile than anywhere else in the country. Wildlife, forests, mountains, rivers, lakes, and vast glaciers that formed the stunning fjords filled my soul.

The purity of Homer's splendor rocked my world, and I couldn't imagine being anywhere else. For me, it was the perfect ecosystem to get transplanted and set roots. But was Homer ready for this granola-crunching hippie wannabe businesswoman? We had landed in the most Republican state in the union, and I was registered with the Green Party. That wasn't going to stop me from chasing my dreams even if I was just *a green dot in a red state*! I wasn't thinking much about politics; I was too busy planning on getting a green business going.

When we arrived in Alaska, the state's revenue came primarily from the oil companies and commercial fishing. Tourism was catching on, appealing to the more rugged travelers — those in search of big fish and wild game. The grandiose scenery was a bonus. Most people worked for the oil industries, school district, government, utility companies, the few existing shops, or in health care. The rest of us had to figure out how to make our way. To start a cottage industry or small business was a risky option I was willing to take. John and I hoped that the quaint community of Homer could provide fertility and nourishment for our next business venture. So, we took a calculated risk with a leap of faith.

Fueled by bold enthusiasm, the journey of thousands of miles had begun with one step. John and I would open our hearts to all the joy and laughter and adapt to the tough times. It was all part of the remarkable journey. Alaska was a place I had yearned to visit, but I had never imagined I'd live there. At twenty-four, I left the lower forty-eight on an adventure to the unsettled territory of the forty-ninth state. At twenty-five, I found my home. As I contemplated the beauty of Homer, I found *reserves of strength* that have fortified me to this day.

Alaska is home to 365,000,000 glorious acres — that's one-fifth the size of the lower forty-eight states — the largest geographical state in the union. Alaska increased the size of the U.S. by nearly 20 percent. It is also the home of Denali, the tallest mountain in North America. Alaska has thirty-nine mountain ranges containing seventeen of the twenty highest peaks in the United States. Over three thousand rivers grace its rugged terrain.

On March 30, 1867, Secretary of State William H. Seward agreed to purchase Alaska from Russia for $7.2 million. Critics thought Seward was crazy and called the deal "Seward's Folly." Buying Alaska proved to be a great move. They made significant gold discoveries in the 1880s and 1890s. In 1946, Alaskans approved statehood and adopted a constitution in 1955. On January 3, 1959, President Eisenhower announced Alaska's entrance into the Union as the 49th state.

Adaptation

*It takes a lot of courage to release the familiar and seemingly
secure, to embrace the new. But there is no real security in
what is no longer meaningful. There is more security in the
adventurous and exciting, for in movement there is life,
and in change there is power.*
~ Alan Cohen

One of Homer's nicknames is The End of the Road. Tom Bodett, author
and creator of the nationally syndicated radio program, *The End of the Road*,
popularized the phrase. There is only one road: The Sterling Highway.
The highway hugs the shore of Kachemak Bay, on the southwest side of
the Kenai Peninsula, and ends at the tip of the Homer Spit – a long narrow
finger of beautiful land jutting 4.5 miles into Kachemak Bay, literally at
the end of the road.

*For good reason, Homer is also referred to as the Cosmic Hamlet by the
Sea and the Halibut Fishing Capital of the World. I'll get to that later.*

There were around 2,200 residents when we pulled into town. The
community has seen little growth in the decades since. Many residents who
could afford to travel would leave in the winter in search of warmth and
sunshine. In the summer, flocks of tourists replaced commercial fishermen,
who went on extended fishing trips. A steady stream of motorhomes from
the Lower 48 made their way to the quaint village of Homer and parked
their rigs on the Homer Spit, sometimes for weeks or months. Many people
in the community welcomed the influx of seasonal tourists since they
brought in extra revenue.

When we arrived, downtown Homer had one doughnut shop, a few greasy spoon restaurants, a couple of real estate offices, a post office, a bank, and June Umiskie's General Store. There were many churches and even more bars. A couple of mom-and-pop grocery stores and a handful of other small shops scattered throughout the town made up the rest of the business community. Most roads were still dirt and gravel.

The residents were a good mix of fishermen and *fisherwomen*, rednecks and environmentalists, Republicans and Liberals, as well as homesteaders and hippies. Artists, musicians, and entrepreneurs were coming out of the woods to help reshape the community. There were probably more entrepreneurial risk-taking characters than contented folks. I had a feeling we would fit right in. But we needed to adjust to what appeared to us to be a new species of human in a place with different resources. This would take some effort after growing up in one of the most *civilized* populated areas in the United States. Many hearty folks still lived off-the-grid; a challenge in Alaska to say the least. It was also a bit lawless in the Last Frontier. There was an independent streak among those who settled in the largest and least populated state in the union.

The long, dark, cold winters and the intense daylight of the summer months — void of stars and moon — was a startling reality. Then, there were the unpaved, rutted roads, limited snow removal, dry cabin living (no running water), and wilted vegetables in the grocery stores. Subsistence was a way of life. Fishing, hunting, berry-picking, and home gardening were commonplace. There were no freeways, shopping malls, fast-food restaurants, small farms, Google, Amazon.com, or Whole Foods. To ship anything in or out of town was costly.

John and I were ready to settle for more wilderness and less stuff. We did our share of hauling water and heating with wood, or from the poor-quality coal gathered from the Homer beaches. We wore layers of clothes to stay warm, conserve resources, and save money. I was five thousand miles from the Garden State and not missing the skyscraper views. Settled into a landscape with vast open, rugged spaces and far-reaching vistas, I was home. The ecology of our lifestyle was about to transform at the end of the road. If we were to make it, we had to adapt.

The connection we made with Yule Kilcher at Fantasy Farm helped us to get established. He welcomed us and shared insights that fortified our will to adapt. The unpredictable weather and the hardened personalities of some of the old-timers were challenging at times. Yule's work ethic shamed us at first, but then we realized we needed to *buck up* if we were to make it in the Last Frontier. His stoic ways reminded me of my father. I would look to him for guidance, never letting him intimidate me, which only made me stronger for what was yet to come. Favorite topics of discussion were history, politics, and learning about his past. Yule's back-to-the-land stories inspired John and me to get over our pampered pasts and adjust to this new ecosystem.

Yule was born in Switzerland in 1913 and left Europe as the Nazis were rising to power. He came to Alaska in 1936 and fell in love with the place. He had a vision and a deep desire to live a more peaceful and self-sufficient lifestyle. Five years later, his dear friend from Switzerland, Ruth Weber, crossed the ocean and became Yule's pioneering wife. Together with their eight children, they cared for their 660 acres on some of Homer's most pristine land.

Yule and Ruth raised their family in a small hand-hewn cabin heated by wood and coal. The family foraged for edibles and hunted for wild game from Nature's bounty. They had extensive gardens from which they preserved food for the winter. Root crops filled their root cellar, and jars of berries, salmon, and vegetables filled their pantry. They also raised cows and chickens. When they were not working to maintain their lifestyle, this Last Frontier family spent time either singing and yodeling around a small piano or playing games. Yule also liked to play chess and loved to win.

The lifestyle came with unforeseeable circumstances. Unpredictable weather and unmaintained roads could make it impossible to leave the homestead. Town was 13 miles away. Once you made it to Homer, groceries and other necessities were limited. The lack of infrastructure, rugged terrain, raging storms, and long, cold dark winters could be hard on a family.

After years of living off the land, Yule became a state senator. He helped write the Alaskan Constitution. With passion and determination, he strived to keep Alaska independent. Yule attracted prominent people who helped shape both the state and Homer. Although he was charismatic, he was also a vocal critic of almost everything and challenged anyone who knew him. Yule had an unstoppable drive to get people to be all they could be. He'd be the first to tow you out of a mudhole. Then he'd give you maximum shit about the grueling task, so you would never get stuck again. EVER!

Still, Yule was a friend and mentor, as well as an avid sourdough baker. He helped us to master our recipes with gusto and shared the real flavor of the

Alaskan homestead lifestyle. His home was a haven for us, a place to take piping hot saunas and cool off with a plunge into his earthen-dug waterhole. Then we'd gather for a homesteader's meal, often moose meat or beef from one of his cows, beer-battered fiddlehead ferns, and wild or garden greens. The final touch was the hard-crusted, dense sourdough bread he laced with dried nettles and baked in his coal-fired cook stove. Yule also introduced us to the right people who would help guide us. I am forever grateful.

Yule died in 1998 with all his children at his bedside. His legacy lives on through the Discovery Channel program, Alaska: The Last Frontier. Many of his family members share the homestead lifestyle and values through this popular program.

Budding

The measure of intelligence is the ability to change.
~ Albert Einstein

W ithout buds, there are no blooms. A bud is small and often overlooked. People seem to prefer a fragrant, showy flower. What a shame, as a bud is so beautiful, packed with energy and potential. If a bud has the right conditions, it will bloom. Some buds, like people, are late bloomers. Storms and uncertain events can kill a bud — just like a promising idea, or a budding business can likewise get destroyed if conditions are not right. For people, as with plants or animals, getting transplanted can be shocking making it difficult to bud. John and I would endure the shock.

We'd learn to weather storms and droughts and adjust to the systems and cycles in the Cosmic Hamlet by the Sea. Courageous, determined, and focused, we'd search for answers. Our tenacious, idealistic spirits, and unwavering faith drove us to take an unconventional risk in settling in a foreign land. Persistence and passion would help us evolve from bud to bloom. Guided by intuition and bolstered by resilience, we'd plant our dreams in fertile ground. Homer was reshaping itself, and our future business would become a part of the new design. With bold enthusiasm, we dove in. We embraced the wild-spirited Alaskans, and they welcomed us with open hearts.

 Lessons I would learn as a budding Soil to Soul Entrepreneur:

- *When you find the good in everything, life is good.*
- *You can't always choose what will happen, but you can decide how you will react.*
- *From bud to bloom, it is a beautiful experience worth pursuing multiple times.*
- *The most important clause to put into a business plan: "Things may change, and so may I." A plan is only as good as your actions.*

Establishing a Strong Foundation

*The foundation stones for a balanced success are
honesty, character, integrity, faith, love, and loyalty.*
~ Zig Ziglar

There was no turning back now. We were emotionally ready to take root in our new environment. But how were we going to do this? With no formal business education, was I prepared to deal with start-up costs, cash flows, budgets, balance sheets, profits, and losses? As a food enthusiast and a Voice for Nature, I set my intentions to make a difference. I would do everything I could to heighten people's awareness about how our food choices affect the Earth. Whether the community was favorable to a natural food bakery or not, to start any new business —especially in a new place — appeared complicated and overwhelming.

We set up camp and our bakery business at the base of the Homer Spit — the most southern point on the contiguous Alaska Highway system. The average temperature in Homer during May was 35-50 degrees. With the wind chill factor, it could feel like below zero. Thankfully, the days were getting longer than the nights in the Land of the Midnight Sun. We appreciated the stunning, 360-degree view of Kachemak Bay, glaciers, mountains, and the Homer hillsides.

On the summer solstice, it is bright daylight in Homer for eighteen hours.

We lived and worked in or outside of our drafty van 24/7. We hand-mixed each recipe, and the dough rose in big wooden bowls on the dashboard where the van's two enormous windows would capture any possible solar heat. It was sometimes so freakin' cold that for the dough to rise, we'd drive

156

around town with the heater blasting. In all honesty, it was a fun way to get to know the area.

We mixed enough dough for thirty-six loaves every day, but since our trustworthy oven could only bake six loaves at a time, we had a full day's work ahead of us. With our funky scale, we weighed the dough out into approximately two-pound loaves which sold for $3 a pop. This worked out to be $108 a day in sales. While the bread baked, we mixed batches of dough for the next day. The resident bald eagles and ravens circled the campsite in anticipation of the microbial-rich crumbs. Curiosity and the aroma hooked anyone who walked by our campsite. Those folks became our initial Homer customers. We often traded bread for fish. There was nothing better than meeting new friends who warmed our spirits and shared their Alaskan fresh catch!

The laundromat had reasonably priced showers and was a warm place to hang out and sell bread. Many locals did not have running water and used the facilities as well. We let everyone we met know when we'd be at the laundromat with fresh bread and the couple who ran the business, informed their patrons. The place was always busier when folks knew we'd be there. This symbiotic relationship with the owners made our operation more efficient and profitable. It was a good lesson in the benefits and value of cross-marketing and collaboration.

Our main expense was the gasoline needed to get into town. Start-up and operating costs were nearly nothing. We still had plenty of goods in our trailer, paid no rent (free camping), and drew free water from the laundromat spigot. The sun and our fire pit covered the other utilities. To top it off, our outfitted laundry advertised our bakery on wheels.

After two weeks, we opened a bank account and deposited $800. In 1982, $800 had the same buying power as $2,082.76 in 2019. We created a budget to include money for showers, gas, and groceries. Tired of eating bread, cheese, dried apples, and pickles, we could now afford to splurge on a variety of foods! Our spirited work ethic was infectious, stimulating sales and attracting new patrons. We were profitable right off the bat. Blind faith was on our side.

Peddling bread on the beaches of the Homer Spit and in downtown Homer opened many doors for John and me. We approached our new business with honesty, character, integrity, faith, love, and optimism as we steadily grasped the concepts of cash flow and budgeting. Our new receptive community reinforced our hope and faith.

Growing Pains Lead to Gains

Pay it forward. Know when to take a hand-up, not a handout.

The demand for our bread rose so fast we outgrew our campsite bakery location in just two weeks. Several establishments heard about our sourdough and pursued us. The local natural foods store, a few restaurants, and the Wagon Wheel, an all-in-one operation of garden supplies, health food, and general store became our first wholesale customers. To keep up with the demand, we had to find a place to expand our shoestring operation. Desperate to find a facility, we knocked on every restaurant and church door with a commercial kitchen. Just as we began to lose hope, our persistence paid off. We found a place in the Old Town Homer district. The historical settlement dates back to pre-World War II days. It was an old transport site for people, mail, and goods. In this seaside setting, Joe and Winnie, owners of the Waterfront Bar and Grill, provided us the opportunity to bake in our first commercial kitchen. We were thrilled!

We struck a deal with the hard-working Alaskan couple. In exchange for using their kitchen, we would provide them with Sourdough rolls to serve their clientele. Joe and Winnie appreciated what it took to get a business off the ground at The End of the Road. They felt good about giving budding entrepreneurs a hand up, not a handout. Customers loved the fresh, fermented rolls. Our warm intentions cultivated new customers for all of us. It was a win-win mutualistic, symbiotic relationship.

Mutualism is a symbiotic relationship, a special type of interaction in the natural world where two species are mutually beneficial to each other, such as a bird and its flower or the specialized bacteria in your gut that enhances digestion. The unique interactions and balance between specific species, including humans, are essential to survival and can only be achieved by working together.

Since the Waterfront served dinner until 9 p.m., the earliest we could get into the kitchen was 10 p.m. I was usually an early-to-bed, early-to-rise gal, so the hours were taxing. We mixed large batches of bread in the antiquated mixer, which was an upgrade from hand-mixing. Everything in that kitchen showed signs of aging. A big plus was that we were in a warm place, so our bacteria-rich dough rose in half the time. During the rising time, we would clean the kitchen and then take a snappy nap on the hard floor in the dining room. After an uncomfortable rest, we handcrafted each loaf, followed by another two-hour rise, and then hours of baking. We had just enough time to bake the rolls for the Waterfront, and fill orders for our wholesale customers and laundromat clientele before the chef came in to prep for the day.

After bread and butter for breakfast, John and I packed up the warm loaves into large hand-woven baskets, and hit the road with the goods and a great attitude. We spent the rest of the day selling, delivering, and sleeping barely enough to do it all over again. The sunlit spring evenings brightened our days.

We listened to people who said, "You can do this," not those who said, "You're crazy!" The business was on the rise, and we were the hot new business in town, ready to create on a grander scale and serve our newfound community. Optimism built confidence — a sturdy trunk that was forming the foundation for our budding business. It all started with creating a little momentum that eventually multiplied until we were unstoppable. Growing pains never felt so good.

Don't Be Afraid to Ask

Let's face it, there's lots of questions when you move to a new
place and start a new career. You get to play the dumb card
and make mistakes. Sometimes, that's what it takes
to stand out in a crowd.

It seemed like we asked questions of every person we met. We weren't dumb, but let's face it, we knew little about the area or how to start a retail bakery. Also, we needed to find a place to live. Back then, we used word of mouth and bulletin boards to communicate. Fortunately, we had a local radio station that made daily announcements about everything from saddles for sale to rooms for rent, on their segment called the *Bush Line*. After all, Craigslist's did not exist. Camping was getting old, and we longed for a place to stand up while we changed our clothes. On Memorial Day weekend, I hit the wall! The tourist season had begun, and we woke up surrounded by a caravan of motorhomes. It was time for us to get the heck off the Spit and lay our bodies into a real bed.

Jim and Jan Preston, the local locksmiths and bread customers, came to our rescue and paid it forward. They pioneered their family business in 1979, just four years before we arrived. The compassionate couple graciously answered our questions and gave us a temporary place to stay. The smelly fish shack had two rooms. One with a bunk bed and a sink with no running water and the other was piled high with colorful floats, crab pots, and fishing nets. It was a mini upgrade from the van that had been our home for months. I was relieved to have kind neighbors a stone's throw away, and to be able to get dressed standing up! The location was ideal, within walking distance of town, the laundromat, and only a few miles from the Spit.

We asked our customers a lot of newbie questions, too. They were happy to answer them since it was in their best interest to keep the new bakers in town. Their encouragement helped to propel our dreams. We welcomed gratitude to be our driving force, which contributed to a positive attitude. Our sincere questions and eagerness to learn made us stand out. Now it was time to find a location to open a real bakery.

Gratitude
changes your
Attitude.

Persistent and Authentic

*And the day came when the risk to remain tight in a bud
was more painful than the risk it took to blossom.*
~ Elizabeth Appell

The day we deposited our first pile of cash in the bank, I felt confident, proud, and maybe even a little cocky. It was time to call my parents and gloat. I was nervous, but also eager to share the good news. My parents had no idea where I was or what I was doing. I was also concerned about my sweet mama's health and not sure what to expect. The guilt weighed heavy on my mind. But the risk to remain tight in a bud was not an option. I saw blooms on the horizon as my courage built. It was time to check-in, speak my truth, and declare my intentions.

I prepared myself for the confrontation in front of the van's cracked rear-view mirror before making the call. I would tell my parents, "My plan is to take a leap of faith and open a natural foods bakery in Homer, Alaska. Your blessings would mean the world." What could be more convincing than that? Besides, I'd tell them, "I'm determined to live on my own, on my terms, and to make a real difference in the world, come hell or high water." Basically, you can't stop me!

There was only one payphone in town at the Sterling Cafe, a local hangout for the true *old-time sourdoughs* — slang for an old-timer in Alaska. Here you'd find coffee with the grounds floating in your cup. Most everyone smoked as they ate greasy bacon and eggs while talking politics and fishing. I was out of my element as I stepped into the Sterling to use the payphone.

My father had given me a prepaid calling card, leaving me no excuses to call. After entering the long-distance phone number, plus the 11-digit calling card number, I postured myself and waited. After four rings, that felt like an eternity, my dad answered, "Goodman Residence," and the conversation went like this:

"Hey, Dad, how ya doing? How is Mom feeling?"

He belted back in his intimidating, deep baritone voice, "Where the hell are you kid?"

With exuberant excitement, I said, "Homer, Alaska."

"What the hell are you doing there?"

Off guard, I lost the words to my prepared speech.

"I'm moving here, Dad."

He blurted back, "What? Are you kidding me?"

With a quivering, yet defiant voice, I said, "No, Dad. We have been here for two weeks, and we love it! To top it off, we made $800 selling sourdough bread in just one week! We plan to stay and open a bakery!"

Before I could catch my breath, he hung up on me, leaving me standing there, humiliated, like a fish out of water, with my emotions flopping this way and that. I slumped and stared in disbelief at the clunky black receiver connected to the payphone by a three-foot wire cord; without my dad's blessings.

Two weeks later — after we had made an additional $1,000 — I called home again. The conversation did not change much, and I got the same negative dial tone at the end of another one-sided discussion.

Charging Forward with Courage

Life requires courage to shift and propel your dreams.

A few days after the second disheartening, one-sided conversation with my dad, John and I took a trip to Anchorage to look for used equipment. The seven-hour drive on winding roads gave us plenty of time to think, talk, and consider our options. We did a lot of soul-searching and committed to each other and our new business venture.

We found everything we would need at one used restaurant supply store in Anchorage: two convection ovens, a 20-quart mixer, sheet pans, a commercial sink, a funky old wooden showcase, racks, prep tables, sinks, a commercial coffee machine, a four-burner cooktop for soups, and some miscellaneous necessities including two wooden tables and eight chairs for customers to dine. The price tag was $8,000 — the man selling the used equipment offered to finance us. We would need to put down $2,000 and pay 15 percent interest. Not the best option, but at least we had one. The salesman was willing to put the equipment on hold for a week. Now it was time to scramble and find a location.

I called Jules Rabin to share our exciting news and get the contact for the grain mill they used. I could tell by the tone in his voice he was delighted we were opening a bakery — five thousand miles away. Jules gave us the contact info and encouragement. It would cost $1,800 to deliver it to our door in Homer. The grain mill was the only new piece of equipment, and the final piece that would make our tangy bread exceptional. I contacted the company and put them on alert for their first shipment to the Last Frontier.

We had nearly $2,000 saved in the bank since my first call with my resistant father, and plenty of ingredients still in the trailer. I gathered my wits and called my dad for the third time. Besides sharing my determination, I would ask him to lend me the $10,000 with better terms than 15 percent interest. There was no time for pleasantries. The one-sided conversation went like this:

"Dad, I have nearly two grand in the bank. We are looking for a location to start the bakery, and I need a $10,000 loan to buy equipment. I will pay you interest! And, I want you and mom to come to Homer and deliver the funds!"

Then I hung up on him!

I was twenty-five, full of conviction, chutzpah, and tenacity, and driven by a courageous dream that would soon come true. When I called back a few days later, I readied myself for the worst. To my great relief and surprise, my father said, "We got our tickets. We'll be there in two weeks!" All I had to say was, "I love ya, Dad!"

Persistence and authenticity had paid off. My father, who had been my greatest resistor, would become my greatest assistor. I still had my doubts. I knew how sick my mother was and felt conflicted about my decision to move five thousand miles away. In my heart, I felt my mom wanted what was best for me. After all, she had moved from California to New Jersey to follow her dreams and be with my father. It was my time to grow into the woman I would become. All the same, it was disconcerting.

Those brief and tense conversations with my father were my first lesson in the art of negotiation. The confidence gained from the positive results of me being authentic helped me with negotiations I would have soon with bankers, employees, and customers. Little did I know I was living like the future mattered. It took courage to bet on a new dream, and nerve to take action. My sharp instincts and steadfast conviction would serve me well on my one-of-a-kind journey.

Location, Location, Location

We must be rooted to grow.

———————————❧———————————

Our business outgrew the Waterfront in a matter of weeks. With cash in the bank, a steady income, and a guaranteed loan from my dad, John and I were ready to rise with the demand and get rooted. Proudly, we put down the first and last month's rent on a 375-square-foot room in a building nestled in the woods on Ocean Drive. This convenient location was close to town, on the way to the Homer Spit, and somewhat visible from the road. The old real estate adage, Location–Location–Location, soon proved true for us.

Many of the locals in the '80s made their living working on the Homer Spit. So, there was always a steady stream of traffic. The small boat harbor at the tail end of the Spit hosted a few dozen fishing charter boats outfitted for tourists. A handful of businesses catered to the tourists, including gift shops, a few eateries, Land's End Hotel, and the Salty Dawg Saloon. There was a small fleet of commercial fishing vessels and the Icicle Seafood processing cannery which kept many folks employed in the summer. Camping was free anywhere you pitched your tent or parked your rig. It was an ideal situation for the influx of temporary workers referred to as *spit rats* who would soon become our best customers and employees.

Love and Acceptance

At every step of life, it would be ideal if our parents allowed us to bloom.
It is their job to make sure we are happy, healthy, and safe—not to
put a thorn in our sides. It helps when we can prove to them we have
met their expectations, even if it is through different achievements.

When my folks arrived in Homer, they found us entrenched in our lives, baking, making deliveries, and working around the clock. We were still pulling graveyard shifts at the Waterfront while scrambling to get our new facility up and running. Mom and Dad stepped into my world to find me sleeping in a fish shack and earning a meager living out of an old laundry van with my *sort of* husband. I looked like a *woods-woman*. OH, MY GOD, what my folks must have thought! They got a good dose of my reality and initially, were not impressed. Boy, did they let me know it! I'm sure if I had been younger, they would have grounded their Jewish American Princess for foolishness and misconduct. Their comments, actions, and postures toward me pushed my emotional buttons. But there was way too much to do, and no time for draining arguments. It was apparent to them; I was not going to budge!

When my parents realized how hard we were working and how determined we were to succeed, they bucked up and offered to help. After a few days, their suburban edginess calmed down as they absorbed the beauty of this wild place.

Mom loved to go out on deliveries with me, enchanted by the stunning wildflowers, majestic views, and colorful Homer personalities. While we connected on a deeper level surrounded by Nature, it was as if she was also budding. As sick as she was, Mom never let on how bad she felt. I have priceless memories of her joy when we dropped off our sourdough and got *money-dough* back. After deliveries one day, sitting in the van in our new bakery parking lot, my mother looked out of the big windows at our facility and asked, "Donna, honestly, are you happy, healthy, and safe?" I looked deep into her big brown eyes, eager for her approval, put a grin on my face, and gave her an exuberant "YES!" She smiled back and reached for a hug. It was a great embrace! She had always been the best mom, but this was when we bonded as women. Acceptance is powerful! What more could a mother or daughter want? We shared respect and unconditional love, both of us choosing to embrace the best in each other. AMEN! Just thinking about that moment brings tears of happiness. From that day forward, we told each other everything. The two times she made it to Alaska and saw me in my element were some of the most joyous times in both our lives.

Dad jumped right in as well. After experiencing his first halibut fishing trip with Jim Preston and getting to know the man who took us in, he was sold on the place. He could see we were happy, healthy, and safe. My dad always had a love for Nature growing up with my bird-loving grandmother. But he never would have experienced the raw and majestic Alaskan wilderness had his tree-hugging, Eco-Bohemian Entrepreneurial daughter not transplanted herself there. He fell in love with the Last Frontier too. That made it easier to accept I would be thousands of miles away, live in a four-hour time zone difference, and it would take a fourteen-hour flight to visit one another.

Within days of overcoming the shock of his only daughter's new reality, Dad was on his hands and knees, helping John install the new floor. They worked tirelessly to get the space ready for the grand opening, which was only a week away. There were plenty of things to do before we could open our doors. Luckily, several carpenters and a variety of handymen and women came out of the woodwork and offered their skills. With their help, we painted walls, washed windows, installed equipment, and buffed out the whole place.

It was my first experience hiring anyone, and I found it very rewarding. Before we opened our doors, we tested the equipment and some new recipes. Then we threw a party for all the fine folks who generously helped us get our dream off the ground. After feasting on sourdough pizza and beer, John and Dad hung the rustic, hand-painted Fantasy Farm sign to remind us of the value of the small farm. Then they placed a rusty old horseshoe over the entryway door to our bakery. We were in luck and business. Even though we didn't have much money, John and I had each other and knew everything would bring a chain of love and prosperity.

My dad also kicked my ass into gear when needed. He insisted on giving me a crash course in *Boot Camp Business 101*. I had no experience running a retail bakery, and being dyslexic was a challenge when it came to doing the numbers. Dad simplified the business details and drilled them into me. Well aware of my shortcomings and my hyper personality, he understood better than anyone how to guide and mentor me. Mistakes would be part of the learning curve.

Dad's Main Lessons:

- *"Donna, keep the cash flowing at all times. The tighter you run the ship, the more profit."*
- *"Donna, keep your hands in the till at all times." Translation: Always keep track of the money.*
- *"Donna, work towards a 30-30-30-10 margin — 30 percent cost of goods, 30 percent overhead, 30 percent payroll, leaving you a minimum of 10 percent profit."*
- *"Donna, NEVER be late on payroll. Your employees are your greatest assets or biggest asses. Know when to promote, and when it's time to kick some ass."*
- *"Donna, keep your eye on the big picture. Do not agonize over the details. Procrastination is a killer."*

He taught me how to do basic business math, and to round numbers up and down in my head, which enabled me to adjust and make smart decisions readily. He made sure I knew the difference between cash flow and income, how to read an income statement and a balance sheet, and that budgeting was essential. It was all excellent advice, and it's not that complicated. Really. The tough part is figuring out who you are, what you love to do, and being willing to ignore those who say, "You should do *this*" and, "Because that's the way it is, so deal with it!" Compost those scripts!

As I digested my father's strong-willed, homegrown business sense, I absorbed most of the knowledge of the financial end of running a business and would learn the rest by trial and error. When I was open-minded, my mind expanded. I began to understand my *happiness-flow*, in relation to the cash flow, and how important it was to balance this relationship. I also learned that when you plant an idea and nurture it, it will grow.

CYCLE 7

Taking Root

An anchor of strength supports intentions.

The root system of a tree or any plant, provides the stems and leaves with water and dissolved minerals. The roots must grow into new regions of the soil to perform their functions: Absorption, aeration, food storage, and anchorage for support. When rooted, a plant can bud, bloom and fruit. Like trees, we must root deeply, firmly, and spread out to grow. When we absorb the right nutrients and are rooted in a supportive environment, we can develop into the best version of ourselves.

Six months after graduating from Evergreen State College, I was the pioneering proprietress of the first natural foods bakery and cafe in Alaska highlighting local and organic food. I was twenty-five years old, and at the age when the brain becomes fully developed. You are less inclined to be sculpted and more prone to be the sculptor. In this coming cycle, I continued to gain the skills to adapt and grow as I anchored my roots. At times, I was out of my comfort zone. These times were when I grew the most. Support from family and our new community provided the anchor and strength. As I gained confidence, I'd take more calculated risks. I'd learn that an entrepreneur must be flexible and have a positive attitude even in the worst of times. Also essential, was the willingness to reposition, dig deeper, and reach further to survive and thrive.

Interconnecting humanity and business to the systems and cycles of Nature made smart business sense. I was determined to prove it. Alaska was the perfect place for me to take root. It was my idea of nirvana. I was willing and able to climb the Alaskan trees and mountains to build something meant to last. But was John? Time would tell.

Building Something Meant to Last

To be successful, you have to have your heart in your business,
and your business in your heart.
~ Sr. Thomas Watson

I saw an opportunity to help transform the unethical foodservice industry and was prepared to act. I got into the food business with the notion that nourishment is our lifeline, and our bodies are temples for our souls. Food is beyond just taste. Food unites us in ritual, in tradition, and in something holy that comes from the bounty of the Earth. Somehow this way of thinking was being lost, and I had my heart set to preserve it, even though the odds were against me.

The grain mill was our last piece of equipment to arrive. The South Carolina manufacturer was pleased to ship his first grain mill to the 49th state in the union. We ground the grain daily. The fresh flour was the essential ingredient that made the best tasting and most nutritious bread you could buy. As more organic and fresh ingredients became available, we incorporated them into our recipes.

The steel grain mill was such a well-built machine it is still in operation nearly four decades later. What a concept — to make something useful, meant to last a lifetime or longer! Meanwhile, modern, poorly made products, often manufactured in other countries, get added to our overflowing landfills. Something is wrong with that picture!

The EPA estimates that nine million refrigerators and freezers are thrown away in the U.S. each year. Appliances get replaced long before they wear out. Changes in style, technology, and consumer preferences make newer products more desirable. According to This Old House, of the major appliances in a home, gas ranges have the longest life expectancy: 15 years. Dryers and refrigerators last about 13 years. Appliances with the shortest lifespan are compactors (6 years), dishwashers (9 years), and microwave ovens (9 years). There's an old adage that goes, "If it ain't broke, don't fix it." Why should that apply to only some things in our life?

173

Mission-Dedication-Intention

Food for People and the Planet Served with Peace and Love.

OUR MISSION: To broaden the awareness of the healing power of fresh whole foods and how our food choices affect the environment and humanity.

OUR DEDICATION: To serve responsibly raised and produced food, and offer diners healthy, delicious meals, and memorable experiences.

OUR INTENTION: To stimulate the local economy and serve food made for people and the planet, and to shift the way we consume – from convenience to conscious eating.

Our goal was to create a conscious business, with substance meant to last.

We were known as the granola-crunching hippie place to eat. A colorful handmade sign adorned the bakery display case that quoted Wendell Berry, "Eat Responsibly." I also printed on our menus our tagline, "Food for People and the Planet." Some customers did not appreciate what we were doing. Serving Peace and Love was a new concept. With education, persistence, and excellent tasting food, we made inroads.

To fulfill our Mission, Dedication, and Intention, we made commitments never to use Styrofoam, to recycle, re-purpose and repair old equipment, to be energy efficient, and to donate any food scraps to farmers. We donated money and food to environmental causes and organizations. As an incentive to gain regular customers and reduce clutter in the landfills, we offered discounts on beverages when folks brought their own to-go cups. We educated the staff and clientele on the impact of our food choices on the environment. And we were the only non-smoking eatery in town — all revolutionary stuff in 1982. Being ahead of the times was not always easy, but necessary if we were to stay true to our values.

Boston University reported, "Americans love their coffee. By some estimates, Americans drink over 100 billion cups of coffee every year. A staggering 14.4 billion are bought in disposable paper cups that end up in a landfill or litter beaches, streets ... everywhere. Placed end-to-end, these cups would wrap around the earth 55 times and weigh around 900 million pounds." Don't get me started on the sleeves, plastic stirrers, and lids.

According to an article in CNN Money, Jan 5th 2018, "To tackle the problem, a group of British lawmakers is calling for a new £0.25 ($0.34) tax on disposable coffee cups. They hope a 'latte levy' will force consumers to use recyclable cups and reduce waste." Not a bad idea.

Choosing a Name

It's about what you do with your identity that matters.

The name we chose for our shoestring business, The Fresh Sourdough Express, had deep meaning for me.

Fresh represents the products we serve that come from responsible farmers, fishermen and women, and ranchers. All meals are made fresh with fresh ingredients. We are always in search of fresh ideas to show the vital role food has in the intricate web of life.

Sourdough is a fermented culture that comprises probiotic-bacteria and natural yeast. These properties make the bread easier to digest than bread made with processed yeast. Lactobacillus in the sourdough neutralizes the negative effects of phytic acid, an anti-nutrient that impairs the absorption of iron, zinc, and calcium that our bodies need to function properly. Sourdough was already a popular word in Alaska. You earn the name Sourdough once you have lived in the state for 25 years or more. The early settlers and prospectors are known as sourdoughs.

Express is something we associate with fast, rapid, and direct. The word also means to convey or to communicate. We chose the word to convey our intention: to provide the opposite of fast food that was becoming the norm and to express Nature's beauty through our baked goods and our food.

Evolving with Intention

*We have the ability to bud, bloom, share the fruits of our labor,
and contribute to a better way of life.*

We started with what we knew how to do best: A variety of our tried-and-true, fermented sourdough bread, rolls, savory pastries, muffins, cakes, and soups, along with some organic teas and coffee. We listened to our customers and catered to their palates to the best of our ability. As we continued to learn more, small bites created big leaps, and we gained momentum.

Tourism was on the rise, and residents and visitors stopped by out of curiosity. For some, it became a delightful habit. Within a month, The Fresh Sourdough Express was cranking. Between our wholesale and retail customers, we were busier than the two of us could handle. To harvest the fruits of our labor, we needed to hire staff. Several colorful Homer characters applied. We hired a few exceptional young women and nice guys around my age — all of whom embraced our Eco-Bohemian concepts and values. The new staff contributed recipes and ideas. The smartest thing I did was to hire people who were smarter and more skilled than I. Not only did the new staff help ease the load on our shoulders and allow us to take full advantage of our situation, they also contributed several new recipes and ideas to build the business.

One of our first hires was a former competitor of ours whom we befriended. Hans was a traveler from Switzerland who had landed in Homer for the summer. To support his adventurous time in Alaska, he sold braided Swiss bread made from his grandmother's recipe. Hans had a good following for his sweet bread, known as Zopf. One day John and I tracked him down and asked him to join our team. Like us, he found it challenging to bake on the Spit, so he took us up on our offer. We learned a lot from each other, culturally and culinary-wise: Another symbiotic win-win experience. Hans found a warm, clean place to be creative and make money, and we gained an experienced baker with great recipes.

Once folks got trained, our menu expanded, and production increased. We encouraged the staff to create and express themselves. In return, the business flourished. One of the most rewarding feelings I've ever felt was the joy that came from co-creating in the kitchen with these inspired beings. My college years taught me how fun and effective collaborating with like-minded people could be. Building a trustworthy crew that aligned with our vision was essential to the growth and development of the business. Because we embraced and empowered the staff, and acknowledged we were all part of the team, our work felt more like play.

The bakery provided a hip culture to work in. We thought and acted out of the box, offering unique food and a welcoming atmosphere. New Age music and light rock 'n' roll playing on our reel-to-reel tape recorder, added to the ambiance. The cafe smelled of fresh-baked goods and patchouli oil — irresistible! The air was full of contagious energy. We created a bartering system with customers and never turned anyone away who could not afford to pay. An hour of work earned you a hearty, healthy meal. Some of those folks became the best employees. My dad had taught me well.

After hours, we often gathered with the staff at the beach for a bonfire. We shared food and innovative ideas that helped to reshape the culture of our community. The expansive sandy grey beaches were accented with a variety of shorebirds, resilient vegetation, chunks of black coal, shapely driftwood, and polished rocks from the rough seas. Soaring eagles and the dramatic Alaskan landscape all inspired us to preserve the beauty. Magic moments like this reaffirmed that I was in the right place. What could be better than evolving together with intention? We worked hard, played hard, laughed a lot, and learned from one another.

Our tiny yet productive kitchen extended into our dining room. An old wooden showcase full of tempting baked goods was the only thing that separated us from the customers. The used wooden tables and eight chairs we purchased added to the welcoming atmosphere. Customers often hung out for hours. The staff and I enjoyed meaningful conversations while folks enjoyed a freshly brewed cup of coffee and a warm pastry, or a steaming bowl of seafood chowder and sourdough bread. I felt my best while engaging with our loyal clientele. Listening to great music and sharing delicious food that we served with peace and love was a recipe for success.

A bakery was the perfect business for me, a warm and fuzzy place that provided space for the community. The kitchen was the place where my family gathered for nourishment and conversation that started and ended each day. Creating an environment like that made me feel at home. My parents and Mother Dear had raised our family with good intentions, and I had the privilege to cultivate those intentions to our new, extended family.

You could say I grew up at The Fresh Sourdough Express. I learned my hardest and most effervescent lessons on Ocean Drive, often with a wooden spoon in my hand. Doing what I loved, I was creating abundance in my life and building relationships meant-to-last. I was evolving with intention.

Rooted Endeavors

*What you do makes a difference, and you have to decide
what kind of difference you want to make.*
~ Jane Goodall

We shared the 1,200-square-foot building with an accounting office that served commercial fishermen and fisherwomen. The people who worked there, smoked so much that it stained the office walls with nicotine. Despite that, they were friendly folks and built-in customers. A lot of clients came into their office to talk finance, and that kind of talk always built up an appetite.

When we got tired of the smell at the Prestons' fish shack, we wised up, bought a used-sleeper couch, and often slept in the small waiting room that separated the two businesses. Since we worked ten to twelve-hour days, we figured we might as well crash there. This frugal yet savvy move saved us money on gas and allowed us to get extra sleep. It felt good to get rooted. To top it off, it turned out we had landed a gold mine of a location.

Our first winter, we made enough money to rent a comfortable cabin across Beluga Lake. They built this *human-made* lake as a landing place for floatplanes. The lake was a block away from The Sourdough Express. As the cold winter settled in and the lake froze, I often snowshoed to the bakery. It was exhilarating to be out in the crisp, clean air under a moonlit sky, on an early Alaska winter morning. These chilly morning treks reminded me how vital it was to care for my body and commune with Nature.

I was chillin' into my new reality.

Within six months of moving to Homer, I was already engaged in community and environmental activism. Branching out and networking was the best marketing approach to help grow our business, plus it was free and fun. I was elected president of the local Conservation Society and became a board member of the newly established Center for Alaskan Coastal Studies (CACS).

The CACS was founded in 1982 by an exceptional Nature mentor, Michael McBride, founder of Kachemak Bay Wilderness Lodge and author of *The Last Wilderness: Alaska's Rugged Coast.* He exemplified how a person could love Nature and still earn a living while educating people about how to preserve it. My intentions and business model were in harmonious alignment with his sincere, entrepreneurial vision.

Our business also became a member of the Homer Chamber of Commerce, which operated out of a small trailer. The enthusiastic staff made up for the dingy headquarters with their heartfelt desire to see Homer thrive.

The moose and crows seemed to appreciate our new little bakery in the woods. We often sighted moose grazing on or bedding down in our yard. When we baked, all the crows in town made the bakery their central hangout. They took a liking to our sourdough, too.

That fall, while all of us kids were off living our lives, my parents sold our childhood home on Pine Hill Road and moved into a condominium closer to my mom's medical care. Brutus, our family Alaskan husky who had camped out in the backyard with me ten years earlier, needed a new home. I welcomed him with open arms to Alaska! He had spent his entire life pampered in the suburbs, so it was up to me to help him acclimate and animalize into his new environment. I taught my old dog new tricks, which helped him adjust to the ebbs and flows. Brutus became the cafe mascot, adored by staff and customers.

Adding to the Course of the River

Time is a sort of river of passing events, and strong is its current; no sooner is a thing brought to sight than it is swept by and another takes its place, and this too will be swept away.
~ Marcus Aurelius

There was a transient population in Homer, and like a flowing river, people often got swept away to pursue other opportunities. Many also left, disenchanted by the weather. Meanwhile, every day my roots grew more profound, and I adjusted to the ebbs and flows. The Sourdough team became my extended family. All of us were very stylish in our aprons covered in flour, and God knows what else, as we created calories of yumminess. To top it off, I got to show off my art and share love every day. It was a great way to earn a respectable living. It was a beautiful exchange. I was living the old adage, "Choose a job you love, and you will never have to work a day in your life."

My Jersey friends would jokingly ask me if I was freezing my ass off and living in an igloo. They thought I'd lost my mind. Maybe I had, but I was safe, happy, and healthy, and I had found my purposeful why. I thought perhaps they lost their minds in the mainstream world.

In the early '80s, the organic movement was barely catching on. The small-scale farm movement in Alaska was nearly dormant. Most people did not give a hoot about organic food. Others did not appreciate our slightly higher prices for the increased value we offered. Customers would ask, "Why use organic? What's the difference? Why is it so expensive?" I did my best to answer the questions and did not let adverse reactions stop me. In actuality, it made me more driven to educate our staff and clientele about the positive impact of organic agriculture. We focused our attention on innovation and on serving the customers who appreciated what we were doing. The more I gave of my time, the busier we got. *What we focused on grew.*

Alaska's climate, sea, and terrain were suitable for fishing, hunting, and berry-picking. We loved to trade cookies for crab, chowder for halibut, and other food for rhubarb and wild berries, which we incorporated into our baked goods. Considering the growing season was only ninety days long, local produce was scarce. We had little choice but to purchase conventional produce from local distributors. My previous connection with the Seattle-based distributor while at Fantasy Farm made it possible for me obtain quality and organic bulk goods. Depending on the weather, transporting the bulk grains, beans, coffee, teas, and other dry goods could take up to two weeks.

Back then the natural foods order catalog was about forty pages. Today the catalogs are like an encyclopedia.

To set up an account with a new vendor with no credit was not an easy task. To come up with enough money to pre-pay for the first several orders was a challenge. Limited technology added to the frustrations. Credit card payments were not common, so we wrote a lot of checks. It may be hard for Americans born after 1980 to imagine a society without credit and debit cards.

Once we got a thirty-day credit option, we took advantage of it and learned to budget and pay our bills on time, relying on snail mail from Alaska to the Lower 48. My experience managing Earth Artisans came in very handy. I understood how to order and had a read on what folks seeking natural foods might enjoy in a food service environment. It was all clicking for me.

Thriving with My Tribe

*Live and act within the limit of your knowledge
and keep expanding it to the limit of your life.*
~ Ayn Rand

The business was generating enough money to support eight full-time employees. We were outgrowing the 375-square-foot facility, and customers requested more meal choices. It was clear there was a need for more seating. The accounting firm that leased the other half of the building wanted out, so I jumped in. I hit my dad up for another loan to cover the cost of the expansion. To remodel the 1,200-square-foot facility would cost around $10,000. When I called my dad for the loan this time, he did not hang up on me. Instead, he wired funds into my bank account. This was a lot of responsibility for a twenty-seven-year-old woman who uprooted and transplanted herself so far from home and had never gone to business or culinary school.

In a matter of weeks, we knocked down walls, tripling the size of the kitchen and doubling the size of the dining room. We also added a separate area just for the bakery and installed two brand new ovens. The cafe's seating capacity increased from eight to forty-eight. Our rent tripled, and so did the staff, sales, and my responsibilities.

It all somehow balanced out. We had changed the course of the river as the business transitioned from a bakery to a full-blown bakery and cafe.

We decorated the new dining area with an Alaskan motif, installed pine wainscoting and custom-made booths which made the place feel homier. Local artists' creations adorned the walls. We made room for musicians and other entertainers to share their talents and replaced the reel-to-reel player with a tape deck and speakers. The new bakery display area was alive with

a more robust variety of baked goods, including a line of savories I created and named — *Stuffs*.

We made the Stuffs using our French Onion Garlic sourdough recipe, stuffing the dough with a variety of different fillings. We also made savory croissants with various fillings and topped the hot pockets with homemade salsa and sour cream. The savories were a big hit and a terrific grab-and-go item. They brought in more business and satisfied happy customers looking for a quick hunger fix. The cafe would get so busy that people could wait an hour for a table, so this decision helped to satisfy those customers on the go. In the slower months, we held various nonprofit meetings at The Sourdough as well as realtor and banking luncheons. We also delivered custom catered platters to several businesses in town.

One thing I loved the most about the cafe was that it was like a party every day as we mindfully crafted ingredients into nourishment with positive energy. I listened to our customers and our staff and looked to them for guidance to make the cafe a welcoming environment to hang out. With valuable input, we added new menu items, live music, poetry slams, art openings, fundraising events, private parties, catering, wholesale, Friday Night Pizza, and Sunday brunch. We even baked our customers' grandmothers' favorite recipes, as a lot of folks had no oven. Diversifying and extending ourselves connected us with the needs of the community and brought in extra revenue. There was neither time nor place for a big ego.

The nature of the business brought people together to celebrate. Birthdays have always been special at The Sourdough, and God knows we had plenty of cake! We offered a complimentary piece of whatever delicious dessert the birthday customers wanted. The Happy Birthday song accompanied the treat, sung by the enthusiastic staff and diners. When a staff member had a birthday, we celebrated with cake, a song, and sometimes a kindhearted and yummy pie in the face!

As Homer grew as a tourist destination, our popular eatery attracted more travelers. With growth came growing pains. Some locals felt we had sold out to the tourists, mostly because they could no longer find a parking space. This accusation was a big blow to my heart as I never intended to cater only to the tourist industry. I swallowed my hurt from the backlash as best I could and charged forward. I often reminded myself to be in the present moment, *to be here now*. The present moment was all I had time for. If I didn't flow with the course of the river, I became exhausted like the salmon that swim upstream to lay their eggs and die. The sky was the limit when I expanded my mindset to the limits of my life and welcomed the ebbs and flows. I did my best to accommodate everyone. I would later find out this was not always a good idea.

My success was not measured by the cash in the register at the end of the day or by what was on my balance sheet. I found success and thrived when I served the community and made a difference in the food industry. I had also found my tribe. Relationship building with the staff was essential. The support of the incredible, expanding team — Bohemian and woodsy women and men — were a large part of what built The Fresh Sourdough Express. Our warm, mission-driven, earthy eatery was on the rise. It was a dream come true!

This stunning stained glass by Janey Wing Kenyon,
was installed in the Café in 1984.

Path to Peace

Right livelihood
is reflecting
our loving-kindness
and compassion
in the way we earn our living.
It is nurturing and
caring for others
with our work.

— Shi Wuling

Evolving with the Ebbs & Flows

*The only way to make sense out of change is to plunge into it,
move with it and join the dance.*
~ Alan Watts

Word of our excellent food and vibe grew statewide. Fuel was relatively inexpensive, and folks from Anchorage and other parts of the state looking for a fun outing would take their motorhomes or the scenic flight down to Homer. Many people had float planes and parked them on Beluga Lake. They walked from the lake and came to enjoy a friendly visit and a meal at our Bohemian cafe. They also loaded up on baked goods and never complained about the wait or the prices. The city visitors appreciated our unique flair and kind customer service.

Our wholesale accounts expanded around the state. We sent our sought-after sourdough bread via a small passenger plane to Anchorage restaurants, and often to rural village customers. We baked a hundred or more loaves a day, along with pounds of delicious treats to keep up with the demand.

As business grew, my time spent doing anything except run the company shrank. I had to resign as president of the Conservation Society and bowed out gracefully from the CACS board, but I remained a supporting member of both groups. The only way for me to make sense of the changes was to plunge into it.

Over the years several dedicated conservation organizations emerged in Homer. Thanks to their efforts, Kachemak Bay is one of the most beautiful places on Earth.

Living in a small community where the bulk of the income comes during the summer meant we had to adapt, as Nature does. In Nature and business, there are recurrent patterns of decline and growth. In business, this means knowing when to hire and when it's time to pare down. We had to learn how to gear up and gear down and control inputs and outputs for each season. We needed to budget wisely so there was a constant cash flow. Like squirrels that store acorns for the lean winter months, we did the same with our inventory.

I was *strong like a bull*, which allowed me to carry fifty-pound sacks of flour or knead thirty pounds of dough at one time. I was a *she-he* woman, capable of doing a man's job. I thrived on the challenges and changes. John did not embrace the ebbs and flows as I did. Two intense summers and two long, dark, cold winters, burned John out, and he became disillusioned. We worked long hours, and seven days a week in the summer. In the Land of the Midnight sun that's eighteen hours a day. This was fine for me as there never seemed to be enough hours in the day to satisfy my drive.

John did not mind the long, sunlit summers or the intensive work schedule, but like so many others living 59 degrees north of the Earth's equator, he suffered from Seasonal Affective Disorder, SAD, a type of depression that occurs during the darkest months of winter. On the darkest days, the sun in Homer is up for only about six hours. It looks less like sunshine and more like dawn or twilight between 10:02 a.m. and 4:06 p.m. To make matters worse, with the mountains to the southeast rising over 4,000 feet, the sun does not crest over them until after 11 a.m. in Homer.

Unlike John who struggled with the darkness and changes, I welcomed the shorter days of fall and winter. We shortened the cafe hours, and I enjoyed starry nights, potlucks with friends, moonlit walks, the northern lights, and catching up on sleep.

Sadly, in the spring of 1984, John took off to follow a different dream. It was heart-wrenching to see our four-year relationship fall like a bad batch of bread. We agreed on $25,000 as a fair price for his piece of the business that we had grown together. Red, our sweet, loyal dog, passed away shortly after that. For me, this was a time of both immense sadness and growth, filled with significant, heartfelt changes. My vulnerability became my strength as I pushed through the grief.

For a few months following John's departure, I did my share of both flirtatious dating and grieving. Mostly I focused on business and community and turned my grief into growth in any way I could. Often after the day was over and no one was around, I cranked up the music, danced, and cried in the cafe dining room with Brutus.

Hire for Good Reasons

Do not hire a man who does your work for money,
but him who does it for the love of it.
~ Henry David Thoreau

Business picked up during the 1984 summer season. Without John, the jack-of-all-trades and head baker, it was time to beef up the staff. I posted a groovy handcrafted sign at the bakery counter with colorful flowers and peace signs that read, "Bakers Needed – Inquire Within." Within hours of my posting that sign, our new baker and the future love of my life wandered into The Fresh Sourdough to purchase a loaf of our hand-crafted caraway rye. Two years previously, when John and I were selling out of our van, Kevin bought one of our first loaves. It was *love at first bite*! He had searched every bakery since his first bite to find more of the tangy, chewy bread.

Kevin was on his way to Kodiak Island to work for the Department of Fish and Game when he stumbled upon my Bohemian cafe. He recalled walking through the door, intoxicated by the experience, ". . . beautiful hippie chicks, the aroma of fresh-baked goods, and dozens of handcrafted sourdough loaves of bread displayed on a wooden bread rack." He was smitten! Not only did he think twice about heading off to count fish for the summer, but he also bought two loaves of caraway rye and, "inquired within!"

I was across the Bay working on a project at the Center for Alaskan Coastal Studies that day. Meg, who had introduced me to Yule in Olympia, was now on staff. She had the great pleasure of having that first encounter with Kevin. On my return to The Sourdough, she relayed news of her visit with the enthusiastic, twenty-five-year-old, handsome, blue-eyed man. She handed me his application, which revealed that he had baking experience. She emphatically said, "You have to hire this guy; he is so cute!" I responded to Meg by saying, "I will hire him for you, but if it doesn't work out, I'll have to let him go." Everyone knew I was good at hiring the *right* people. I'm proud to say that, to date, I have fired no one.

Kevin joined the team as the head baker and worked his way to the top. Yes, I hired my future husband, and to this day we continue to work together in every way — sweet, sour, savory, tart, and sometimes bittersweet. He has been with me every inch of the way helping to grow all our businesses, our family, and our beautiful life together. Both of us are still smitten, and caraway rye is still our favorite bread.

Letting Go — Moving On

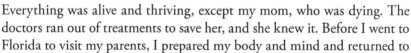

Holding on is not always a sign of strength.
There are times when it takes more strength and courage to accept and let go.
Love is more potent than anything, and it outlives death.

Everything was alive and thriving, except my mom, who was dying. The doctors ran out of treatments to save her, and she knew it. Before I went to Florida to visit my parents, I prepared my body and mind and returned to a yoga ashram in the Bahamas. During the winters, this relaxing place had been a refuse for me to recoup before visiting my folks in their winter Boca Raton residence. The tropical island was just a short flight away.

Surrounded by supportive spiritual people in an idyllic setting, I reflected on the significant changes in my life. We meditated and chanted twice a day for hours in the open-air temple, practiced yoga between nutritious meals, and enjoyed an hour of beach time every day.

I connected with a woman attending the yoga retreat who had just lost her mother to cancer. One day, we strolled down the beach together and I asked, "How were you able to cope with your mom's death?" Her insightful words of wisdom were, "Let her go, as she will always be with you."

I let go right there! I cried harder than I had ever cried in my whole life. On that white sandy beach, both of us bawled our eyes out, fully experiencing profound grief interwoven with the celebration of life. We held space for each other as the sea lapped against the shore and the warm sand embraced our feet. I gained more enlightenment from our conversation in Nature than I had received from a week of chanting, meditating, and doing yoga.

After the retreat, my mom and I had our last earnest conversation that would change my life forever. It was a sunny, hot, beautiful day at the condo. My mom, wrapped in a white wool blanket, was sitting on her recliner chair, her back to the large window. As I sat across from her, the palm trees swaying, and the sun streaming in, she confided in me, saying, "I'm ready to go, Donna." I did not resist. She asked me to talk to my dad and brothers. "Please tell them to stop treating me like a sporting event, pushing me to beat this damn thing." She continued, "I'm done fighting, Donna."

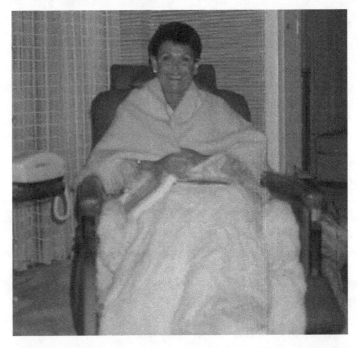

Even though it wasn't easy, I was ready for this conversation, which started the letting-go process for both of us. Doing my best to soothe the tense moment, I asked my mom, "What will you do in your next lifetime?" How was my atheist mom going to answer that question? She paused for a long minute, slipped her reading glasses down from the bridge of her nose, and looked me straight in the eyes. Her big beautiful brown eyes pierced my soul even before a word came out of her mouth, and then she spoke.

"I'll come back as a successful businesswoman. Yes, that's what I'd love to do."

While I wrote this story, I felt her presence in my soul and bawled. How awesome was my mom?! She knew this was what I wanted. This was her way of giving me the ultimate blessing and approval for how I was conducting my life.

Six months later, I held space for this beautiful being as she took her last breath in a sterile hospital room. My father and brothers were at the annual father-son golf tournament, trying to enjoy some quality time as they too had been by my mother's bedside for days. I promised my father I'd be sure my mother wasn't in any pain and I would not leave her side until he got back. Within an hour after they went, my mom took a turn. The doctor informed me that there was nothing they could do and that she was passing. Unable to contact my dad and brothers, I lay down next to my mother in the hospital bed, and held her until her last breath. It was paramount for me to recognize that it was time to let go of my sweet mama so that she could go with grace.

With tears streaming down my face, I talked her through her passing, helping to take her mind to a peaceful place, a better life without pain, and into a new embodiment. I told her how much I loved her and how much her life meant to me and all those who knew her. I felt my mother acknowledge my presence, and knew she felt safe with me. I witnessed her magnificent aura transcend, and we embraced in spirit. I was twenty-seven, and she was fifty. We both let go.

Her genuine and compassionate ways and unconditional love, are gifts that live on within every fiber of my being. I came to understand that the fertility of love never dies, and precious memories last for eternity. I still have that white blanket.

The Power of Love and Mentors

You can get a blood transfusion, but you can't live without water.

My parents were in a loving marriage for thirty-two years. My father had endearingly cared for my mom every day of her life. They communicated about the future, understanding that my father would outlive my mother. My mom knew my dad would need a good woman in his life to help him get through the sadness and carry on. My father was a successful, passionate, attractive, fifty-eight-year-old man when my mom passed away. After his grieving process, he dated several women until the next woman of his dreams entered his life.

If my family was from Pluto, my stepmother Rosemary and her family were from Saturn or some undiscovered planet. The initial blending of our families was awkward for me at times. To begin with, I came from a liberal, more or less Jewish family with a touch of Baptist (Mother Dear) and a dose of atheism. Rosemary came from a conservative Italian Catholic family. She ate a lot of pasta while I grew up eating meat and potatoes. It was tough love at first, but once we opened our hearts, we digested our differences.

She and my dad shared a deep love that overflowed into our blended family. Rosemary honored my mother and never tried to replace her. Instead, she added to and enriched my life. She became a role model and mentor. Besides being a terrific grandmother, now in her eighties, Rosemary spends time as a volunteer for multiple causes. I often call her Saint Rosemary as she is one of the most generous and kind people I know: An unexpected treasure!

My dad and Rosemary came to Alaska every summer for three weeks. They helped us stay in touch with the restaurant trends, offering East Coast wisdom and savvy marketing ideas. They both took a sincere interest in the business and shared some of their favorite recipes, some of which became menu items at the cafe. Dad continued to mentor me and had the foresight to boss me around. He wanted to be sure I absorbed all his wisdom. His heartfelt tough love paid off. The valuable lessons he passed on enriched my life. Love is essential to a flourishing life, as is change.

Through the strong bonds of Mother Dear and her girls, my extended Homer family, and now the beautiful addition of Rosemary, I came to a new realization: You can get a blood transfusion, but you can't live without water. Blood may make us related, but relationships that are sincere, loving, and loyal are like the vitality of the water, which I consider the true essence of what it means to be family. Mother Dear and her family, Rosemary, my husband and dear friends all have different DNA than I do. What matters is the love and support that brings us together.

Life is a roller coaster, so fill your ride with those whom you consider family. Inspire others with your passion and purpose and get inspired by others. There will be highs and lows, but the key is to stay true to your morals and enjoy the ride. New realizations come with each day.

Choose a Partner Wisely

*Some people spend their whole life in search of love
when it might be right in front of them.*

Kevin was the lead baker for years and chose not to get too involved in the business. It took four years and a wedding ring to form our business partnership. We more-or-less eloped — something else my dad was not happy about. I was his only daughter, and he had already endured a *non-wedding* when John and I shared our vows in a barn.

I was still not the kind of gal who wanted a fancy-pants wedding. Instead, our Bohemian ceremony took place on a crisp magical winter solstice day in our home. A handful of our close friends gathered for the ceremony and the home-cooked meal I made. Brother Asaiah, the soulful character who dubbed Homer, *The Cosmic Hamlet by the Sea*, married Kevin and I. Tall and thin, with fine gray hair tied in a ponytail and piercing blue eyes, he brought so much love and light to the Homer community. We felt blessed to have his spirit join ours.

Asaiah, a follower of South Asian Mysticism, arrived in Alaska in 1955 and homesteaded at the remote head of Kachemak Bay, about twenty-five rural miles east of Homer. The followers of this group, known as the Barefooters, vowed not to wear shoes or cut their hair until the world was at peace and hunger was eradicated. The group eventually disbanded, and the shoes came back on. But Brother Asaiah kept his long, gray ponytail and his moral values until he passed away at seventy-eight. I'm forever grateful that I knew this man, a soulful mentor whose values continue to influence me to this day. My hair is getting long and walking barefoot is a lot easier now that I live in Hawaii.

In the fall of 1989, nearly eight months after our official wedding day, my thoughtful father rented a big house and flew my two brothers and their families, Mother Dear, Kevin's mother, and my aunt to Homer. Rosemary and my dad worked for days to prepare a feast and told us to invite the community. Asaiah recapped the wedding ceremony, and then we all celebrated and feasted at The Sourdough. Kevin and I were now life partners in the eyes of our families — a wise and most heartfelt decision.

By observing my parents' and others' relationships, both healthy and not, I managed to absorb the wisdom that helped me to navigate the various waters in my relationship with my husband. Trial and error got us through the rest. We had to learn which emotional buttons could be pressed, and which ones to avoid. There was always a lot to talk about, and plenty of things to resolve. Any time communication lines shut down, Kevin and I headed for the hills with our dogs for a hike. We got clarity as we relaxed, breathed, and connected. By the time we got back to the cafe, we were solid again, ready to get back into our groove.

My business strength was in customer service. I managed the *front of the house* where I enjoyed engaging with the customers. In addition, I oversaw the marketing, menu planning, catering, and ordering of everything we needed to keep the business running smoothly. I also worked in the bakery and loved to produce great food in the remolded kitchen. Kevin's business strength was in the *back of the house*, where he did the bulk of the production. He worked with the bakers and cooks. He was organized and able to cope with production demands. He also took charge of scheduling, banking, and the day-to-day nuts and bolts necessary to maintain the facility. This is where Kevin flourished as an intuitive entrepreneur. It was when we respected each other's strengths that the operation ran smoothly.

Most of the time, we worked together like a well-oiled machine. There were also tense times that made us reevaluate our priorities. My glass was always overflowing, and Kevin's was often half full, so we balanced each other out more often than not. Regardless, our love was real, and I figured if I loved someone that much, I wanted to spend as much time with him as possible, even in the hard times.

Like a river flowing to the sea, there could be fast and slow currents, obstacles, and debris along the way. In order to stay afloat, and avoid muddying the waters, we learned to navigate the various channels and rivers of our relationship. We cherished and shared time and our deepest feelings, which was imperative to balance our personal lives. As we weathered storms,

we embraced the opportunities to learn how to flow through stressful times.

Since 1984, Kevin and I have had a symbiotic relationship. The decision to spend the rest of my life with someone encompassed a great deal more than I expected. To me marriage is the grandest commitment, and the most demanding yet rewarding of relationships. I have learned that true love settles for less than perfection and makes allowances for our weaknesses. When we radiate compassion from our hearts, we share from the depths of our souls our most intimate thoughts and aspirations.

Blooming

*"How does the Meadow-flower its bloom unfold? Because the lovely
little flower is free down to its root, and, in that freedom, bold."*
~ William Wordsworth

Without a bloom, there's no fruit. Many flowers have brightly colored
petals, scented with sweet-smelling nectar, which attracts insects,
birds, bees, and bats, which pollinate the flowers. The role of the flower
is to produce eggs and pollen: The reproductive system necessary for the
fruit to develop. Flowers are sensitive and light-dependent. In the right

environment, once exposed to enough light, they go into full bloom, and double, or even triple in size. Like flowers, humans continually bloom if conditions are optimal. When a bud is ready, it blossoms.

Some are late bloomers while others bloom too
early and can get caught in a freeze.

After we remodeled the Sourdough, business cranked up that summer to a whole new level and vibration. I was on fire, high on life, and in love. Buds were plentiful. With newfound courage, I released the familiar and seemingly secure and embraced the new and unfamiliar. I gathered and harvested life ingredients that enhanced my convictions. Now it was time to root and shoot in unexpected directions.

As I bloomed into adulthood in this fertile environment, what would take me by surprise? I would learn in this cycle that my external shoots and internal roots had a different energy and purpose, and I would have to learn how to harness that power in order to blossom. Sometimes even if I appeared mature, I honestly muddling through uncharted waters.

The responsibilities of adulthood were trying at times. How was I to figure out this grown-up stuff? How was I to maintain my own beliefs, my dogma, and not get misperceived by others? With experience, I would become more resilient, capable of bursting into full bloom multiple times, sometimes too early, sometimes too late, but most of the time, at just the right time.

Money Mindset

We must not forget that the Earth is our most important bank.
It's time we invested in her well-being.

In the spring of 1985, the landlords wanted to sell 1316 Ocean Drive, the home of The Fresh Sourdough Express. The cafe was situated on a half-acre of prime real estate including a 1,200-square-foot building. They gave me the first option to purchase. I had invested a lot of time and money into the building's remodel, so I needed to decide whether to jump in, and fast. I was a twenty-seven-year-old budding entrepreneur not entirely sure of my ability to take on so much responsibility. Even though business was good, things happened faster than expected and I had experienced growing pains for sure. My CFO (chief financial officer) dad, on the other hand, believed in me. When I called to let him know what I was up against, he said, "Go for it Donna, and if you need it, I'll co-sign on a mortgage." This is the same guy who hung up on me two years earlier, telling me I was crazy. His support motivated me deeply.

Applying for my first mortgage took a multitude of skills. With blind faith and my dad's encouragement, I took the next calculated risk. Kevin and I headed to Anchorage and made a camping trip out of the occasion. In the morning I disguised my identity. I slicked back my wild, long, hippie hairdo, washed off the patchouli oil, and put on a professional-looking dress I bought at a thrift store. Off I went to the bank, with enthusiasm and damn good-looking financials.

I number crunched with a terrific banker in Anchorage who was a kick-ass, brilliant woman. She saw that I had my act together, or at least that's how I appeared. We enjoyed sharing our Alaskan stories. I had learned from my father that it never hurt to be charming. She got the loan approved within days, without my father co-signing the note. Eureka!

In those days, Alaskan banks were eager to help small businesses. More loans meant more money circulating through their banks. Alaska was in a boom period, and lenders were banking on a bright future. With only 400,000 people in the state, the more businesses the better, especially ones that hired Alaskans. It was excellent timing for me!

The price for the building was $150,000. With inflation, today it would have cost $337,400. I had $30,000 from my summer profits to put down on the mortgage for a fifteen-year note at 10 percent interest. My payment was

$1,800 a month which was a big leap from $1,200 rental payments. With the banker's support and my parents' encouragement, my self-esteem rose, and I embraced the challenge with a healthy money mindset.

Before I got into business, I thought money was the root of all evil. My new mindset was to not let money define who I was; to not let my net worth outweigh my self-worth. I constantly reminded myself that money is merely a social/cultural construct. It was the intention I gave to the money's purpose that mattered. I was in control of my relationship with prosperity and what it meant to my identity.

When I started to make more money than I ever imagined, I realized it had the power to both empower and create, or disempower and destroy. A *make more money* mindset was most effective when I was grateful and shared the wealth. Making more money meant business was good. I provided a service that people appreciated and I created opportunities for people to work in an environment that fostered good intentions. It felt good to donate money to causes I believed in and to lend money to others. To build true wealth meant to put my money into helping others and the Earth. All these reasons made money meaningful. My power lay in not letting money rob my soul and in cultivating good intentions.

No matter how much money I made, I continued to shop (and still do) at thrift stores. I still buy used cars, furniture and just about everything else. It's not because I am cheap — it's out of principle. Why rob the finite resources of our beautiful Earth when the landfills are overflowing with perfectly good things? Money matters. It puts food on the table, clothes on our backs, and roofs over our heads. Without it, our most basic needs are threatened. I am reminded that paper money is made from cotton and linen, coins from metals and minerals, food from the soil and the sea, clothes from plants and animals, and homes from various materials of the Earth. It matters how we spend it!

The word "currency," is derived from the Latin word "currens," meaning current. A current is a steady and continuous flowing movement in a river, lake, or sea. Money comes, and money goes like the currents. Maybe that's why it's called currency. A business income is like a current in a flowing river. The riverbanks support the flow, allowing it to continue moving in the right direction: It holds the river. The idea is to build up your bank so that you're prepared for both floods and droughts, and ebbs and flows.

Growing with Gratitude

Develop an attitude of gratitude, and give thanks for everything that happens to you, knowing that every step forward is a step toward achieving something bigger and better than your current situation.
~ Brian Tracy

When we hired people, we let them know, "You will work *with us*, not *for us*." We offered a position, not a job. We often remind the staff, "It is the customers who pay you, we just sign the paychecks." The wait staff and baristas received better tips when they were gracious to the customers, and the team shone when we let them know we appreciate them. Staff members who showed a sincere interest in the business, over time moved from dishwasher to head chef or baker.

As the business grew, communication with the staff was paramount to a harmonious work environment. Team meetings were as essential as one-on-one meetings. It was an opportunity for us to clear the air of any tension and to strategize how best to grow the business together. We shared appreciation for one another. Overall, we were fortunate to work with some of the most wonderful people.

Gratitude always fosters a better attitude.

In the early days of the Sourdough, all our sales were cash or checks. When I prepared the bank deposits, it took two to three deposit slips to list all the checks and a lot of time to add them up! Not an easy task for a busy dyslexic person. Nine times out of ten, I made a mistake. I dreaded going to the bank!

At first, the bank tellers were not too happy to see me step in line with wads of cash and checks stuffed into vinyl bank bags. I could feel their vibe. They finally gave up and told me to organize the cash, and they'd do the rest. My attitude was full of gratitude, and I showed it by bringing a treat from the bakery for the lucky teller who was now excited to see me. A chocolate chip cookie or berry-cheese Danish turned out to be the perfect exchange for filling out the deposit slips.

When the bank hosted parties or held events, they often chose The Fresh Sourdough Express as their caterers. There were still times during the bustling high summer season when going to the bank was not a priority. Like a squirrel that hoards acorns for a winter day, I hid piles of cash. During the cold winter months, it was a welcome surprise to retrieve thousands of dollars from under the mattress or in between the cushions! When Kevin took over the banking, it was a huge relief.

Growing Influence

We do not have to struggle to change an existing, antiquated paradigm.
We can create a new and better one.

Our counter-cultural cafe grew in popularity each year. We were in full bloom! Not a day went by when a customer wouldn't say to us, "Wish there was a Fresh Sourdough Express in our town," or "You guys need to franchise." To please everyone was a challenge, especially when we were trying to influence customers tainted by the rapidly growing fast-food franchises. Many people in the '80s were served BS propaganda. They accepted eating out of Styrofoam, and expected the hyper-speed-drive-thru, cheap meal experience. Super-sized meals were just around the corner.

Although business was booming, it was not living up to my expectations. The more I learned about our corrupt food system, the more my spirit yearned to do more. But how was I going to influence more people to eat responsibly and make healthier choices for their bodies and the planet?

It frustrated me to no end that people acted ignorant to the environmental damage caused by their food choices. How could people not know or care how crops grow, and how the meat industry treats animals? The resources of the Earth were being gobbled up as the demand for Big Macs grew.

The Sourdough had proven that it had *staying power*, and I thought I could help create a new franchise model that would make the current food franchises obsolete! I was a restless serial entrepreneur and ready for the next challenge.

Flirting with Franchise

Our biggest opportunities might be staring us in the face.
What we focus on grows.

McDonald's was the first fast-food franchise that forged its way into our small community in 1985. But not without a fight! Members of the community, including myself, were not keen on a corporation squashing small businesses. It concerned others that the massive golden arches would disrupt the view of the choice corner lot and serve up Big Macs and fries full of trans-fats within walking distance of the high school. Within months, McDonald's was *killing it*, devouring the other small eateries' incomes. We had one small victory: We got a sign ordinance passed that reduced the size of the golden arches, and for everyone else who wanted to put up a sign in town.

As I witnessed McDonald's success, franchising appeared to be the best way for us to reach the masses. Our one little Alaskan-themed cafe in the Last Frontier was not doing the job. I seriously considered the option, and I sought counsel from my closest friends and father. My biggest concerns were that people would accuse me of being arrogant, self-righteous, or a sellout. My dad asked me some profound and confusing questions: "Donna, ask yourself, is it your conviction or your ego talking? Are you ready to change your life dramatically?" A woman in a man's business world played against the odds. Yet I felt strongly that if I spread the message of *healthy food, healthy body, healthy planet* via a franchise, it would have a significant impact.

I saw how our cafe had become part of the vibrant culture in our community, a hub for commerce, and an effective way to educate people. I could only imagine how it might be if every eatery served regional food. You would think it would stimulate the local economy, create jobs, and have a far-reaching effect, right? I was convinced a conscious cafe with soil to soul awareness, could thrive and be part of the social fabric of any place.

What if in every university town the students had the option to eat at a Fresh Sourdough Express, rather than at unhealthy fast-food eateries that were infiltrating college towns? I figured this would be the perfect demographic to start the chain. If more students ate quality food, it would positively affect the young minds of the future. We could save the Last Frontier and other endangered places if people were well-fed and educated! I was on a mission with conviction.

> *How fragile that sounds — The Last Frontier — suggesting the last of the wilderness, along with clean air and water.*

I imagined pristine scenes of the Alaskan wilderness, instead of images of subway stations plastered on walls. I also pictured a menu that included the nutritional profile for each meal, and how far that meal traveled to get to a customer's plate: A visionary idea at the time. A list of the local farmers with photos of the farm would welcome diners at the door. Yes, I thought out the details!

Serious about exploring the possibilities, I flew to Chicago to meet with a company that specialized in franchise development. Once again, I transformed my hippie act, washed off the patchouli oil, braided my wild hair, and wore my fancy thrift store outfits. I attended several black suit meetings. Even in my most professional business attire, I was still wearing a dress, so I had to posture myself to prove that I was as driven and intelligent as they were; that I was worthy of their time. I suspected that the men in black had never seen anyone like me before, nor the franchise concept I proposed. Remember, this was 1988, and the healthiest food franchise was Subway.

To my surprise, the men in suits were all over my ideas — in a big way! They wined and dined me and drove me around in a limousine. The Alaskan theme and the concept of the Last Frontier intrigued them. Alaska was fast becoming a hot destination. The franchise company was ready to eat up my ideas and fast! My ego inflated.

It was all glamorous and persuasive. At the same time, it frightened and confused me. It would take a buttload of work to set up a new distribution system of responsibly raised, regional food. The money and legal stuff overwhelmed me. A leap of blind faith would mean a more corporate lifestyle and a lot of travel. And besides, was the world ready for this? Was I? Could my Fresh Sourdough Express make it in this business climate?

Taking a look at the history of franchise restaurants is a way to track the growth of the industrial food complex. The first food franchise started in 1916, with the successful model of Nathan's All-American Hot Dog. In an article written by Tracy V. Wilson, How Fast Food Works, *she states, "The McDonald brothers opened their redesigned restaurant in 1948. Several fast-food chains that exist today opened soon after. Burger King and Taco Bell got their start in the 1950s, and Wendy's began in 1969." Americans' diets shifted from a local whole foods diet, based on sound, small-scale ecological farming, to a junk food diet influenced by corporate conglomerates.*

Justifying Decisions

It is in your moments of decision that your destiny is shaped.
~ Tony Robbins

Kevin adamantly disliked the franchise idea. He expressed that he thought it would challenge our cafe's core values, and the additional workload would erode our relationship. I learned the hard way that when both parties have substantial arguments, it's hard to decide which vision is the best choice. For weeks I struggled with the decision. I concluded there was no way I was giving up on my sweet husband. I justified my decision by promising myself I would find a different way to pursue my purpose and mission.

When I look back on that time, I remember feeling everything from failure and resentment to relief. I wondered how my life would have been different if there were hundreds, or perhaps thousands, of Sourdough restaurants nationwide, or around the world. Maybe I would have more money, but my heart would be bankrupt. Kevin was right. Homer, Alaska was our small-town home. Keeping to our core values brought more peace and love to our relationship, and as our love continued to grow my regrets vanished. I would come to accept that I was years ahead of my time.

Customer feedback helped us to grow the business and could catch me off guard. There were uneasy decisions to make at the cafe that could be hard to justify. Let's be honest, there are unreasonable customers, and the customer is NOT always right. I tried to view any uncomfortable situations as opportunities to do a better job and be a better person.

In response to the demand for faster service, our ready-to-eat savories offered a solution to fast-food junkies and the locals in a hurry. Then there was the soda dilemma. The soda manufacturers switched to high fructose corn syrup (HFCS) in the '80s, a cheaper, addictive sweetener. The super-sized, low priced sodas doubled people's consumption, and addiction to soda became commonplace. Consumers were not aware that HFCS was a leading culprit that causes inflammation and increases the risk of obesity, diabetes, heart disease, and cancer. To appease the soda drinkers, I brought in a line of all-natural sodas. A lot of customers balked at even the thought of an alternative to Coke or Pepsi. They wanted their corn syrup sweetened drink! As I tried to justify my decisions, I'd often make compromises. Even with my education, it was hard to digest the magnitude of how mammoth corporations had taken over every aspect of our once wholesome food system. From farms to our tables, from cafes to supermarkets, we became victims. The industrial food complex had taken over our diets and expanded our waistlines.

To get our mission across and help lessen customer skepticism, I made educational table tents that informed about our Eco-Bohemian Cafe principles. Rather than alienate, I educated. The more honest and sincere I was the larger the customer base grew. Most people were grateful and showed it by bringing in friends and family. Our loyal customers were the best PR anyone could have wished for. They helped build the business. I continued to focus on our mission, doing my best to stay fit and healthy. I had re-shaped my destiny.

There are fast-food franchises and eateries that have made better choices — but not enough, or fast enough. There is too much misinformation fed to us about food and health to undo easily. It is up to us to unravel the truth and make choices like the future matters. If more consumers questioned owners of franchise eateries and restaurants about how the food they use is grown, raised, manufactured, and transported, how might things change? Ask the owners, managers, and servers if what they are serving is chemical-free and antibiotic-free or made using GMO products. Ask them to tell the truth! If they don't have answers, ask why? They should know what they are serving you, right? As more people become aware and demand to know what's in our food and how it's grown and raised, we stand a better chance to rebuild our economy from the soil to our souls.

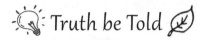 Truth be Told

Imagine if the food industry advocated environmental, humane, and animal justice. And what if food service workers got treated like human beings — not as a disposable human resource?!

In the last two decades due to the work of exceptional journalists, authors, and filmmakers, information is readily available for consumers to make the right choices. When the documentary *Super-Size Me* came out in 2004, it awakened a small population of the world to the growth of the problem. The movie showed how a fast-food franchise diet affects more than just your waistline. One of my favorite books is *The Omnivore's Dilemma*, published in 2006 by Michael Pollan. He wrote a well-documented and thought-provoking view of how far gone our country has become regarding what we eat. We innocently have become a super-sized, corn-fed nation. In 2009, documentary filmmaker Robert Kenner released *Food, Inc.* showing how the corporate food chain has taken over the American Diet. The film, *Cowspiracy* released in 2014, will make you think twice about eating meat ever again! Martha Rosenberg reports on recent raids of U.S. slaughterhouses. The factory farm industry, which exploded with the fast-food franchises, is responsible for billions of tons of GMO corn grown to feed beef cattle.

Billions of acres of other GMO monoculture crops such as soy, sugar beets, and cotton, dominate once fertile farmland. The toxic chemicals used on the GMO crops have far-reaching effects. The corrupt industry is the source of widespread water pollution, the horrendous animal cruelty, air pollution, and the alarming contamination of our food. Industry workers are often undocumented and paid less than 6 dollars an hour! Human beings are being subjected to unsafe and unhealthy working conditions, knowing that the workers can't fight back.

White Wash, a book by Carey Gillam, won the Rachael Carson award for good reason. Like Carson and her work combatting the reckless use of pesticides, Gillam has worked to unfold the dark truth about Monsanto's Roundup product. The chemical known to scientists as glyphosate is the world's most popular weed killer, and it has been found to kill more than just weeds.

These are just a few examples of in-depth studies, by heroic people, that offer the truth and Soulutions to what we can all do to make a difference. There are more in the Soulution section.

The Battle of the Bulge

Health is our real wealth not pieces of gold and silver.

The frustration from my high-intensity franchise attempt and the restlessness brought on by my tenacious personality spurred unhealthy habits. Long workdays and overeating began to re-shape my figure. I came up with a simple solution to reduce stress and my waistline. I signed up for aerobic classes, which were all the rage in the late '80s. I enjoyed a break from the business while dancing and sweating with other women. I'm still baffled by skinny chefs and bakers.

After a few months of classes, and being a savvy businesswoman, I figured *why pay to attend when I could get paid to teach*? I had ideas on how to make classes more fulfilling and fun. Winter months were slower at the cafe, and I made enough money in the busy season of 1989 to take off for two months to get trained. I chose a program called "Strong, Stretched, and Centered." The bonus, it was in Hawaii. The program was run by an entrepreneurial and dynamic woman named Gloria Keeling, who became one of my fondest mentors. Her innovative, whole-systems approach to a healthy body, mind, and soul jived with me.

Besides taking classes in anatomy, physiology, weight training, and aerobic dance steps, Gloria guided twelve eager students to dig deeper into self-actualization. She emphasized, "It's not about how skinny you are, but how healthy you are." She reminded us daily, *"Health is your greatest wealth!"* I realized I had been hanging on to a body image that negatively affected my life. It was liberating to finally cast aside that archaic script! We ate a whole-foods, vegetarian diet and trained four to six hours a day. Yoga, meditation, and mindfulness were part of the course. I gained a new level of confidence and lost twenty pounds. After the training, I was a certified fitness instructor and had enough confidence to be an innovative teacher.

I created a whole-systems program based on the Strong, Stretched, and Centered approach and philosophy. For several years, I taught classes to an active following of fabulous women, kept my weight off, and gained new cafe customers.

One of the *bible books* in my library is *Diet for a Small Planet* (1971) by Frances Moore Lappé. I was doing my best to live up to her high standards in a fast-food, meat-and-potatoes world. Grateful for Frances's wisdom, I honored her knowledge and brought it forward in our business. We incorporated more vegetarian meals into The Sourdough menu which cost less and had less of a detrimental impact on the Earth. We also offered meal plans for special dietary needs, catering to another new niche market. Being innovative and conscious of budding changes in demand paid dividends and pleased a new clientele.

Health is your greatest wealth!

Soil Soulution

We have neglected the truth that a good farmer
is a craftsman of the highest order, a kind of artist.
~ Wendell Berry

Now strong, stretched, and centered, I was motivated to do more. I bought five acres of beautiful, fertile land near The Sourdough. Kevin and I had a dream to raise organic food for the café. We also understood getting food to Alaska had a huge carbon footprint. After being transported to the docks in the Lower 48, supplies were barged thousands of miles across the North Pacific to the port of Anchorage where they were transferred into gas-guzzling, refrigerated trucks by enormous forklifts before being hauled across the final 225 mountainous miles to Homer. This process could be called nothing less than arduous.

Buying natural and organic food was still more expensive than conventional products, so Kevin and I either settled for less profit or worked extra hours to make up for the higher costs. Buying our dry goods in bulk did help bring the cost down, which offset some of the shipping expenses — but not all. When a barge was late because of stormy weather, we were at the mercy of conventional distributors who carried nothing organic.

We attempted to run both the cafe and our farm for three years but realized it took too much time and effort. To find experienced organic farmers to help us run the farm was nearly impossible. Besides, the big harvest came in the fall when the cafe slowed down — too much produce at the wrong time! It became a hard lesson in trying to do it all. We sold the fertile land to a real farmer who continued to be a supplier of our organic produce. It was a good reminder of the benefits of working in collaboration with experts and doing what you can. We surrendered with the notion that you *can't do it all, but it's worth trying*. Whether I was a farmer or not, I had planted myself in Homer and continued to fertilize my soul and business with healthy amendments.

The same year we bought the farmland, we purchased our first home with a drop-dead gorgeous view of the bay, located down a lovely *soil road* a few miles from town. I was twenty-nine. Kevin and I had been house-sitting and pet-sitting for years, which helped us save money for a down payment.

Now that we had a home, it was time to fill it with joy. We got two droopy-eyed, big-eared cocker spaniels and inherited a pregnant kitty. Then Simba arrived, a handsome husky-wolf mixed breed that ended up on our doorstep and never left. His wild, gray-blue eyes and gentle temperament settled my soul. Simba was my most amazing animalizing mentor yet. We all took a lot of trailblazing Nature hikes, which helped me to stay strong, stretched, and centered. Kevin eventually planted a small garden, and we got chickens. That winter, Brutus, our beloved husky, joined Brandy in doggie heaven.

High Tunnels, also known as "hoop houses,'" have ignited the small farm movement. The government-funded High Tunnel program has helped growers expand their variety of crops and extended the growing season in northern climates. We now enjoy homegrown tomatoes and cucumbers in Homer!

Digging Deeper III
Fuel, Food, Plastics, and the
Banking Connections

The fossil fuel, banking, and food industry feed off each other.
A bull market, in bear country.

In 1969, just ten years after Alaska achieved statehood, oil was discovered on the northern coastline. The state held the Prudhoe Bay Oil and Gas lease sale in September 1969, which brought in $900 million in revenue. Many of the state's decision-makers supported putting a portion of the expected revenues into a permanent fund known as The Alaska Dividend, or PFD. These funds would be out of reach of day-to-day government spending and would generate income in perpetuity. The state government paid a yearly dividend, financed indirectly from oil revenues. Initially, if you were a resident for six months, you received a check. The legislature changed the residency period from 6 months to 24 months in 1989. As the price of oil fluctuated, so did the size of the PFD check.

The first dividend checks, distributed in 1982, were for $1,000: The equivalent of $2,500 today. It was like a gold rush for John and me when we opened the envelope to find the crisp government checks — a welcome bonus to living in the most beautiful place on Earth. When Kevin and I discovered the truth of the not-so-free money years later, we were in moral agony, and saw it less as a gift and more as a bribe to keep people in the state. In the following years, we continued to take the bribe, but we always used that money wisely or donated it to environmental causes.

The construction of the Alaska pipeline began in 1971 and was completed in 1979. The price of crude oil was at a peak, and Alaska was in the middle of an economic boom in the '80s. Meanwhile, the rest of America experienced its worst recession since the Great Depression. It's hard to believe that by 1982, unemployment reached nine million, the highest rate since the Depression. 17,000 businesses failed, the second highest number since 1933. Oil prices in Alaska were $32 per barrel, and the state's petroleum revenue exceeded $3.5 billion. For some, the Last Frontier was their last hope for employment opportunities. Alaska is beautiful, but unpredictable. Its extreme weather and short daylight hours in the long, cold winter months are not for the faint of heart.

Art by Calley O'Neil

The money from the PFD encouraged residents to help stimulate the economy. A flood of opportunities spilled across the state. A more sophisticated infrastructure was built, and social programs expanded. New roads, schools, and municipal buildings made Alaska more attractive to newcomers and residents alike. Mid-sized and small businesses sprouted up and anticipated success. It was a bull market in bear country. People flocked north with dollar signs in their eyes.

In 2015, the dividend amount reached its peak, and each resident received $2,072. In 2016 Governor Bill Walker vetoed about half of the allocations to the PFD because of failing economic times in Alaska. In a statement, Walker said, "I believe we must find a balance between the wants of today and the needs of tomorrow. If we don't make changes, we're on a course to economic disaster. It's a 100 percent preventable disaster, and I will do everything I can to prevent it."

As usual, with new leadership comes new problems. Governor Mike Dunleavy created riffs because of his vetoes of some 440 million dollars of operating budget when he came into office. The services looking to have their funding cut included the University of Alaska system and Medicaid. One of his goals behind this controversial move was his desire to reallocate funds towards an increased Alaskan PFD of $3,000. Majorities in the House and Senate did not share his position on the Permanent Fund Dividend. On August 19, 2019, the Governor was disappointed when the state legislators vetoed his bill, which would have paid Alaskans nearly double what they are used to, and forced the Governor to settle on a figure of $1600 for the PFD that year. Pressure from Alaskans wanting to recall the Governor across party lines, forced him to scale back his aggressive budget cuts that would have dramatically affected education and Medicaid. Yes, the power of the people came together on things that matter. We need to see more of this!

The Alaska Oil and Gas Association reports that: "Alaska is the only state in the Union that is so dependent on one industry to fund its government services. Since the completion of the Trans-Alaska Oil Pipeline, petroleum revenues to the State of Alaska have averaged over 85 percent. In the state's 2013 fiscal year, oil and gas revenues represented 92 percent of Alaska's unrestricted revenue. Oil tax revenue has a significant effect on the state's ability to provide services to Alaskans." This sounds like an invasive species to me.

> *Everyone wants instant everything, and they want*
> *instant success, but I always think you should treat things*
> *in the arts like a garden and let them grow.*
> ~ Penelope Keith

With the oil glut in the '80s, manufacturers had greater leverage to produce cheaper goods. Food manufacturers were on a binge and produced an excessive variety of unhealthy, processed and packaged, addictive products like Cool Ranch Doritos, Fruit Roll-ups, and Teddy Grahams. High calorie and chemical beverages such as Crystal Light, Capri Sun, and Diet Coke became household items. Meat and dairy sales soared as cheeseburgers grew. Corruption of the industrial food complex infiltrated our food system to please the addicted palettes they created. If people took the time to read and understand the long list of incomprehensible ingredients, maybe they would think twice.

Most of what is consumed can barely be considered food. Many did not question — they consumed what was fed to them. Fad diets, processed packaged goods, and the fast food franchise industry boomed. As the size of Americans bulged, profits soared for the few. Meanwhile, I bucked a fierce tide as our natural foods cafe defied the odds and flourished. While I was out to change the way people viewed food, the American mindset was in super-size-me mode — the bigger and cheaper, the better. Vegetarian meals were a hard sell.

Finite resources and entire ecosystems, including the rainforests, were being devoured for the sake of cheaper, nutritionally deficient products.

As I write, the rainforests are burning up in
Brazil and in Africa the fires blaze.

According to Raintree, more than "200,000 acres of rainforest are burned every day. That is over 150 acres lost every minute of every day, and 78 million acres every year!" Over 20 percent of the Amazon rainforest is gone, and much more is severely threatened as the destruction continues. The Rainforest Alliance reported that "Agriculture drives 80 percent of tropical deforestation and billions of tons of greenhouse gas emissions each year." The soil is disturbed, culture is affected, and the landscapes scarred. The rainforests are considered the lungs of the Earth because they produce most of the world's oxygen and sequester carbon. Grazing cattle to supply cut-rate meat for cheap franchise meals became a bigger business, and the forest shrank.

The fossil fuel-driven packaging industry marched right alongside the food industry, creating demand for plastics and Styrofoam containers. The industries feed off each other as revealed in an investigative series *Fueling Plastics*, launched on September 20th, 2017 by The Center for International Environmental Law (CIEL). The publication examines the deep linkages between polluting fossil fuels, the plastics industries, and the products they produce and distribute. In the US and Gulf Coast, plastics production is localized to particular regions where fossil fuel development is present. When Hurricane Harvey hit the Gulf Region, reports from the CIEL proved the devastating implications of the growing fossil fuel movement. The infrastructure that the US shale gas boom has created, fuels a massive build-out of plastics globally. Wars are being fought over the black gold, and non-renewable resources continue to get gobbled up in the name of progress. Most things are purchased with a plastic credit card, issued from a bank invested in fossil fuels. *What's in your wallet?*

To make matters worse, many fossil fuel companies own plastics manufacturers, and many plastics companies own fossil fuel companies. Steven Feit, Staff Attorney at CIEL, states, "Exxon is both the gas in your car and the plastic in your water bottle." If trends in oil consumption and plastics production continue as expected, plastics will account for 20% of total oil consumption by 2050, and there will be more plastic in the sea than fish. Who wants to live in a fast-food nation driven by a corrupt fossil fuel economy? Banning single-use plastic is one step towards living like the future matters.

This was the era of making everything appear larger than life, from shoulder pads and big hairdos to stock portfolios. Consumer debt was also large, and the masses were on a destructive path, investing in the superficial extravagance and denying the consequences. The recession that began in the early '80s started with a decline in income and was then fueled by consumers' desire to continue purchasing. Plastic credit cards provided the means to a misguided, fake reality. It was as if consumption were the antidote for feeling the pinch of the recession. This blind desire brought big debt. The use of plastic credit cards enabled the ordinary person to buy futures, to acquire more than they could afford in the present, and to satisfy their current desires. This led to excessive entitlement and compulsive spending habits. Once inflation was under control, the banks stood to make big profits from consumer lending via credit cards. And when inflation looked like it was under control, consumers upped the ante.

Every time we swipe a credit card (made from fossil fuels), we must question what our investments are supporting. We should also challenge the bank fees that are going toward the discretionary decisions of bank lords. According to numerous articles, some of the world's top banks continue to lend tens of billions of dollars to extract the most carbon-intensive fossil fuels. How long can this corrosive oil-based plastic economy last?

Sure, credit cards help shorten business deposit slips, but they add fees to the business owner. They also add debt to consumers who can't pay the card off on time. The addictive mindset to borrow now, pay later, and ignore the repercussions continues to take its toll. It is parallel to our natural world. The bottom line is, if we don't consider the long-term consequences of our behavior and take action, we will bankrupt the finite resources that support us all.

Renewable energy was in its infancy. The fossil fuel industry had built walls of opposition, making it hard for innovative, energy efficient companies to get through. Big business and oil tycoons spilled into the political system, diluting democracy. Meanwhile, in April 1986, the largest nuclear catastrophe devastated an area in Ukraine when the Chernobyl Nuclear Power Plant discovered a flaw in a Soviet reactor design. The Cold War isolation attributed to poor management and lack of safety measures. More than a thousand square miles of land around Chernobyl remain officially uninhabitable, a radioactive hot zone for thousands of years.

We did the best we could to conserve our resources at home and at the cafe. We switched to energy-efficient light bulbs, low flush toilets, and drove more fuel-efficient cars when they came available. Gas-guzzling pickup trucks and sport utility vehicles (SUVs) were especially popular in Alaska. Hybrid and electric vehicles were not on anyone's mind.

In an article for Scientific America, Annie Sneed says, "In 1985 scientists reported something very unsettling: They found a hole in the planet's ozone layer over Antarctica. The culprits, they said, were humans emitting chemicals that depleted atmospheric ozone above the South Pole and the rest of the globe. Because the ozone layer protects us and other organisms from harmful solar radiation, the international community united in 1987 to sign the Montreal Protocol, which phased out the use of such chemicals."

I embraced an attitude that money made me more of who I was. The energy I put into the money was purposeful. Money is not the problem; it's what you do with it that matters. That is where the power was for me! I was able to make changes. It could exasperate me, and yet be so rewarding. It was time to focus on birthing and evolving into the next cycle of my life.

EVOLUTION IV

Transformation

Principles that influenced my life in this Evolution:

- Offer encouragement.
- What we focus on grows.
- Act with a purposeful-why.
- Mentors are essential, regardless of your age.
- Time is our most valuable currency; spend it wisely.
- Know your truth, who you are, and what you love to do.
- Stimulate an economic system that is ecologically viable.
- Embody your highest potential to be the best version of yourse

Fruiting

It is not necessary to struggle to reach the fruits of life;
nourish your soul, and the bounty will follow.

———————

As a plant transforms from a flower to fruit, it goes through cycles; from pollination to fertilization and finally into maturity. While the seeds develop, the fruit serves as a barrier and protects them from the external environment. If there are seeds, there will be fruits, grains, nuts, medicine, fiber, and timber. The seed is the child of the plant; it is the next generation.

Like everything in Nature, we must bear fruit and seed (birth) to survive; this is how life has lasted for billions of years. How we take care of the sacred womb of the mother reflects the outcome of life within and without. Nothing compares to the feminine power of birth.

228

If nourished, a tree — or a life — will produce a more fruitful yield. The harvest — the outcome — is up to us. One apple seed will grow into a tree that can provide over 800 pounds of fruit a year! Most fruit trees are highly productive and bear fruit for 20 plus years, which is as long as many people stick with a career. With the fruits of our labor, we produce products and services to get a return on investment (ROI). Long-lasting success depends on the seeds we sow and how well we nurture our intentions.

The fruitful years were mind-boggling, thrilling, and mountains of work. During this cycle of life, harvests were abundant. For years, I developed the cafe with as much conscious food as people would ingest. A healthy money mindset enabled me to adapt to rapid growth, the floods, and the droughts. I understood how to store seeds and grains for the winter and beef up inventory for the busy summer season.

With a solid trunk, I could confidently defend my principles and was very fruitful. Yet, with boundless yearly harvests there came increased demands, expenses, and unexpected responsibilities, which would lead to unforeseen consequences. At times, I doubted if my roots were strong enough to harvest the abundance. In spite of these doubts, my perseverance prevailed.

The Harvest Cycle produced some of the most precious memories of my life. Something growing inside of me would change my life forever! I'd learn how much nourishment and focused energy it takes to birth a new business idea and a child at the same time! Most importantly, I learned that it's love that gets us through hard times.

Pollination

Without seeds, there would be no fruit; there would be no life.

―――――――――⸱⸱◦◉◎◉◎◉◎◉◦⸱⸱――――――――――

The next cafe remodel was in 1989, when we more than doubled the size of the facility. It was like giving birth to twins! In peak season we were open seven days a week, serving breakfast, lunch, and dinner, and enjoying bumper harvests. People lined up out the door to get a table. Our staff peaked at forty-five, and we became one of the larger employers in town. We were proud to provide meaningful employment and to be part of the positive growth in our community.

Over the years, Kevin and I shared in the joy of others as many friends raised their families. Up to this point we had been too busy raising our first baby (The Fresh Sourdough Express) to think about bringing a child into our world. With the success of our business, I no longer had to put my dreams on hold to have a child. I had one more meaningful reason to pursue my dreams. Kevin and I decided we were as ready as we could be to pollinate. I was thirty-four.

It was New Year's Eve, so we're not sure if I conceived in 1990 or 1991. We were visiting friends in Sheep Mountain, a rural community in the Alaskan interior a couple of hours northeast of Anchorage. It was minus 10 degrees outside, with a rare blue moon — a magical freakin' cold and gorgeous night! Our lodging was in the upstairs of an uninsulated carport, heated by a portable space heater. Most of the night, except for the pollination part, we felt like we were trying to sleep in our walk-in freezer.

The next day we flew to Thailand for eight weeks, unaware that I might be pregnant. Kevin and I were overdue for a vacation and ready to unwind and warm up. Within a week, I felt sick, especially in the morning. It soon became clear that I was not suffering from chronic food poisoning. Instead, a new addition to our family was growing inside of me. Along with morning sickness, other unexpected circumstances came while traveling in an "underdeveloped" country.

It disturbed me that a country could be classified as a first, second, or third world. I questioned what "more developed" meant. It warmed my heart to see how Thai culture engages its elders and youth in everyday life. They embed intergenerational respect and values in the culture. It delighted me to see how food and culture were woven into their lifestyle. Meals were a celebration, and we were often invited to join in. There was not a fast-food chain or box store to be found. The Thai people we met lived with less stuff and had more developed souls than most people we knew. People's happiness was gauged by how much they enjoyed life. It may have looked like poverty, but it felt so rich. There was an attitude of gratitude amongst the people — even in a country undergoing a military coup at the time we were there. This "underdeveloped" country had a lot going for it despite poverty, crime, sadness, and poor sanitation. I had seen all of that in Harlem NYC. It seems like whoever was making these determinations about development were only gauging the worth through a lens of materialism.

I experienced how cultural differences can be the bridge for the whole of humanity when we respect our differences and share the wealth. My world views reshaped as my senses awakened to a whole new world.

Without diversity and balance, humans,
like a weed, are an invasive species.

Although efforts have led to achievements in reducing global poverty, the UN reports that more than 700 million people live below the international poverty line of $1.90 a day. About 10 percent of the world's workers live with their families on less than $1.90 per person per day. The majority of people living below the poverty are found in Southern Asia and sub-Saharan Africa. High poverty rates are often found in small, fragile, and conflict-affected countries.

In the United States, we do not have to travel far to witness poverty. According to Poverty Rate USA, 13.5 percent — 43.1 million people — are living in poverty. Solutions for a fair distribution of wealth are yet to be discovered. There are opportunities for us all to figure out this unethical injustice.

Our trip also coincided with the winter in which the first Gulf War began. They canceled flights for days on end, and we thought we might have to birth our son in Thailand. Kevin freaked out and went into a cold sweat. Meanwhile, I imagined how awesome it would be to be in a warm climate and start a sanctuary for the monkeys who were treated like third world citizens. Once things calmed down, including my morning sickness, we could rest and recharge.

Relaxed and with great tans, we returned to a wet, muddy Alaskan *spring break-up*. We were excited to share our memorable stories and the news we were going to be parents!

> Solutions for a
> fair distribution of
> wealth are yet to be
> discovered. There
> are opportunities
> for us all to figure
> out this unethical
> injustice.

Entrepreneurial Surge

Whether you seed an idea, a business, or a child; to give birth is an honor and a commitment. Be prepared to spend a lot of time fostering growth.

I worked every day at the cafe during my pregnancy and taught my Strong, Stretched, and Centered classes until I was eight months pregnant. I felt fantastic! I smiled and radiated from the inside out. While pregnant, I also had another entrepreneurial surge. I figured out a way to run a new business from home that complimented motherhood and fortified my will to heighten people's awareness of the environmental impact of our food choices. My unstoppable drive soared like an eagle. It was the most creative and soulful time in my life! AH!LASKA was the brand I incubated while my child grew inside me. When I gave birth, the new company came to life.

For the entire pregnancy, Kevin, the midwife, the doctor, and I were all convinced that our child would be a girl. Shanti Rose would be her name. Shanti is a Sanskrit word that means "peace," but it is also translated as "calm" or "bliss." I would rub my belly many times a day and chant, Shanti, Shanti, Peace, Peace, repeatedly. Creative bliss shifted within, and our darling son, Daniel Jazz was born. OMG, we had a son. He was calm natured, and has brought me a lot of peace, even during turbulent times. We called him Jazz.

Jazz was a spirited soul who became the brightest light and most precious being in my life; he would strengthen and guide my visions. Never could I have imagined the amount of love a mother feels for her child. The day I held Jazz in my arms for the first time was the day I truly understood my mother's unwavering love for me. Kevin was equally in awe, and we expressed our love openly.

We recognized when Jazz needed mommy or daddy and accepted our specific roles. For instance, I'm a gagger, so extra-stinky diapers put me over the edge and Kevin had no problem with rank diapers! If he needed a break from the Sourdough, he'd take a walk with Jazz, and I'd pick up the slack at the cafe. There was no room for head or power trips around parenting, just love. I breastfed for two-and-a-half years, never once giving our son a bottle nor a reason to worry, as I had worried for his sake since the day my baby brother came home from the hospital years before. Unwilling to be away from Jazz for any extended period, I rearranged my life and career to accommodate motherhood.

A family is one of Nature's miraculous works of art.

The Goose that Laid the Golden Egg

Do not let go of the goose until your next endeavor is nested in success.

———————•:•⊙⊙⊙⊙⊙⊙⊙•:•———————

AH!LASKA was a creative outlet that satisfied my mission-driven mania and gave me maximum mommy time. It was a business I could run from home on my schedule. The brand initially comprised six baking mixes. I chose the most popular recipes from test samples taken in our bakery and capitalized on them, turning them into dry mixes that people could make at home.

The names I chose for the product line were: Grizzly Bear Brownies, Moose Fudge Cake, Puffin Muffins, and Field of Poppy Seed Pound Cake. Each one-pound, eye-catching package, came with a factual insert that included information about the animal or plant and their relationship to their dwindling habitats. The line also included Fisherman Biscuits and a dry Sourdough Starter Mix. The insert for these mixes told the stories of Alaskan fishermen, fisherwomen, and gold miners, and explained their impact on the environment. I included recipes on how to use each product in multiple ways. A variety of recipes for each mix proved to increase sales. Customers wanted to take home a taste of The Fresh Sourdough Express, and I hoped they would get the environmental message.

We also wholesaled the line to gift shops throughout the state. The company grew faster than we could have imagined, so we rented another location in downtown Homer for retail, production, and storage. Our wholesale customers asked us to expand the line. They assured us they could sell whatever we sold them since the brand was so popular. One day on a sales trip to Anchorage and the North Pole (and yes, there is a town in Alaska called the North Pole), Kevin and I came up with the idea to make cocoa mixes. We called this line, AH!LASKA HO HO Cocoa.

Between the cafe and bakery mixes, we used thousands of pounds of non-organic sugar, cocoa, and flour. There had to be a better way. I vowed to find one before I came out with any more products. I spent countless hours in search of consciously grown, organic commodities. The new cocoa formula called for sugar, cocoa powder, and vanilla. All these organic commodities, at the time, were grown in third world countries.

I knew that the people who live and work in industrial agriculture areas were at the mercy of big corporations; and they lose their ability to be self-sufficient. When mono-crop farming takes over, the culture of the place, human health, and the environment get degraded. Children are often forced to work! Now that I had a child of my own, this notion of a child working and not in school, was amplified! Is it greed that drives these unsustainable and inhumane practices? Or is it ignorance, or politics? Whatever the reasons, it appalled me that my livelihood depended on the commodities these human beings grew. I was not willing to let the inconvenient truths of the corrupt food systems stop me from exposing the truth and finding Soulutions.

How to Start a National Company

Since the Ice Age, nothing has changed the world faster than business.
It is ethical businesses, led by morally courageous people, that can
rapidly transform our world for the better.

It took me months to find a trustworthy organic commodity broker. When I finally found Steve, I was thrilled. He got into the business because he too understood the industrial food complex was screwed up. Steve assured me that all the goods he sourced were chemical-free and the working conditions were humane for the growers, harvesters, and producers — and farmers got paid a fair price! The Fair Trade Movement in the USA, was in its infancy. We built our relationship based on trust and ethics and to be part of this movement.

Fair Trade is a global movement that works on trading partnerships, and seeks greater transparency and equity throughout the entire food production chain. Better trading conditions secure the rights of marginalized producers and workers. There is a diverse network of organizations, producers, companies, shoppers, and advocates that are striving to put people and planet first.

Steve had sourced a line of organic raw sugar in Brazil. The new sweetener, called Sucanat, was dark brown and had a light, but delicious molasses flavor. It was the first organic sugar to get shipped to North America. He also found an unsulfured organic cocoa powder grown in Latin America — the two main ingredients in our soon-to-be-launched in Alaska: AH!LASKA Cocoa mixes.

A talented graphic artist in Homer assisted me in designing an endearing label and professional marketing materials. The branded mascot was a fun-loving, cartoon polar bear. I called him AH!BEAR and gave him the honorary title, "A Voice for Habitat." For me, AH!BEAR was the spirit of our son.

Steve set me up with a certified organic co-packer and warehouse facility on the east coast, where the raw materials were turned into cocoa mixes. Consolidating the operation under one roof made the process efficient and cost-effective. Steve also sold me thousands of pounds of organic sugar and cocoa which we used at our cafe and in the baking mixes. It was an achievement to convert our recipes using the new unrefined natural ingredients.

I found an affordable shipping company and had the bulk cocoa, sugar, and cocoa mixes shipped and barged to Homer. Yes, the carbon footprint to ship the commodities from their origin on the East Coast, I justified it because I could serve more organic products. At the very least, I had solved one problem.

The initial cocoa launch had three flavors of Ho Ho Cocoa: Glacier Mint, Arctic Amaretto, and Tundra Vanilla Spice. I named the flavors after these three priceless ecosystems. Like the baking mixes, they had an Alaskan theme. An insert with a strong environmental and social justice message went under the lid of each can. The cocoa was a HOT HIT and outsold my baking mixes in Alaska!

A few months after the statewide launch, Steve took a sample of our Cocoa mixes to the national natural foods trade show in Baltimore. He wanted to show off to his clients what a large manufacturer in the industry could do with his commodities. Up to this point, no one had launched a national organic cocoa product. Steve called me from the show with excitement in his voice. "Donna, all the major distributors have been by my booth and they want to purchase YOUR branded concept! They love the image of sipping a cup of hot cocoa made by an Alaskan. If you want to leap into the national market, you can ride my coattails and be the first organic cocoa in the nation!" Gulp and silence. Finally, with trepidation in my voice, I spoke. "What do I have to do?" Blind faith again led me to take the next leap.

It would take focus, support, and dedication to take the products nationwide. It appeared to be a more straightforward way to have a broader impact than my franchise idea. I was more mature and ready to follow through with my promise to myself. Steve stood by his word and introduced me to the best sales brokers and distributors in the industry and helped me refine the initial recipes. The first organic cocoa mix in the United States was born! I was psyched!

The brand and its mission had broad appeal to the brokers and distributors. My challenge was to market the unfashionable benefits of organic ingredients and *Fair Trade* to the masses. I had advantages, as the products looked and tasted great, and Steve, a great mentor, was there to assist and encourage me.

At first it all appeared daunting as the sugary, addictive, insanely popular cocoa brands were marketed mercilessly to children! Cocoa was even found in vending machines and in schools. I hoped that with AH!LASKA cocoa and my kid-friendly AH!BEAR mascot, we could be a "Voice for Nature" and offset some conventional cocoa sales. I wanted the message that we advocated to truly reach the masses. With logistical help from my younger brother on the East Coast and a $25,000 loan from my supportive father (who at this point believed in me whole-heartedly), I was in business.

The national brand launched in just a few months. The money went to finance the inventory, package design, and marketing materials. This left just enough to purchase booth space at the next natural foods trade show in Anaheim, California, where Jazz, (who was 6 months old), my brother, and Kevin and I made our first appearance with AH!BEAR. The show was a great success. We gave out a lot of samples, got a few orders, and generated tons of interest.

A week later, I awoke at 4 a.m. to the ring of the fax machine (it was 9 a.m. Eastern Standard Time). There lay a $20,000 order from just one distributor! I had to look at the glossy fax paper a dozen times before it sank in that all the zeros were for real. Several other purchase orders rolled in that week, totaling over $100,000! Holy Shit!

To purchase the ingredients and additional packaging materials to fulfill all these orders, I would need an influx of cash, and fast. A good challenge for a dyslexic sleep-deprived new mom! A line of credit would give me a source of funds I could tap into at my discretion. And when I paid it back, I could reuse it again.

With more than $100,000 in purchase orders, I dove in 110 percent to get everything required to receive a $200,000 line of credit. (That equates to about $360,336.42 in 2019.) Between my father's coaching and moral support, steady income from the cafe, and help from the Small Business Association (SBA), I pulled it off!

Todd Grinman, the banker from our local branch, had watched our fruitful cafe grow and was a loyal cafe customer. He worked with SBA and me to quickly get the necessary line of credit. He respected my tenacious personality, and I appreciated his business savvy. We inspired each other. Todd became another great business mentor. He believed in me and gave me great advice. I saw our relationship as a partnership.

Todd's profound words have stuck with me to this day: "Donna, the cafe is the goose that laid the golden egg. Do not let go of that goose until your next endeavor is nested in success. Build something positive, meant to last, and your nest will support many prosperous golden eggs, eager and ready to hatch." He went on to clarify, "Always build upon your success. What you appreciate will appreciate. Let your failures be lessons learned." Excellent advice! I wove all my experiences into our foundation (the nest), providing a secure space to hatch new ideas into reality. I would learn how to choose my twigs and branches wisely.

To build a national company in small-town Homer came with a big learning curve. Wholesaling a national product line differed greatly from a retail cafe. The business model had different systems and operated on different cycles. It felt like someone transplanted me into a new ecosystem. Todd Grinman was right to advise me to use and build from the wisdom gained from the cafe. Doing so, it strengthened my ability and gave me the added confidence to leverage this new company. It was a natural progression to diversify and birth another product line in the food business. Like siblings, each business was different, yet nested in similar values. I dove in and learned!

I recognize that not everyone has a family benefactor with the means to lend money. If you have a solid idea, are a hard worker, and are determined, you will find the support and money. Funding noble endeavors is a reality! You can find possible funders and other resources at the back of the book.

Marketing 101

Marketing should be about educating customers and be truthful; not bullshit.

With the line of credit, I paid my father back and purchased the ingredients and packaging supplies to fulfill orders. The rest of the money was used to develop a marketing plan and run the company. I learned from running my businesses and helping others with theirs that 80 percent of business success is attributed to marketing and collaboration. The word marketing, for me, translates into educating. It is the creative process that ignited my passion for business.

AH!LASKA hit the national market in 1992, and I witnessed the power of business on a grander scale. To the masses, it was still *woo-woo* to be an organic farmer or producer. The natural food industry was pumped up with innovative brands ready to break the groovy stigma. Many of the new products even tasted good.

The industry hummed with socially and ecologically minded entrepreneurs. I rubbed elbows with some of the most ethical CEOs (Chief Executive Officers) from good companies. Many of us were determined to prove to the industrial food complex that a sustainable and organic food system could work! It was a challenge. The word *organic* was not commonly used to describe food or agricultural practices. The only times I heard people outside the industry say the word, was when they were referring to organic chemistry or compounds or when customers questioned me … "Why organic? Doesn't it cost more?"

> *Unsustainable business models will transform with consumer*
> *demands. It is up to each of us to shift our wants and needs*
> *to help reshape and heal humanity and the Earth. The*
> *more educated we are, the better choices we make.*

The opportunity to help transform the broken food system came as a surprise this time. It more or less fell into my lap, and I wanted to be sure my efforts made a difference. I focused my energy on what I did best and hired a terrific office manager. Natalie reminded me of my wonderful roommate, Mary, from college. We appreciated each other's talents and accepted each other's weaknesses. Respectively, Natalie was anally retentive, and I, overly creative. We balanced each other out and ended up having fun while making a difference.

I featured The Fresh Sourdough Express on the cocoa packaging as the home base of AH!LASKA and highlighted the cocoa at our cafe. It was awesome when AH!LASKA fans found our little restaurant in Homer. AH!LASKA customers loved the story of how we founded our company and they appreciated the food we served. Cross marketing created a symbiotic relationship that helped build both of my businesses, and our nest-egg grew as did our mission.

Promoting a brand in the natural foods industry had a long to-do list. I provided marketing slicks and ran ads with distributors and attended trade shows. Retailers expected coupons, shelf talkers, and demos. There were store slotting fees to get on the shelves. Also, distributors and retailers expected ongoing discounts.

My marketing plan also included the publication of my first children's book in 1992, *Yummy Recipes ~Wilderness Wonders for Kids and Adults.* I also published a cocoa recipe booklet. The educational activity book and cocoa booklet complemented and promoted both the AH!LASKA brand and The Fresh Sourdough Express cafe concept. I sent the cocoa booklet to stores when they bought ten cases or more of the cocoa. Customers who bought a can of cocoa received a free cocoa recipe booklet which had twenty ways to use AH!LASKA cocoa. More ways to use cocoa meant more cocoa sales. Both books highlighted how our food choices affected all life on Earth and proved to be excellent marketing tools.

In-store demos were a great success. I collaborated with ethical brands such as Organic Valley, Straus Family Creamery, Eden Foods, and Westbrae to do passive demos. Customers could sample the cocoa with milk or a nondairy option while they shopped. I united with Pamela, the founder of Pamela's Bakery, who made great gluten-free cookies. Free samples of cocoa and cookies on a cold winter's day made the customers and retailers happy. It was a smart move to position AH!LASKA with industry leaders. Creative marketing and collaboration were the essential ingredients that helped AH!LASKA become the best-selling organic cocoa in the nation!

Once the new golden egg (the cocoa) hatched and was productive, I diversified the brand and launched the first organic chocolate syrup in the nation. As I had seen my dad work to expand his business, I employed the same tactics and strategies. Once in the chocolate business, I captured all the seasons with a variety of similar products. At the cafe, we branched out into more catering and wedding services. Each business leveraged existing products or services.

AH!LASKA took off as Jazz grew bigger. Over the years I developed more products. Some made it to the shelves, others did not, but I had fun trying. Jazz was with me almost every minute. His calm and innocent presence helped me to stay rooted as my mental shoots branched out in many directions.

I ran the company for ten years and saw the brand reach the shelves of every natural food store and supermarket that carried a healthy line of products. AH!LASKA was a brand built with substance and was built to last. The chocolate syrup remains number one in the nation in its category today.

I proudly donated a percentage of the AH!LASKA profits to wildlife organizations.

Buyer beware: *Many mainstream corporations have compromised the word "natural." Today there are several natural foods distributors with catalogs hundreds of pages long with thousands of items, many of them not worth eating. A good way to save money, the environment, and stay healthy is to shop the perimeters of the stores where the food is fresher, less processed, and has the least amount of packaging.*

Making a Choice to Delegate

Delegate to empower others.

After Jazz was born, Kevin and I had our hands full! We were running two growing companies, taking care of our house, three spoiled dogs, and several cats. Add to this the mounds of snow to shovel, wood to chop, and cars to maintain in the cold Alaskan winters, and we could get pretty burnt out. We had little time for each other, Nature hikes, or friends. I was grateful to have a supportive husband who understood that the business of running a family and a household is all-consuming. Kevin accepted more responsibilities at the cafe, and I focused on being a full-time parent and running AH!LASKA. Many big cocoa and syrup deals happened while in the bathtub or in the sandbox with my son.

Being too busy fizzled the fun and was not sustainable. It came down to delegate or break down, so we delegated and empowered others. I created a *working parenting recipe* that made it possible for me to focus on what I loved to do, while my assistants enjoyed other tasks. They were grateful for their role, and I was thankful to them. Win-Win!

It's about trusting, giving, and receiving.
Empowered, we become ambassadors for a common cause.

Recipe for Working Parents

Time is your most valuable currency, so spend it wisely.

- *Before anything, create a network of family, friends, and neighbors to help out with enhancing your child's life.*

- *Sleep whenever you can and take time for yourself.*

- *If you are in business for yourself, hire a trustworthy office manager.*

- *If business is good, hire a personal assistant/nanny, someone to keep the house clean and orderly, go to the post office, and attend to all things personal, even changing poopy diapers.*

- *Make sure that your work environment is away from home or separated from your living space.*

- *Bottom line and most important and essential: Make family life a priority and value your friendships!*

Creative Habitats

*All children deserve to be safe, happy, healthy,
and to have a connection with the Earth.*

Jazz and I hung out at the cafe plenty. Motherly instincts prompted me to create a kid-friendly atmosphere at the cafe — a place where Jazz could be safe and have plenty of fun outdoors while connecting with Nature.

We had a big sandbox built in the front yard surrounded by trees, grass, colorful flowers, and herbs. We filled the sandbox with toys purchased from the thrift store and old cafe measuring cups, pots, and pans. Kids loved it! The sandbox was in view from several of the dining room tables and visible from the road. We arranged outdoor seating to accommodate families, and those without children.

The legendary Sourdough Express van was inoperable by this time, yet still productive as signage. We moved it to the front lawn of the cafe and turned it into a playhouse for children to enjoy. We let the children know that the van only drove if no adults were inside. The magic van brought out the children's wildest dreams. As they took hold of the gigantic steering wheel and took off in their minds, they explored uncharted territory in their imagination. Between the sandbox and the magic van, our place became the eatery of choice for families with kids. The new habitat encouraged folks to eat outdoors. A busy yard attracted more customers. We were the only business in town with an outdoor, kid-friendly place to play. I never imagined how good this would be for business.

Me in 2015 with my granddaughter.

The property next to the cafe was still wooded. When Jazz got older, it was a safe environment for him to wander under our watchful eyes. In his special woods, he was in touch with Nature, where imaginary friends were OK for they were kin.

Our eatery exposed Jazz to both family and business values. He experienced how we conducted our day-to-day operations, absorbing our work ethics, much as I had during my childhood. He was safe and happy hanging out at the cafe.

The nanny watched Jazz at The Sourdough if Kevin needed me at the café. She also attended the other children playing in the sandbox. Her presence created a more relaxed environment for adults to eat. Jazz met with children from around the country and the world. Just as Mother Dear had done for me, Jazz's nannies exposed him to new ideas and people. The staff and regular customers enjoyed and interacted with him too. The intergenerational influence was good for us all. Our family did a lot of growing up at The Sourdough. I was never more than a mile or an hour away from Jazz until he started daycare: Two half-days a week, at age four.

Jazz started to get migraines in second grade, and we also found out he had dysgraphia, which is the inability to write coherently. I started homeschooling him since the school environment, with its fluorescent lights, lots of noise, and peer pressure, amplified the migraines. At first, homeschooling terrified me. Being dumb is no fun: I was still getting over that useless, old script.

That winter we vacationed in Hawaii, where Jazz learned to write the alphabet on the white beaches, etching the alphabet into the sand with his hand. Words followed. We did not adhere to a strict curriculum but used guidelines from a homeschool program offered by the Alaska school district instead. A lot of kids lived remotely in the state, and homeschooling was a good option. I listened to Jazz and focused on his interests. I played the dumb card again and asked tons of questions. Other homeschool parents were happy to help, and I was glad to help them. We created a supportive learning environment for Jazz, hired qualified tutors, and joined homeschool groups. We also spent a lot of our time out in Nature.

Jazz benefited from some TV programs, the History and Discovery channels in particular. He learned to enjoy science from *Bill Nye the Science Guy* and *The Magic School Bus,* and he fostered a love for history with *Liberty's Kids.* He also loved to time travel while he watched the program *Wishbone,* starring a smart fox terrier known as "the little dog with a big imagination." These educational programs with NO commercials sparked Jazz's desire to learn more. He did not spend much time in front of the *boob tube.* When he did, it was educational, with an occasional reward of an episode of *Power Rangers.*

The homeschool habitat provided an alternative to traditional education that worked for our family. It also allowed Kevin and me to be involved with our child's education. We all had the privilege to relearn or learn new cool things. I saw my role in Jazz's education as teaching him to love to learn. We got the basic subjects down, and the rest we let Jazz choose what he wanted to learn. As I watched him thrive in this environment, I realized that homeschooling would have been the better choice for me if it had been an option.

Having the instinctual ways of a child, Jazz continually reminded Kevin and me what was important: To be flexible with the ingredients in our lives, to be quick to adapt and to change a recipe if it wasn't working. He often knew before we did when things were wrong and set us straight. He reminded us of what was really important. The privilege of raising Jazz was the most meaningful and extraordinary thing I have done. Motherhood was my sanctuary and my strength. I am forever grateful for all the *essential mentors* and teachers who have *offered encouragement* and inspired him; and to Jazz for putting up with my shortcomings. "It takes a village to raise a child."

Root Rot: The Tipping Point

Harsh drought, parched, windblown, beaten by relentless sun,
roots dig deep to find reserves of strength.

I n the gardener's world, root rot is caused by a dangerous fungus. Fungi thrive in wet soil. Root rot infects plants when there is inadequate drainage. Just like its name, the roots rot when they are over-saturated. When an infected plant gets transplanted from one part of the garden to another, it is a threat to the other plants. When we transplant old baggage, burdens of the past, or long-held negative ideas, it impedes our experiences.

Things can go rotten in business and life. When this happens, it's essential to address the root cause and correct it. It's a choice we get to make. Rotten things happen to the best of us, yet often people settle for the *dis-ease*. The faster we take care of a wound, the sooner it will heal, unless we pick at the scab.

Remove the rot, and the healing begins.

250

When the fungal-infested soil is removed, and we clean the plant's roots, it will heal. Once treated and replanted in rich, clean humus, it can flourish. We too, can recover when we replant ourselves in the right environment with positive thoughts and people. Like an infected plant, the longer we have suffered, the longer it might take for the rot to get eradicated.

The Fruiting Cycle, with all its glory, came with unexpected hardships. I birthed a beautiful child and a national company. I was a proud mama and embraced life and business with passion and a purposeful why and got rewarded both financially and soulfully. I literally and figuratively had my cake and ate it too — at least for a while; I was on blissful overdrive.

With all the creative habitats and joyful times, there were unpredictable currents that began to shift my well-being. Eventually, the currents got too strong and swept me away into a negative vortex. Positive experiences masked the depth of my physical pain, which resulted from the unexpected knee surgery I had a year after Jazz was born. I could not accept these unfortunate consequences. Blinded by the rushes and entrepreneurial surges, my fighting, yes-I-can spirit kicked in. Like a roller coaster, there would be highs and lows. I did my best to stay true to my morals and enjoy the ride.

I learned from the Root Rot Cycle that I was not immune to the trials and tribulations that happened in my life. This cycle recaps some of the underlying currents that took place in my subconscious mind as I grew all our businesses and my family in the fruitful years.

In summary, being a woman in a man's business world was difficult! Physical pain made it even harder. Over the years, the build-up of negativity, non-cooperative employees, and unreasonable customer demands dragged me down. As the hurdles came in from every direction, my relationship with my sweet husband began to sour. For a few years, I lost focus and my ability to deal with the workload. Nagging emotional pain grew as I witnessed more people spiral into the supersize-me-mode.

I fell into the persuasive trap of chasing the unattainable, unsustainable American Dream. It belittled me as I succumbed to the artificial human systems and cycles that I had resisted for so long. I lost sight of why I got into business in the first place. Ignoring the fungal environment that slowly grew inside me, I ended up getting to the lowest point in my life; the best version of myself disappeared. Moral agony sucked! Like a plant, when conditions were NOT favorable, I became saturated — emotionally flooded, spiritually drained, and physically bloated. I experienced root rot as I morphed into a powerless workaholic, foodaholic, and sugaraholic. It was a lonely place to be, and I eventually had nowhere to turn but the mirror. I was definitely not living like the future mattered.

I share my misfortune in this Cycle to help others recognize the signs and act on them before you spiral out of control as I did. How we deal with the highs and lows determines everything. If it were not for love and a village of friends and mentors who helped me remove the rot, God only knows where I would be right now. I wish to thank you; you know who you are.

> How we deal with the highs and lows determines everything.

Painful Baggage Leading to Addiction

Blamers are Complainers and Drainers.

———————

And so, the hardships began. It all started with a bum knee.

I planned to get back into aerobics after Jazz turned one. Teaching had given me joy, kept me fit, and balanced out my workaholic tendencies. As I trained to get back in shape, I blew out my knee.

My persuasive, loving dad insisted I come east to have the knee operation. He knew one of the best surgeons in New York City, and he also wanted to see his grandson. It was New Year's Eve day, 1992, when I went in for a simple torn meniscus operation and came out of the operating room discouraged. Back then, MRIs were not commonplace. The doctor informed me that the x-ray did not pick up on the severity of the tear. It also detected arthritis. Bone on bone meant a long, agonizing recovery, and arthritis meant I would most likely always have pain. The added prognosis was that I would never dance again or walk more than ten city blocks until I had a total knee replacement. No skiing, snowshoeing, hiking, or anything else I loved to do that got me into Nature. He suggested I wait as long as possible to have the knee replacement as they only lasted 10 years, and I should wear a cumbersome knee brace unless I was sleeping.

For the first and only time in my life I became depressed. This depression lasted for a couple of months. I had most of my thick auburn hair chopped off so I could fit my head into a swim cap and begin physical therapy in heavily chlorinated pools. The chlorine worked against my overall health, disinfecting everything, including my beneficial gut flora. Like Samson, whose God-given supernatural strength diminished when his hair got cut, so too would I lose my insatiable drive. I truly believed I had given up my power!

Despite the many obstacles that caused my despair, strong like a bull, I pulled my life together for my son. For several years I put up a good front and continued to grow AH!LASKA and spend quality time with Jazz.

That knee surgery began the slow downward spiral into territory I had never known existed. I was in my mid-thirties and still a high-functioning workaholic, with a bum knee, lower back pain, and a young child. The battle between my subconscious and conscious minds began.

Food for People and the Planet?

The industrial food complex does NOT solve problems — it creates them personally, ecologically, and globally.

There were food and mood issues.

As fun and as exciting as it was, growing a natural foods cafe in Homer, Alaska had its challenges —nothing I couldn't handle, or so I thought. The word "Express" in our name occasionally bit us hard. When we got swamped, the service could be slow. Some impatient customers did not appreciate waiting longer than twenty minutes to get served. We tried our best to make up for the wait and offered free samples, and refills on coffee and tried to explain, "Real food takes time to prepare." We intended to provide quality food, not serve fast food or piss people off.

By the 1980s, fast food fascination had hijacked people's palates. The double drive through made it easier and faster to get a fix. The masses were led to believe that fast and filling empty calories were okay. No one seemed to know or care that most food service establishments dished up food from cans, plastic bags, pre-made frozen meals, or were deep fried. These products had a list of ingredients only a scientist could understand. Frozen pizzas, chicken, processed sliced meat, hamburger patties, canned soups, and ready to eat cordon bleu were easier to deal with and more profitable. It appeared the longer the list of ingredients on a label, the more alluring they became to the consumer. Cool Whip replaced real whipped cream, and not even one ingredient came from a cow! It was hard to comprehend the lack of transparency in our food system — the system that can improve the quality of life the fastest — because everybody eats!

An addictive society is excellent for business!

The new convenience products made most restaurateurs happy. Distributors catered to the trends, which meant the choice to buy quality goods was limited. By the time produce got to Alaska it was second-rate. It became increasingly frustrating to run our natural foods cafe in this business climate. After all, we had bills to pay and a hefty payroll supporting many young adults and families. We sometimes caved into the pressure and served things that did not make us proud. It pained me to see this happen. We even served Coca-Cola for a while after several customers walked out with noses turned up at our natural sodas. There were now dozens of eateries down the road and competition became an added issue.

Not enough people cared about "Food for People and The Planet" or being "part of the Soulution, not the pollution." The public was skeptical of the high cost of organic food. Most consumers didn't think about economic or social costs, nor the long-term global consequences. It exhausted me trying to educate the staff, customers, and purveyors. No one wanted to hear about the closely guarded dark secrets of the industrial food complex. Some people thought I was full of shit: a granola-eating, tree-hugging hippie. They viewed the truth about what was happening to our health and the Earth like a bunch of hype rather than an inconvenient reality. Moral agony came when we had no choice but to accommodate and cater to the growing society of habitual foodaholics. It hurt the most when an employee felt that way!

Healthier foods and baked goods cost more to produce. If customers did not care or want to buy what we were offering, why make it? Would you choose a gigantic gooey pecan sticky bun or an organic wheat germ, sunflower seed, apple bran muffin? The demand for our hard-crusted, dense sourdough bread shifted as more consumers became infatuated with the Standard American Diet. Their taste buds and wants had adapted to fluffy sliced bread, settling for quantity, not quality. We went from selling artisan, round, whole-grain sourdough bread to adding yeast to some doughs. We baked them in loaf pans to satisfy requests for lighter, more practical, sliced loaves. It was hard to digest that people preferred to eat this way.

On the surface, everything appeared to be in sync, but the reality was all upside down. I struggled to find my place in the American Dream while serving and educating people about healthy food. The masses got addicted to unhealthy (could barely be called) food. As my effectiveness wore off, I would become weary from my attempts to buck a sick system.

Today, we get inundated with opinions on social media sites, such as TripAdvisor, Yelp, and the like, but this isn't always helpful since there are conflicting views. Besides, 5-star reviews for a place that serves a reasonably priced, greasy gourmet bacon cheeseburger and hand-cut deep-fried potatoes is not a positive review for your health or the planet. Persuasive — yes, and good for the business owners. But how might things be different if these review sites rated business by its conservation efforts? Such as, what is their carbon footprint, or their carbon offset plan? How do they source their ingredients, and how far did they travel to get to the plate? How are the fruits and vegetables grown and how are the animals they serve treated? What are their recyclable and composting practices?

Food service establishments are usually wasteful and use more energy than other retail businesses. If not done right, the carbon footprint of a restaurant is GIGANTIC. "More than 80 percent of the $10 billion annual energy bill for the commercial foodservice sector is spent on inefficient food cooking, holding, and storage equipment." Food and packaged waste can be excessive. To ship oranges to Alaska, and salmon to Florida takes a lot of energy and packaging. The cost to the environment does not get calculated into the price of our food.

Biggest Asses or Greatest Assets

Being resilient and growing intuitively when others do not can be challenging.

There were staffing issues.

Business owners, particularly in small tourist towns, know how difficult it is to find good help. Foodservice professionals and mission-driven people with a strong work ethic were scarce in the '90s. The fast-food industry had tainted restaurant workers. Culinary schools' taught students to use trendy processed ingredients.

Kevin and I did our best to hire people who resonated with our core values: Who worked with us, not for us. Unfortunately, this did not always work out. As the business grew, so did the need for more employees. We got so busy that sometimes we hired whoever walked in the door and wanted a job. They were usually there for one reason: A paycheck.

Many young seasonal restaurant workers were from a generation of entitlements, decades after the Great Depression. They came with an attitude — "I'll do what I want." They didn't understand how hard it could be to get a job, or an education, or put food on the table.

If an employee did not agree with the Sourdough policies and philosophy, they tended to act disrespectfully. I felt like my morals were constantly being tested. Kevin and I did our best to stand by one another, but sometimes things got testy with the staff. Some employees preferred Kevin's management style, while others preferred mine.

It broke my heart when someone came to work with a Coke in their hand. I'd later see the aluminum can wind up in the trash, located right next to the recycle bin. A hungover employee reeking from alcohol was especially hard to take. Kevin and I learned to tolerate a plethora of misconduct; we sucked up the negativity and bucked up. Otherwise, we were the ones washing the dishes, prepping, cooking, and waiting tables. In retrospect, pleasing everyone was not the answer. A better idea would have been too close for the day, put up a sign; "gone fishing" and regroup. In retrospect, it was not worth having a rotten apple in the bushel.

On the other hand, many of the local millennials were the best staff! They worked through their high school years, and once they went off to college, came back to work in the summers. Many eventually started Eco-Bohemian careers. It has been a joy and an honor to watch these kids turn into contributing adults, and to have mentored and inspired them.

When we worked as a team, we strived for the good of the business. We had each other's backs. In harmony, we grew the business into an epic eatery. For years, the Sourdough had been on fire! I missed those times.

United with
a purposeful
'WHY' is when
we thrive.

Communicate ~ Communicate ~ Communicate

True love makes allowances for another's weaknesses. Getting to the core of an issue may bring conflict at first. Being willing to communicate brings peace.

There were relationship issues.

Kevin and I were long overdue for a serious conversation. We took the opportunity on a drive to Anchorage to get supplies for the cafe and drop off AH!LASKA orders. We bundled up our darling son and hit the road. On a blustery winter day, we got to the meat of the matter. Once Jazz fell asleep, I spoke honestly: "I want to sell the cafe," I said. "I'm tired of the struggles that are souring our relationship. I want to move somewhere warm. The cold weather is creating more pain in my body, and I'm disillusioned with my efforts in Alaska."

The moving part did not come as a surprise to him. What shocked him was the thought of giving up the cafe! His identity was entrenched in providing for his family and the only thing he felt confident in doing at the time was running The Sourdough. I still remember the look on his sweet face. There was a long silence as we gazed out the frosty windshield. Lost in our emotions, we were unaware of the surrounding beauty. Finally, Kevin looked at me, confused and lost. Then, finding his inner voice, he said, "What would I do?" He was clearly not ready to let go of the business, nor was he prepared to move from Alaska. This conversation was a pinnacle turning point for us.

The six-hour drive to Anchorage on icy roads gave us time to listen to each other and express our feelings. What we said pushed us to the depths of our souls. We acknowledged that our priorities of late, were not straight. It was hurtful when we disagreed and did not resolve our arguments. We agreed to STOP THE CRAZINESS! This meant we had to honor each other's wishes, be supportive, and respect our differences. We agreed more communication was essential for personal growth, our relationship, and business matters. We agreed that our health and our family were our highest priorities. The conversation brought us both to tears more than once. It also brought us closer together. At one point I grabbed Kevin's hand and looked into his teary eyes and said, "I love YOU; life is too damn short to harbor regrets." He squeezed my hand back and looked at me with a new level of love.

So, what came out of this impasse? I sold the prosperous Sourdough Express business to Kevin for $1, intending to relinquish my involvement in major decision-making. I would focus on being the best mother and run AH!LASKA. Part of the year we agreed to spend somewhere in the Lower 48, where it was warm and close to an airport, as I traveled a lot for AH!LASKA business. The cafe became seasonal, open for six months of the year after running year-round for fifteen years. Kevin would help me in the winter months with AH!LASKA.

I also insisted that he get medical treatment for his migraines, as this was a source of the problems. He had suffered from these severe headaches since his early twenties, and they greatly affected his well-being and our relationship. As most migraine sufferers know, there is no quick fix. From that day forward, whenever we hit rough places in our relationship, we did not wait to communicate our feelings.

Kevin's love and support helped with all the trials and tribulations. Sometimes it was not enough to keep me from going dark. He too struggled with the rise of the industrial food complex and a growing complacent population. But we had our priorities straight, and with our willingness to communicate we grew together even in the hardest of times.

It takes nourishment and time to have a long-lasting love relationship.

Today, Kevin and I still take the time to work through tough times. We learned how important it is to forgive each other for our shortcomings. Let's face it, shit happens when you live and work together twenty-four-seven. Patience, communication and honoring each other's strengths have been vital to our healthy, long-lasting relationship. Common interests continue to strengthen us. We have a joint mission for the present and the future that helps get us through the best and worst of times. We both love Nature, animals, children, and good food. Love, trust, and fun are the primary ingredients in our relationship — they are the macronutrients that solidify our connection. Kevin is the yang to my yin and yin to my yang. He is the light in my darkest hours, my best friend in the world, and the sweetest, most kindhearted person I know. As most loved ones do, he also pushes my buttons the hardest. It is all worth it!

A healthy relationship at any age fosters maturity, stability, and trust. When there is trust, we can have faith and feel comfortable with ourselves and with each other. For any relationship to flourish, like a garden, it requires tending. Yes, this takes doing the work, but when you love what you are doing, it does not feel like work. Over the years, friends and clients have asked for relationship advice. The main question has been, "How do you stay in a loving, long-lasting relationship?" I offer three pieces of advice:

1. Communicate 2. Communicate 3. Communicate

Moral Agony

*When you admit and accept that part of success
is screwing up, you can succeed.*

There were other moral agony issues.

Running a national company was a tremendous experience. The good times gave me a lot of satisfaction. I enjoyed developing products and creative marketing plans that expressed the company's mission. I felt I was making a difference in the industry. But after eight years, AH!LASKA ran into trouble. There were problems with the cocoa packers, escalated costs to get on the shelves, and fierce competition.

Greed and big *not-green dollars* infiltrated the industry at a rapid pace. Simultaneously, small businesses got bought out or went extinct. Mainstream companies with big names such as Kellogg's, Kraft Foods, and General Mills wanted a piece of the action. Threatened by the growing natural food market share, they started buying up brands with potential and swallowing a market share they didn't understand. With one hand, they fed us the "organic" label, and out of the other hand pushed their unhealthy, mainstream goods and agendas. Most consumers were unaware and feasted on what was marketed to them.

ConAgra got into the game and bought Lightlife Foods, and Coca-Cola bought Odwalla for $181 million in 2001! It disturbed me to see the industry succumb to the corporate conglomerate. Other natural food companies skyrocketed in the industry, such as Annie's Homegrown with its beloved bunny mascot and went public in 2011. AH!BEAR was jealous.

*It was time for companies like mine, to either
get eaten up by another company
or eat up other brands.*

The cost of doing business and competing with big corporations became so high it was out of reach for a gal from Homer who was already doing too much! As I searched for superficial glory, it only brought feelings of jealousy and insecurity, leaving me with a bruised and confused ego. As the competition attempted to eat me alive, I lost touch with what was important. I questioned if I had failed, rather than honor my successes. It would take years to acknowledge that I had done my best and to respect myself for what I did, not what I should have done. Sometimes it's just who you know, timing, and luck.

According to Business Insider, "Only 10 companies control almost every large food and beverage brand in the world. These companies — Nestlé, PepsiCo, Coca-Cola, Unilever, Danone, General Mills, Kellogg's, Mars, Associated British Foods, and Mondelez — each employ thousands and make billions of dollars in revenue every year." Like an invasive species, these corporations stifle free enterprise. Their intentions affect our health, the environment, and the economy. The tipping point from capitalism to "corrupt-ism," has seesawed in the wrong direction.

Before I caved in and sold out, I gave it one last push in 1997 and partnered with a reputable marketing and design firm that believed in me and the brand's mission. If the brand would keep up in this industry, it needed a significant makeover. At this point, I was reaching *overwhelmed* mode and was relieved to have partners. I gave up a 40 percent interest in the company. For this, my new partners poured in thousands of dollars to re-brand and reposition AH!LASKA in the marketplace. I got to help. It was an opportunity to develop more skills. Up to that point, I had made all the decisions and designed the packaging and marketing materials.

This partnership worked well for a couple of years until the marketing firm grew too broad and could not give the brand its 40 percent worth of attention. I negotiated an agreement to get AH!LASKA back 100 percent. But was that what I wanted or needed? I put up a good front, and did my best to smile as I continued to grow the company and my own body.

Today, there are some good companies and products. Yet, I came to appreciate that anything processed and packaged, put in a box or plastic, is not as good as eating food directly from its natural state. In the greed for profit, we lose the intrinsic value of our food. Read labels and do your research. The word "natural" has gotten distorted and diluted. If a product is truly organic, fair trade, GMO-free, humanely raised and packaged responsibly, then there's a chance you're supporting an ethical company.

Mounting Trials and Tribulations

Whether it be a person or the environment,
if you do not nurture it, it will erode or vanish forever.

There were multiple other issues.

I worked tirelessly to grow AH!LASKA, which excited me, but could be hard on my health and family. Closing the cafe in the winter made room for new restaurants, some of which were started by former employees. More pieces of the pie brought forth a variety of competitive choices. Customers we saw every day came in once a week if at all. This crushed my spirit. The fierce competition in Homer could take the joy out of business.

Each year the woods on Ocean Drive shrank as the demand for commercial real estate grew, and our cafe in the woods was steadily encircled by developers on all sides. As each tree got taken down, the moose population declined and so did the beauty that once surrounded our cafe. I shed many tears as the sound of the bulldozers conjured up memories of Pine Hill Road. I wished I had enough money to buy up all the land and save the beautiful trees and moose habitat!

I must have read *The Giving Tree* by Shel Silverstein to our son one hundred times. The book reminded me and taught Jazz of the importance to give more than we take and to respect Nature or risk its destruction. The words also speak to unconditional love, and to be a giver, a nurturer, and a cultivator: Whether it be for a person, a tree, or the environment. As I whittled away to a stump (except I was getting plump), I'd ask myself, why am I not giving to myself!?

Kevin's migraines, even with treatment, were not any better. If he was down with a headache, often for days at a time, I'd step in at The Sourdough, full throttle! Over the next several years, I watched the Sourdough turn into something else as the sales slid. Without enough support, the challenges gained momentum. I became saturated with problems I could not handle; the ugly fungi process began to take root. Bad habits brewed deep within as the unsustainable system wielded its power over me. I would increasingly require additional stimulants to keep up with the pace of the workload.

Family Challenges

Relatives can be pillars of support, or they can be weak links.

—————————••©©©©©©••————————

OMG, the family issues.

Every fall, Jazz, Kevin, and I went to New Jersey to visit my side of the family. Perceived as the psychedelic sheep, I often felt judged as being self-righteous, a nonconformist hippie, and politically incorrect. My path and views were so different that often conversations got heated.

My dad had supported me financially and with business advice, but I yearned to bridge our different perspectives on life. I wanted him to be more like me, and he assumed I would be more like him. It hurt me to disappoint him, yet worse to disappoint myself. He could never grasp that it was the Earth that was my home, not his house.

Regardless, I adored my dad and my stepmom, and when I more or less adapted to their lifestyle while visiting, all went well. Before each visit, I hit the thrift stores to buy a whole new wardrobe to please my dad. After all, we'd be dining at the country club and other fine eateries. Kevin also complied, and Jazz loved it all: The food, museums, Broadway shows, and family gatherings. There was so much love — like a chameleon — I blended in and indulged with the attitude of "When in Rome..." I must admit, it was a blast when I was on my best behavior.

Rosemary and Dad had a relatively healthy diet for a middle-aged couple in the '90s, or so they thought. My dad insisted on eating meat at every meal. Thank goodness both his wives served salad or other fresh vegetables with the otherwise carnivorous diet. Rosemary snuck in a fish dinner on Fridays.

Unfortunately, the meats were pumped up with antibiotics, hormones, dyes, and sodium nitrate. Angus beef was all the rage, but no one thought about the cows that lived a miserable life and spent their last days in inhumane feedlots. Don't get me started on how they raised veal. I had the guts to bring my dad an article about veal production. It was graphic and disturbing. Somehow, my dad didn't give a damn; that really bothered me!

Dad and Rosemary loved to cook, entertain, and grocery shop. When I shopped with them, if I could find organic foods, I'd slip them into the cart. Believe me, they let me know how ridiculous I was! Their kitchen had a big pantry full of packaged goods. Pasta, crackers, chips, condiments, Maxwell House coffee, soft drinks, and plenty more processed products with daunting lists of unhealthy ingredients. A beautiful fruit bowl decorated the kitchen counter. The refrigerator was always full of conventional milk, a variety of cheeses, yogurt, and cold cuts full of nitrates. There was almost always an assortment of supermarket produce unless it was in the summer when you'd find a fresh bounty from their garden.

My folks had a small productive garden filled with eggplant, tomatoes, peppers, and herbs. Rosemary, a fantastic Italian cook, made the best eggplant Parmesan, and her homemade tomato sauce — over the top! My dad and her also made delicious soups and stews from the garden surplus and stashed them in the freezer so that in the dead of winter, they could enjoy a taste of summer. The basement of the house had two freezers full of meat and a backup of everything including ice cream. Despite the abundance, there was nothing organic or free range except Dad's catch of Alaskan fish and Rosemary's garden delights.

I did my best not to be judgmental, kept my mouth shut, and swallowed my pride; *I mindfully refreshed and tamed my ego.* I ate the food and killed negativity with kindness. Meals full of flavor and made with love pacified my deep-rooted discouragement and feelings of ineffectiveness. If my family didn't accept or appreciate my values, how was I going to make any difference!?

For years, my family did not accept my psychedelic sheep ways. Gradually they'd shift to healthier choices: Basically, back to the way their parents ate. When organic food showed up at their house, I felt more at home. It took time, but we learned to respect our differences and become more tolerant of each other's opinions. I would come to appreciate that my parents had provided a loving place to visit and had cared for me even when I was at my lowest point.

I learned that when there are hard-set rules and opinions, we are more likely to rebel. When we are open-minded, we can change our minds and influence others. Discussions about the environment and politics would become more civil between my stoic father and I as we grew closer and closer throughout the years.

Being a psychedelic sheep can be hard. Parents and siblings can be excessively critical and cause confusion and grief. They can stress you out to the max and get under your skin because they think they know you best, are jealous or resentful of your progress, or have their own issues. Align yourself with those who bring out the best in you. Find your tribe — psychedelic, black or white — be open to others and let your true colors shine through. Nurture the meaningful relationships in your life. Persistence pays off. Those who judge you, but love you, will eventually accept you. If not, then carry on. Love and acceptance come in every color of the rainbow. Let go of the shades that wash out your true colors! Never give up on being you-er than you.

Align yourself with those who bring out the best in you.

Mission-Driven Business Woman

STOP IT! Stop the craziness!

The bitch issues!

In 1980, when I was 22, I dug into my first business without considering the odds of being a woman. The pressures to subscribe to the American Dream stayed present, as did the daunting stereotypic role of a bitchy businesswoman. I continually tried to prove myself in the male-dominated business world; it could be HARD, and the physical pain I endured all those years made it even harder!

The entrepreneurial traits I inherited from my, "strong-like-bull," innovative father were to be a rule-breaker, to be full of tenacity and passion, and to have a bold vision. They worked for him, so why not for me: A smart woman with a strong personality?

I was on a mission to heighten people's awareness of our Mother Earth's majesty and the grandeur of a woman's ingenuity — a bold vision. God knows I had passion and tenacity! Being intensely mission-driven with so many obstacles, there were times I couldn't see the light at the end of the tunnel and everything around me appeared dark. I could feel boxed in by societal rules and norms that were unacceptable to me. I often could feel the pressure stifling my creativity and drive. Yet I never let on and persevered as best I could as a woman in these times.

In the media, women were portrayed as witches, superheroes, or sex objects. These superficial and unrealistic expectations of what a woman should be created confusion and resentment among strong-willed women. You were expected to have a fashion model figure or a Hollywood appearance. Flaunting tits and ass, or at least lots of cleavage, was a way to make progress. It did not matter if you were smart; sex was the fastest way to the top. Have things changed?

I could not understand why women throughout history were labeled as either a Madonna or a whore, and now added into the mix, a bitch! Why are strong, intelligent women in leadership roles thrown into these degrading categories? There was no shortage of mixed messages and I found myself with an identity crisis.

During those few years when I struggled, some people labeled me a "bitch." It was a heavy burden being looked upon as a self-righteous, bitchy boss. On top of that, the self-sabotage was brutal. Extra weight became a shield of armor, protecting my pained body and aching heart from predators and slander.

I chose not to give up my business to be a mother! Unfortunately, other women were doing just that: Claiming it was too hard or they were tired of fighting the male-dominated work culture. They were fed up trying to climb the corporate ladder with unequal treatment and pay. It is ludicrous that the oppression of women is still prevalent today. Women have so much to offer the male-dominated business world. They add tremendous value, intuition, and insight!

I also witnessed women being harder on one another in the competitive world. I wondered if women were set up by insensitive men to fail, to keep us in our place, and to keep us weak. I learned if we respect and honor our different gender roles and strengths, we find harmony. Undermining each other's values is *backassward*!

In America, the first female CEO of a Fortune 500 company did not even exist until 1998. As of 2019, women only represent approximately 5.2 percent of the top CEOs. To think we have not settled the gender pay gap! According to Payscale, "The uncontrolled gender pay gap, which takes the ratio of median earnings of all women to all men, decreased by $0.05 since 2015. However, women still make only $0.79 for every dollar men make in 2019." Several articles over the years have provided substantial evidence that women in leadership roles are more likely to outperform their male counterparts on points of return on sales, equity, and invested capital, as well as on issues *concerning the engagement with employees. How come the pay gap remains such a substantial issue, when female leaders are consistently putting up better figures and providing a higher quality experience for their employees?*

Motherhood and Business
When I was balanced, it worked out.

The haunting stigma that women must give up a fulfilling career to have a family, or that a woman's place is in the home and to then be disrespected, is ridiculous! It's the 21st century! If you're a woman who is facing these stigmas, do whatever you can to avoid being in a compromised position. Quit your job, start your own company, and unite with other righteous women and men. Ask yourself this, "What is important? What is my self-worth, worth?" Find the tools and use them!

I learned the hard way that running a business and raising a child are all-consuming, hard to balance, and complicated. I could have it all, couldn't I? Yeah, if I only knew what I know now. A child changes the dynamics. And if you do not adjust, things get out of adjustment.

Whenever I put too much emphasis on business, it tipped the scale in the wrong direction and left Jazz and Kevin resentful. When I was balanced, it all worked out. Since I was not equipped with the tools to stay balanced, it felt like I was on a seesaw for four years. I'm glad my child got to see his mother be successful, and yes, it was wonderful to have him there to comfort me when times were tough. He helped me to keep it real, and I prioritized motherhood over everything.

I adopted the role of a superficial superhero. To make sure Jazz was happy and did not feel excluded, I sometimes gave into his normal childish desires and bought him cheap, made-in-China plastic toys (often made by children): Beanie Babies, Pogs, Pokémon, and Power Rangers. At least most of what we bought came from garage sales and thrift stores. Pacifying him with occasional trips to McDonald's and Subway were the worst of these motherly moral agony indulgences. I didn't understand at the time that children learn from what they observe, not what we tell them to do. All the same, Kevin and I filled Jazz up with great food and a variety of experiences: culture, music and the arts, time in Nature, and we always had animals. His friends were always welcome at our home.

When Jazz got older, he shared his feelings about my workaholic tendencies. He let me know our business endeavors sometimes took away from what he might have considered an ideal childhood. Once I reflected on his perception and appreciated his honesty, I could admit, at times, my priorities got twisted. Forgiveness and compassion freed both of us to move forward with more grace. We agreed it was better to nourish the best memories and to compost unpleasant ones. Jazz is now a father and has a better understanding of the joys and challenges of parenting. He has learned by observation, as I had from my father, that persistence, passion, and determination are excellent qualities to have. It warms my heart to see how much good he absorbed from his youth and to watch him evolve into a bright, independent man.

Jazz has grown up to be a bright young man like his Papa.

Temporary Pleasures

Hungry for connection, we blindly consume.
Whether it be food or booze. Is it worth choosing a toxic
altered state of consciousness for a fleeting moment of pleasure?

Addiction came forth because of all these issues!

As the trials and tribulations tested my patience and endurance, overeating and overworking was my way to deal with life. At the Sourdough, I was like a moose grazing my way through the cafe. I would start off with tasting whatever came out of the oven: A warm, gooey sticky bun, a berry cheesecake Danish or a lemon poppy seed muffin. Then I would cruise into the afternoon devouring a fresh-out-of-the-oven chocolate chip cookie. I regularly indulged in a loaf of warm sourdough bread smothered in butter or, better yet, Brie cheese. YUM! Mix that up with a few Americanos, sip on some milkshakes and smoothies daily and... you get the picture. I rationalized consumption of a few extra cookies, leftover muffins, and big meals, as what I needed to get through the day. My idea of making a better choice was to have oatmeal cookies, justifying that they were full of fiber. Have you ever done that?

I got superb at fooling myself. Between ibuprofen and a cocktail of sugar substances and caffeine, I conned myself into thinking I could carry on this way. Studies now show that sugar is more addictive than cocaine. It became my drug of choice! After knee surgery, I started my coffee addiction. The caffeine compounded my sugar buzz and gave me immediate gratification. Afternoon espresso drinks and belly aches led to sleepless nights. I needed a sleeping pill to get even a few hours of sleep. My insulin and cortisol levels soared!

To mask my despair, I ate and ate and ate, and I worked and worked and worked. In Alaska, that's a long day of eating and working in the summer.

Dr. Mark Hyman, a renowned doctor of integrative medicine, writes, "The science of food addiction is clearer now than ever before. A powerful study published in the American Journal of Clinical Nutrition proves that higher-sugar; higher-glycemic foods are addictive in the same way as cocaine and heroin."

My nickname at the cafe was the "cooler clean-out lady." God forbid something was found rotten in the coolers. Since we only used quality ingredients, and they were expensive, I let nothing go to waste. This included licking spoons and scraping every bowl clean. I'd make twenty to forty thick, creamy, delicious milkshakes a day preparing them so that there was little waste. Super sneaky, I'd scraped out every last drop and put the shake remains in a coffee mug to make a one-of-a-kind concoction just for me. Folks thought I was sipping coffee. Really, I was only fooling myself. It was a compulsion with multiple layers.

The heavier I got, the more she-he like I became. I had the strong like-bull external persona. Losing my compassion, sensitivity, and sensibility, I numbed myself towards almost everyone except my son.

I was not only compelled to eat everything at the cafe, when I got home, I often devoured whatever I could! Jazz used to crave saltine crackers and Rice Krispies Treats, and since these products seemed to have a placebo response calming his migraines, we both ate lots. Since I knew about nutrition, and we had access to fresh-caught salmon, halibut, mussels, and crab, I made sure to eat healthy meals between my sweet and salty obsessions. If I were eating the SAD diet on top of my sugar addiction, I'd be dead! I gave myself permission to eat the same size portions as my husband, who was five times more active than me. After all, you can't get to 205 pounds at 5 feet 2 ¾ tall, and not eat like a hungry man. In four years, I gained 60 pounds!

I was worse than an addict — I was a legal drug dealer. I pushed the white powdery substances, even if they were organic! Besides selling over-the-counter baked goods — made with powdery flour and sugar — I bought the first forty-foot container of organic sugar in the nation, to make AH!LASKA Cocoa. Our small company bought several containers a year to fill cocoa and chocolate syrup orders. Even though we used more ethical ingredients, it was still packaging sugar into a canister or plastic bottle. We pushed more sugar in one year to make the first round of cocoa mixes than all the previous years of the cafe combined! Finite resources were used to produce and transport these non-essential products. Moral agony was hard to digest and felt nothing like success.

According to the World Wildlife Fund (WWF), roughly 145 million tons of sugars are produced in 121 countries each year. And sugar production does indeed take its toll on surrounding soil, water and air, especially in threatened tropical ecosystems near the equator.

Denial

We feel rotten, empty, and lost if we do not follow our hearts and dreams.

———————— ₒₒₒₒₒₒₒₒₒₒₒ ————————

The reason for it all!

As the years went by, I played the victim game. Feeling unfulfilled and in denial brought uncertainty, and I felt inadequate. I gave away my power to empty calories, rather than deal with the demands. Being honest hurt too much. Living in crisis turned into a stifling habit. Choosing work and food over fulfilling connections was no way to live. The only bird songs — or more like sounds — came from the crows scavenging in the cafe parking lot and the shrills of the bald eagles soaring by.

It was impossible to change my ways when I was in denial. Who wants to admit they have a problem? Like most addicts, mine was a gradual progression I had kept hidden, or so I thought. As the stress mounted, my passion waned, and my deep-seated despair had nowhere to hide. The dopamine rush I had received from the businesses wore off, and the rose-colored glasses fell off the bridge of my nose. Harmful emotional bacteria (baggage) crept in to conquer this tree-hugging, Eco-Bohemian woman, and saturated me with negativity. Stress, pain, lack of exercise, and overeating made for a disastrous recipe. I rotted from the inside out and suffered from irritable bowel syndrome (IBS), anxiety, and adrenal fatigue. While aspiring to help others get healthy, I made myself sick! How contradictory is that!?

Being present was hard, and it was hard to communicate with others when I was in denial. Excessive work and toxic consumption habits could no longer mask the pain! Being driven and determined were positive characteristics until I took them to an extreme! I lost sight of the present and the principles that helped me stay balanced. I reached a tipping point and had fallen into an addictive state and refused to admit it.

My workaholic tendencies and self-destructive patterns, which isolated me socially, have long been known as symptoms of depression. My superficial smile for the customers provided a necessary front. I was anxious about the future and let worries from my past nag at me. Like a bear with a toothache, I'd sometimes get agitated, mean, aggressive, or curl up in a corner and sulk. I'd blame, criticize, and put down others to make myself feel better, saying things like "You drive me to eat," and "You're not doing enough." This criticizing was abusive and toxic. Denial is stubborn and ugly. It distanced me from my higher purpose, and I earned the title of "bitch." Harsh criticism and judgment diminished my humaneness. In my mind, I judged myself as failing — which proved to be a painful, emotional punishment. My self-worth drowned in a sea of despair and left me with a bruised and confused ego. I had one pity party after another, and I was the only one who attended. To put it mildly, I was a miserable mess! Root rot sucked!

Among the joys of giving birth, the obstacles during this
evolutionary period seemed as vast as Mount Denali.
How was I going to lift myself out of this one?

Digging Deeper IV

*The compulsive need to chase the American Dream
can rot a well-intended spirit.*

───────── ⚜ ─────────

My ridiculous justifications that allowed me to compromise my values were partially due to what was happening in the world. I absorbed the societal messages and events and did my best to ignore how I felt about them. Like annoying background noise, the current affairs added to the erosion of my optimistic spirit. Drug wars and the crack/cocaine epidemics were all over the news. The workaholic and foodaholic epidemics were not newsworthy, nor considered to be the illnesses they are. I did not relate that my addictions stemmed from similar reasons to those of drug and alcohol abusers. Listening to the news made things worse.

WebMD sheds light on this disorder: "Compulsive overeating is a type of behavioral addiction, meaning that someone can become preoccupied with a behavior (such as eating, or gambling, or shopping) that triggers intense pleasure. People with food addictions lose control over their eating behavior and find themselves spending excessive amounts of time involved with food and overeating or anticipating the emotional effects of compulsive overeating." This article also says: "Experiments in animals and humans show that, for some people, the same reward and pleasure centers of the brain that are triggered by addictive drugs like cocaine and heroin are also activated by food, especially highly palatable foods. Highly palatable foods are foods rich in sugar, fat, and salt. Like addictive drugs, highly palatable foods trigger feel-good brain chemicals such as dopamine."

The rapid growth of the industrial food complex was monstrous, and out of control, like me. Corn syrup was the bane of the American diet in the '80s and '90. The justification for processed foods and beverages is that they were easier to ship, produced less waste, were compact for storage, had a longer shelf life, and could be non-perishable. The bottom line: big profit for corporations at the expense of human health and the environment. People got bigger too as they ate into the fast lifestyle and food. The health care system expanded to take care of new ailments: Obesity and diabetes. At the same time, I had classmates die of Aids.

The industrial food complex was composed of the 'Big 6' — Monsanto, BASF, Bayer CropScience, DuPont Pioneer, Dow Chemicals, and Syngenta at the time. These corporations dominated our food system with the new agriculture biotechnology: Government regulations and subsidies favoring big corporations. Large-scale agribusiness raped the soil. Our global food systems, from the land, to the seas, and to our tables, were being depleted. The idea that bigger is better made it harder for small farmers and businesses.

According to the National Sustainable Agriculture Coalition, "A recent pair of reports from the Economic Research Service (ERS) confirms that federal subsidies to farms are increasingly going to larger and larger farms, thus supporting the cycle of the big getting bigger. Access to land is a huge problem for young farmers, and big farms contribute to this problem. Fewer and bigger farms mean less money circulating in local economies, fewer farm jobs in rural areas, and less opportunities for beginning farmers to get into the business." These issues haven't gone away and are likely to get worse with the current administration and beyond if we don't pay attention.

Organic Certification standards evolved through the '90s — well-endowed lobbyists funded by agribusiness watered down the well-intended measures. Even today, although government-regulated, many aspects of organic food production are misleading.

The middle class needed to be on high alert. As "big business" grew, free enterprise shrank: Fierce competition stifled the idealism. The Haves and the Have-Nots continued to grow further apart. It was still a man's world of finance with ruthless marketing practices. Land and Americans were becoming more compromised, gentrified, and homogenized. The corporate world projected itself as the "good guys" who would make the world safer and life easier. As companies merged to form larger conglomerates, the lack of balance of power turned capitalism into "corrupt-ism." Economic growth trumped living as if the future mattered.

Our appetite for bargain goods encouraged the newly minted coal industry in China to explode. As we grappled with pollution at home, we exported the problem, as if the Earth's air had political boundaries and poisoning people in other countries didn't count.

The backdrop of the times brought opportunities and obstacles.

The year 1990 started with promising news when Germany reunited after forty-five years of repressive separation. Then the Cold War officially ended with the fall of the Soviet Union on Christmas Day, 1991. Meanwhile, Operation Desert Storm — also called the First Gulf War (the Oil War) — began. The terrorist attack bombing in 1993 on New York's World Trade Center alarmed our country and shook our freedom. That same year, we thought there was hope for the environmental movement when Vice President Al Gore pushed for implementing a carbon tax to modify incentives to reduce fossil fuel consumption.

I remember how I felt when Nelson Mandela was awarded the Nobel Peace Prize in 1993 after being imprisoned for 27 years. This high honor was rewarded for his "work for the peaceful termination of the apartheid regime, and for laying the foundations for a new, democratic South Africa." By overcoming adversity, he bravely rose to be president of South Africa in 1994 as genocide was occurring in the African nation of Rwanda. Mandela's will to stand up for his beliefs gave me the incentive and strength to carry on. There was also hope for women when Ruth Bader Ginsburg co-founded the Women's Rights Project and was appointed associate justice of the Supreme Court of the United States by President Bill Clinton. In her early career, this brilliant Jewish woman championed laws that gave women and other minorities more equal rights. The second female justice, Ginsburg took the oath of office on August 10, 1993.

The much-heralded NAFTA (North American Free Trade Agreement) of 1994 made it possible to bring to market out-of-season "fresh" fruits and vegetables. Unfortunately, many crops are fertilized with chemicals banned in the United States. The produce could even be sprayed with a petroleum-based wax for longer shelf life, leaving the harvest devoid of many natural nutrients and taste. Meanwhile, America exported unhealthy, cheap, processed, packaged foods to the grocery stores of Mexico and Canada. That same year, Jeff Bezos — the technology entrepreneur who founded Amazon — eventually took consumer usage of a wide range of products and materials to a whole new level. E-commerce exploded, eventually making it even easier to buy cheap, packaged food.

In 1996, Dolly the Sheep became the first cloned mammal, and it concerned many that this was the way of the future. In 1997, Steve Jobs went back to his post at Apple as the CEO, and his innovative creations like the iPhone, iPad, MacBook, and more streamlined desktop Macs quickly changed the world. That same year Madeleine Albright made history as the first female secretary of state. But like many women, she struggled to get her voice heard and acted upon. That same year, the tragic death of 36-year-old Princess Diana stunned the world.

Al Gore helped broker the Kyoto protocol in 1997, and pushed for passing the treaty which called for a reduction in greenhouse gas emissions. He also tried to educate the public about the relationship between human-caused emissions and global warming. Getting people's attention was an uphill battle for Gore, as it was for me. As he said later when introducing his film, *An Inconvenient Truth*, "I've been trying to tell this story for a long time, and I feel as if I've failed to get the message across."

Meanwhile, the media was relentless with their distractions, diluting the American Dream. People Magazine, the increase in TV sitcoms, and O. J. Simpson's murder trial consumed people's time and attention. Fast-food commercials and the latest trends in processed food dominated the airwaves, along with over-the-counter medications developed to ward off the effects of foods that were advertised. Addiction was on the rise in every category, including sex. By 1998, it was on everyone's mind as President Clinton was going through impeachment, and Viagra hit the market — hard.

Just as we were all getting addicted to the digital age, the year 2000 "Y2K," or the "millennium bug," arrived and threatened our way of life. Computer programmers became concerned about a potential design flaw moving from the 1990s to the year 2000. They expected problems because 20th-century software often represented the four-digit year with only the final two digits, making the 2000s indistinguishable from the 1900s. Panic hit in 1999 when we heard of the potential disaster and stocked up on everything from generators to canned food. When the Y2K fallout was averted, computer use, and the Internet exploded. Meanwhile, global climate change was more apparent, and seventy-four tornadoes touched down in Kansas and Oklahoma that same year.

From genetically altered seeds that promised to make crops free of disease to digital music technology, everything changed! The technology movement was on steroids. People became more fascinated with the Internet than with what they put in and on their bodies, and the Earth. The Internet became the 21st century's compulsion. The masses grew further away from the value of the soil and each other's souls. The pace of change was staggering.

Our lives changed forever. In my eyes, the Earth itself — the masses and I — were on an unsustainable trajectory. It would take years to regenerate my well-being. I needed to first crash and then relearn; living like the future mattered, and being part of the Soulution would be a saner reality!

Maturity

Principles that influenced my life in this Evolution:

• Know your truth.

• Be part of the Soulution.

• Health is your greatest wealth.

• The present is a gift. Receive it in the Now.

• Live like the future matters, in harmony with Nature.

• Time is your greatest currency. Think, and take action.

• Connect, collaborate, and celebrate life from the depth of your soul.

Restoration: Planting Seeds for the Future

Restoration is the act of returning something to a former, and often better, condition.

———————————•⚬⚬◉◎◉◎◉⚬⚬•———————————

Nature teaches us about restoration and recovery. A clear-cut forest will eventually recover, as can a polluted river. A broken bone will mend in time. Take care of a wound, and it will heal if you do not pick at the scab. If we are compromised, we can rehabilitate. In Nature, a diversified ecosystem has no addictions; it is healthy and balanced when it is respected.

When a natural environment is disturbed, drilled, mined, fracked, or dumped on, it deteriorates under the pressure of over-production. To some people, this looks like progress. Like the spirit of the trampled Earth, our fragile internal landscape can get stripped when our good intentions are dumped on or shunned. When our productivity is devalued, it disturbs our souls. Desperate and drained, we fill ourselves with something — anything! A restorative mindset allows no room for such nonsense.

When the soil gets nourished, like our souls, there is no need for artificial substances. It takes attention, not toxins, to heal depleted and distressed souls. Temporary relief from these toxins only masks the problem. Eventually, the substances wear off and are ineffective. It then takes stronger substances to perform. These substances interfere with life and can even interfere with the ability to produce healthy offspring. Addiction takes over like an invasive species. Balance and nourishment are the keys to success in every sense of the word. We can learn so much from Nature.

Humankind desperately needs restoration. For Nature and people, returning to a former state takes time and attention. The time to heal is contingent on the level of damage. For example, restoring a tree can involve pruning dead and damaged parts, often many times. Although it is difficult to restore a tree to its original state, if cared for it can double and even triple in stature and be highly productive. Our self-worth can also get reset. We can again, love, be open, and be free.

In this cycle of my life, I share with you what I did to rebound. I experienced how fear robs, weakens, and paralyzes. The restoration process is ongoing. It required dedication, courage, and patience to change and rebuild. Rather than run away, I embraced the opportunity to heal, reshape, and cherish my life again. I gravitated to the 13th-century Persian poet and scholar, Rumi, who advised, "Be like a tree and let the dead leaves drop." As I came to terms with the challenges, it forced me to dig deep into the root of my pain, and then prune destructive superficial patterns. I had to purge parasites and ward off energy vampires, internally and externally. I accepted that there would be dark times. I gained a healthy attitude of gratitude and learned to embrace the changes with respect and balance. But first I had to fall hard!

Demons or Truth

*Sometimes we may have to hit rock bottom to
receive the alarming wake-up call,
"Get your shit together or else!"*

Disconnected from others and from Nature, unfit to dance and hike, and full of moral agony, I was at the lowest time in my life. My wake-up call came in the fall of 1999 after four years of unruly behavior. By this time, I had gotten good at dressing in loose, comfortable dresses and dark colors that helped hide my girth. At my annual health checkup, the nurse asked me to step on the scale. First, I removed my jewelry, shoes, and as much clothing as possible, and peed. It shocked me when I stepped on to the antiquated scale! My aching body, all 5 feet 2 ¾ inches, weighed in at 205 pounds!

After the reality of my heart-wrenching checkup, I wandered to a nearby park and had a pathetic pity party under a native spruce tree. Defeated, fat, and older than my years, an epiphany hit me like a ton of chocolate chip cookie dough! I was not only destroying myself and my relationships, my actions also contributed to the detriment of the Earth. My addictions had morphed me into a hypocrite! I hated that fact more than my fat body! This peace-loving, granola crunching, tree hugger was about to go to war with herself!

I missed my intuitive mother! I was now forty-two years old, and at my age she had been very sick. I wondered what my brave mother would have expected of me in my condition. If she had been around to support me, would I have gotten into such a HOT MESS? I thought of my nine-year-old son, someday with the memory of me in my current state, and that hurt the worst! Buckets of tears and negative, self-berating talk released as I examined and let go of toxic emotional baggage.

I asked myself these questions as I drowned in self-pity:

How come most of my life I was told what I should do, and how I should be?

How come in camp, gym class, and life, I was not encouraged to have a mind, heart, and soul connection to my body, but instead to compete, to win or to be a loser!?

How come propaganda was legal and allowed to spread the message that smoking and eating processed junk food was normal?

How come being a businesswoman, trying to make a positive difference in the world, was so frickin' hard?

How come I couldn't do it all!? How had I allowed negative self-sabotaging messages to take over my being?

I knew that food was life, food was love, and that food was my livelihood. I knew darn well that what I ate affected my body, moods, those around me, and the health of the planet.

Being stuck in self-loathing sucked! Ruminating on my past to find something or someone to blame did not work. Only a brutal *babble-out* with my inner demons would shift my thought process! Confronting the barriers I faced triggered raw places in me I never knew existed. Blamers are drainers and complainers! It was time to stop! Time to end the craziness!

The babble-out came down like this:

"Good grief, Donna, you're a certified aerobics instructor who owns a successful restaurant and a national company. You have a husband who loves you and a precious son! And you have Mother Dear, Dad, Rosemary, friends, and cash in the bank! You live in one of the most beautiful places on Earth! You have a comfortable home with more privileges than most people in the world! And you're pissing your life away!? STOP BEING such a pissant: worthless and contemptible!" Bursts of tears and gut-wrenching emotion poured out of me.

"Donna... get over yourself! SHUT UP, YOU inner demons and energy vampires STOP! STOP eating me alive... BE GONE! This is your life, Donna! LET GO of these toxins and the Bull SHIT. Forgive yourself, forgive everyone. Excuses BEGONE! Enough is ENOUGH!"

Nearly delirious and exhausted, this babble-out changed my life! Glassy-eyed, I looked up to the treetop above me for answers; the branches reached out with pride in all directions. Bright, yellow poplar leaves from a nearby tree swirled in the wind and gracefully fell to the ground at my feet. The leaves reminded me of my sweet mama, and I welcomed the comforting feeling. I received the sacred wisdom to go out on a limb and change my ways.

I would rise like a phoenix and let old growth die!

Not willing to be empty and disconnected from my truth, friends, and family, I acknowledged the signs and surrendered. This took doing the work! I assessed the trauma head-on, which came with anger and joy. It was time to reclaim my pride and dignity, as my mother had taught me to in her darkest hours. I had gotten the successful businesswoman thing down; now it was time to get my priorities straight.

Full Disclosure: Writing about this time in my blessed life, I must admit, I relapsed into some destructive patterns as I conjured up unpleasant memories. I breathe a sigh of relief, grateful for the solace and wisdom gained from my experiences. The heartache is over, but I recognize that if I'm not true to myself I can fall off the wagon. That's why they're called addictions. A lack of knowing one's truth is hard to digest. Inner demons and energy vampires are always lurking. I have learned that it is the fire of your passions and the light of your heart that keeps you balanced.

> *For far too long we have been seduced into walking a path*
> *that did not lead us to ourselves. For far too long we have*
> *said yes when we wanted to say no. And for far too long*
> *we have said no when we desperately wanted to say yes.*
> *When we don't listen to our intuition, we abandon*
> *our souls. And we abandon our souls because we are*
> *afraid if we don't, others will abandon us.*
> ~ Terry Tempest Williams

Destiny is a Matter of Choice

*The best years of your life are the ones in which you decide your problems
are your own. You do not blame them on your mother, the ecology,
or the president. You realize that you control your own destiny.*
~ Albert Ellis

At first it felt like I lost my freedom of choice when I gave up the things
that made me sick. I often fell back a step and then learned how to take
two steps forward. Most important was to forgive myself. I aimed to accept
myself each step of the way to recovery. I knew the world was in crisis and
I needed to focus on my turmoil before I could help anyone else.

When I finally admitted I had a problem, it released me. It wasn't easy to
relearn to love myself again, to be happy and non-judgmental. It did not happen
overnight. Half the battle was to accept the source of pain. Agony came from
clinging to what did not serve me. Living in an artificial bubble of prosperity,
or worrying about cycling into debt, would no longer be options. Thoughts
that I was not doing enough or good enough, or feelings of envy that someone
had something I should have, were BS! Blamers are drainers and complainers!

Gratitude changed my attitude.

That autumn big decisions happened fast and intentionally. It was time
to lighten the load and sell AH!LASKA. A buyer stepped up within three
months. With more time on my hands, I dove into self-care, homeschooling,
and family life. When needed, I rolled up my sleeves and assisted at The
Sourdough. Quality food and family time eased Jazz's and Kevin's migraines.
I added in more of what mattered and deleted what didn't. I spent more

time in Nature and less time watching the news. I replaced disrespect with respect for myself. With awakened gratitude, forgiveness, and devotion, I steadily evolved. My time became my most valuable currency.

What I fed my mind was as critical as what I fed my body. As I gained clarity, I trusted my gut emotions and listened to my inner voice. If things got out of my control, I separated myself from the situation. I asked for help from those I trusted and took downtime to reevaluate. I rebuilt trust with our staff and friends. This required being sincere and honest — sometimes brutally honest. Being hypercritical had only caused alienation. I chose to muster up courage and compassion for myself rather than allow the fear, anger, and grief to eat away at my soul. A bad experience is not a self-fulfilling prophecy, nor did it have to define my destiny. Freedom came with finding Soulutions to problems. Conscious vigilance led me to do the next right thing. Being balanced proved to be liberating: A wholesome destiny! Everything was better when I thought better of myself.

I lost weight and started to gain back my well-being. The pain in my body and soul eased, which helped to build momentum. The love of family and dear friends proved to be better than wealth and privilege. As I nourished everything from the soil to my soul, my chances of staying healthy elevated.

The present is a gift, receive it in the Now.

Of all the businesses I took great pride in birthing and running, nothing, absolutely NOTHING compares to parenting. NOTHING! I cherished the role of motherhood. Being a devoted and loving spouse fell right in line with being a mom. I embraced this affirmation: "I have my priorities straight."

To run a household with children is the most important business and a noble career. Anyone who values a business or career over being a parent does not have their priorities straight. That's not to say you cannot do both. Destiny is a matter of choice. So is balance and patience, which are vital if you choose to do both. Navigating the ups and downs can burn you out if you do not have the right support, are in denial, are over driven, and do not have the right tools. Most important is to never forget that health is your greatest wealth.

I choose both with newfound clarity and balance. I gained more respect for stay-at-home parents who multitask all day. They are both the CEO and CFO of the household, in charge of everything from scheduling, managing play dates, finding tutors, and shopping, to paying the bills. This takes a lot of time and energy. I figured out how to change my attitude and this made the endless tasks fun! I also shifted the direction of my career that suited parenthood and accommodated my healing journey. Gratitude became my favorite tool. *When you are grateful, you are never in bad company.*

To raise a child, or grow a business, takes time and nourishment. Both require inputs and outputs to stay balanced. For parents, there are (inputs) receivables — such as our child's first steps — and (outputs) payables, such as medical bills. For families with more than one child I can only imagine. Each child would be like a separate business entity — each with different inputs, outputs, and needs that require individual care. Balance and support are vital to sustain and thrive, no matter what we do.

The Wi-Fi age has given us opportunities I could never have imagined when I was a mom. Today we can get a degree and work from home while we raise a family. You can be a health coach, social media expert, web designer, editor, marketer, or tutor, and there are so many more options. There is also no reason we cannot have several careers in our lifetimes, including the most rewarding and meaningful of them all: Being a parent-preneur!

Working Mother gives further suggestions to get into a career at home. Thinking out of the cubical and doing something you love to do, and that your children can be a part of, works the best.

PBS Parents tells how gardening with children affects their brains, bodies, and souls. Gardening with children not only cuts food costs, it provides a gratifying way to teach children about the most important things for their survival in this rapidly changing world. What could be more important than fueling your family's body, soul, and mind with nourishing food as you take care of the soil and Mother Earth?

A Memorable Experience

Home is where you feel at home.

That winter, Kevin and I sold our first home and purchased a lovely three-bedroom house with a cabin on two acres of land in a park-like setting. The stunning views of Kachemak Bay and the Homer Spit made it hard to leave home. We shared the property with majestic moose, nesting eagles, Sandhill cranes, and an occasional black bear. In the spring our yard was a nursery for the baby moose and crane colts (chicks). Nature was at my door all day long: A heavenly place to live and heal.

We turned the two bedrooms downstairs into a lovely bed-and-breakfast. We called our new business *A Memorable Experience*. The new creative endeavor filled me with positivity and helped me focus on doing something I loved with a purposeful why. I got inspired to decorate our new home and landscape the property. The Alaskan wildlife theme I picked for the bed-and-breakfast rooms, the view, flowers, and our hospitality delighted guests.

Travelers came from around the world. Conversations covered everything from war and peace to poverty and opulence. I traveled the world in my mind and gathered real news from real people about their homeland. My mind awakened as I listened to their realities, especially how foreigners viewed America and Americans. Most people came from populated urban areas for a once in a lifetime visit. The beauty and vastness of Alaska astonished them all. It was a joy to share the splendor. I fantasized about how the world could be if William Shakespeare was right when he said, "One touch of Nature makes the world kin."

It turns out that *heads in beds* was a lucrative way to earn extra income. To top it off, the B&B guests ate at the cafe! The best part of the business was that I could be home more with Jazz. Bingo! My Soil to Soul Entrepreneurial spirit rekindled as I adapted to the changes within and evolved. I continually reminded myself to move forward with grace.

Big Island, Big Changes

Manifesting is powerful!

During the winters we often vacationed on the Big Island of Hawaii for a few weeks, and we always wished we could spend more time there. With AH!LASKA sold, and the passing of Simba, our last animalizing wolf-husky friend, we were free to spend months in paradise. Here, I would accelerate my recovery.

In the fall of 2001, I contacted a realtor in Hawaii to find a place to rent or house-sit for the winter. The realtor landed us a great spot. She let us know that the property was down a country road, and the people who owned the house, Marty and Linda, were nice folks.

On our visits to the Big Island, Kevin and I often drove down that county road to whale watch and picnic on the rugged, rocky shoreline. There were only two homes on the two-mile rutted road that ended at the Pacific Ocean. When I first saw the property and the small bungalow home, I said to Kevin, "I could live and die right here!"

Before we left to housesit, Linda gave us directions and a vague description of the place. There were no Google Maps or GPS. Could it be possible we were about to house-sit in the same bungalow which I had fantasized about living and dying in ten years before!? When I walked into their lovely new home on the same property, it stunned me. Manifesting is powerful!

Marty and Linda were longtime residents of North Kohala and had two big dogs. They decided to start a vacation rental business on their property. They wanted to turn their original bungalow and another house they had built for Linda's mother and visitors, into rentals. Our experience from running our bed-and-breakfast and being dog lovers, made Kevin and me a great fit. We helped get the business off the ground, and Marty and Linda got us familiar with the area and the lovely people in Kohala — a symbiotic, synergistic relationship. Once the couple saw we knew what we were doing, they left for a three-month trip. We grew their business and I continued to gain strength, courage, and wisdom in this tropical paradise.

Ecological and Economic Mindset Plan

To break free, it takes willpower and a healthy mindset, as well as a relentless subscription to an attitude of — there is no turning back.

Have you heard the phrase "failing to plan is planning to fail?" Well, my personality, combined with dyslexia, resulted in someone who doesn't like to plan, nor follow a strict diet or exercise routine. Once I accepted that a plan was an essential part of recovery, things happened faster. I did my due diligence and checked out plenty of trendy self-help and weight loss books at the library.

My favorite book, *The Body Ecology Diet* by Donna Gates, ignited my action steps. The title itself was a wake-up call; after all, we are Nature, part of the ecology. I learned from Gates' research how the body and ecology interconnect in more ways than just a title. Our digestive system works much like compost or soil; the soil is considered the stomach of the Planet. Our stomach is where we breakdown (decompose) organic matter.

Our body is home to about 100 trillion bacteria and other microbes, collectively known as our microbiome. The healthier our microbiome, the stronger our immune system is. The vast majority of microbiome live in our digestive system. The diversity of these mini microbes is essential to stay balanced! They help us digest food, produce vitamins, and ward off nasty germs. When we are balanced, vitality is the outcome.

YEA for fermented foods and other natural probiotics that strengthen our bodies' ecology. NAY to processed foods. The stomach is also referred to as our second brain because of the enteric nervous system in our bellies. That's why we can feel things at a gut level. When the body, the temple of our soul flows, we flourish.

Based on my knowledge of food and business, and my new gut wisdom, I established a strong interconnection with my entire being that guided me to develop a plan that worked for me. I figured if I paid as much attention to my health as I did to my businesses, I'd turn my life around faster. The foundations of a business are cash flow, balanced books, profit, and loss. I put my business savvy to work. I monitored how much I ate, slept, drank, and exercised, and I balanced intake and output. I added in more fun, healthy food, exercise, new friendships, and absorbed the tropical lifestyle. My efforts equated to weight loss and profitable energy — the capital gain!

Small and large victories were put into my memory bank. My accomplishments were noted and stored as excellent investments that compounded interest. Positive thoughts became assets! I accrued self-worth and mastered a new mindset. My workaholic mania morphed into one of a health-aholic. The bottom line: I would gain health and lose toxins.

Our precious body
is the temple
for our souls.

Gaining Health, Losing Toxins

Affirmations are more powerful than requests,
for they remind you that you already have what you seek.
~ Alan Cohen

My clear plan fostered doable action steps. I relearned how to have a healthy relationship with food, my mind, and exercise. I ate whole-foods, mostly plant-based with calories that gave me long-term energy. I accepted I was the protagonist of my life and tended my inner garden with probiotic-rich food (lots of homemade fermented sauerkraut), and my mind with nourishing thoughts. As I restored my microbiome, my gut functioned like a well-managed compost pile that heated my metabolism and activated my digestion. I turned the gunk (mental, material, and emotional) and burned up what did not work for me. Yes, sometimes it had to get HOT to break down the BS. Voila, the results: Microbial rich amendments that built my immune system and helped me to gain health and lose toxins! Strong and healthy, I could spread the love!!

> *Properly cultivated soils are fertile and antimicrobial*
> *because the balance of life wants to keep things in order.*
> *That's why compost always helps clean up the mess.*
> ~ Peter Risley, dear friend and farmer

I hooked up with an incredible practitioner of traditional Chinese medicine. Dr. Alvita Soleil tested my blood, urine, and saliva, and routinely checked my pulse and tongue. Acupuncture got my chi in order. I got deep tissue massages twice a month from Rebecca, an incredible healer who learned from a master in the Philippines. Both wise women gave me support and guidance. I wove in the good ideas from other sources and incorporated the whole systems' approach from the Strong Stretched and Centered training.

My bum knee prevented me from doing aerobics, but there were other things I could do. NO more excuses! Getting back into Nature was part of my plan. Two times a day I gingerly walked up and down the steep country road animalizing with Marty and Linda's two 75-pound dogs, Dusty and Doobie. Often, I felt they were the ones taking care of me. Within a month I could hike up the hill twice as fast without my knee brace.

As I walked, I was mindful and reconnected with my inner voice and the natural world. I cleansed my mind of toxic thoughts and welcomed in what was possible. Daily swims in the warm, vibrant Pacific that teemed with tropical fish and dolphins, soothed my body and soul. When the whales breached, it was the best! Nature — the ultimate regenerator — filled me up once again! Focused on self-actualization, there was no room for self-sabotage. A healthy attitude was my foundation for success. A mindful relationship with myself brought more peace, which balanced out my hormones and helped me sleep.

I got on a regular sleep pattern, early to bed and early to rise. Sleep deprivation had activated my need to eat and was partially responsible for my lack of energy. Sound sleep is when we repair our bodies and spirits, and fewer worries make for sweet dreams. I drank only water, lots, and lost sugar cravings. Our bodies are made up of over 70 percent water. When dehydrated, we have cravings.

Family time was of the utmost importance. As I continued to feel better, our family life got better. I engaged with the community and made new friends who did not know my past and therefore did not judge me for my successes and failures. The locals informed me that whatever one wishes for can manifest in the tropical paradise. I had manifested living in this place, and now I was manifesting my plan to live like the future matters.

My plan was only as good as the actions I took to follow it. Many business plans never make it off the shelf, and most diet plans do not work unless you put the program into action. As my life changed, I'd adjust my plan. If I reached a plateau, I'd shift and up the ante. I proceeded by understanding that no amount of money or fame would make me happy if I were not living in a place of truth. Personal growth outweighed the financial gain.

No More Resistance or Fiery Dragons

Life is a series of natural and spontaneous changes.
Don't resist them — that only creates sorrow.
~ Lao Tzu

One book I reached for that winter was the *Tao Te Ching* by Lao Tzu, also identified as Laozi. He was a philosopher and poet of ancient China and the founder of Taoism. I studied his profound words, stopped resisting, and started to go with the flow. I read Alan Cohen's insightful book *The Dragon Doesn't Live Here Anymore*. The book reinforced my desire to purge pounds and toxic emotional dragons. As I gathered wisdom, I reconciled and made peace with my past. When I let go of fiery dragons, seeds of positive change grew more robustly. I could propel forward with empathy for myself and listen more deeply to my inner desires.

A new friend, who had struggled with several addictions, gave me a little book full of big ideas. *Meditations for Women Who Do Too Much* by Anne Wilson, is still in my library. When I opened the beautiful card that she left inside the book, some dead dried flowers fell to the ground. Her words stick with me to this day: "Donna, I'm so glad to see you are taking your addictions seriously. This little book I offer you helped me get through hard times. I now celebrate life from the depth of my soul and addiction is my past. I wish the same for you, my dear friend. Make room for new blooms, let the dead leaves fall as you move into your vibrant future. – Aloha"

I have gifted this book to others who do too much, and who are mostly women. Yes, I still may do too much, but at least now I'm more aware and know when to STOP IT.

Communication once again was the headliner on my journey forward.

Kevin and I had been together for eighteen years. The business had become the driving force of our relationship. Our marriage was in a different place. Always being in charge had left little room to be vulnerable. I had hidden behind a protective shield of emotional armor, and assumed being strong and tolerant was expected of me. Breaking down is not an attractive side of anyone, yet armor is heavy and hard. Kevin was a trooper. He was there for me. As we dismantled the emotional defenses between us, we both felt lighter. When we communicated from the depths of our souls without fear or judgment, there was no need for armor. Our vulnerability is part of our strength.

We vowed to reboot our relationship and infused it with more love, trust, and respect. Kevin and I grew like a well-cared for orchard bearing an abundance of fruit year after year. When in tune with each other's emotions, as Nature adapts to moody weather, we are more prepared for unpredictable and hard times. When one of us gets down, the other is there to help. Sometimes that means giving each other space. We communicate, "I love you; I just need space."

Jazz continued to be homeschooled, and Kevin and I encouraged him to love to learn. I found experts who could teach him what was beyond our ability, and we learned and laughed together. While I helped Jazz resolve his dysgraphia and other challenges, I found solutions to help me with my dyslexia and dragons. Once we got Jazz a computer, his dysgraphia was no longer a problem! Without resistance, we both excelled.

Jazz and I read most of the Harry Potter books out loud, which conjured up many thoughtful discussions. Inspired by J. K. Rowling, a humble, creative female writer who went from rags to riches, I sought other women role models. I started the very first draft of this book. Writing became a tool to heal.

The Big Island lived up to its reputation as the healing island. The spirit of Pele, the goddess of the volcano, had rejuvenating energy. The tropical breeze, oxygen-rich landscapes, salty sea, and Aloha lifestyle were a powerful formula to invite healing. One pound at a time, one step at a time, one positive thought at a time, persistently and patiently I progressed. My plan and affirmations were working. I lost thirty pounds of toxins that winter and gained a healthy attitude. I was too busy for pity parties. With more faith and the promise to stop ignoring my desires, I reunited with my truth — the principles that guide me to this day.

The Systems and Cycles of Nature

Be patient with yourself. Self-growth is tender; it's holy ground.
There's no greater investment.
~ Stephen Covey

————————————•:•◉◉◎◎◎◎◎◎•:•————————————

The tools I gained in Hawaii helped keep the fiery dragons away. There were still toxins and weight to lose and knowledge to gain. Adhering to the Ecological Economic Mindset Plan was not as easy in Alaska, but essential if I were to live without invasive pathogens. Patience and tenderness for myself would be an adjustment.

The sweet temptations at arm's length were hard to resist. But I resisted most of the time. Relapsing was part of the journey. If I felt weak, I refused to ignore it, as that's when I was most susceptible to giving in and spiraling out of control. Each time I reached for a quart of ice cream or another decadent food, and then resisted, strengthened me. I learned to relax, a challenge for someone who anxiously tries to figure out ways to do more. I admitted that self-inflicted tension had not served me. It was dysfunctional and had only made me weaker. Problems were not the problem; it was how I coped with them. I accepted that I would make mistakes, learn from them, and move forward. That is when mistakes become strengths. With the right attitude, challenges become opportunities.

My most significant successes would follow my failures.

Every day, Kevin and I took walks in Nature. The beauty of the Alaskan paradise inspired me to stay on the right path. I paid close attention to how Nature naturally repairs and rebuilds itself, and I could do the same! Natural

303

things continually decompose and turn back into fertile, loamy soil. Diverse ecosystems support and balance each other as life *metamorphoses*. With respect for the systems and cycles of nature, I incorporated the wisdom that it was natural to transform, which made my healing journey more inclusive.

> *Nothing in Nature is continuous except change, such as a butterfly metamorphoses from egg to larva to pupa and finally to an adult.*

For the next two winters, we continued to manage the vacation rental in Hawaii. In the winter of 2004, we bought a small house ten miles outside of town near Pololu Valley. Over the next seven years we split our time between Hawi, Hawaii and Homer, Alaska. I continued to invest my time in personal development, Nature, and healthy entrepreneurial endeavors. I reminded myself that time was my most valuable currency and must be used wisely.

Homeschooling and running seasonal businesses gave us the freedom to commute between Alaska and Hawaii — two extraordinary places. Each is home to one of the most massive mountains on Earth. Hawaii is the most remote landmass in the world, and Alaska is the largest state in the union.

Mauna Kea is the highest point in the state of Hawaii, and stands 4,205 m (13,800 ft) above sea level. Measured from its base on the ocean floor, it rises over 10,000 m (33,000 ft), significantly greater than the elevation of Mount Everest and Denali above sea level. The highest mountain is determined by measuring a mountain's highest point above sea level. The tallest mountain is measured from base to summit. Using that measurement, Denali is taller than Mount Everest. The world's tallest mountain technically is not Mount Everest. Mount Everest is the tallest mountain above sea level, but if we're talking sheer height here, base to summit, then the tallest mountain is Mauna Kea on the Island of Hawaii.

In Alaska, we leveraged our B&B venue by offering intimate wedding packages. Back on track, I approached this new venture with heartfelt enthusiasm. It was fun to consult with the bride and groom and help them plan their special day. For fourteen years, I had the privilege to perform over one hundred ceremonies, each time renewing my love for my dear husband. I took the photos, conducted the services, and made the bouquets and boutonnieres. The Fresh Sourdough Express provided the wedding cakes and catered the receptions. Jazz was often the flower boy, ring bearer, and a great help. Again, doing what I loved paid off. Monetarily and personally, I was on track. The three months of income from heads in beds and wedding services paid our house mortgage and expenses for the year!

Craving ✤ Gaining ✤ Sharing Wisdom

Knowledge is a path of gathering information,
and wisdom is walking that path.

Building Bridges

My father spent his life doing his best to save teeth, but when it came time to pull a rotten tooth, he did. I know from experience that removing a tooth can be painful and emotional. After all, it is an intimate part of us, and it never grows back. Even if the tooth once served you, it can still make you sick — if it's rotten, yank it! Some people's teeth get so rotten they can become ill and cannot recover.

Why is it that sometimes we feel we cannot bear to lose, whether it is a tooth, game, toxic relationship, dysfunctional marriage, or mediocre career? What about an unhealthy habit we talk ourselves into? Is this way of thinking okay? Trying too hard can leave us empty and defeated, even if we win. Who says you have to win or be a loser?

After my father pulled a tooth, he would build his patients a functional bridge. Likewise, in Nature and life, there are ways to rebuild. With the right conditions, a spider weaves a new web, and a tree grows new limbs. Engagement with friends and mentors provided the right conditions to break destructive patterns and stay clean as I rebuilt my self-worth. The best part — healthy relationships — have no toxins or calories. Besides, it was none of my business what negative people thought about me.

Many successful people say, "You're the average of the five people you spend the most time with." My desires were to be a better parent, wife, business owner, and free of destructive habits, so, I hung around those types of people. Others who loved and cared about me were an infinite source of nourishment I never took for granted. I built bridges. Imagine if we all built bridges that bettered our health, relationships, and the world.

Deconstructing the Unappetizing Parts of My Ego

A big part of recovery was to let go of the distasteful parts of my ego which had taken over my identity. It was up to me to change and come to terms with what success meant. Freud defines the ego as the part of the mind that mediates between the conscious and the unconscious, and is responsible for reality testing and a sense of personal identity. In many spiritual traditions, there has long been an understanding that the ego is not what we are; instead it is how we identify ourselves. I came to believe we are not purely ego. The ego seeks judgments and opinions; the soul seeks the truth.

Our ego is not inherently bad, but it can get misdirected. If we are in pain or out of balance, this gets broadcast externally through our ego. For example, as criticism and judgment built up, my lack of self-worth made me defensive, and I blamed others. My damaged ego, like a bull in a china shop, believed it was trapped, frustrated, hurt, angry, stuck! Once I abandoned these constipated beliefs, and listened to my inner voice, there was room to grow back into my wholesome self. Change began with awareness and acceptance.

As I healed, I searched deep for my higher calling, and what was truthful for me that would set me free and help me ascend. I reflected on some of the happiest times in my life, taking me back to my college years and early days at the cafe. Back then, I had no compulsive, destructive habits or addictions. I was more productive in an environment where collective consciousness propelled my actions. We kept our egos in check as we tilled the soil and our minds. At the cafe, we kneaded the dough and concentrated on being of service. Our actions brought out the best in us.

Understanding the interconnection between my gut and mind was another way to reclaim the genuine and productive parts of my ego. The stomach is referred to as our second brain for a good reason. It is where we first process our food and emotions. Healthy gut flora is made up of 15 percent *bad* bacteria and 85 percent *good*. The bad bacteria are like the critics of our digestive system. Too much harmful bacteria, like an overly big-headed ego, is burdensome and knocks us off center. When the ego is in perspective, our senses heighten, and the *good guys* run the show. A balanced ego functions better than a deflated or inflated one. High on forgiveness and low on fear, I had the strength to ward off the *bad guys and keep them in check*. Flexible, and with good intentions, daily I could change, and let go of bad habits. I adjusted to situations and circumstances and persevered with a healthy pea-sized, digestible ego. The more I trusted my intuition, the more my temptations, lower desires, and the distasteful part of my ego ended up in the toilet bowl. That's where the crap that has no value belongs.

To let go of my sick habits that had captured my ego, took guts. Once I understood that habits aren't in themselves the problem and that they are indeed not always bad, new healthy habits became my foundation. It was a choice, an agreement with my intuitive inner voice. As my good intentions and habits replaced the addictive patterns, I was free.

Adding in healthy habits that supported the best version of me, cured my addictions. Excellence is not one single act to accomplish, it is a result, achieved through repeated decisions and the formation of healthy habits.

Choose Mindful Thoughts and Words

A new mindset evolves with awareness and
acceptance of our thoughts and word.

A big shift came when I changed my use of words. For example, I eliminated saying "I have to, got to, should have." I stopped "wanting" and "needing," and started "choosing." Changing my language helped rewire my brain. I *chose* a mindset of opportunity and awe, as opposed to one of doubt and desperation. It was a *choice* to *choose* love and compassion as my driving forces. I *chose* to have a healthy, pea-sized ego. I did not want or need to do something; it was my *choice*. It's a *choice* to make the best of every situation. *Choosing* to unplug from the news and ignore propaganda helped reprogram my mind. I *chose* to switch to healthy habits and nurturing habitats. When I changed the way I thought, I made better *choices*.

It's Your Choice to Change.

Meditation was another tool that put me in the driver's seat of my emotional wellbeing. Stopping the mental chatter was difficult and took time. My preferred method to relax my mind is to walk mindfully in Nature. I turn off the cell phone, focus on my breath and steps, and turn my attention to the beauty around me and within. Nature Therapy, tuning into the present moment, and letting go of any emotional junk, proved to be my most exceptional medicine.

Understanding the Darkness

Great minds discuss ideas; average minds discuss
events; small minds discuss people.
-Eleanor Roosevelt

Part of the process to heal was to stop doubting myself and to share my story. In my quest to recover, it was clear that I was not alone. Overindulging and bingeing had become commonplace. Some friends and regular customers noticed the shift in me and were eager to find out how I got back on track. It was as if people came out of the closet. They talked to me without shame as they spoke their truth rather than small talk and gossip. Their sincere interest gave me the courage to be honest and vulnerable with them. They too felt the heavy armor, especially the women who struggled in their male-dominated careers or in destructive relationships. Understanding my darkness helped me guide others to find their light. Like tossing a pebble in a still pond, my good intentions, energy, and strength reverberated.

I was no longer moved by factors that boxed me into an unflattering shape.

Craving, gaining, and sharing wisdom, I re-learned that true happiness is to enjoy the present and to appreciate that nothing in Nature is constant except change. As I identified and abstained from unhealthy substances, eliminating pathogens became natural. I gained insight into myself and others, listened to my instincts, and communicated. With awareness and acceptance, I reshaped my thought patterns and habits, and built a bridge that would support a future I could be proud to live. Still, however, there was a shield of armor protecting my half-healed heart. The rest of my rooted pain would get addressed as I continued to regenerate and evolve.

> *Although the time was painful, I am grateful for the*
> *experiences and tools I have mastered to stay clean.*
> *Looking back on my life, I can respect what I*
> *have done and all I have become.*
> *Believing the future is bright, my spirits shined.*

Leave NO room for obsessions, resentments, or desperations.
Fiery dragons will burn you up and out.

No More Excuses

What would you do if you learned that you're more
powerful than you have ever been taught?
~ Bruce Lipton

A few years later, a good friend who recovered from food addiction turned me on to epigenetics and neuroplasticity. She was one of the few people who understood what I had gone through. She said to me, "Donna, you are the architect of your brain," and handed me a book by Bruce Lipton, *The Biology of Belief.* After I read the book, I accepted that my brain was NOT hardwired, and I understood and accepted that I had already reshaped my brain and body. Now I had an affirmative source from a PhD biologist to support my findings.

Neuroplasticity and epigenetics were revolutionary concepts. Studies have proven we can rewire our brains and reshape our genes to create lasting changes. We can create our thought processes in response to our experiences. Neurological changes are our brain's way of shifting to meet our needs. I learned that this nuanced understanding of the brain's plasticity offers hope for people who suffer from addiction. I looked at it this way: If I exercise my body, I can get stronger. Since my brain controls my muscles, I can exercise it too. Our brain is a remarkable organ. Our genes are unique and receptive to our choices. Why blame my brain and genes for my compulsive behavior, when I can use them to fight it?

Your mind is the garden, your thoughts are the seeds,
the harvest can either be flowers or weeds.
~ William Wordsworth

The last of the so-called Five Good Emperors, Marcus Aurelius, born in 161 A.D., is thought to have said, "The things you think about determine the quality of your mind. Your soul takes on the color of your thoughts." Somehow this insight has gotten lost for nearly 2,000 years.

It makes sense that the mind and our genes, like everything in Nature, can change and adapt in response to experience. This knowledge gave me the confidence to shift my experiences until that new state became *normal*. For example, my *babble-out* was an intensely charged event, so powerful that it disrupted my brain's addictive patterns and started the creation of new neural grooves. During my downward cycle, neuroplasticity had worked against me. I gave into destructive desires and believed I needed sugar and caffeine to get through the day. We can get motivated by what we don't wish to be, as well as by what we want to be. We can change our brain and change our lives. It's a choice we get to make!

I wish there had been somebody to tell me all this.

We can change our brain and change our lives. It's a choice we get to make!

Reflection

When you're in a dark place, it can feel like you've been buried alive,
when perhaps you have planted yourself in preparation to sprout.

───────────◦∘◦◉◦◉◉◦◉◦◦∘◦───────────

After a long drought, the forest is parched and uncomfortable, brown from the radiant sun. Wisdom and reserves of strength lie deep in the roots, and the layers of bark protect the trees. Even though it appears the forest is dying, it is not. Nourishment runs deep, as resilience and strength are stored in the DNA. Patience allows us to see the predictable rains and quench our thirst. In life, when there is a drought, we must dig deep. The further we dig and the more we explore what is not seen on the surface, the more resilient we become. This makes us stronger. Our inner strength is found when we dig deep for answers.

Nourish yourself as you recover, including feeding and watering both mind and soul. All of this builds resilience and strength that helps us through times of drought.

Compulsive behavior is a sign of destructive cravings that can lead to addiction. These obsessions include food, work, porn, opioids, cell phones, negative relationships, or the over-consumption of anything. The longer we are in denial, the harder it is to break a dysfunctional cycle. Addiction and substance disorders are complex conditions which affect how our brains and bodies function; they are comprised of both a psychological and a physical inability to stop consuming. It results in compulsive substance use and abuse, despite the consequences. When the issues are not addressed, they can lead to broken marriages, resentful children, loss of friendships, unemployment, and poor health. When we need to, but cannot, will not, or do not know when to stop, there is a problem.

> *Dependence on the excess of anything is detrimental.*
> *Work, sugar, and toxic relationships are no exception.*

The prison of addiction does not discriminate. Many people are not even aware they have a problem. Each of us has different triggers and tolerances. Chasing the American Dream, or any unattainable dream, can also be addictive. Aspiring to do something or be somebody you're not robs your soul. Thinking you need stuff you do not need can spiral you into debt. A house full of stuff can leave you empty.

When we're in a state of equilibrium, we remain upright and sturdy. There is no room for constricting beliefs or harmful behavior in our lives. Balance is stability; when we're stable, we are less inclined to fall into addictive behavior.

> *Being part of the Soulution, we ward off Earthly and personal pollution.*

In most circumstances, it is possible to change our brains and our lives. We can overcome adversity. I recognize that we must each find our way through difficult times. No matter how low you feel, you are never alone. If there is no other solace to count on, all things can and will change. When you're going through tough times, remember that the sun will always rise; darkness is a natural part of life. We must go through dark times to find the light. It is up to each of us to choose our destiny and how we perceive the world. Love and compassion are the greatest medicines, along with surrounding ourselves with the right conditions and people. An excellent exercise is to ask yourself, "What can I add into my life, to live the life I desire?" As you prune unhealthy habits, you can regenerate your commitment to your purposeful passions. When you choose to focus on the good things in your life, life is good.

I wish there had been somebody to tell me all this before I fell short of my potential. Whether you're at the beginning or mid-career, I hope my story can help you get out of or avoid unnecessary grief. We all resonate to a different vibration, so find others you resonate with and get connected.

Throughout this book, I have quoted and mentioned many of the influential people, mentors, books, and quotes that have either helped shape my life, set me straight, or set me free. There are countless guides, inspirational leaders, and mentors available to us. I have listed many of them in the Soulution section at the back of the book.

Regeneration

Life is constantly pointing us towards our higher calling.
We just have to open our eyes and begin to walk that path.

꙳꙳◦◉◉◉◉◎◎◉◎◦꙳꙳

very species, from bacteria to humans, is capable of regeneration, rebirth, and renewal. When conditions are right, the process happens faster. Regeneration is the act of improving a place or system so it can be more productive. The context of the word regeneration also means rebirth, renewal, and to grow again. A starfish can regenerate its whole body from just one leg. Deer can regrow antlers, lizards regrow their tails, and sharks replace lost teeth: As many as 24,000 teeth in a lifetime! Decaying trees will regenerate into nutrient-dense humus.

The cells in our bodies are always regenerating. Our skin renews itself every 27 days. Humans can regenerate some organs, such as the liver. Although some human tissues cannot regenerate, we can revive our careers, lifestyles, and relationships. We can also be restored spiritually, as well as the way we think, feel, and act.

In this cycle, I reached another level of maturity. I learned that being sustainable was not enough to solve my problems or the world. If my health was just OK, why sustain what I was doing, when I could do better? Twenty-five years after I graduated from college, humans began to acknowledge their role in climate change. We know that human activity is responsible for pollution and depleting resources so continuing the way we live is not sustainable. We can do better! A regenerative approach is necessary to deal with the health issues of people and the planet. Living like the future matters, from the soil to our souls, matters more than ever.

The opportunity to heal and evolve was not something I took for granted. As I dove into purposeful endeavors, I became resilient and was, therefore, more resistant to root rot. With healthy roots, I could dig deep — far and wide — to make a difference as my mindset evolved from a degenerative to a regenerative one. This required me to be true to myself and do the work. Rooted in this mindset, it enabled me to seed, sprout, bud, bloom, and fruit again. Yes, there would be storms, outbreaks, death, and rebirth along my journey. I would feel the Earth move under my feet. Balance is fragile.

Bold Initiatives

We are called to assist the Earth to heal her wounds and, in the process, heal our own — indeed to embrace the whole of creation in all its diversity, beauty, and wonder.
~ Wangarĩ Muta Maathai

The Story of Stuff with Annie Leonard was released in December 2007. This twenty-minute film, on consumption unleashed a torrent of pent-up demand for an honest conversation about the impact humans have on the Earth. The film blew me away! It was my time again to *take action and to be part of the Soulution.* There was no room for compulsive behavior. I was on a mission with intention!

With my mojo restored, in the spring of 2007 I co-founded an organization with two remarkable women, Kat Haber and Kyra Wagner. Out of grave concern for the environment, we were determined to do something, and Sustainable Homer was born. Our mission was to unite the local municipality, businesses, nonprofits, and residents on the pressing issues, and get them to take action! We gathered weekly with a small group of other dedicated activists to come up with a plan. With a bold initiative to focus on, I had a resurgence of energy.

Our efforts lead us to host a two-day conference. The objective was to gather experts and members of the community to strategize and formulate solutions to the escalating environmental crises. We invited speakers who had a stake in energy, water, sanitation, ocean acidification, threatened and endangered species, and food security issues. Who were these people managing the resources that we all depend on? We asked the speakers to address their plans to deal with the environmental crises. Kat, Kyra, and I figured if the community was engaged, and all the departments could work together, we could solve some problems.

Other than catering a wedding for 200 people, this was my first time co-creating and coordinating such a big event. The gathering boasted a packed audience which left many attendees standing. I was the MC and a nervous wreck. Pumped with adrenaline and emotions, I stood on the stage behind a podium and explained the intention of the conference. With pride, I introduced speakers and helped facilitate panel discussions. Yes, I was scared but proud to stand before our community at the forefront of a movement, and united with others who did not think I was out of my mind. At least I did not feel like a salmon swimming upstream by myself.

At the same time that Sustainable Homer was established, the Mayor and City Council joined the International Council for Local Environmental Initiatives (ICLEI). They made a commitment with more than 700 governments around the world to take part in the Cities for Climate Protection Campaign. A task force of highly educated and motivated local individuals created a Climate Action Plan for our city. The action plan team put on a presentation at the conference, which added great value to the outcome of the event. The action plan was a step in the right direction for Homer's future, but like any plans, they need to be updated and are only as good as the actions taken.

United we were stronger. It was hopeful to see the conservation organizations work with each other and policymakers toward a more sustainable Homer. The organization helped bridge the gaps. It was a lot of work, but it was fun and rewarding to be part of this initiative to help save the planet. Kyra went on to stimulate the growth of the farmers market and continues to keep the community up to date on Sustainable Homer happenings.

Earthquake

Probably the most visible example of unintended consequences is what
happens every time humans try to change the natural ecology of a place.
~ Margaret J. Wheatley

On October 14, 2007, Kevin and I returned to the Big Island, while Jazz stayed in Homer to experience public school as a freshman. One of his trustworthy childcare providers moved in for a couple of months to hold down the fort in our absence. Jazz, being a teenager, was more than okay with his parents being away for a short period of time.

On October 15, I woke up at sunrise to the sound of birds and the delightful Kohala trade winds. Excited to be back in Hawaii, I jumped out of bed for my morning walk with our dog, Benjie, a feisty Jack Russell Fox Terrier that joined our family the previous winter. As we walked up the soil road from our house, I breathed in the balmy clean air and tropical scents. The tension in my body after another busy season at our cafe and B&B dissipated as I tuned into Nature's songs. Then, a deafening silence, followed by an abrupt, intense rumble, shook me to the ground. A shocking 6.7 magnitude earthquake lasting nearly two minutes shook my entire world, seemingly without end! It rippled through me like shock therapy and left me wondering if this was the end of my life. The land rocked back and forth as palm trees swayed like elongated balloons in the wind. The trees held strong: Like steadfast sentinels watching a child receive their punishment, they sympathetically witnessed the trial of a fallen woman. They stood witness, as I weathered the brunt of Nature's tremendous wrath and lay there, helpless. My four-legged, animalizing friend ran for his life toward our home, seesawing in my vision. I called out, "Goodbye, I love you, Benji." I prayed for peace, gave thanks for my life, and prepared myself for the end as I breathed in the Earthy scents. It moved me to my core as the Earth rebelled, rocked, and rolled.

When the Earth calmed down, I began to regain my senses. I lifted my head and then kissed the ground. I stood up, patted my body, and yelled at the top of my lungs, "I'm alive!" Wobbling, I headed home to my dear husband. Kevin had been in bed with a migraine during the onset of the quake. As dishes crashed to the kitchen floor and pictures fell from the walls, he dodged broken glass and ran out the door to search for me. When I reached our yard, our panicked hearts leapt for one another. The rush of adrenaline relieved Kevin of his migraine. Within seven minutes of the first earthquake came the second, a magnitude 6.0 that hit just 15 miles south of our home. From our yard, situated only 500 feet above sea level, we could see the stunning view of the Pacific Ocean with the mountains of Maui in the distance. As we gazed out at the water in disbelief, we witnessed a plume of red particle dust, bursting upwards and stretching for miles in the atmosphere. Yards of mineral-rich land had broken loose from the cliff's edge: Boulders, rocks, trees, soil, meadows, and our hiking trails fell into the sea. In awe, we stood there scared, startled, and stunned.

Given that a tsunami was possible, we prepared for the worst. We gathered with neighbors to assess the reality and share knowledge of our resources. A boulder in the road barricaded our neighborhood and we had no access to town. We were left without power and water for three days. While damage to our house was minimal, some lost precious belongings, and others, their homes.

The power of Mother Nature had transformed the landscape and me. For days afterward, we experienced multiple aftershocks that kept us on full alert. When we walked around the altered landscapes, we saw graves, that once stood in order, shifted out of alignment, roots of trees reshaped, and shorelines altered to form new jagged edges. More aware than ever of how precious and precarious life is, I discovered newfound strength, courage, and wisdom. I was reborn and moved forward with profound gratitude for my life.

S.O.U.P.
Sustainable Outcome, Unified Profits

That winter, a new friend came into my life. Ashley was also a foodie and cared deeply about what was happening to our food systems. One evening, after a couple of glasses of wine and many hours of brainstorming, we came up with a plan to help solve the daunting issue of food insecurity on the island. The North Kohala Resource Center was helping people learn how to write grants for projects that would enhance our community. It was a wonderful opportunity, and for a year, Ashley and I dove in to explore the possibilities of installing a food hub where farmers could aggregate their crops for distribution. Our plan included a community commercial kitchen for making value-added products; the intention was to create a cooperative Kohala Brand with the farmers and producers. One of the ideas was: S.O.U.P. — *Sustainable Outcome, Unified Profits*. Yes, one of the product lines would be soup. The end goal was food security and economic growth that fostered taking care of the people and the 'Aina. We were having so much fun, we forgot how much work we were putting into the idea.

Ashley reminded me of my wonderful roommate in college; smart and witty. With my passion and vision, we were a great team. We enjoyed visiting with all the growers we could find in the area, toured the island's commercial community kitchens, and met with the appropriate agencies that considered funding the project. We really expected this was going to happen. But there were plenty of roadblocks, and more regulation then we could have imagined. Why do they make it so hard to do the right things? The price of doing business in a rural community where real estate prices are high, makes the stakes higher. There were also not enough people, including farmers, who were ready at the time. Unfortunately, the project got stuck on the shelf and Ashley left town.

The disappointment nearly shook me to my core, but I rationalized that maybe I was just again ahead of the times. Rather than go into despair, I used the tools that I had acquired, and I held faith in my heart that something good would come of our hard work. I continued doing my best to find ways to bring the regenerative food movement to the forefront. Patience is a virtue but not always easy. I learned so much from this experience and it would help me launch my next business endeavor a few years later.

Being resilient builds character.

Mama Donna

*It is an honor, and an endearing privilege to be Mama Donna.
I love my name; I love being a Mama.*

After a year, Jazz had enough of public school and consented to finish high school as a homeschooler. That winter in Hawaii, he moved to a nearby *bohemian* startup farm down the road. We managed to see each other enough to accomplish the homeschool requirements and Jazz excelled in maturity while working on the farm.

Kevin continued to run the Sourdough six months of the year. Jazz and I came to Alaska for the bustling summer season. I would manage the B&B and help at the cafe while Jazz learned to bake for The Fresh Sourdough Express. It was exciting and shocking to see our sixteen-year-old son begin to evolve into manhood. I would learn to let him make his own decisions and mistakes. This was not always easy. No one can prepare you for the part of the parenting process of letting go of the child and embracing the new. All kinds of things happen that will shake up your life.

That winter in Hawaii, I earned my new endearing nickname, Mama Donna. It was given to me by a sweet, beautiful blue-eyed, blond-haired, twenty-two-year young lady named Jenny Rose. She is the woman who painted the incredible colorful phoenix above. Jenny came to live on the same communal farms as Jazz. The property was lush with tropical fruit trees and garden, but facilities were marginal, and transportation to town could be an issue as vehicles were scarce. Jenny and the other farmhands, (most of them from urban areas) used our house as a place of refuge when they needed a hot indoor shower, a reliable phone, or to escape a bad storm. Kevin and I often prepared meals for the weary farmhands and listened to the young adult's challenges as well as their exciting revelations. One day Jenny Rose was having a particularly hard time and came by for some extra love and support. After hours of deep heartfelt conversation and release, she said, "Thank you, Mama Donna!" And from that day forward, she called me Mama Donna. My new nickname caught on with many others, and I embraced my new *hānai* family.

Hānai is a term used in the Hawaiian culture that refers to the informal adoption of one person by another.

Put Fear Aside

*Unexpected opportunities and experiences can be shocking
and shake you up. Our fate is not always in our control. No
matter how life moves you, go with it; absorb the lessons.*

In the early fall of 2009, my dear friend and activist, Kat, who helped start Sustainable Homer, brought one of the first TEDx events to our community. She gave me the opportunity to give my first TEDx talk on the "Effects of Plastic on our Planet." In 2010, I delivered my second talk on the consequences of being an Oilaholic. In less than seven minutes, I did my best to convey some of what is in this book. Scared shitless, I stood in front of a couple hundred Alaskans, people who received dividends from the oil investments in our state and blasted the source of their income. I spilled my guts and gave multiple reasons why we needed to divest from oil and how we can do it "One Bite at a Time." This was my first time doing a PowerPoint presentation, so it wasn't perfect. If you decide to watch it on YouTube, you'll see by my size that I still had more toxins to lose and health to gain. I have come a long way since then both in being a presenter and in the presentation of myself.

*Be it on stage, or in an earthquake, these moments
are potent reminders of who we are.*

By the winter of 2009, the Big Island was becoming our primary residence.
Jazz turned 18. He was a bright homeschool graduate, ready for adventure.
In his rite of passage, he journeyed to Ecuador and Peru and began to evolve
into adulthood on his own terms. As long as we knew he was safe, healthy,
and happy, we were OK. Kevin and I were now in a place and position to
seed new endeavors in the winter months in Hawaii. I am so grateful I had
my health and a positive mindset to prepare me for what we would deal
with moving forward.

We felt the pinch of the Great Recession with declining revenues in both
businesses. The Great Recession, which started in December 2007 and
lasted until June 2009, was the most prolonged recession since World War
II. My dependable dad felt the pinch too, and on top of that, he had been
ill for a couple of years. There was no way I was going to ask him to bail us
out. In search of some financial relief, we went to two traditional, regulated
banks to refinance an existing loan, only to be turned down. After 26 years
in business, we were humiliated, but I did not let it get the best of me! It
would have been easy to binge daily on loaves of banana bread, but instead,
I walked and swam in the ocean more, got my wits about me, and called
one last bank.

We put fear aside and persevered! With all our ducks in a row, we let the
banker know, there was no way they could not refinance our loan. We

painted the perfect scenario and presented our reasoning why it was a no-brainer to work with us, even if our cash to debt ratio did not meet their requirements. It took several conversations to convince the local branch manager that our successful business was worthy of refinancing. Our credit was excellent; we had never been late on a payment, and we employed 35 people who would deposit their paychecks in his bank. It took most of the winter to negotiate and get the loan; a grueling process. But we got it!

In May 2009, I marched into the Homer branch of Wells Fargo, carrying two large tote bags, hand in hand. It was deliberately timed so the branch manager, who had turned us down for the refinancing loan request, was there. I propped those bags onto the teller's counter in full view of her office. The teller immediately called the manager over after I asked her kindly to close my account. "Hundreds will do," I said when asked how I would like my money.

The manager scurried out of her glass box and paused before she spoke with a sigh, "Is there anything I could do to keep you as a loyal customer?"

Eagerly, I jumped on her invitation and responded, "Yes, give me a loan with a lower interest rate." She said, "I am so sorry, it is out of my control."

I said, "That is exactly why I am divesting from this corporate bank. And you might consider working for a more ethical company." (She did eventually move to the bank that gave us the loan)

She wrote a cashier's check, and I immediately went to the bank next door that gave us the loan and opened a checking account. I also suggested to our employees to bank with the bank that gave us the loan.

We ended up refinancing our existing loan with better terms and a lower interest rate. This lowered our monthly payments, which helped with our cash flow. Within six months, we were back on our feet financially and able to add an additional $200 a month to our payments, which went directly to paying down the principal. We did this every month for the life of the loan, which saved us thousands of dollars. The bank was happy, and so were we. Another win-win!

How to Start a Farmers Market Business

Green business. It's more than a good idea. It's a powerful, practical strategy for shifting society onto a more socially just and environmentally sound course.
~ Alisa Gravitz

I learned from my grandparents that a grocery business, which got them through the Great Depression, was a good business, as people must eat, even in challenging financial times. The impact of the great recession spurred Kevin and me to start a pop-up cafe at the Hawi Saturday Farmers Market. The great contacts I made with the farmers, while trying to get the food hub off the ground, made the start-up easier and enjoyable. Our experience at

The Sourdough and my experience at the Olympia Farmers Market would also come in handy for this new venture. By now, our nest was well fortified with sturdy branches. We called our business, Always In Season.

Our initial vision was to sell pint jars of fermented vegetables. Fermented food had been a big part of my recovery, so I wanted to share the many benefits of eating these traditional foods. Besides being a potent probiotic, they are the most cost-effective way to enhance your immune system. Kevin and I developed a product line: Sauerkraut, kimchi, zesty daikon radishes, and dill pickles. We also used other seasonal vegetables to make more beautiful combinations. The variety of flavors, colors, and shapes packed in glass jars added to the ambiance of the display. Our vision expanded into a full-blown cafe.

Cost-effectiveness — Adding a small amount of fermented food to each meal will give you the biggest bang for your buck. Why? Because they can contain 100 times more probiotics than a supplement!

To entice people to try the products, we offered a variety of wraps, and paired them with one of our zesty ferments. Like the pairing of fine wine with a meal, it intrigued people to try them. We called the wraps Walkabouts, because customers could walk about the farmer's market while they ate the delicious and nutritious edibles. We prepared everything we served from scratch and used 90 percent local ingredients.

For days, Kevin and I prepped and prepared rotating menu items to go inside the wraps. The fillings included pumpkin taro mash, extreme greens, eggplant tapenade, liver pate, and beef and basil. Customers could personalize their wraps with one or more of the fillings. They also had the choice to add sprouts, lettuce, homemade sauces, or salsas. As the final touch, we recommended which ferment would go best with their one-of-a-kind Walkabout. We also made fresh chutneys, guava spreads, baked goods, and in-season specials. A favorite was the purple sweet potato quiche made with duck eggs. The wrap fillings, along with the jars of ferments, salsas and chutneys, were sold in recyclable containers.

While I cranked out the Walkabouts, Kevin was busy making freshly squeezed juices with a hand juicer. This was a big draw to our booth — orange, grapefruit, and tangerine — whatever citrus was in season. We offered turmeric and ginger juice shots to boost the citrus drinks.

The most rewarding times were our visits to several farms each week to purchase ingredients and build relationships with hard-working farmers. We would buy extra produce and sell it at our booth, adding to its beauty and bounty. Customers loved it, the farmers were grateful, and it thrilled me to share the gifts from the soil and touch people's souls. This diversity provided multiple income streams, and we were happy and profitable. The customers were satisfied.

Besides purchasing from the farmers, when we saw fruit going to waste in people's yards, Kevin and I offered to harvest the fruit, and in exchange, share the harvest with the landowner. It was unbelievable to see how much food was going to waste. The documentary, *Dive! Living off America's Waste*, debuted that year, and I learned that billions of pounds of food were being thrown out in America! Every year the amount of food wasted continues to grow. Food waste has become an epidemic, and most didn't seem to notice.

Food Waste is everyone's business! *According to author Dana Gunders of the Natural Resources Defense Council, "Getting food from the farm to our fork eats up 10 percent of the total U.S. energy budget, uses 50 percent of U.S. land, and swallows 80 percent of all freshwater consumed in the United States. Yet, 40 percent of food in the United States today goes uneaten." Meanwhile, millions of people die from starvation each year and millions of others suffer from malnutrition. According to the World Economic Forum, there is more than enough food to feed the entire planet. Too many people go hungry every day, while approximately 1.3 billion tons of food gets lost or wasted.*

Why is so much food wasted!?

I knew a solid marketing plan and good connections would be 80 percent of the success of the business, so I wrote an informative menu that highlighted what we did and why. On our menu, we honored the farmers and ranchers who supplied us. There was also information about the benefits of fermented foods. Educated customers had more reasons to buy. We created a fun environment for people to relax and eat. Colorful tablecloths and vases of flowers on the tables attracted people like bees to flowers. We made time to engage with our clientele. Good food and conversation are always a good combination. Our connections with the farms and customers, and a solid marketing plan, were essential to our success.

The Walkabouts were a hit! Our busy pop-up cafe attracted customers to the market. This, in turn, drew more vendors. Today, the Hawi Farmers Market is bustling. It was gratifying to create another business that inspired the growth of the local food movement and aligned with the economic hard times to provide healthy and affordable options.

Every winter, my dad and Rosemary came to visit us. I was glad they got to see us and our new business thriving. My father's health had been declining for several years. It was tough for me to see this robust, brilliant man in so much discomfort. Still, his determination to live and make the best of his years gave me faith in the process. This would be the last time he saw Kevin and me in action. Seeing us in our element gave him great satisfaction. I cherish the memory of him eating a Walkabout, scooting around in his electric scooter, telling everyone how good it was!

Farmers markets are a great place for a start-up food business. You get the most bang for your buck. You can do market research with your products while making money and serving your community. Think collaboratively and you will have a better chance to succeed. An overly competitive market is not healthy for any business. Create a unique idea with a well-thought-out marketing plan, have fun, and go for it! The number of retail farmers markets in the USA has grown since I first hit the Olympia Farmers Market. According to Statista.com, "In 2014, there were a total of 8,268 directory listings for farmers markets throughout the United States."

Shield of Armor

The more we bring our individual lives into alignment with the whole of existence, the more we feel nourished and at peace.
~ Joshua Rosenthal

———————⊶⊷◉◎◉◎◉◎⊶⊷————————

In January 2010, Kevin and I got a phone call from the Small Business Development Center in Alaska. We were processing cabbage for a 50-lb. batch of sauerkraut when the call came in on our Hawaii landline.

I answered the call, "Aloha!"

The enthusiastic man on the line replied, "Is this Donna Maltz?"

"It sure is, how can I help you?" I said.

"Well, Mrs. Maltz, I am calling to inform you that you and your husband, Kevin, have been selected as the Small Business Owners of the Year for the State of Alaska, lauded as responsible green pioneers."

Dumbfounded, and then teary-eyed, I took a deep breath, put the phone on speaker, and took Kevin's hand. We walked out onto our deck overlooking the Pacific Ocean towards Alaska. With sincerity in my choked voice, I said, "Whoa, we are so honored." After the gentleman gave us the details about the award and dates for the ceremony, Kevin and I embraced, and I had a good cry. More of my armor loosened. The emotional relief was humbling and overwhelming for both Kevin and me to finally get recognized for our efforts.

The Present is a gift ~ Receive it in the Now.

The award ceremony took place in a fancy hotel conference room. With my devoted husband by my side, I delivered our acceptance speech. The audience, many of whom were once disbelievers in green business, were now respected colleagues. It was a very emotional event, and a proud moment for both of us.

I was further blessed in that my father was still alive. We got to share the news of the award with him and express our gratitude for all his support. He had been my greatest assistor and a loving father. I cannot begin to imagine how my life would have turned out if not for my dad's encouragement and generosity. Investing in me on so many levels, he taught me through example about courage, faith, perseverance, and valuing my life and the lives of others, as well as the importance of being giving, gracious, and charming. He taught me to never give up. He believed in me, even when I did not believe in myself.

Six months after we received the award, on October 3, 2010, my dear dad passed away at 82. I was 53. Watching my overindulgent, vibrant father decline over seven years was hard, yet it helped me to further recover. Just as my mom's illness affirmed that health is our greatest wealth, my father's illness and his passing motivated me to take better care of myself. After Dad's passing, the armor loosened more, and I began shedding more toxins.

Although my dad had been such a positive influence in my life, there was no more trying to prove myself to him, no more seeking his approval, or wishing he would see things my way. His passing brought me so much grief, but it also brought me some relief, knowing that he would be with my sweet mama and was no longer suffering.

Near the end of my father's life, I asked him what he felt were his most significant successes. He replied, "My friends, my family, and my Rosemary." I moved forward with friends, family, and my darling Kevin as the benchmarks of my success.

Like my mother, my father lives on in the fabric of my being. I am forever grateful to both my parents for my existence. I brought their gifts forward and composted what did not serve me. I know in my heart that my caring parents passed away proud of their rebellious daughter.

My father left me a financial gift that enhanced our existing assets, qualifying us to get a loan to invest in another piece of real estate. With business back on track, Kevin and I were in a position to take advantage of the market that resulted from the housing bubble of the Great Recession. Foreclosures were at an all-time high, and the banks were ready to deal. We scored on a beautiful farmstead near our other home in Hawi. Our comfy home sits on three acres of magnificent and fertile acreage overlooking rolling hills, spotted with sheep, cows, and horses, down to the sea. The view of the island of Maui is breathtaking, and the property is abundant

with citrus trees, avocados, pineapples, papayas, bananas, flowers, and herbal and medicinal gardens.

Kevin and I saw the potential to turn our investment into an eco-friendly vacation rental and retreat business. We named it Always in Season Retreat. Again, heads-in-beds helped to pay our mortgage, and we get to continue sharing this stunning property with delightful people from around the world.

A long-term renter moved into our other house for five years, just enough time for the housing market to recover and help pay down our mortgage. My father had taught me to buy low and sell high, and that is what we did.

In 2011, I furthered my commitment to lose more toxins and gain health. I took an Online course to get certified as a health coach from The Institute for Integrative Nutrition (IIN). During this yearlong program, I shed more pounds and dismantled the remaining armor. I fortified my body and my soul. Completing the comprehensive course and receiving the certification gave me the confidence to start my coaching practice and The Culinary Healing Arts Retreats. I rekindled my motivation and drive, and returned to the path toward my destiny. Once again strong, stretched, and centered, I was honored to help others on their healing journey.

Love and support provided me with the courage that enabled me to
continue on a regenerative path.

Engagement

*Each of us has a spark of life inside us, and our highest
endeavor ought to be to set off that spark in one another.*
~ Kenny Ausubel

My love for the 'Aina ("land" in Hawaiian) and natural farming grew stronger as I became a more full-time resident of the Big Island. The community attracted more people who were passionate about social and environmental justice. I was ready to dig in deeper with these innovative change-makers. I weaned myself off of being active in Alaska so as not to be spread too thin.

Living on an island in the middle of the ocean was a choice I made. Kevin was warming up to the idea of making it our full-time residence. I resonated more with politics here in Hawaii than in Alaska, and the tropical weather was without a doubt more regenerative. It was the perfect place for me to engage with issues that mattered to me.

I loved the fact that Hawaii is the most isolated population center on the face of the Earth, and that the air quality is some of the best in the world. What I did not appreciate was that a state that once produced all of its food now imported 85 to 90 percent of its food. I was once again on a mission to be part of the movement to increase food security and food self-sufficiency on the island. Our Always In Season farmers market business had helped increase consumer demand for local produce, but there was more I could do.

Hawaii is 2,390 miles from California; 3,850 miles from Japan; 4,900 miles from China; and 5,280 miles from the Philippines. In his in-depth research report, Gregory Kent states, "As the most geographically isolated state in the country, Hawaii imports approximately ninety-two percent of its food, according to the United States Department of Agriculture. Currently, Hawaii has a supply of fresh produce for no more than ten days. Ninety percent of the beef, sixty- seven percent of the fresh vegetables, sixty- five percent of the fresh fruits, and eighty percent of all milk purchased in the State are imported. The legislature further finds that Hawaii's reliance on out-of-state sources of food places residents directly at risk of food shortages in the event of natural disasters, economic disruption, and other external factors beyond the State's control (Hawaii State Legislature 2012)."

Greater consumer demand and pressure on political leaders is imperative for food security no matter where we live.

Connect and Collaborate

When the North Kohala Community Development Action Plan (CDP) started, I jumped on board. The core of the plan was focused on sustainable development and the community was invited to participate in discussions with county representatives on county policy. The CDP process attracted a diverse group of community members to several inclusive interactive meetings. The plan covers many topics from cultural preservation to land use. We broke into small groups and made headway together. It felt good to collaborate with others and feel like our input mattered. Our efforts helped to coordinate the delivery of county services to our community. I was thrilled that one of the objectives of the CDP was to produce 50 percent of our food by 2050. Does your community have a development plan that you participate with that is making a difference in your community? Social media will never replace community engagement.

Soon after the CDP was established, a grassroots organization formed in North Kohala called Sustainable Kohala. The mindset to regenerate, rather than sustain, was fast becoming a reality as the effects of climate change heated up. Living in an active community, and having engagement with others, kept me on track.

In 2011 the Hawaii Institute for Pacific Agriculture (HIP), an exceptional permaculture school in Kohala, was established by the visionaries, Dash and Erika Kuhr. They invited me to be on their advisory team. It has been a rewarding journey to be part of their noble vision to help train the next generation of farmers. The Kuhrs are rooted in the land; the wisdom of the 'Aina. While raising three free-range children, they and their committed team offer internships, youth programs, community events, and farm tours. The institute has inspired hundreds of new organic farmers and citizens. Most recently, HIP is also responsible for bringing the first Farm to Cafe program to our local schools. Every community would benefit from the powerful knowledge this forward-thinking organization brings forth. I'm delighted to share that HIP is helping to get a food hub going!

The 'Aina (land) is not just soil, sand or dirt; it is a heart issue for Hawaiians. The very word 'Aina brings forth deep emotion evolved from ancestral times when people lived in nature as an integral part of it.

The Kohala Village Hub (KVH), established in 2014, is another aspiring model devoted to regenerative practices, which I helped to develop, and served on the board for 5 years. The multicultural enrichment center brings our community together to learn and have a good time in a wholesome environment. The KVH supports regional efforts to strengthen Kohala's social, economic, and environmental fabric through the programs and services offered. The beautiful campus in the heart of Hawi continues to bring forth new opportunities for our community.

In 2014, the Blue Zone project came to North Hawaii. I became involved in the project, started by Dan Buettner, which works to help transform communities across America into places where healthy choices are made easy. It has been proven that people live longer with a higher quality of life. Engagement and quality food are two factors that have been identified with *centenarians* (longest living people). For a long time, I have let people who are close to me know that I plan to live until I am 120. (I have a lot of living to do.) Therefore, the Blue Zone formula was very attractive to someone like me who loves food and engaging with others.

I share all of this with you as I found the processes of regeneration came when I engaged with others doing things that mattered to me. Being part of something makes me feel whole. It is a delicate balance to know when to cut back and when to branch out. Engagement with tribes of supportive people committed to striving for Soulutions helps me prosper in every sense of the word; keeps me stable and happy. With Aloha, I renewed my belief system and awoke to my next evolution. Forgiveness is a liberating act of self-love.

Live like the Future Matters; in harmony with Nature and dear friends.

Digging Deeper V

To cherish what remains of the Earth and to foster its renewal is our only legitimate hope of survival.
~ Wendell Berry

During this evolution of personal growth and transformation, the problems of climate change became more apparent and marched in step with another financial crisis. In Alaska, I witnessed millions of acres of forest get eaten alive by the spruce bark beetle in the '90s. A decade later, I also observed the stunning recovery processes as the forest rebounded on the Kenai Peninsula. The beetles continue to travel and feast on more mature northern forests. The warming summers contribute to the increased frequency of outbreaks from the natural cycles of the beetles. They were back with a vengeance in 2018, in South Central Alaska. Meanwhile, on the Big Island, I witnessed a seashore take a new shape after a 6.7 magnitude earthquake, and a volcanic eruption sculpted new landscapes.

Around the world, catastrophic "super" storms, unprecedented heat waves, floods, earthquakes, tsunamis, and out-of-control wildfires made the headlines. Countless people died from natural disasters and thousands of acres of carbon-sequestering forests burned to the ground. As the disasters started showing up in more people's backyards, voices got louder, and people started warming up to the reality that something must change. But what and who would do something about it?

To add to the pollution and the climate dilemma of the new millennium, the world population grew at an alarming rate, from just over 6.1 billion to 6.9 billion in the first decade alone. Populations have swelled in areas where catastrophic natural disasters have occurred. The increase in bodies means an increase in demands on the environment, raising the global question of how our lifestyles affect the future. Most population growth comes from the most impoverished nations. Population growth and pollution are synonymous. The growing population's impact on the already mismanaged resources makes the Earth angrier.

Environmental groups gained momentum as quickly as critics tried to dampen the will of millions of citizens. Big business, the media, bankers, and even politicians jumped on the bandwagon as they saw financial gains from carbon-sequestering inventions and investments. Corporate and political greenwashing diluted the true colors of the crisis, pulling the wool over people's eyes. More money and time got spent on fake green campaigns than on implementing business and political practices that had any substantial environmental impact. How green is natural gas? How clean can a "clean" coal plant be? What defines "natural food?" Where do the recyclables go? Who is overseeing the regulations?

Adlai E. Stevenson II, American lawyer, politician, and diplomat said, "A hypocrite is the kind of politician who would cut down a redwood tree, then mount the stump and make a speech for conservation." Why are there not more righteous politicians and businesses to protect their citizens and the children? How can we buck this tide?

The backdrop of the times brought opportunities and obstacles.

In 2001, George Walker Bush began his reign of power after winning the election by a slim (false) margin. The 43rd President of the United States lost the popular vote, yet still beat Al Gore, the climate change activist, due to the electoral college. Bush, the "Oil Man," remained president for eight years. One of the first things he did in office was refuse to endorse the Kyoto Protocol: An international treaty extending the 1992 United Nations Framework Convention on Climate Change (UNFCCC), committed to reducing greenhouse gas emissions, and mitigate climate change. I was frustrated and pissed off. Even with the negotiation of the Kyoto Protocol, sea levels have continued to rise more than 2-1/2 inches annually on average, and "the number of weather and climate disasters worldwide has increased over 42 percent" according to PBS. We need stronger initiatives!

On 9/11/2001, nearly 3,000 people perished at the World Trade Center and the Pentagon to terrorist suicide bombings. The following invasion of Afghanistan ignited the "War on Terror." President Bush signed an executive order which stated that non-citizens suspected terrorists could be detained indefinitely. The high-security prison in Guantanamo Bay, Cuba played a significant role in the atrocities of this period of time. In November 2002, the oil tanker, *Prestige,* spilled its 77,000-ton cargo off the coast of Spain, causing the country's most massive environmental disaster to-date. I witnessed the catastrophic, devastating Exxon Valdez oil spill that occurred in Prince William Sound, Alaska, on March 24, 1989. The far-reaching, long-term effects are not always the most visible, and will continue to impact a community for years to come.

Meanwhile, in 2003, the Bush administration marched into the Second Persian Gulf War. The rationale for the attacks was principally on the assertion that Iraq, which had been viewed by the US as a rogue state since the first Gulf War, possessed weapons of mass destruction. It's clear you can't explain the Iraq War without mentioning oil! Still, George Bush won a second term. Indeed, this was and continues to be a time of War and Oil.

Wall Street was shaken to its core in 2001, as Enron, one of America's largest corporations, collapsed in bankruptcy. This conglomerate that focused primarily on natural gas, electricity, and commodities, left thousands of employees and shareholders financially devastated when shares dropped from $90.75 to $0.67 by January 2002. This political, legal, and investor crisis imposed widespread costs on the U.S. economy, causing regulations to tighten and leaving lingering skepticism of the corruption in our financial markets.

In 2004, Facebook was born, and Google took off, changing the way we relate to one another, get our news, and buy our goods. The advanced online technology launched us into the digital age, confusing business and politics even more. Imagine what would happen if the Internet imploded today.

In 2009, *The Guardian's* former environment editor John Vidal stated, "In 2006, Nicholas Stern, a former World Bank economist at the UK Treasury, reported that 'business as usual in a climate-changing world meant economic meltdown.'" After the housing bubble in 2007, the economy did meltdown. The U.S. government was forced to enact stimulus programs and tax cuts. These programs included the Economic Stimulus Act of 2008 and the American Recovery and Reinvestment Act of 2009. According to the Department of Labor, "Roughly 8.7-million jobs were shed from February 2008 to February 2010, and GDP contracted by 5.1 percent, making the Great Recession the worst since the Great Depression."

Home prices declined by approximately 30 percent and the S&P 500 index would fall to 57 percent by 2009 from its 2007 October peak. But something interesting happened: Carbon emission rates did not rise when the economy declined. Production was low because of the recession. As soon as the economy recovered, the carbon rate rose to unprecedented levels. What does that suggest about the relationship between the human impact, the economy, fossil fuels, and climate change? Do you think there should be a Global Carbon Tax?

In 2008, China overtook the US as the world's largest greenhouse gas emitter. Most of what China produced was for the US market. Seventy percent of China's energy came from mismanaged coal plants. China was, and still is, manufacturing a lot of crap, influenced by the western mindset that neither we nor the Chinese need. A lot of that toxic plastic waste was originally manufactured in China at one of those coal fired plants. For three decades China received 7 million tons of returned plastic trash from the U.S. The influx of additional waste contributed to China's deteriorating air quality to the point that 4,000 innocent human beings died every day from complications caused by the pollution! In 2017, the Chinese government canceled the recycling plastic contract. At least today, China leads the world in new technological solutions to clean up the pollution with new green policies, but where is all the plastic going?

The industrial food complex continued to escalate, adding to the war against Nature. The resistance to a harsh chemical that was attempting to control weeds and insects kept wearing off. Plants and soils required stronger addictive chemicals to be productive. Petroleum-based chemical companies grappled for more quick fixes to relieve the pains of the faulty systems. Imagine dysfunctional agricultural fields as having an addiction to opioids. Pesticides associated with genetically modified foods were engineered to tolerate herbicides such as glyphosate and gluphosinate, and insecticides such as the bacterial toxin bacillus thuringiensis (Bt). In 2009, Monsanto rolled out its new patented product Roundup 2, which was designed to make the first-generation seed obsolete. In 2011, researchers in eastern Quebec found Bt toxins in the blood of pregnant women, indicating that this toxin is passed from the environment to the fetus."

The impact and effects of Genetically Modified Organisms (GMOs) on human health and the environment became public. Toxic chemicals and dangerous GMO seeds were touted as "advances" in science and technology, and the answer to the question of feeding the growing global population. The controversy ignited human and planetary justice issues. Unlabeled genetically modified food began to take over the grocery store shelves, and GMO became an unwanted acronym in most households. Consumers, unaware of the consequences, continue to be subjected to unproven science, and continue to consume as guinea pigs. Who controls the welfare of the people and the planet? Why do they make it so damn complicated?

In 2018, Bayer AG acquired the massive conglomerate Monsanto. The new high-profile agrochemical company was planted in Bayer's pharmaceutical crop science division. Bayer, who touts itself as being a Life Science company, is now a leader in crop science and animal health. What does that mean for our future? It is definitely something to be concerned about, considering one German-owned global corporation has so much control of the genetically engendered seeds and the agrochemical sector. We have the government Food and Drug Administration, and now food and drug corporations in control of the seeds and chemicals — A monopoly on food and drug production. The choice to destroy or rebuild our world is in the hands of a few big businesses and governments, but it is the will of the people that will determine the outcome. Bayer says they are raising the bar on transparency, sustainability, and engagement. We, the people, must hold them accountable. With over 11,000 additional lawsuits inherited from the purchase of Monsanto's cancer-causing agricultural chemicals, there will be a lot of digging up to do at Bayer.

I accepted that it was OK to get mad as hell, as long as I propelled that anger into positive action. Action makes us feel better. It is the children of today that are going to inherit all these problems. It is the elders of today that have to live with themselves, knowing this is the case if they do nothing about the problems.

We feel better when we help make the world a safer, more just place to live. There are times where we have to get mad as hell — after all, we're human. We have the power and the choice to tip the scales in each and every action we take; we can either choose to regress and falter, or we can choose to regenerate and evolve into the best version of ourselves. What would happen if the human species embraced the systems and cycles of Nature, and if regeneration was at the root of our intentions in more ways than just propagation?

> *Although the problems of the world are increasingly complex,*
> *the solutions remain embarrassingly simple.*
> ~ Bill Mollison

EVOLUTION VI

Wise Growth

Soil to Soul Principles that influenced my life in this Evolution:

- Mentors are essential.
- Gratitude changes our attitude.
- Celebrate life from the depth of your soul.
- Strive to bridge the gaps, with love, respect, and compassion.
- Shift the focus from the good of mankind to the good of life-kind.
- Support and take part in creating a resilient, robust community.
- Stimulate a vibrant economy that cultivates unity and reverence for life.

CYCLE
13

Aging & Awakening

Leave a small footprint and have a greater impact.

An adult tree has weathered many storms, potentially enduring acid rains, fevers from fire, heat waves, sub-zero freezes, infestations of parasites, fungi, and infections. Snags and broken branches are common, as is the fear of being cut to the core before its time. Trees become seniors as they age. Gaps may appear in their canopies as prominent limbs begin to die out — just like the gaps in our memories that come with age.

Like trees, humans are more vulnerable to bugs and viruses as they age. The older trees remain responsive and involved in their communities during these latter years. Their DNA circulates through the ecosystem to the younger trees and surrounding life via an underground network. Without the elder trees, diversity becomes compromised, culture is lost, and the forest is weakened. The human species also benefits from the wisdom of its elders. If our elders are endowed with these attributes, then why would we not honor them?

Some trees can live much longer than others. Oddly, the longest living trees survive best in more extreme climates and situations. The bristlecone pine, with their strangely shaped, wind-beaten limbs, can live up to 5,000 years! They are conditioned to be more resilient.

The trees know that someday they will return to the soil and once again regenerate into a new cycle of life. Given this understanding, the trees do not fear death; they are part of the systems and cycles of Nature.

Flashback — My 40ᵗʰ High School Reunion

*There are times to reminisce about the past, and
there are times to anticipate the future.
Being stuck in the past can make us depressed, living only
for the future makes us anxious. By being present and
living like the future matters, we can live in peace.*

My flight took off in the early morning. I got comfortable in my window seat, computer at hand, prepared to write until we landed. I was flying from Newark, NJ, back to my home in Hawaii. It was the fall of 2014. I was 57 years old and had gone back east to attend my 40th high school reunion.

As the plane traveled west, we gained daylight hours and moved through several time zones. The weather was stellar across the country. I recapped my seven days in Jersey, reminiscing about the good times and coming to peace with the heartaches. Seeing old friends conjured up memories, both meaningful and otherwise. I did my best not to pass judgement on some of my classmates, who appeared older than their years. Decades of living an unhealthy lifestyle, immersion in corporate culture, or unfulfilled marriages had taken their toll. With others, I rejoiced. We shared our longevity secrets, achievements, and stories of our children at the Closter Elks Club, where our modest reunion took place. It was hard not to revert to the child I had left behind.

During the 12-hour flight, I took in the magnitude of America through my tiny, peek-a-boo window like never before. Raw and confused from my week in Jersey, I gazed at the vastness for hours as I sorted through my emotions. During take-off and landing, I viewed the sprawl of humanity that criss-crossed through the once natural and native lands.

I saw corporate complexes, shopping malls, and parking lots full of bright yellow school buses. Asphalt roads cut through treeless mountaintops. Grids of power, both renewable and antiquated, connected the once sacred land. The enormous footprint of human-made structures, constructed from materials extracted from the Earth, looked innocent from the air. So did the freeways with vehicles lined up like ants. There were miles of urban sprawl. Skyscrapers and track homes littered the landscape. Some settlements were connected by bridges, others by waterways and highways. The harbors were full of stacks of gigantic transport containers. Enormous vessels came and went.

As the plane grew in elevation, the dramatic landscapes boasted tapestries of ornate agricultural acreage. Seeing miles of rivers, vast lakes, acres of forests, and majestic mountains eased my mind. There were stretches of wilderness, flat plains where buffalo once roamed. There were canyons and cactus-filled deserts. Conversely, there was barren land that had been clear-cut, or scarred by mining. From coast to coast, my flight followed the weather patterns. I saw the changes from the perspective of the clouds, finally finding myself over miles of seemingly pristine open water, before arriving in Hawaii.

It looked as though America was still the land of the free and home of the brave. Yet all of it was owned by someone or claimed by the government. I contemplated how much the scenery had changed in just 40 years, with over 100 million more people in the U.S. I pondered the changes in my personal life, and the memories of my tree forts and my forest, now covered with McMansions. Feeling the sadness of the loss of my parents, grandparents, and high school classmates, who had passed away far too young — I had a good cry, then dried my weary eyes.

I imagined how the landscape would have looked different, had the evolution of our country been designed around ecological systems, rather than profit. What if our education system taught us to value Nature? Why were we not taught to understand the value of biodiversity, and know that natural farming and green buildings were viable sustainable systems? It would have made sense if we knew how to build resilient communities; if we knew where our food and resources came from and understood the impact of our consumption on the Earth. What if human systems got modeled after Nature's systems? I thought, what a beautiful world it could be.

To turn my mood around, I envisioned our world as a place where all of us get to enjoy, learn, and grow, with Nature in our daily lives: A place where everyone lives like the future matters. I reminisced on the happy times in my childhood and remembered how grateful I was for those friends that still remain dear to me.

Interconnect with Purpose

*Everything in our world is sacred and interconnected - and
we're in the midst of an epochal shift to recognizing that truth
in every realm of human endeavor. It's a magnificent time
to be alive and participate in this evolutionary leap.*
~ Stephen Dinan

In November 2014, our granddaughter was born. Freya Luna Moss. This beautiful, innocent seed would put the fire in my belly to complete this body of work. I sure as heck wanted to make sure she knew me and the impact her precious being has had on my life. This unfinished manuscript had been sitting dormant for nearly ten years! At the time of publication, Freya will be four years old, and I sixty-two. Every day, Freya's spirit inspires me to not retire, as do the souls of all the children who deserve a vibrant planet to play, learn, and laugh in. Being a grandmother is beyond words as is being Mama Donna!

My clients were also a big part of my decision to finish this body of work. Especially, Amanda Brannon who created the beautiful Soil to Soul artwork. She was living in Alaska at the time and had followed me on Facebook for years. In 2014, she sent me a private message, asking me if I had considered writing a book, and if so, would I be interested in working out a trade with her. I let her know I had been working on one, on and off, for years, and had just jumped back into the process. She offered to provide graphic design work, in exchange for attending one of my Culinary Healing Arts Retreats. We came up with a plan, and she came to Hawaii for two weeks. Amanda really encouraged me to get this book out into the world and I helped her get healthier. It was a win-win!

I put the bulk of my coaching practice on hold, and almost everything for that matter, and settled into becoming an author with the hopes to inspire more people to become the best version of themselves. In this book, I have woven in many of the principles and resources I use in my coaching practice.

I chose to learn how to be a writer and then focused on the business of being an author. The book went through many metamorphoses; as did I. I dove into my personal past and invested hundreds of hours researching corporate, political, and environmental changes; intending to better understand the circumstances that influenced my reality and the world's. While trying to make sense of it all, I often doubted myself, felt overwhelmed, and almost got depressed at times by what I was learning. Occasionally, I fell into old patterns and compulsive behaviors. Fortunately, those times did not last long, as I had been there, done that BS, and had the tools to overcome these energy vampires. Instead, I was able to dedicate myself to making this my most meaningful evolution. Now I'm on fire!

I found writing mentors, and with their support I was able to conquer my fears and my insecurities of being a dyslexic writer. Encouraged by dear friends and my loving and supportive husband, who all professed that my story mattered, my doubts steadily dwindled. I am eternally grateful for their love and light. To balance out the negative things happening in the world, I turned my focus to the many people who are part of the shift of consciousness toward a higher vibration — Soulutionists.

I invested in my education by attending live seminars from one of the world's leading high-performance coaches, Brendon Burchard. I also graduated from Marie Forleo's B-School, which is an excellent Online business training course for conscientious entrepreneurs. The messages of these younger entrepreneurs, who shared their belief that you can make money and positively change the world; reinforced my long-held convictions, actions, and devotion.

Knowledge helps us navigate the pressing issues.

Now there are many excellent conscious Online programs and podcasts: The Shift Network, the Food Revolution, The Aware Show, Ted Talks, Hay House Radio, Bioneers Radio, and more. I hope you will check these excellent resources out. It's uplifting to hear what other change-makers are doing. There are also several great Online communities striving to connect us to responsible companies, including Green America, Eco-Business Links, Green Plus National Directory, Well.org, and more.

In 2015, I founded Soil to Soul Solutions, intending to start an Online platform that would inspire Soil to Soul entrepreneurs, artists, authors, and musicians to push their products and services out into the world. It was slow going, until my brilliant partner, James Mattie entered my life. James, now twenty-two years old, came to Hawaii for a three-week visit with his buddy Spencer, in 2017. I was in the middle of a Blue Zone sponsored vegan potluck when Free (Rachel Harrington), one of my delightful, free-spirited hānai daughters, popped over to my house for an impromptu visit. In tow with Free, were James and Spencer, who she introduced to me as Nature and Earth. They were all vegans at the time, living in a vegan community down the road. Everyone who came to this community, known as Gentle World, was offered a name that most represented them at the time. Naturally, the three of them joined us for a delicious meal and fertile conversations.

Ah, yes! A name. It becomes part of our identity, as does the name we choose for our business and what we choose to call one another. Like anything in Nature, a name can change and take on new meaning. I call my husband *Lovey*, my dogs *Darlings*, and everybody *Love*. I myself, am honored to be known as Mama Donna.

Earth, Nature, and Mama Donna.

348

A week later, Nature and Earth moved into our Aloha Cottage. These fun and intelligent young men ended up interning on our farmstead for six months. James was a Nature-lover, but he was not a farmhand kind-of-guy. While Spencer helped primarily around the farmstead, James took a real interest in both my Soil to Soul work and this book. For me, that was the best thing that could have happened. James helped me get and stay organized, and we spent hours editing and brainstorming about this book. It turned out that he had the skills that I lacked and was excellent at them all. Truthfully, technology is a whole other world to me, I've always been the hands-in-the-soil — or dough kind of gal. James has taught me so much about the Online world and the benefits of using social media to raise people's vibrations. We are both devoted to growing businesses that puts Nature at the forefront of our endeavors. James is also the marketing manager, webmaster, and social media guru for my persona brand, Donna Maltz ~ at www.donnamaltz.com. Our intergenerational relationship makes growing the companies more fun and meaningful. To this day, I still call James, *Nature*. He is a truly grounded and wise individual, who remains in touch with both Nature and the Earth.

I attended my first Bioneers Conference in 2016. Kenny Ausubel and Nina Simons, two brilliant social entrepreneurs, founded the innovative non-profit in 1990. The devoted couple and their determined team unite people to work on breakthrough solutions for restoring people and planet. I found my international tribe! Every year, I attend the mind-expanding, educational event. It's a creative haven, "a fertile hub," to network with thought leaders of all generations and nations. The speakers and attendees rock my soul! It's my Woodstock. I get so energized and inspired; it lasts me all year. The three-day event takes place in San Rafael, California, at the Marin Center. I hope someday we will meet at the conference. To stay fueled, I listen to Bioneers Radio and Podcasts.

All of these people and events are so valuable to me, but Mother Nature is my most exceptional mentor. Daily I contemplate the magnificence of our existence: Grateful for the privilege to be on this planet. Sometimes sobbing, face down on the Earth, I beg for answers. I ask, "How can I help? What wisdom do you wish for me to convey?" When I ask, I receive guidance. The words I write come from the many voices of Nature — the birds, frogs, the sounds of a mother moose giving birth in our yard in Alaska, and the whale's songs as I swim in the warm Hawaiian sea. Angry storms, dancing northern lights, starry nights, sunsets with green flashes, and tangled roots all speak to me. I often walk and always write, barefoot.

The Earth energizes me and keeps my fire burning! The rickety picnic benches by the sea have become some of my favorite writing studios.

Inspirational wisdom from my mentors and resources help me stay balanced. My reasons to be somebody and act upon my inner desires are reinforced. No longer am I afraid to be ahead of my time. With a renewed attitude of — Yes, I Can… I am ready to go out on a limb. It is my time!

Me and James "Nature"

Holy Land, Holy Words

*It's kind of like childbirth, hard to explain
unless you experience it for yourself.*

⎯⎯⎯⎯⎯ ⦿⦿⦿⦿⦿⦿⦿ ⎯⎯⎯⎯⎯

In June 2017, Kevin and I traveled to Israel to celebrate our niece Lola's marriage to Yanay, a wonderful Israeli man. His loving family lives outside of Tel Aviv. The stunning ceremony and festivities took place at the historic Jerusalem Hotel, overlooking the Old City of Jerusalem and the West Bank. The food was over the top, as was the dancing into the wee hours of the night. Yanay's family shared the beauty of the country with us. We indulged in the rich culture and delicious Israeli cuisine for days. The blending of our two families was better than bagels, lox, and cream cheese!

After our adventures, which included a dip in the salty Dead Sea, a visit to the Old City, and an exploration of Tel Aviv, Kevin headed back to Alaska. I would join him there, after spending an extra ten days in En Hod, an enchanting, Eco-Bohemian artist community in the northern part of the country. The village is situated on a hillside, a few miles from the Mediterranean Sea. The 150 homes in En Hod were built and settled by artists in the 50s and 60s. They were young, idealistic, liberal, bohemian

351

folks who came from around the world to settle in the Holy Land. They had a common interest: To help rebuild the humanities in the war-torn country.

The sweet village was immaculate and beautifully landscaped. It was designed as a walking town with narrow roads and well-maintained paths. There were bronze sculptures, sweet park benches, and galleries throughout. Many of the homes had attached art studios. The artists welcomed visitors, and you could observe them as they worked with clay, stained glass, and paints. There was a sense of community pride. People from around the world who were interested in intentional communities or art, wandered around the quaint village in awe.

I rented an apartment on the outskirts of the village from a family that helped establish the earthy artist colony. The man who ran the rental business also restored antiques and repurposed almost anything. His shop and my comfortable apartment, which was decked out in early-20th-century decor, were attached to the house. His wife was an eccentric and talented painter, whose studio was also on the property. Her art graced the apartment walls. I felt like I was in a surreal time warp surrounded by aged furniture in this provincial town.

Their daughter owned the only coffee shop in the village. Midday, after working for hours, I'd stroll barefoot through the quiet streets. I'd either end up at her rustic, Mediterranean-style coffee shop to enjoy a strong cappuccino and colorful people while working on my manuscript, or I'd go dine at one of the two unique eateries in town. The people who live there are soulful and accepting. Dogs and cats are free to roam the town and lounge at the eateries. I felt right at home.

It was in the enchanting setting of En Hod, at the heart of the Holy Land, that I did one of my final rewrites of this book. I now know why many famous artists and writers retreat there. It is a village full of cultural bliss! The creative and mystical energy stimulated my senses. My soulful well-being recharged. This was an unexpected blessing.

Being in Israel opened my eyes and left me with a lot of questions. Over the years, the bible stories I read and the news I watched influenced and distorted my views of the country. Experiencing the contrast between the country's war-torn history and her modern development gave me some clarity, but it did not answer all my questions.

How could this sacred place develop so fast in just 70 years? How come no one talked about how the development was affecting the environment? It was evident by the littered beaches, congested highways, and air quality, that there were problems. There was barely a kibbutz to be found, modern agriculture had taken over most of the landscape. There were so many lovely people in this beautiful place, how could they not recognize what was happening? I questioned over and over again, why so much political and religious conflict, hatred, resentment, and hypocrisy continues to reign in this sacred place! Why? Why? Why? Why can we not move past our differences? Getting answers to my questions would not happen in three weeks. I did my best to navigate how I felt with the notion that what I experienced was a microcosm of the more significant global issues.

If you have never been to this extraordinary country, with so many contrasts, and so much conflict, diversity, beauty, and culture, it's kind of like childbirth, hard to explain unless you experience it for yourself. The place brought out holy words in me. As deep reflections poured out of me, Mother Dear's words rang through my head daily: "There is so much hatred in this world, there's no room for no more." Love, yes, love was the answer that kept ringing in my ears. We must love more because love conquers hate; it is more powerful than revenge. It takes courage to resolve conflict, not greed and guns.

Let Go ~ Ascend

With all the uncertainties, moving onward and upward is liberating.

There once was a time when I was married to my work and addicted to unsustainable habits. Those days are long behind me. Eighteen years before the completion of this book, I sat under a tree and admitted to being entirely out of balance. Feeling hopeless — a worthless woman — and fearing another ice age or burning planet, was no way to live. It's liberating to be free from destructive behaviors and unhealthy obsessions and to be encouraged by life. Appreciating who I am, knowing what I love to do — my motives for why I do what I do are clear.

In this final story, I share my current affairs. As you well know, nothing in Nature is constant except change; therefore, my present will be the past by the time you read this. Regardless, it is a happy ending, and most days, I'm the happiest person I know.

On my 61st birthday, which happens to be on Mother's Day, I flew Mother Dear, who was now 82, to Hawaii. We enjoyed a glorious two weeks, relaxing and exploring the Big Island together. For my birthday, she got me a lovely gift from the local thrift store (on my request). Enclosed was a card with the perfect message on the cover: "You are not Aging, you are Evolving." Yes, those words struck me, but not as much as her endearing message inside the card. At 61, I was still her "little girl and a bundle of joy." I had the privilege to read this entire book to her while lounging in paradise. We laughed and cried as we shared priceless memories.

Before Mother Dear arrived, I knew she had been ill and hoped the tropical healing of the island would revitalize her, and it did for the time being. However, when Mother Dear returned to Georgia, cancer got the better of her body. It turns out that no one knew how sick she was. I journeyed back east to visit her in the hospital and witness her incredible spirit in this time of great adversity. The hospital workers said she was the most visited patient they'd ever had. Within weeks, I was back on an airplane, looking out the peek-a-boo window, contemplating life, and anticipating gatherings with loved ones to honor her purposeful life. She shared her love with everyone wherever she went. Our love for one another was like no other. While Mother Dear moved onward and upward with her Lord in heaven, alongside all who awaited her, her spirit remains embedded in my soul. I share her inspiring wisdom with others.

Moving onward and upward is liberating.

In 2019, we sold our Alaskan home and retired from A Memorable Experience vacation rental business, but our fond memories remain. It was also our last year running The Fresh Sourdough Express Bakery and Cafe. After 37 years, it was time for the next cycle! Can I get a hallelujah! I must admit, it was very emotional for Kevin and me to let go of this long lasting, priceless evolution. Lots of tears were shed, but now we have more precious time to spend with friends and our son and granddaughter. Our special friendships from Homer will always be a part of our lives, just like those of my best childhood buddies. Like water, these kindred spirits have stood the test of time and kept me afloat in rough seas. We continue to celebrate each other's achievements; we are family. I am grateful!

Gratitude changes the attitude and is very becoming to all who wear it!

Kevin and I are still enthusiastic Soil to Soul Entrepreneurs. I cherish being able to share my life and business aspirations with my precious husband. Our Always in Season Farmstead Vacation Rentals business and Culinary Healing Arts Retreats keep us busy. On top of that, my coaching practice, photography, and writing are all part of my blessed days. I also love being a hānai mom and mentoring others. Let's not forget my dogs. They are with me 24/7.

To this day, time in Nature brings Kevin and me closer together. We may not be native Hawaiians or have Native American blood, but we too connect deeply with the natural world. Our land offers a bounty of fresh organic fruits, vegetables, and herbs. For the bulk of our day, we are surrounded by Nature; here is where I get my strength, courage, and wisdom. I believe our love of Nature has been a core value that keeps Kevin and me together. When we are walking the Kohala cliffs, or hiking the Homer trails, we communicate more deeply. Kevin and I believe that we must protect the precious, limited natural resources, and the kingdoms of plants and animals.

The Hawaii state motto — "Ua mau ke ea o ka ʻāina i ka pono," means the life of the land is perpetuated in righteousness. These words hold great value in my heart.

Our home runs on solar power, and our hybrid car saves us money, and hopefully, helps to limit our carbon footprint. It also helps that we don't drive much. We entertain friends from all parts of the world at our beautiful farmstead retreat. Art, music, healthy food, and business development are all part of our blessed life. Our hānai family continues to grow.

Mentoring others who are striving to live like the future matters brings us joy! I'm incredibly grateful for these intergenerational relationships that help keep me in touch with the youth and keep me youthful. The greatest joy of all is the privilege of being a grandmother! Every chance that Kevin and I get to visit our son and our granddaughter in the mountains of North Carolina is a blessing. Living as if the future matters has never made more sense.

Living as if the future matters has never made more sense.

Daily Rituals

Taking time for rituals and routines, we make more time.

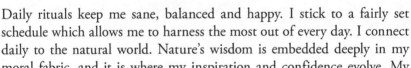

Daily rituals keep me sane, balanced and happy. I stick to a fairly set schedule which allows me to harness the most out of every day. I connect daily to the natural world. Nature's wisdom is embedded deeply in my moral fabric, and it is where my inspiration and confidence evolve. My emotional intelligence comes from looking into the eyes of others and connecting with my heart.

I rise with the sun, devoted to a balanced master plan, which includes daily practices that bridge passion with action and set the pace of my day. The fresh, tropical air and the songs of the morning birds offer inspiration. After Kevin and I share a gratitude hug, he brings me hot lemon water. The lemon is freshly picked from our tree. Then, it's coffee time with my love! We sit on the deck of our beautiful Hawaiian home, where we communicate about the day before checking into our virtual world.

By 9 A.M., we are off for a walk to a remote place with our intuitive, canine friends. Chester, a handsome Catahoula mix breed and Sadie, his sweet bitch. Midway through the hike, I do a *Sky-Walk Active Meditation*: Lying

358

on my back on a slight incline, so the blood goes toward my heart, I raise my feet toward the sky. It releases my body, mind, and spirit as I gently stretch and go within. A peaceful plunge in the ocean caps off the morning ritual. I'm a treader, not a swimmer. I'm sure it's a sight to see, my head bobbing above the water with my long, thick auburn hair piled up on top. I also wear a big-brim visor as I perform my perfect doggie paddle. The dogs swim too, and we work out our bodies and minds together. I often rejoice on these outings with friends or clients.

I eat breakfast like a princess, lunch like a queen, and dinner like a pauper. Michael Pollan's advice, "Eat food, not too much, mostly plants," works for me. Admittedly, now and again, I'm tempted to pig out on a freshly baked macadamia nut pie I purchase at the Hawi farmers' market. To offset temptation, I'll eat a fiber-filled, fluorescent sweet mango, passion fruit, or dragon fruit, along with some macadamia nuts to balance out the high-glycemic, nutrient-dense treats. No longer do I relapse for more than a day, before I am back into the systems and cycles that nourish the philosophy I adhere to.

The afternoons are my time for concentrated writing and business. I get more accomplished in these six hours because I have taken the time to commune with Nature and do my daily rituals. Once 5 P.M. hits, I'm off on another walk, to clear my mind and reflect on the day. Most evenings, I put in another two to three hours of writing, posting on social media, and research. After a gentle gratitude hug, it's lights out by 10 P.M. for a restful slumber. OK… I admit, sometimes if I'm on a roll, I'll work until midnight or beyond. After all, I'm still as passionate and determined as ever!

Twice a month, I get a deep massage from a special hānai daughter, Sarah. She is one of my primary care *healers,* friend, and health mentor. As is

Alvita, my seventy-year-old Chinese medicine doctor and dear friend since 2002. Their love, care, and intergenerational wisdom have helped me melt away the toxins, and have kept me fit in body and mind. Still no knee replacement! Although my knee is not perfect, my attitude about it makes up for the imperfection. I love my knee — in fact, both of them. Prioritizing my health has made all the difference, which includes spending more time with friends and engaging with my community. These essentials help me thrive in these chaotic times. It all comes down to how we choose to look at the world.

Nature is where I get my daily news. I observe how the Earth's natural communities' function, how storms impact entire ecosystems, and how the sun and rain and all of Nature's diversity makes it possible for us all to live. Spending time in Nature helps put things in perspective and keeps me balanced.

My daily rituals awaken me to what is possible. My body feels better at 62 than it did at 42. I feel as if I'm getting younger in every sense of the word. This anti-aging formula is working — and you can't find that in a face cream.

Spending time in Nature helps put things in perspective and keeps you balanced.

Digging Deeper VI
Awakened

*Adults keep saying we owe it to the young people, to give them
hope, but I don't want your hope. I don't want you to be hopeful.
I want you to panic. I want you to feel the fear I feel every day.
I want you to act. I want you to act as you would in a crisis.
I want you to act as if the house is on fire, because it is.*
~ Greta Thunberg, 16-year-old climate activist

Unlike in previous Digging Deeper sections, where I have highlighted significant events throughout history that impacted my life, this one has a new feel. I have experienced so much joy, abundance, success, and yes, some anger, pain, and sorrow. Like a tree that weathers many storms and has received the blessings of the sunshine and rain, I am resilient and happy. My happiness comes from the way I choose to look at the world.

I am inspired by people like Greta Thunberg, and so many other youths, peers, and elders, who are relentlessly speaking out and taking action to bring forth justice. It's time for all of us to step it up and be part of the changes that need to happen in the world. By its nature, the world is a fruitful place to live. Quality of life is a core value for success. The quality of life has improved for some, but not for most. The more awakened we are the more we help bridge and heal the gaps that divide and dehumanize humanity.

Awakened to Reality

Living on the surface is shallow. We must go deep and grow.

In October of 2016, right before the presidential election, a documentary was released about the effects of climate change. Kevin and I watched the film with some friends when we were in North Carolina. *Before the Flood*, presented and produced by Leonardo DiCaprio, addressed the dangers of climate change and explored several solutions. We thought for sure that no one in their right mind would ever elect a politician who ignored the importance of climate-related issues. The outcome of the 2016 elections crushed my spirit and those of everyone I knew.

It's not just the changing climate that awakens my deep desire to see radical change. Each day, we witness the impact of the debris created by the addictive human condition. The reality is this: Pollution, ocean acidification, dying coral, oil spills, floating plastic garbage islands, filthy beaches, contaminated rivers, failing crops, scarred landscapes, rampant fires, littered cities, poor air quality, global pandemics, lack of potable water, starvation, overpopulation, and the extinction of countless species are all products of our actions. Along with the recent COVID-19 pandemic, these casualties of overconsumption are a clear sign of our disrespect for the Earth. It is unacceptable to allow them to persist.

Meanwhile, America's current administration has made catastrophic decisions regarding the environment. An article from the New York Times reported that, "All told, the Trump administration's environmental rollbacks could significantly increase greenhouse gas emissions and lead to thousands of extra deaths from poor air quality every year." This information comes from a recent report prepared by New York University Law School's State Energy and Environmental Impact Center. In addition to the environmental atrocities — which included withdrawing from the Paris Agreement — food security under the current administration has plummeted.

At the time of completion of this book, we will be well into the 2020 elections. Many experts predict we are in the midst of an environmental crisis that has hit so hard, we better do something about it. It's unconscionable that the fossil-fuel driven America is both the world's largest economy and the second-biggest polluter. *The Economist* says, "Amid the clamor is a single, jarring truth. Demand for oil is rising and the energy industry, in America and globally, is planning multi-trillion-dollar investments to satisfy it." Compared to the other species on our planet, humans use more resources than we need. A wasteful society creates enormous pressure and imbalances on the ecosystems that make up this life-support system we call our Mother Earth. We cannot deny this any longer. We must coexist with Nature if we are to exist at all.

> *I do not see a delegation for the four-footed. I see no seat for the eagles. We forget and we consider ourselves superior, but we are after all a mere part of the Creation. And we must continue to understand where we are. And we stand between the mountain and the ant, somewhere and there only, as part of the Creation.*
> ~ Oren Lyons

How long can we stand for misguided political and corporate leadership that puts our nation and the world in great danger of environmental and economic catastrophe? I'm sure by looking at recent polls that not everyone agrees with me; so be it.

There was a survey by the American Psychological Association which concluded, "More than half of Americans (59 percent) said they consider this the lowest point in U.S. history that they can remember — a figure spanning every generation, including those who lived through World War II and Vietnam, the Cuban Missile Crisis and the September 11 terrorist attacks." Apathy and addiction are common conditions that result from suffering. Substance abuse of any kind robs people of their basic needs, such as housing and food. An article in City Journal stated, "According to the Office of National Drug Control Policy, the average heavy-opioid user consumes $1,834 in drugs per month." Food, shopping, electronics addiction; any addiction, for that matter, is costly. In addition, addictive habits are detrimental to society and the Earth.

Surveys and opinions are not answers, neither is living in La-La Land or Doom-and-Gloomville. To be blinded by the truth or caught up in a superficial reality is shallow. We can no longer afford to ignore or drown in our sorrows if things are to change. The powers that be are doing their best to separate us from each other and from the light. We can, and must, break the spell of greed and fear that evokes compulsive behavior if we choose to live a happy and purposeful life. Who wants to live in a tug of war with personal demons and energy vampires? Neither the Earth nor humans can continue to absorb the assaults without radical self-defense. We must rectify the current governments and divest from those corporations that are not cooperating with the laws of Nature and have turned our society into compulsive consumers. We must vote and spend our dollars wisely.

Yes, I am sickened that America, the supposedly shining model, sets the example for the rest of the world. It has gone backassward, and the American Dream has turned into an addicted, disastrous nightmare on so many levels. But this does not have to be our reality. I fall into the 41 percent of people who does not believe this is the lowest point in U.S. history. I think we can turn things around. But what will it take to fix a dysfunctional political and economic system from the ground up? What role will you play?

Our bodies, mind, and the Earth could use a stimulus package that is transparent and regulated by the systems and cycles of Nature. We are part of the Soulutions when we act accordingly.

Awakened to a New Paradigm

We've got to think now, in real terms, for that seventh generation . . .
We've got to get back to spiritual law if we are to survive.
~ Oren Lyons

I choose to look at the realities from a visionary perspective, determined to do my part to ensure that future generations can enjoy the wonders of the world as they are intended to be. I believe that if people live from their hearts and act with integrity, they can be part of the Soulutions, and united, we can make this the best time in history. Is it really so idealistic to hope all life would have the opportunity to interconnect and be part of the beautiful web of life? In shifting our focus from the good of mankind to the good of *life-kind*, we can create an evolving paradigm and improve the quality of life for all. Imagine what the world could be like if the human systems and cycles we created served life-kind, and eliminated the systems that have been corrupted by greed and built to conquer and exploit?

There are intelligent and compassionate role models, leaders, and countries setting examples, like Finland, Iceland, Sweden, and Denmark. Other countries are also making great progress in protecting both human health and natural ecosystems. Ecuador is the first country to recognize the rights of Nature in its constitution.

Rights for Nature articles acknowledge, "Nature in all its life forms has the right to exist, persist, maintain and regenerate its vital cycles. And we—the people—have the legal authority to enforce these rights on behalf of ecosystems. The ecosystem itself can be named as the defendant."

They say history repeats itself. That can be disturbing if we consider the wars and greed that have plagued humanity. There are likewise parts of history that offer us ancestral wisdom to live in harmony with Nature and each other. Much of the traditional wisdom our ancestors offer can help save our lives. The stress of our modern, fast-paced, addictive society was not part of their everyday lives. People lived close to the land communally and laughed a lot. There was a more harmonious connection to the Earth and there was solidarity.

As I have mentioned, business has changed the world faster than anything since the Ice Age. Corporations, politics, education etc... It is all business, once there is an exchange. After all, it's your business how you run your life. Every day, we are constantly exchanging, whether it be money for groceries or gas for our cars. We also exchange with others, our energy and emotions, even our experiences. We deal with inputs and outputs all day long. Like a business, our lives are better when everything is balanced.

> *We are not apart from nature, we are a part of Nature.*
> *And to betray Nature is to betray us, to save Nature, is to save us.*
> ~ Prince Ea

To live harmoniously, we must address human rights and the rights of Nature, which means we must consider the inalienable rights of all life. By championing "Life, Liberty, and the pursuit of Happiness" for the birds and the bees, the flowers and the trees, and all sentient beings, we can help redefine the choices we enact as we move into the future. To do this, we must have a sense of self. And be educated.

We are biological organisms, and therefore, we are part of the web of life, not above the laws of Nature. All life is interconnected, from the cosmos to the tiniest microorganisms. The Earth, our lifestyles, and our careers interconnect each day far more than we realize. When we take into consideration the food, culture, and ecology in the place we live, and improve it, we all benefit. Our connections can result in a shared benefit, or end in mutual destruction.

Nature is the master of balance and diversity. Diversity brings balance and adds value to the whole. Without it, there is a risk of extinction. We evolve with integrity when we honor all life. A homogenized culture of any kind is unbalanced and lacks integrity. When we respect and support diversity and embrace our unique gifts, there is a higher chance of success. These principles go hand in hand with business models: The more natural and diversified the business, the better the chance of its survival.

The closer we get to Nature and understand its value, the less inclined we are to destroy it. Awakened, we can regenerate our human nature and Nature herself. We then go forth with grace and help guide the human race. It's a choice we get to make.

There are numerous examples of individuals, politicians, businesses and organizations making headway. Hawaii Congresswoman Tulsi Gabbard states, "Protecting our environment is not just a policy discussion; it is a way of life, embedded in the fabric of our culture and society. To preserve and protect the 'Aina, we must continue to conserve our precious, limited natural resources and promote sustainable practices."

Paul Hawken, entrepreneur, activist and author, started Project Drawdown in 2001 with fellow entrepreneurs, scientists, and thought leaders. Their research led to the ground-breaking book published in 2017, *Drawdown: The Most Comprehensive Plan Ever Proposed to Reverse Global Warming.* Included in the book are 100 of the most substantive solutions to climate change. "Many, if not most, of these solutions can be undertaken with little or no new laws or policy and can be financed profitably by companies and capital markets." This well-documented book and ongoing work provide a compass and a toolkit. It is full of reasons for why and how to bring life back into balance.

When the eight-part series, *Our Planet,* narrated by David Attenborough, was released in 2019, I watched each episode twice. If everyone watched this series, they might think twice about how they live on this beautiful planet. The breathtaking cinematography and compelling narrative left me feeling hopeful, and more determined than ever to play a significant role in the discovery and enacting of Soulutions.

I am sincerely grateful that nations, people and organizations exist who are striving to balance out the less thoughtful examples in the world. You can find many more examples in the Soulution Section at the back of the book. But is it enough? Is the work done by these few nations and courageous leaders and organizations enough to allow my granddaughter's generation and those generations to come to be able to say that we did enough?

Awakened: A Choice We Get to Make

We are in a time of significant challenges, but there are endless opportunities to help restore life-kind and the planet. It's a choice we get to make.

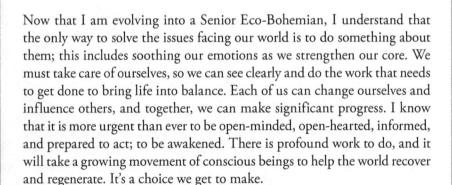

Now that I am evolving into a Senior Eco-Bohemian, I understand that the only way to solve the issues facing our world is to do something about them; this includes soothing our emotions as we strengthen our core. We must take care of ourselves, so we can see clearly and do the work that needs to get done to bring life into balance. Each of us can change ourselves and influence others, and together, we can make significant progress. I know that it is more urgent than ever to be open-minded, open-hearted, informed, and prepared to act; to be awakened. There is profound work to do, and it will take a growing movement of conscious beings to help the world recover and regenerate. It's a choice we get to make.

I get it; at times, we might feel ineffective, discouraged, fed up, and want to give up. It's hard to see through the darkness. It hurts to see our fellow humans behave in ways that are violent, selfish, or insensitive. Especially, when we know that people can behave in ways that come from a place of awareness. It's natural to feel disappointed and overwhelmed. It's fair to say that most everyone feels the effects of the environmental and humanitarian crises. The political tension and economic uncertainty are results of that very strife.

To rebel can feel like a burden. But sometimes, it is the most important thing we can do. Standing up for something that will make life more vibrant is not only a viable option, but a necessary and rewarding path. Here, the discomfort of parting ways with the old and established represents an opportunity to make a difference. To truly serve and support progress, we must know when our resistance is right, and when to set it aside. When we are present with a healthy ego, we are more aware and effective. The world needs more conscious leaders and enterprises with moral courage and caring, active citizens, to support and balance life-kind. Conscious contributions that consider everything from the soil to our souls create value for humanity and the Earth. It is noble and a valuable use of one's time and energy to support environmental, political, and economic systems that serve and support future generations. They are counting on us. It's a choice we get to make.

I've learned that being anxious about the future serves little purpose, except in a healthy dose, if it motivates you to work harder for something meaningful. Sometimes, we all could use some help, and we must find the courage to ask for it. We can get through the darkness when we believe we are ready. I've also learned that forgiveness is powerful, especially the forgiveness of one's past transgressions. It is essential to take care of our emotional wellbeing to fully prosper. I believe that, whatever ill fortune we may have had, with the right support, we can transform our reality into a life we value. Forgiveness and courage increase our chances of co-creating a more harmonious world. Remember, the faster you take care of a wound, the quicker it heals. Not living in vain, stuck in fear, or dwelling on the past, we have the energy to heighten our chances for success. It's a choice we get to make.

Where we find ourselves today is the culmination of all our thoughts, choices, and beliefs. If you have personal issues that weigh you down, it's much harder to be part of the Soulutions. Whether it is grief, fear, illness, or rejection — pain is real. The armor we don to escape these emotions is heavy and hard. Being frustrated and angry sucks. It takes the willingness to experience and express anger, pain, and sorrow so that we can move beyond our limitations. Fulfilling our ambitions and creating a life we are proud of takes doing the work. Doing so, we can dismantle old, stagnant armor and share our light. Each individual's energy has a role in the shift of consciousness.

We wear our energy around us like clothing everywhere we go. You may not think people can see or feel it, but they can. So can you. Our spirits are both unique and malleable. The motivation and drive we reflect determine the quality of this energy.

Just as healthy soil creates the conditions for the tree to grow from seed to maturity, so too do our souls and bodies become enriched if we feed them well. The energy that we give off will be sharper, more transparent, and more brilliant. It is the ripple effect: Like a pebble tossed into a still pond, our intentional actions can make positive waves.

At any time in our lives, we have the choice to change. Nothing is constant in Nature except change. When we focus on our personal development from a soulful place, it elevates our vibration and helps us reach our highest potential. By allowing ourselves to rise to a higher frequency, we ascend.

The journey from our smaller self, to our more significant being, takes doing the work, courage, and support. It is liberating to compost what does not serve us and feels so good to nourish what does. By remaining true to our inner guidance, what's next for us to be and to do is clear. We have the ability to face any destructive or addictive habits, beliefs, and behaviors. We must clean our own house before we can clean up the homes of others.

When we find our purpose, something bigger than ourselves to devote our lives to, this becomes the best time in our lives. To live consciously is a choice we get to make. Conscious living takes into consideration all life. When we are present in our surroundings, we are in-tune with how people, places, and things affect us, and how we affect them. We come into greater service to the world when we give more than we take. It's a choice we get to make.

Awakened, We Believe in Our Potential

Dreams don't work unless you do!

Once we are awake, we are ready to activate our dreams and be part of the Soulutions. With a positive attitude, the political, economic, and environmental crises present new opportunities. I believe that through 21st-century education and the advances in technology, we can take more conscious actions to inspire the global community to restore, protect, and cultivate more stewards of the Earth. I believe that the world is ready to transform and experience the joys of life as we co-create and solve problems.

Sometimes, the solutions to problems are not always found in increasing complexity but in simplicity. So too are our dreams: They are what we make of them. No dream is too big or too small if they are our dreams. Dreams, like everything in life, change. Dreams do not usually happen by chance; we make them happen.

We all have our own way. There are things each of us can do, whether it is to share content on social media, sign petitions, march for freedom, campaign for conscious leadership or start an action group. We can plant a garden, feed the homeless, hug more, and love more. It makes a difference in how we spend and don't spend our dollars, how we vote, raise our voices, and what career we put our time into. We can consume less, donate money, drive less and divest from fossil fuels. It can be as simple as not buying into negative thoughts, and not buying things that are bad for you and the Earth. It feels good to regenerate our human nature, and our health.

Something we can all immediately do to build a better world, is to value the food we consume. All 7.7 billion of us (and counting) eat. What we ingest has a significant impact on our economy, environment, and health. Eating is a simple daily task which we can all wrap our mouths around to help heal and regenerate the world. If you are already doing this, you know what I mean.

> *The plain fact is that the planet does not need more successful people. But it does desperately need more peacemakers, healers, restorers, storytellers, and lovers of every kind. It needs people who live well in their places. It needs people of moral courage willing to join the fight to make the world habitable and humane. These qualities have little to do with success as we have defined it.*
> ~ David Orr

A Soulution-driven mindset fills you with nourishment and attracts positive people. The more fortified we are, the more energy we have to solve our problems and the closer we get to our dreams. Being balanced and happy allows us to live longer the way we wish to live. When we love ourselves and are happy with whom we are, we're more resistant to negative influences and can accept and love others more fully. We can detect unbalanced behavior in others, and feel what needs to get done, and know how we can best contribute. The more love and compassion we cultivate, the more we receive, and the less we need to wear armor and bear arms. Our differences align with others when we awaken to our own beauty and strengths. When we embrace each passing moment with clarity, we can stand rooted in our truth, with integrity. We are better people when we can accept others for the blessings they bring forth — without judgment — even if their values do not align fully with ours. Allow your loving voice to take precedence, and compassion and courage will guide you.

How quickly things have changed in my short life! I can only imagine what's possible over the next sixty years if we consider everything from the soil to our souls. With the COVID-19 crisis fresh in our minds, we have an incredible opportunity to get to the root cause and heal life-kind. When enough of us commit to living like the future matters, we will create the world we wish to inhabit. Like a tree in a healthy ecosystem, you can stand proud, plant seeds so that others can breathe, sit in the shade, and enjoy the future. Strength to grow lies within. When we stand our ground with the belief that we make a ubiquitous difference, we are not living in vain. We provide oxygen; we add to life and live like the future matters. I wish for all life to have the opportunity to interconnect and be part of the beautiful web of life.

Imagine a world without crises. A place where we all feel safe, have plenty to eat, breathe clean air, and drink clean water. A world where everyone has a place to sleep and feel loved, and have basic needs met. A place where we shared our abundance. Imagine if Earth was a place where all inhabitants, from the largest mammal to the tiniest microorganisms, were respected in the web of life. What does that look like to you?

The future matters to us, but it matters even more for our children, our grandchildren, and generations beyond. What seeds will you plant for them to harvest? Let's ask ourselves what messages, dreams, and values we are passing on to them, and what stories will you share? What gifts and burdens will they inherit? Let's share our stories and help others adapt, accept, and rejoice in the beauty we create! I ask you to make a promise to yourself that your purpose in life goes beyond judgment and fear.

Let us evolve, awaken, and continue to unfold the petals of our lives. Strive to be the best version of yourself and a bright light in the world so you can be part of the Soulutions. Remember, our life is the total of what we believe. The more energy we put into living like the future matters, the faster it will manifest. Encourage each other to do right in life. I hope you stay faithful to the blessings given to you and allow them to guide you to serve the greater good.

I'm honored to have shared a glimpse of my life with you and hope my words have inspired you to live like the future matters. As I move gracefully and graciously in this present cycle of my life, the future is bright.

What Now? What Next?

Why Retire When I Can Inspire

Now that I have finished this book, I'm in a place in my life I never imagined was possible. It has been a long and inspirational process, and with a sense of relief and accomplishment, I'm ready to move onto the next book.

Helping others continues to be the most rewarding part of my journey. Being the CEO of my life (Conscientious Enthusiastic Optimist) is a privilege and a joy, as is being a voice for Nature. As a seasoned businesswoman, Life and Business Coach, I am equipped with a toolbox of skills to offer others. Nature Therapy and the Culinary Healing Arts are part of my practice, which I use to guide clients to healing lifestyle changes: Eating healthy, Nature bathing, and living from the heart. Nature photography has become another form of meditation for me, enhancing my time with the natural world. I share this beautiful practice with my clients. I enjoy helping others find their inspiration, reclaim their health, and stick with the program. Sometimes it just takes a little help.

I help clients to compost what does not serve them and to nourish what does, so they can have a more fulfilling life. My mission is to guide them to clear energy blocks that they might not even know they have so they can break through stagnant barriers and manifest what they desire. The key is to learn how to balance our lifestyles with our livelihoods. With an appetite for self-improvement, clients have experienced life-changing results. I take pride in seeing results, knowing people are making a more significant difference in the world. The more people are aware that they can make decisions on behalf of future generations so the children of the future can enjoy what we have today, the better.

I believe you don't have to struggle, worry, or stress to build an amazing life and business. Yes, there is work to be done, but if you love what you are doing, it will not feel like work. If you keep doing the same things, you get the same results. Our lives are a product of our thoughts, words, and actions. We can transform our lives from the inside out and manifest the life of our dreams. It begins with our connection to the divine and our love within. It is vital to have faith and believe in your own abilities. It is equally important to have a clear vision of where you want to go, and who you choose to become. Mentors and coaches are essential when you choose to awaken to your highest potential. Building a culture of dignity within ourselves strengthens our core, so we can do more good in the world.

If you would like more information about my practice, and how I can help you realize your dreams, go to www.donnamaltz.com and schedule a complimentary consultation. At the very least, we will get to know one another a little better.

I look forward to sharing great things with you as we foster further Soulutions for a vibrant world. The trees seem to have many of the answers.

If a Tree Could Talk

When we plant trees, we plant the seed of peace and hope.
~ Professor Wangari Maathai

Humans cease to be without trees like me, so please listen up! My wisdom is embedded in the soul of the Earth and all of life's creations. I am a universe unto myself, full of wisdom and wonder, as are you.

When you breathe in oxygen, you exhale carbon dioxide (CO_2). Meanwhile, I, the selfless tree, absorbs all that nasty CO_2. I am kind enough and smart enough to exhale pure oxygen into the air, so you and all life may breathe. Unless you burn me down, cut me down, or I get struck by lightning or disease, I'll store this toxic carbon until I can no more. When I begin to decline, I will leach this stored carbon back into the atmosphere. Even as I decay, I bring balance through my death, as I transform into fertile, carbon-sequestering soil. I embody a precise system of yin and yang, giving and receiving.

Not only do I provide oxygen and sequester carbon, think of the shade, food, medicine, clothing, warmth, building materials, musical instruments, books, and toilet paper I provide you. Most humans, after they die, are planted in a box made from me. Some of us trees will sacrifice our lives to serve others, as do all creatures in Nature. But my question to you is this: Why take so many trees? Many things humans think they need are useless and disrespectful. If you take me for granted, please stop!

You may feel you cannot live without certain things that my tree friends and I provide for you. I understand. But there is so much more you can do. Consume less. Don't be wasteful. Contribute more. You can also adorn your yard with productive carbon-sequestering trees and witness how our blossoms and fruits attract pollinating bees and other useful insects. If you can, plant a garden, or better yet, a food forest. You will be healthier, and so will all of us. Hug a tree every day to remind yourself of our connection to each other.

Most importantly, humans must stop cutting down diversified, old-growth forests if they wish to survive on Mother Earth. You can live without one lung, but not two.

My tree friends and I are happier and healthier when surrounded by a mixture of dead, old, and young trees. We depend on intergenerational wisdom as do all the other sentient beings and plants; it keeps the Earth's kingdom in balance and resilient. Still, many of my forest kin are being displaced or are gone forever. This notion of disrespect pains me at my core. None of you appreciate being disregarded or disturbed, so you can understand our plight.

I am a living example of Nature's perfection, and like you, I am made up of self-regulating intuitive systems. My outer bark is my protector, my inner pipeline bark distributes nutrients, my cambium tissue produces new cells, my sapwood distributes water, and my heartwood supports my soul. My leaves carry out photosynthesis, making food for you and me. To be healthy, I must have stability, nutrients, sun, and rain. My roots are always reaching — soul-searching for answers. These functions are essential to all of us.

Often, you look at a tree, and all you see is the outer beauty: the leaves, the branches, the fruit or flowers. I hear you say, "Ah, that tree is gorgeous." You may take for granted my pleasant smells and satisfy yourself with my delicious fruit, without recognizing that the most significant energy to produce the essence of trees lies beneath my surface. It is the richness of the soil that nourishes me; these parts unseen make my bounty possible. Interconnected, we maintain a healthy balance.

My roots provide a sophisticated underground network that helps sustain life. In exchange, I depend on the miraculous insects, vital soil bacteria, and active fungi to fix nitrogen and fertilize my roots. Animals, from rodents to birds, spread my seeds. Their excrement is an essential part of both the living and dying process. It enhances the soil, and at the same time, it rots away carcasses and the forest's dead remains. All of us understand that we depend on one another for survival. It is our differences that make the difference. I cherish living and building respectful relationships. A strong foundation rooted in compassion and justice benefits future generations.

For as long as I can, I shall honorably welcome others to perch on my limbs. I will provide homes and nourishment for plants and animals to live in harmony and grow in symbiotic relationships. I will teach my young how to thrive in a healthy ecosystem. I know the way.

You see, we are all part of Nature. Let me show you how everything is interconnected, from the soil to your soul. There is much to learn from me. The kernel of life is held in my seeds. Allow me to inspire you to stand proudly, branch out, evolve, and grow in the right direction. I will teach you how to fearlessly reach for the sky, adapt to changing times and to live harmoniously with our beautiful Mother Earth. Sit, observe, and talk with me. I will offer you my fruit, my shade, and a limb to recline on. I will listen to you as you have listened to me now. Together, we can figure out how to live like the future matters and to be part of the Soul-ution.

"The forest is much more than what you see," says ecologist Suzanne Simard, professor and leader of The Mother Tree Project. Simard's work, and her discovery of the idea of a hub tree, or "Mother Tree," is vital to our understanding of forests. These "mother trees are the largest trees in forests that act as central hubs for vast below ground mycorrhizal networks. They support young trees or seedlings by infecting them with fungi and ferrying them the nutrients they need to grow." This discovery is fascinating, and I encourage each of you to go and watch her thought-provoking Ted Talk to get more in tune with the social lives of trees.

Acknowledgments and Gratitude

Writing this book has been an incredible journey. Having the vision to write a book is one thing, it is another to do it, and yes, for me, it was as hard as it sounds. The experience has been both challenging and rewarding and would never have happened without the love and support from so many that stood by me.

First, I wish to thank all the visionary leaders working to bring social and environmental justice to the forefront. And to the organic farmers, and stewards of the Earth that have nurtured me and others. The world is a better place because of you. What makes it even a better world are all you people who are sharing wisdom and are mentoring the next generation to do the same. Thank you for not retiring, and for inspiring.

Over the years, so many people generously gave of themselves, their time, their ideas, and their support. I am forever grateful for your trust in me, your faith in the process, and your commitment to stand by me through it all. You all mean the world to me and have taught me so much. Thank you for reminding me to stand by my words, laugh, dance, play, and enjoy my precious life. My heart is full thanks to you.

A special thank you goes out to James Mattie: My amazing hānai son, business partner, mentor, editor, webmaster, and social media guru. He has been with me almost every step of the way, and I could not have done this without him. He has touched my heart and strengthened my commitment to help build a more humane world. James is of the next generation working to bring social and environmental justice to the forefront. I am honored to work so closely with him. You're AWESOME!

I wish to express my love and gratitude to my other patient editors. They all have taught me to be a better writer and have encouraged me never to give up. All of my editors gave me the confidence to launch this body of work. Landry Fuller, who was my first editor, and one of my last editors, and a dear soul Sistah! Julie Clayton, for believing in me, and helping me get the structural editing in order. Carla Orellana, my dear friend, who read the entire MS out loud with me and helped me get rid of at least 100 *ings*. Sharon Reese, for proofreading and also reading the book out loud with me via the phone, making sure we had the Chicago Manual Style down. We even had fun doing it. Meg Schadee, for proofreading an earlier draft, and her faith in me and my work. And Janey Wing Kenyon, final proofreader and extraordinary friend: you ROCK my world! And finally, Evan Boyer, another hānai son, who helped me with the citation notes, edits, and fact-checked my endless hours of research. I am forever grateful to all these word mentors and conscious people!

I also wish to acknowledge the beta readers who gave of their time to read this body of work. Their valuable feedback helped me get over my insecurities and get through the final drafts: Suzanne Jennings, Jimmy Anderson, Aziza Mondi, Evelyn Tymrak, Priscilla Mendenhall, Judd Pillot, Angela Rosa, Jane Tollefsrud, Be Hambright, Alvita Soleil and my fantastic stepmom, Rosemary Goodman. You all have my endless love and respect.

Many thanks go to my friends, clients, and colleagues who generously offered feedback and encouragement along the way. And to the amazing artist, Kirsten English, who did the stunning art for the cover. Amanda Brannon for the magnificent Soil to Soul Logo, and for a meaningful friendship. My first hānai daughter, Jenny Rose, who honored me with the name Mama Donna. Her majestic Phoenix art soars above my bed, reminding me to rise each day with a fiery passion. Stained glass and musical artist, Janey Wing Kenyon who has been a dear friend since 1982, celebrated life with your original music in our café; your beautiful stained glass window will follow us to Hawaii. And to Calley O'Neill, girlfriend and fellow Earth mama, and Rama the Elephant for the magical art of The Sun Bear.

Special thanks to my favorite business mentor other than my fearless fantastic father, Bryan Zak, from The Alaska Small Business Development Center. And to the Homer Chamber of Commerce and the spirited Homer community, who supported our businesses and fed my soul. It has been an honor to feed you all these years.

Mahalo to my hānai family in Hawaii who enriches my life; especially Teliece Price, our home-keeper and vacation rental manager, and Emmanuel Volf, our gardener and handyman. They both help to keep my life in order and keep our home a sanctuary for me to pursue my writing. To each and every one who has ever helped us make our house a home. And to those of you who will help us in the future, I am forever grateful for your love and care.

Then there are the hundreds of people who have worked, *not for us, but with us,* in any of our numerous businesses. Thank you; you know who you are. Without you, I would not have such a good story to tell.

Also, a big shout-out to the millions of customers who have supported me. Whether you bought the first cucumber or loaf of bread, stayed at our vacation rental or trusted in me to marry you, I thank you. Or perhaps you purchased my first book: *Yummy Recipes ~Wilderness Wonders for Kids and Adults,* or drizzled AH!LASKA chocolate syrup on your ice cream. MAHALO.

To my extraordinary family, starting with the man of my dreams, *my lovey,* and patient husband, Kevin. I give my endless gratitude. Thank you for your generosity, moral encouragement, and willingness to provide me the time and space to learn to be a writer and stick by me, even pushing me to reach the finish line. Thank you for the many read-throughs, suggestions, memories, and support that have helped to strengthen my voice. Thank you to my precious son, Jazz, and my sweet and inspiring granddaughter, Freya, who give me the most reasons to live like the future matters. They are my darlings, and I am forever grateful for their inspiration, love, and light. My son lives like the future matters, and he is teaching this to his insightful, wise nature-loving daughter. I am honored to be his mother and Freya's Tutu (that's "grandma" in Hawaiian). I thank them for always reminding me of what is really important. Oh, I cannot forget my unconditionally loving animals, Chester and Sadie, who are with me twenty-four seven, and Buddha our annoying cat. And to all my animalizing friends over my lifetime, who have kept me calm, taken me on walks, and have never let me down.

And finally, to my most excellent teacher and mentor, our generous Earth and to all of Nature's inhabitants that make our lives possible. I am beyond grateful! MAHALO.

And my gratitude to YOU for taking the time to receive my words.

Honorary Soulutions and Soulutionists

Okay, here's the deal: Our world is faced with many challenges, but there are just as many Soulutions as there are problems. Below I've put together a list of some of my favorite which have helped to empower and inspire me. For the sake of this publication, I put the resources in order of the cycles where they are most relevant to my stories. Many of them cross over to the other cycles. There are also other Soulutions that can be found in the Notes section and throughout the book. I hope you will take the time to check them out and find new ones as you continue to live like the future matters.

If you go to my website, www.donnamaltz.com, you will find summaries and active links for all the Soulutions. All of them are star resources; celebrities in my eyes. If you know other people or organizations that you feel should be added, please email me at dm1aloha@gmail.com. United, we will have a more significant impact to help make our world a more just and habitable place to live. If you are part of one of these organizations, or a Soulutionist yourself, I wish to thank you for the vital work you do!

All are current sources as of January 2020.

Cycle 1: Seed to Sprout

- The World Health Organization
- Global Ecovillage Network
- Eco-Cycle Solutions Hub
- Blue Zones
- Transition Town

Cycle 2: Seeding

- Slow Food
- Food Politics
- Vani Hari- Food Babe
- EWG
- Center for Food Safety
- Food Tank
- Civil Eats
- The China Study
- River Keeper
- The Center for Ecoliteracy
- Richard Louv
- The Institute for Earth Education (IEE)
- John Hunter
- Ensia Media
- NatureBridge
- Landmark School
- Natasha Campbell-McBride

Cycle 3: Sapling

- Chef Anne
- Let's Move
- Edible School Yard
- Real Food Media
- Good Food Purchasing
- Stephen Ritz
- 16 School Garden Initiatives
- Growing Minds Growing Schools
- Urban School Food Alliance
- Protect Our Schools
- The Children's Music Network

Cycle 4: The Education of an Eco-Bohemian

- Eight Shields
- Wilderness Awareness School
- Permaculture Institute
- Hawaii Institute of Pacific Agriculture
- Expedition Education Institute
- Nature Lover Colleges
- Top-20 Coolest Schools
- The Foundation for Deep Ecology
- David Suzuki Foundation
- Satish Kumar
- WWOOF Program

- Vandana Shiva
- Kiss the Ground
- The Soil Association
- E.O. Wilson
- Center for Biological Diversity
- Regeneration International
- The Organic Consumers Association
- Heal Food Alliance
- The Worldwatch Institute
- Agroforestry
- IFOM Organic International
- Rodale Institute
- Food Systems Journal
- Rudolf Steiner Web
- Mother Earth News
- Utne Reader

Cycle 5: Budding

- Defenders of Wildlife
- Conservation International
- The Walden Woods
- Earth Guardians

Cycle 6: Rooting

- Fresh Sourdough Express
- Chefs Collaborative
- Truth Love and Clean Cutlery

Cycle 7: Branching Out

- Center for Alaska Coastal Studies
- Alaska Conservation Society
- Kachemak Bay Heritage Land Trust
- Cook Inlet Keepers

Cycle 8: Blooming

- SBA Small Business Administration
- Funders
- School of Natural Cookery
- Culinary Schools.org
- The Culinary Institute of America Sustainable Table
- Forks Over Knives
- Earth Talk
- Green America
- Large Hoop Greenhouses

Cycle 9: Fruiting

- WWF
- Ethical Traveler
- Impact Travel Alliance
- Green Global Travels
- Earth Stewards
- Food Is Power
- The Gift Economy
- Conscious Capitalism
- Humanity's Team
- Slow Money Woody Tash
- USDA Grants
- Wallace Center
- Food Shot Global

Cycle 10: Root Rot

- Dr. Mark Hyman
- Psychology of Eating
- Zen Recovery
- Arianna Huffington

Cycle 11: Restoration

- Body Ecology
- Brain HQ
- Bruce Lipton
- Institute for Integrative Nutrition

Cycle 12: Regeneration & Rebirth

- TED Talks
- Growing for Market
- Kohala Village Hub
- Real Leaders
- Woman Earth and Climate Action International

Cycle 13: Awakened

- Biomimicry
- Terra Genesis
- Right of Nature
- Stone Soup for the World
- Conservation international
- The Sierra Club
- Project Drawdown
- 350.0rg
- Union of Concerned Citizens Scientists
- Earth Island Institute

- Bioneers
- The Shift Network
- The Food Revolution
- Well.org
- The Aware Show
- Hay House Radio
- Bioneers Radio
- Brendon Burchard
- Marie Forleo's B-School
- Mrs. Green's World Gina Murphy-Darling
- Eco-Business Link
- Green Plus National Directory
- Earth Citizens
- Tree Sisters
- Green Belt Movement
- Stand for Trees

Suggested Reading:

- *The N.D.D. Book* – Dr. Spears
- *The Business & Biology of Raising Composting Worms* – Duncan Carver
- *The Ecology of Freedom* – Murray Bookchin
- *Small is Beautiful* – E. F. Schumacher
- *Be Here Now* – Ram Dass
- *Seven Arrows* – Hyemeyohsts Storm
- *Living the Good Life* – Helen and Scott Nearing
- *Good Morning Beautiful Business* – Judy Wicks
- *Diet for a Small Planet* – Frances Moore Lappé
- *Diet for A Hot Planet* – Anna Lappé
- *The Nourished Kitchen* – Jennifer McGruther
- *The Art of Fermentation* – Sandor Ellix Katz
- *Thrive* – Arianna Huffington
- *Kiss the Ground* – Terry Tamminen
- *Animal, Vegetable, Miracle* – Barbara Kingsolver
- *The Dragon Doesn't Live Here Anymore* – Alan Cohen
- *The Last Wilderness: Alaska's Rugged Coast* – Michael McBride
- *The Omnivore's Dilemma* – Michael Pollan
- *White Wash* – Carey Gillam
- *Drawdown: The Most Comprehensive Plan Ever Proposed to Reverse Global Warming* – Paul Hawken and Tom Steyer – All Paul's books are recommended
- *Deep Economy: The Wealth of Communities and the Durable Future* – Bill McKibben – All his books are recommended
- *Five Love Languages* – Dr. Gary Chapman
- Fox Fire Books: More awesome books to read can be found here
- Chelsea Green Publishing: has an array of other great books I suggest reading
- *The Sleep Revolution* – Arianna Huffington

Suggested Viewing:

- Food Inc. and other related films
- Conspiracy
- Super-Size Me
- Before the Flood
- From Paris to Pittsburgh
- Our Planet

Suggested Magazines and Online News Sources:

- Mother Jones
- Ensia
- Huffington Post
- The Guardian
- Resurgence Magazine
- Huffington Post
- National Public Radio (NPR)

Inspiring Musicians:

- Playing for Change
- Spinditty
- MindfulXpansion
- Nahko Medicine for the People
- Trevor Hall
- Amber Lily
- Paul Izak
- Drew Daniels Band
- O2 Change
- Kaahele
- Ydine
- Tiana Malone
- Mila Polevia
- Xiuhtezcatl Martinez

Cover Design Artist

Kirsten English

I have been creating nature-themed art as part of my daily meditations since 2012. I have been revitalized and inspired by Mother Nature & her steady current of growth and change. I appreciate our earth more than ever and like trying to show off its beauty. Mama Donna's work inspires me. I follow her on Twitter, and when I see one of her beautiful photos, I'm inspired to turn it into a work of art.

I've found a great balance that includes these very important, small, everyday activities: eating right, exercising the mind and body, and having a grateful attitude about all the ups & downs that come along with this life. In fact, none of this could be possible without those three.

I live on a little happy island in British Columbia. My community consists of fewer than 3000 people, mostly artists. The scenery here is endlessly inspiring.

One of my favorite things to do is to make art for other people. This usually involves getting inspired by a photo or portrait and turning it into its own spectacular work of art.

I really feel people should be celebrated more for all their hard work and accomplishments. So, I am celebrating them, and every day I get to be a part of this universe is my way of sharing love with them.

Notes

Listed below, by cycle, are the sources referenced in this body of work, along with others that have influenced me and my writing. You can see that I have done my homework. Each source has contributed to my work, and I have learned so much from all of them. Evan Boyer, my proofreader and citation manager, has helped me immensely, and I am forever grateful. He is a recent graduate from Claremont McKenna College, where he majored in International Relations. We dug deep into the resources and have ensured they are fact-checked and worthy of your time and consideration. The information you will find in each article, book, website, and peer-reviewed academic journal will dig deeper into the many topics I have touched on in this book. They will help you to better understand these significant issues and events that have impacted my life and the world around us. The website URLs are all current as of January 2020.

INTRODUCTION

"22 Dyslexic Billionaires." *Dyslexia.com*. http://dyslexia.com.au/dyslexic-billionaires/.

"Introduction to FTSG." *For The Seventh Generation*. https://www.fortheseventhgeneration.org/introduction-to-ftsg/.

Sofield, Deb. "The Only Person you are destined to become is the person you decide to be." *Vunela*, October 1, 2017. https://magazine.vunela.com/the-only-person-you-are-destined-to-become-is-the-person-you-decide-to-be-57be70cb5ae.

EVOLUTION I: THE BEGINNING CYCLE 1: SEED TO SPROUT

"1950's Cost of Living." *History of Humble Independent School District*. https://www.humbleisd.net/Page/101516.

"1950s Important News and Events, Key Technology Fashion and Popular Culture." *The People History*. http://www.thepeoplehistory.com/1950s.html.

Adams, James Truslow. *The Epic of America*. Boston: Little, Brown, and Company, 1931.

Amadeo, Kimberly. "Who Really Owns the Federal Reserve? Is It a Secret Conspiracy to Create a One World Bank?" https://www.thebalance.com/who-owns-the-federal-reserve-3305974.

"Anniversary of the Federal Highway Act of 1956." *Government Publishing Office*, June 29, 2016. https://www.govinfo.gov/features/federal-highway-act-1956.

Bellis, Mary. "Who Invented the Green Garbage Bag?" *ThoughtCo*, March 22, 2019. https://www.thoughtco.com/who-invented-the-green-garbage-bag-1991843.

Dietz, Robert. "Single-Family Home Size Increases at the Start of 2018." *National Association of Home Builders*, May 21, 2018. http://eyeonhousing.org/2018/05/single-family-home-size-increases-at-the-start-of-2018/.

Ehrlich, Paul R. *The Population Bomb*. Sierra Club/Ballantine Books, 1968.

Emerson, Ralph Waldo, Robert Ernest Spiller, Alfred R Ferguson, Joseph Slater, and Jean Ferguson Carr. *The Collected Works of Ralph Waldo Emerson*. Cambridge, Mass.: Belknap Press, 1971.

Fry, Richard. "Millennials Projected to Overtake Baby Boomers as America's Largest Generation." *Pew Research Center*, March 1, 2018. https://www.pewresearch.org/fact-tank/2018/03/01/millennials-overtake-baby-boomers/.

Gleisner, Tina. "Home Trends – What's Changed Since 1950?" *Home Tips for Women*. https://hometipsforwomen.com/home-trends-whats-changed-since-1950.

"Global Strategy: Breastfeeding Critical for Child Survival." *World Health Organization*. https://www.who.int/mediacentre/news/releases/2004/pr19/en/.

Harris, Alexander. "U.S. Self-Storage Industry Statistics." *SquareFoot. com*, March 11, 2019. https://www.sparefoot.com/self-storage/ news/1432-self-storage-industry-statistics/.

History.com Editors. "The Interstate Highway System." *History.com*, May 27, 2010. https://www.history.com/topics/us-states/interstate-highway-system.

Loughrey, Clarisse. "The John Lennon Quotes That Are Still Painfully Relevant in This Troubled World." *Independent*, December 8, 2016. https://www.independent.co.uk/ arts-entertainment/music/news/john-lennon-death-anniversary-mark-david-chap-man-the-beatles-yoko-ono-a6765266.html.

"Malvina Reynolds - Little Boxes (Weeds Theme Song) Full Version with Lyrics." YouTube Video. 2:11. "Souled Out," January 30, 2012. https://www.youtube.com/ watch?v=VUoXtddNPAM.

"Municipal Solid Waste." *United State Environmental Protection Agency*. Five. https:// archive.epa.gov/epawaste/nonhaz/municipal/web/html/.

"Panic of 1907: J.P. Morgan Saves the Day." *United States History*. https://www.u-s-his-tory.com/pages/h952.html.

Tan, Amy. *The Bonesetter's Daughter*. New York: G.P. Putnam's, 2001.

"The American Dream: What is the American Dream." *Library of Congress*. https:// www.loc.gov/teachers/classroommaterials/lessons/american-dream/students/the-dream.html.

"The Postwar Economy: 1945-1960." *American History: From Revolution to Reconstruction and Beyond*, Accessed June 15, 2019. http://www.let.rug.nl/usa/out-lines/history-2005/postwar-america/the-postwar-economy-1945-1960.php.

"The Ultimate Purpose of an Economy Is to Produce More Consumer Goods." *Quote Investigator*. https://quoteinvestigator.com/2014/08/23/more-goods/.

"Thomas Edison." *History.com*, November 9, 2009. https://www.history.com/topics/ inventions/thomas-edison.

"Time is Running Out for the World's Forests: Total Area is Shrinking by the Day." *Food and Agriculture Organization of the United Nations*. http://www.fao.org/ americas/noticias/ver/en/c/1144234/.

CYCLE 2: SEEDLING

Allen, James. *As A Man Thinketh*. New York: Project Gutenberg, 1902. https://www. gutenberg.org/files/4507/4507-h/4507-h.htm.

Altaf, Maham. "Teach How to Think, Not What to Think." *Daily Times*, October 26, 2018. https://dailytimes.com.pk/314636/teach-how-to-think-not-what-to-think/.

Barclay, Eliza. "Your Grandparents Spent More of Their Money on Food than You Do." *National Public Radio*, March 2, 2015. https://www.npr.org/sections/thesalt/2015/03/02/389578089/ your-grandparents-spent-more-of-their-money-on-food-than-you-do.

Bierce, Ambrose, David E. Schultz, and S. T. Joshi. *The Unabridged Devil's Dictionary*. Athens: University of Georgia Press, 2000.

Black, Nicole. "Justice Ruth Bader Ginsburg: A Dedicated Crusader for Women's Equality." *Above the Law*, April 5, 2018. https://abovethelaw.com/2018/04/ justice-ruth-bader-ginsburg-a-dedicated-crusader-for-womens-equality/.

Braverman, Beth. "The Older the Woman, the Wider the Gender Pay Gap." *The Ladders*, April 2, 2019. https://www.theladders.com/career-advice/ the-older-the-woman-the-wider-the-gender-pay-gap.

Byrd, Deborah. "This Date in Science: Sweden Goes First to Ban Aerosol Sprays." *EarthSky*, January 23, 2015. https://earthsky.org/earth/this-date-in-science-sweden-goes-first-to-ban-aerosol-sprays.

"CFCs." *The Ozone Hole*. http://www.theozonehole.com/cfc.htm.

Davis Dyslexia Association International. "Achievers with the Gift of Dyslexia." https://www.dyslexia.com/about-dyslexia/dyslexic-achievers/.

"Dr. Martin Luther King Jr. Quotations." *Lovearth Network*. https://www.drmartinlutherkingjr.com/mlkquotes.htm.

"Earthworm Functions." *The Earthworm Society of Britain*. https://www.earthwormsoc.org.uk/earthworm-functionshe.

"Eating Disorder Statistics." *National Eating Disorders Association*. https://www.nationaleatingdisorders.org/toolkit/parent-toolkit/statistics.

"Food Prices and Spending." *United States Department of Agriculture: Economic Research Service*, June 11, 2019. https://www.ers.usda.gov/data-products/ag-and-food-statistics-charting-the-essentials/food-prices-and-spending/.

"Great Education Quotes." *Teacher Certification*. http://www.teachercertification.org/a/great-education-quotes.html.

Hay, Louise L. *You Can Heal Your Life*. California: Hay House Inc,1984.

Heltne, Chris. "The Insect Apocalypse Is Here." *The Half-Earth Project*, November 28, 2018. https://www.half-earthproject.org/the-insect-apocalypse-is-here/.

Holland, Stephanie. "Marketing to Women Quick Facts." http://she-conomy.com/facts-on-women.

"Hudson River PCBs." *Riverkeeper*. https://www.riverkeeper.org/campaigns/stop-polluters/pcbs/.

Jeffrey, Terrence P. "1,773,000: Homeschooled Children Up 61.8% in 10 Years." *CNS News*, May 19, 2015. https://www.cnsnews.com/news/article/terence-p-jeffrey/1773000-homeschooled-children-618-10-years.

Kelly, Jack. "Martin Luther King Jr. Said, 'The Time Is Always Right to Do What Is Right': Here's How You Can Start." *Forbes*, January 18, 2019. https://www.forbes.com/sites/jackkelly/2019/01/18/martin-luther-king-jr-said-the-time-is-always-right-to-do-what-is-right-heres-how-you-can-start/#6493d28235d9.

Lyons, Libby. "Eating Disorders on the Rise All Around the World: An Overview." *Eating Disorder Hope*, June 10, 2019. https://www.eatingdisorderhope.com/blog/eating-disorders-world-overview.

Murray, Matt. "A Woman's Place Is in Her UNION; A Look at The Women of Steel." *NH Labor News*, March 13, 2013. https://nhlabornews.com/2013/03/a-womans-place-is-in-her-union-a-look-a-the-women-of-steel/.

Olivardia, Roberto. "The ADHD-Dyslexia Connection." *Attitude Magazine*, January 25, 2018. https://www.additudemag.com/adhd-dyslexia-connection/.

Ray, Brian D. "Homeschooling Growing: Multiple Data Points Show Increase 2012 to 2016 and Later." *National Home Research Education Institute*, April 20, 2018. https://www.nheri.org/homeschool-population-size-growing/.

Schlesinger, Bill. "The Decline and Fall of Insects." *Translational Ecology*, August 1, 2018. https://blogs.nicholas.duke.edu/citizenscientist/the-decline-and-fall-of-insects/.

Shaywitz, Sally E. *Overcoming Dyslexia: A New and Complete Science-Based Program for Reading Problems at Any Level*. 1st ed. New York: A.A. Knopf, 2003.

Steinmetz, Katy. "How Ruth Bader Ginsburg Found Her Voice: A New Study of the Supreme Court Justice's Accent Says Something About the

Way We All Talk." *Time*, Accessed August 1, 2019. https://time.com/
ruth-bader-ginsburg-supreme-court/.

Teen Kids News. "How Jane Goodall Revolutionized Our Knowledge of Chimpanzee
Behavior." *Teen Kids News*, May 23, 2019. https://teenkidsnews.com/tkn-news/
careers/how-jane-goodall-revolutionized-our-knowledge-of-chimpanzee-behavior/.

"The Cost of Living During the Cold War." *Living History Farm.* https://livinghistory-
farm.org/farminginthe50s/money_01.html.

"The Ozone Layer." *UCAR Center for Science Education.* 2018. https://scied.ucar.edu/
ozone-layer.

Vagins, Deborah J. "The Simple Truth about the Gender Pay Gap." *American
Association of University Women.* https://www.aauw.org/research/
the-simple-truth-about-the-gender-pay-gap/.

Weller, Chris. "Americans are Rejecting the 'Homeschool Myth' — and Experts Say the
Misunderstood Education Might Be Better than Public or Charter
Schools." *Business Insider*, January 23, 2017. https://www.businessinsider.com/
homeschooing-more-popular-than-ever-2017-1.

CYCLE 3: SAPLING

"11 Facts About Food Deserts." *DoSomething.* https://www.dosomething.org/us/
facts/11-facts-about-food-deserts.

"28 Inspiring Urban Agriculture Projects." *Foodtank.* https://foodtank.com/
news/2015/07/urban-farms-and-gardens-are-feeding-cities-around-the-world/.

Barker, Vicki. "The Real Story Behind Britain's Rock 'N' Roll Pirates." *NPR*, November
13, 2009. https://www.npr.org/templates/story/story.php?storyId=120358447.

"Betty Ford's Battle with Breast Cancer." *PBS*, July 29, 2014. http://cancerfilms.org/
blog/betty-fords-battle-with-breast-cancer/.

"Childhood Obesity Causes & Consequences." *Center for Disease Control and
Prevention.* https://www.cdc.gov/obesity/childhood/causes.html.

"Childhood Obesity Facts." *Center for Disease Control and Prevention.* https://www.cdc.
gov/healthyschools/obesity/facts.htm.

"Eating Unhealthy Food." *BreastCancer.org.* https://www.breastcancer.org/risk/factors/
unhealthy_food.

Epicurious. "Alice Waters on Simple Food, the Future of Chez Panisse, and Dinner
With Jay Z." *HuffPost*, December 7, 2017. https://www.huffpost.com/entry/
alice-waters-on-simple-fo_b_4564038.

Funk, Kristi. "Debunking Breast Cancer Myths: The Truth About Genes, Gender, and
Destiny." *KevinMD.com*, April 24, 2018. https://www.kevinmd.com/blog/2018/04/
debunking-breast-cancer-myths-the-truth-about-genes-gender-and-destiny.html.

Gonsalves, Gabriel. "The Courage to Become Who You Really Are."
Gabriel Gonsalves, June 11, 2015. https://www.gabrielgonsalves.com/
the-courage-to-become-who-you-really-are/.

Johnson, Jackie. "The Interesting Story Behind Victory Gardens." *Herbal Academy*, July
17, 2017. https://theherbalacademy.com/victory-gardens/.

Leach, Nicola. "Facts about Cycling." *Alliance Work Partners*, May 12, 2017. https://
www.awpnow.com/main/2017/05/12/fun-fact-friday-46/.

Mørch, Lina S., Charlotte W. Skovlund, Philip C. Hannaford, Lisa Iversen,
Shona Fielding, and Øjvind Lidegaard. "Contemporary Hormonal
Contraception and the Risk of Breast Cancer." *New England Journal of
Medicine*, December 7, 2017. https://www.nejm.org/doi/full/10.1056/
NEJMoa1700732?query=featured_home#article_citing_articles.

Rabinowitz, Adam N. "Crime and Supermarket Locations: Implications for Food Access." *University of Connecticut Graduate School*, August 22, 2014. https://pdfs. semanticscholar.org/3a87/2322c47245a8d9260a6f4bdbc15f7473f80c.pdf.

"Should Military Recruiters Be Allowed in High Schools?" *Scholastic.* http://www.scholastic.com/browse/article.jsp?id=10852.

"Slow Food Movement: Our History." *Slow Food* https://www.slowfood.com/about-us/our-history/.

"Study Shows that Fast Food Advertising Penetrates Schools." *American Heart Association*, January 13, 2014. https://newsarchive.heart.org/study-shows-that-fast-food-advertising-penetrates-schools/

Terry-McElrath, Yvonne M., Lindsey Turner, Anna Sandoval, Lloyd D. Johnston, and Frank J. Chaloupka. "Commercialism in US Elementary and Secondary School Nutrition Environments: Trends From 2007 to 2012." *JAMA Pediatrics.* 2014;168(3):234–242. https://jamanetwork.com/journals/jamapediatrics/fullarticle/1812294.

"The State of Consumption Today." *World Watch Institute.* Accessed 7/25/19. http://www.worldwatch.org/node/810.

Thompson, Kirsten M. J. "A Brief History of Birth Control in the U.S." *Our Bodies Our Selves*, December 14, 2013. https://www.ourbodiesourselves.org/book-excerpts/health-article/a-brief-history-of-birth-control/.

Tucker, Erika. "Top 10 Memorable David Suzuki Quotes." *Global News*, April 13, 2012. https://globalnews.ca/news/233616/top-10-memorable-david-suzuki-quotes/.

United States Department of Agriculture Economic Research Service. "Access to Affordable and Nutritious Food: Measuring and Understanding Food Deserts and Their Consequences." *United States Department of Agriculture*, 2009. https://www.ers.usda.gov/webdocs/publications/42711/12716_ap036_1_.pdf.

Voices for Healthy Kids. "Food Companies Marketing to Kids." *ScienceDaily.* www.sciencedaily.com/releases/2014/01/140113163658.htm.

DIGGING DEEPER I

Cote, Jacqueline Burt. "20 River Phoenix Quotes on the 20th Anniversary of His Death." *CafeMom*, October 31, 2013. https://thestir.cafemom.com/celebrities/163385/20_river_phoenix_quotes_on.

Ganzel, Bill and Claudia Reinhardt. "Postwar Fertilizer Explodes." *Living History Farm.* https://livinghistoryfarm.org/farminginthe40s/crops_04.html.

History.com Editors. "The 1950s." *History.com*, June 17, 2010. https://www.history.com/topics/cold-war/1950s.

"How Much of the World's Energy Does the United States Use?" *American Geosciences Institute.* https://www.americangeosciences.org/critical-issues/faq/how-much-worlds-energy-does-united-states-use.

"Nutrient Pollution: The Issue." *United States Environmental Protection Agency.* https://www.epa.gov/nutrientpollution/issue.

Ogburn, Stephanie. "The Dark Side of Nitrogen." *Grist*, February 5, 2010. https://grist.org/article/2009-11-11-the-dark-side-of-nitrogen/.

Warhol, Andy. *The Philosophy of Andy Warhol: From a to B and Back Again.* Harbrace Paperbound Library, Hpl 75. New York: Harcourt, 1977.

"What is the United States' Share of World Energy Consumption?" *U.S Energy Information Administration.* https://www.eia.gov/tools/faqs/faq.php?id=87&t=1.

EVOLUTION II: BRANCHING OUT
CYCLE 4: OUT ON A LIMB

"1970's Food and Groceries Prices." *People's History*. http://www.thepeoplehistory.com/70sfood.html.

"1978: Economy/Prices." *1970s Flashback*. http://www.1970sflashback.com/1978/Economy.asp.

"A Guide to The Three Sisters Diorama." *New York State Museum*. http://exhibitions.nysm.nysed.gov/iroquoisvillage/sistersone.html.

"Aldo Leopold Quotes from Green Fire." *The Aldo Leopold Foundation*. https://www.aldoleopold.org/teach-learn/green-fire-film/leopold-quotes/.

Authority Nutrition. "Today's Wheat: Old Diet Staple Turned Modern Health Nightmare." *Care2*, February 8, 2014. https://www.care2.com/greenliving/modern-wheat-old-diet-staple-turned-modern-health-nightmare.html.

Bookchin, Murray. *The Ecology of Freedom: The Emergence and Dissolution of Hierarchy*. Palo Alto: Cheshire Books, 1982.

Bruner, Jerome. *On Knowing: Essays for the Left Hand*. Cambridge, MA: Belknap Press of Harvard University Press. 1979. (Original work published in 1962).

"Can Organic Farming Feed Us All?" *World Watch Institute*, June 2006. http://www.worldwatch.org/node/4060.

"Can the Greatness of a Nation…" *PETA*. https://www.peta.org/features/gandhi/.

Carrington, Damian. "What is Biodiversity and Why Does It Matter to Us?" *The Guardian*, March 12, 2018. https://www.theguardian.com/news/2018/mar/12/what-is-biodiversity-and-why-does-it-matter-to-us.

Carson, Rachel. *Silent Spring*. Boston: Houghton Mifflin Publishing, 1962.

"Celiac Disease, Non-Celiac Gluten Sensitivity, and Food Allergy: How Are They Different?" *American Academy of Allergy, Asthma, and Immunology*. https://www.aaaai.org/conditions-and-treatments/library/allergy-library/celiac-disease.

Cooper, Bob. "Small farmers from around the world learn how they can grow far more food." https://www.pri.org/stories/2016-08-24/small-farmers-around-world-learn-how-they-can-grow-far-more-food.

Drengson, Alan. "Some Thought on the Deep Ecology Movement." *Foundation for Deep Ecology*. http://www.deepecology.org/deepecology.htm.

"Energy Crisis." National Museum of American History. https://americanhistory.si.edu/american-enterprise-exhibition/consumer-era/energy-crisis.

Foundation for Deep Ecology. http://www.deepecology.org/.

Gunnars, Kris. "Why Modern Wheat is Worse Than Older Wheat." *Expand Your Consciousness*, July 10, 2017. http://expand-your-consciousness.com/modern-wheat-worse-older-wheat/.

Henderson, Diedtra. "A Natural Eye -- Wildlife Photographer Frans Lanting Tries to Adapt to the World of His Subjects." *The Seattle Times*, February 22, 1999. http://community.seattletimes.nwsource.com/archive/?date=19990222&slug=2945591.

Henderson, Elizabeth. "Why Sustainable Agriculture Should Support a Green New Deal." *Independent Science*, January 14, 2019. https://www.independentsciencenews.org/health/why-sustainable-agriculture-should-support-a-green-new-deal/.

"History: Ideas and Action." *Foundation for Deep Ecology*. http://www.deepecology.org/history.htm.

Inside Garden City Neighbor. ""How Can a Nation be Called Great if Its Bread Tastes Like Kleenex?" Julia Child." *Patch.com*, February 10, 2014. https://patch.com/

new-york/gardencity/how-can-a-nation-be-called-
great-if-its-bread-tastes-like-kleenex-julia-child.

Jacobs, Meg. "America's Never-Ending Oil Consumption." *The Atlantic*,
May 15, 2016. https://www.theatlantic.com/politics/archive/2016/05/
american-oil-consumption/482532/.

Lee, Marc. "Moon Landing Anniversary: One Small Step 40 Years On." *The Telegraph*,
July 7, 2009. https://www.telegraph.co.uk/news/science/space/5711257/Moon-
landing-anniversary-one-small-step-40-years-on.html.

Lindsey, Rebecca. "Climate Change: Atmospheric Carbon Dioxide." *NOAA Climate.
gov*, August 1, 2018. https://www.climate.gov/news-features/understanding-climate/
climate-change-atmospheric-carbon-dioxide.

"Losing Ground: Re-thinking Soil As a Renewal Resource." *FEWResources.org*. https://
www.fewresources.org/soil-science-and-society-were-running-out-of-dirt.html.

Lowe, Lindsay. "13 Beautiful Nature Quotes in Honor of David Attenborough's
Birthday." *Parade* May 8, 2019. https://parade.com/879373/lindsaylowe/
13-beautiful-nature-quotes/.

Malik, Arshad. "Gluten Sensitivity - Symptoms and Diet | Arshad Malik, MD." https://
www.arshadmalikmd.com/blog/post/is-gluten-sensitivity-real-or-just-a-fad.html.

"Marie Forleo." https://www.marieforleo.com/.

Marx, Karl. *Economic and Philosophic Manuscripts of 1844*. Moscow: Progress Publishers,
1959.

Mattern, Jessica Leigh. "30 Camping Quotes That'll Get You Pumped for Your Next
Adventure." *Country Living*, May 1, 2019. https://www.countryliving.com/life/
travel/g20916937/camping-quotes/?slide=4.

Mayo Clinic. "Celiac Disease Four Times More Common Than In 1950s." *ScienceDaily*.
July 2, 2009. www.sciencedaily.com/releases/2009/07/090701082911.htm (accessed
August 6, 2019).

Nearing, Helen, and Scott Nearing. *The Good Life: Helen and Scott Nearing's Sixty Years
of Self-Sufficient Living*. 1st Schocken Books ed. New York: Schocken Books, 1989.

Nestle, Marion. "Gluten Intolerance Becoming More Commonplace." *San Francisco
Gate*, May 31, 2009. https://www.sfgate.com/food/article/Gluten-intolerance-
becoming-more-commonplace-3296755.php.

Nield, David. "There's Another Huge Plastic Garbage Patch in The Pacific
Ocean." *Science Alert*, July 25, 2017. https://www.sciencealert.com/
scientists-just-found-another-huge-plastic-garbage-patch-in-the-pacific-ocean.

Norsigian, Judy. *Our Bodies Ourselves*. New York: Simon & Schuster, 1970.

"Oren Lyons." *Americans Who Tell the Truth*. https://www.americanswhotellthetruth.
org/portraits/oren-lyons.

Paddock, Catherine. "Soil Bacteria Work In Similar Way To Antidepressants." *Medical
News Today*, April 2, 2007. https://www.medicalnewstoday.com/articles/66840.
php.

"Purchase of Alaska, 1867." *Office of the Historian*. https://history.state.gov/
milestones/1866-1898/alaska-purchase.

"Ratification Info State by State." *Equal Rights Amendment*. https://www.equal-
rightsamendment.org/era-ratification-map.

Rogosa, Eli. *Restoring Heritage Grains: The Culture, Biodiversity, Resilience, and Cuisine
of Ancient Wheats*. Chelsea Green Publishing, 2016.

Schafer, Carol. "The World Has Only 60 Years of Topsoil Left, Experts Say."
Planet Experts, December 10, 2014. http://www.planetexperts.com/
world-60-years-topsoil-left-experts-say/.

Schumacher, Ernest Friedrich. *Small Is Beautiful: Economics as if People Mattered*. Blond and Briggs, 1973.

Silva, Jason. "Why We Could All Use a Heavy Dose of Techno-Optimism." *Vanity Fair*, May 7, 2010. https://www.vanityfair.com/news/2010/05/why-we-could-all-use-a-heavy-does-of-techno-optimism.

Smith, Carol. "Fifty-Three-Year-Old Quote Still Rings True Today." *Corn South*, 2009. https://cornsouth.com/2009/october-2009/fifty-three-year-old-quote-still-rings-true-today/.

"Soil Erosion and Degradation." *WorldWildlife.org*. https://www.worldwildlife.org/threats/soil-erosion-and-degradation.

"Soil Formation: How Long Does It Take to Form?" *Eniscuala*. http://www.eniscuola.net/en/argomento/soil/soil-formation/how-long-does-it-take-to-form/.

"The Biodynamic French Intensive System: Techniques Employed by Alan Chadwick." *Alan Chadwick: A Gardener of Souls*. http://www.alan-chadwick.org/html%20pages/techniques.html.

"The Elements of Biodiversity: What and Where It Is." *Center for Biological Diversity*. https://www.biologicaldiversity.org/programs/biodiversity/elements_of_biodiversity/.

Toole, Michael. "Modern Wheat - Old Diet Staple Turned into a Modern Health Nightmare." http://www.namaskarhealing.com/files/namaskarhealing/files/articles/Modern_Wheat__A_Health_Nightmare.pdf.

Townsend, Janet. "The Last Tree." *New York Times: Archives*, August 17, 1995. https://www.nytimes.com/1995/08/17/opinion/l-the-last-tree-420195.html.

Vighi, G, F Marcucci, L Sensi, G Di Cara, and F Frati. "Allergy and the Gastrointestinal System." September 2008. https://www.ncbi.nlm.nih.gov/pmc/articles/PMC2515351/.

"What is Biodynamics?" *Biodynamics Association*. https://www.biodynamics.com/what-is-biodynamics.

"What Is WWOOF?" *Federation of WWOOF Organization*. https://wwoof.net/what-is-wwoof/.

"Who was Rudolf Steiner?" *Biodynamics Association*. https://www.biodynamics.com/steiner.html.

Wilder, Bill. "When the Student is Ready, the Teacher Will Appear." *Industry Weekly*, October 31, 2013. https://www.industryweek.com/blog/when-student-ready-teacher-will-appear.

DIGGING DEEPER II

"Bottled Water Facts." *Ban the Bottle*. https://www.banthebottle.net/bottled-water-facts/.

Cowen, Edward. "Carter Gasoline Plan Could Increase Taxes 50 Cents in 10 Years." *New York Times*, April 14, 1977. https://www.nytimes.com/1977/04/14/archives/carter-gasoline-plan-could-increase-taxes-50-cents-in-10-years-help.html.

Frieden, Zach. "Student Loan Debt Statistics In 2018: A $1.5 Trillion Crisis." *Forbes*, June 13, 2018. https://www.forbes.com/sites/zackfriedman/2018/06/13/student-loan-debt-statistics-2018/#50ad8b327310.

"If You Are Planning for a Year, Sow Rice." *Winkler Partners*, October 28, 2014. http://www.winklerpartners.com/?p=5383.

Jamrisko, Michelle, and Ilan Kolet. "College Costs Surge 500% in U.S. Since 1985: Chart of the Day." *Bloomberg*, August 26, 2013. https://www.bloomberg.com/news/articles/2013-08-26/college-costs-surge-500-in-u-s-since-1985-chart-of-the-day.

Lutz, Ashley. "These 6 Corporations Control 90% Of the Media in America." *Business Insider*, June 14, 2012. https://www.businessinsider.com/these-6-corporations-control-90-of-the-media-in-america-2012-6.

"Percentage of Undergraduates Receiving Financial Aid, By Type and Source of Aid and Selected Student Characteristics: 2011-12." *National Center for Education Statistics*. https://nces.ed.gov/programs/digest/d15/tables/dt15_331.10.asp.

"Scholarships and Grants for College Students." *Debt.org*. https://www.debt.org/students/scholarships-and-grants/.

"Students and Debt." *Debt.org*. https://www.debt.org/students/.

"The Story of Plastic: Learn." https://www.storyofplastic.org/learn.

"The Story of Plastic: Watch." https://www.storyofplastic.org/watch.

EVOLUTION III: GROWTH AND DEVELOPMENT
CYCLE 5: GETTING GROUNDED

"Alaska Inspiration Guide." *Alaska Wildland Adventures*. https://www.alaskawildland.com/reservations/2019%20AWA%20Inspiration%20Guide.pdf.

America's Story from America's Library. "Purchase of Alaska: March 30, 1867." *America's Library*. http://www.americaslibrary.gov/jb/recon/jb_recon_alaska_1.html.

Carter, Laura Lee. "Midlife: Finding the Courage to Release What is Familiar and Seemingly Secure…" *Adventuresofthenewoldfarts*, March 11, 2016. https://adventuresofthenewoldfarts.com/2016/03/11/find-the-power-to-release-a-bit-of-familiar-today/.

"Lao Tzu." *BBC*. http://www.bbc.co.uk/worldservice/learningenglish/movingwords/shortlist/laotzu.shtml.

London, Jack. *Jack London: Novels, Short Stories, Poems, Plays, Memoirs & Essays*. Musaicum Publishers, 2017.

"Nina Simons." *DoOneThing.org*. http://www.doonething.org/heroes/pages-s/simons-quotes.htm.

"Population in the United States: Alaska." *U.S Census* https://www.google.com/publicdata/explore?ds=kf7tgg1uo9ude_&met_y=population&idim=state:02:56:15&hl=en&dl=en.

Shreckengast, Brian. "How Big Is Alaska?" *Alaska Business*, April 4, 2016. https://www.akbizmag.com/industry/education/how-big-is-alaska/.

"The Last Homesteader." *National Park Service*. https://www.nps.gov/home/learn/historyculture/lasthomesteader.htm.

CYCLE 6: BUDDING

Hardy, Benjamin. "How to Become More Intelligent (According to Einstein)." *Mission.org*, July 19, 2018. https://medium.com/the-mission/if-youre-not-changing-as-a-person-then-you-re-not-intelligent-according-to-einstein-73ba950d99d5.

Rodenhizer, Samuel. "Quotation Celebration: The Measure of Intelligence is the Ability to Change." *Wordpress*, January 15, 2018. https://quotationcelebration.wordpress.com/2018/01/15/the-measure-of-intelligence-is-the-ability-to-change-albert-einstein/.

"Symbiotic Relationships: Mutualism, Commensalism & Parasitism." *Study.com*. https://study.com/academy/lesson/symbiotic-relationships-mutualism-commensalism-amensalism.html.

Ziglar, Zig. "Foundation Stones." *Ziglar.com*. https://www.ziglar.com/quotes/foundation-stones/.

CYCLE 7: TAKING ROOT

"7 Reasons I Eat Sourdough Bread." *Cultured Food Life.* https://www.culturedfoodlife. com/7-reasons-i-eat-sourdough-bread/.

"At What Age Is the Brain Fully Developed?" *Mental Health Daily.* https://mental-healthdaily.com/2015/02/18/at-what-age-is-the-brain-fully-developed/.

Kottasová, Ivana. "Would You Pay a Tax on Coffee Cups?" *CNN Money*, January 5, 2018. https://money.cnn.com/2018/01/05/news/coffee-cup-tax-latte-levy/index. html.

Loristillman. "The Role of Heart in Business." *Wordpress.* February 4, 2013. https:// loristillman.wordpress.com/2013/02/04/the-role-of-heart-in-business/.

McCallum, Tom. "Writing I love – Alan Watts and the meaning of life." *Tom McCallum*, January 23, 2018. https://tommccallum.com/2018/01/23/ writing-i-love-alan-watts-and-the-meaning-of-life/.

Miles, Michael. "Marcus Aurelius' Six Timeless Observations on Life." *Pick the Brain*, August 8, 2018. https://www.pickthebrain.com/blog/marcus-aurelius/.

Pollan, Michael. *The Omnivore's Dilemma: A Natural History of Four Meals.* New York: Penguin Press, 2006.

Rand, Ayn. *Atlas Shrugged.* New York: Plume, 1999.

"Responsible Appliance Disposal: Disposing of Appliances Responsibly." *United States Environmental Protection Agency.* https://19january2017snapshot.epa.gov/rad/dispos-ing-appliances-responsibly .html.

Sustainability @ BU. "Join the September Challenge." *Boston University Sustainability.* https://www.bu.edu/sustainability/join-the-september-challenge/.

Tardif, Rachel. "The Facts About Refrigerator Recycling." *Recycle Nation*, March 12, 2013. https://recyclenation.com/2013/03/facts-refrigerator-recycling/.

This Old House. "How Long Things Last." https://www.thisoldhouse.com/ideas/ how-long-things-last.

Women in the World Staff. "Jane Goodall Responds to Ivanka Trump's Use of Her Quote in New Book." *Women in the World*, May 3, 2017. https://womenintheworld. com/2017/05/03/jane-goodall-responds-to-ivanka-trumps-use-of-her-quote-in-new-book/.

Wuling, Shi. *Path to Peace.* Amitabha Publications, 2006.

CYCLE 8: BLOOMING

Berry, Wendall. *The Gift of Good Land: Further Essays Cultural and Agricultural.* San Francisco: North Point Press, 1981.

"Factory Farms." *ASPCA.* https://www.aspca.org/animal-cruelty/farm-animal-welfare.

Garfield, Leanna. "10 Up-and-Coming Healthy Fast Food Chains that Should Scare McDonald's." *Business Insider*, February 19, 2018. https://www.businessinsider. com/new-healthy-fast-food-chains-better-than-mcdonalds-2017-2/.

Gillam, Carey. "Whitewash: The Story of a Weed Killer, Cancer, and the Corruption of Science." https://careygillam.com/book.

King, Debbi. "10 Tony Robbins Quotes About Success and Motivation." *Everyday Power*, January 9, 2019. https://everydaypower.com/tony-robbins-quotes-3/.

Nordstrom, Todd. "7 Quotes About Gratitude That Will Inspire You This Thanksgiving." *Inc*, November 20, 2018. https://www.inc.com/todd-nordstrom/7-quotes-about-gratitude-that-will-inspire-you-this-thanksgiving.html.

O'Brien, Robyn. "How Coke & Pepsi Could Save Us from High Fructose Corn Syrup." *Huffpost*, September 7, 2010. https://www.huffpost.com/entry/ why-coke-and-pepsi-should_b_707250?guccounter=1.

Paul, Katherine. "From 'Sea to Shining Sea,' Industrial Ag Fouls America's Waterways." *EcoWatch*, March 22, 2018. https://www.ecowatch.com/industrial-agriculture-water-pollution-2551396477.html.

Rosenburg, Martha. "What Big Meat Doesn't Want You to Know about Slaughterhouses." *Organic Consumers Association*, May 15, 2018. https://www.organicconsumers.org/blog/what-big-meat-doesnt-want-you-know-about-slaughterhouses.

Shahbandeh, M. "Percentage of Genetically Modified Crops in the U.S. in 1997 and 2018, by Type (as Percent of Total Acreage)." *Statista*, April 24, 2019. https://www.statista.com/statistics/217108/level-of-genetically-modified-crops-in-the-us/.

Shanker, Deena. "There Could be Ketamine in Your 'Natural' Chicken." *Bloomberg*, June 22, 2017. https://www.bloomberg.com/news/articles/2017-06-22/there-could-be-ketamine-in-your-natural-chicken.

"Sugary Drinks." *Harvard T. H. Chan School of Public Health*. https://www.hsph.harvard.edu/nutritionsource/healthy-drinks/sugary-drinks/.

"Tony Robbins - It's in the Moments of Decision that Your Destiny Is Shaped." YouTube Video. 12:25. "Duc H. Nguyen," March 29, 2015. https://www.youtube.com/watch?v=_ZqyoXudii4.

Viegas, Susana, Vanessa Mateus Faísca, Hermínia Brites Dias, Anália Clérigo, Elisabete Carolino, and Carla Viegas. "Occupational Exposure to Poultry Dust and Effects on the Respiratory System in Workers." *J Toxicol Environ Health A*. 2013;76(4-5):230-9.

"What is a GMO?" *Non-GMO Project*. https://www.nongmoproject.org/gmo-facts/what-is-gmo/.

Wilson, Tracy V. "How Fast Food Works." *HowStuffWorks.com*, August 22, 2006. https://science.howstuffworks.com/innovation/edible-innovations/fast-food.htm.

DIGGING DEEPER III

"About the Rainforest: Rainforest Facts." *Raintree*. http://www.rain-tree.com/facts.htm.

"Agriculture's Greenhouse Gas Emissions on the Rise." *Food and Agriculture Organization of the United Nations*, April 11, 2014. http://www.fao.org/news/story/en/item/216137/icode/.

Bohrer, Becky. "Embattled Alaska Governor Scales Back Budget Cuts, Approves Oil-Wealth Dividend of $1,600." *NBC News*, August 20, 2019. https://www.nbcnews.com/news/us-news/embattled-alaska-governor-scales-back-budget-cuts-approves-oil-wealth-n1044446.

Brooks, James. "Dunleavy Vetoes $444 Million from Operating Budget." *Anchorage Daily News*, July 11, 2019. https://www.adn.com/politics/alaska-legislature/2019/06/28/gov-mike-dunleavy-vetoes-444-million-from-alaska-state-operating-budget/.

"Chernobyl Accident 1989." *World-Nuclear.org*. https://www.world-nuclear.org/information-library/safety-and-security/safety-of-plants/chernobyl-accident.aspx.

"Facts and Figures: State Revenue." *Alaska Oil and Gas Association*. https://www.aoga.org/facts-and-figures/state-revenue.

"Food and Farming: Conserving Forests and Improving Livelihoods." *Rainforest Alliance*. https://www.rainforest-alliance.org/issues/food.

"Fueling Plastics: Fossils, Plastics, & Petrochemical Feedstocks." *Center for International Environmental Law*. http://www.ciel.org/wp-content/uploads/2017/09/Fueling-Plastics-Fossils-Plastics-Petrochemical-Feedstocks.pdf.

"Fueling Plastics: New Research Details Fossil Fuel Role in Plastics Proliferation." *Center for International Environmental Law.* September 21, 2017. https://www.ciel. org/news/fueling-plastics/.

"Fueling Plastics: Series Examines Deep Linkages Between the Fossil Fuels and Plastics Industries, and the Products They Produce." *Center for International Environmental Law.* https://www.ciel.org/reports/fuelingplastics/.

"Gas & Oil Prices - A Chronology." *NPR.* https://www.npr.org/news/specials/oil/gas-prices.chronology.html.

Harvey, Fiona. "Top Global Banks Still Lend Billions to Extract Fossil Fuels." *The Guardian*, June 21, 2017. https://www.theguardian.com/environment/2017/jun/21/top-global-banks-still-lend-billions-extract-fossil-fuels.

Hershey Jr., Robert D. "The Dark Side of the Oil Glut." March 21, 1982. https://www.nytimes.com/1982/03/21/business/the-dark-side-of-the-oil-glut.html.

"Historical Timeline." *Alaska Department of Revenue: Permanent Fund Dividend Division.* https://pfd.alaska.gov/Division-Info/Historical-Timeline.

"History of the Alaska Permanent Fund." *Alaska Permanent Fund Corporation.* https://apfc.org/who-we-are/history-of-the-alaska-permanent-fund/.

Kesslen, Ben. "Many Alaskans Mount Effort to Recall Governor as Huge Budget Cuts Threaten Education, Medicaid." *NBC News*, August 12, 2019. https://www.nbcnews.com/news/us-news/alaskans-mount-effort-recall-governor-huge-budget-cuts-threaten-education-n1040951.

KTOO News. "Watch: Dunleavy Signs Off on $1,600 PFD, Agrees to Restore Funds to Multiple Budget Items." *Alaska Public Media.* August 19, 2019. https://www.alaska-public.org/2019/08/19/watch-dunleavy-to-announce-decisions-on-pfd-budget-vetoes/.

Nikkhah, Roya. "Penelope Keith Interview: Art Needs to Be Allowed to Grow." *Telegraph*, November 14, 2010. https://www.telegraph.co.uk/culture/8131158/Penelope-Keith-interview-Art-needs-to-be-allowed-to-grow.html.

Potts, Cliff. *Wealth, Women and War.* Word Techs, 2008.

Sneed, Annie. "Wait—The Ozone Layer Is Still Declining?" *Scientific America*, February 6, 2018. https://www.scientificamerican.com/article/wait-the-ozone-layer-is-still-declining1/.

"What Is Ozone?" *National Aeronautics and Space Administration.* https://ozonewatch.gsfc.nasa.gov/facts/SH.html.

EVOLUTION IV: HARVEST TO ROT
CYCLE 9: FRUITING

Ahmed, Mohsen Al Attar. "Monocultures of the Law: Legal Sameness in Restructuring of Global Agriculture." *The National Agriculture Law Center*, 2006. http://www.nationalaglawcenter.org/wp-content/uploads/assets/bibarticles/ahmed_monocultures.pdf.

"Child Labor and Slavery in the Chocolate Market." *Food Empowerment Project.* http://foodispower.org/human-labor-slavery/slavery-chocolate/.

Dean, Rochelle R. "Poverty in America." *The Borgen Project*, April 27, 2017. https://borgenproject.org/poverty-in-america/.

"Definition of Fair Trade." *Home of Fair Trade Enterprises.* https://wfto.com/fair-trade/definition-fair-trade.

"Fruit Trees." *Eartheasy.* https://learn.eartheasy.com/guides/fruit-trees/.

"How Long Do Fruit Trees Live?" *Dave Wilson Nursery.* https://www.davewilson.com/question/how-long-do-fruit-trees-live.

"Industrial Agriculture." *Union of Concerned Scientists.* https://www.ucsusa.org/
our-work/food-agriculture/our-failing-food-system/industrial-agriculture.

Naidoo, Kumi. "The Food System We Choose Affects Biodiversity: Do We Want
Monocultures?" *The Guardian*, May 22, 2014. https://www.theguardian.com/
sustainable-business/food-system-monocultures-gm-un-diversity-day.

"Sustainable Development Goals." *United Nations.* http://www.un.org/
sustainabledevelopment/poverty/.

"Sustainable Development Goal 1: End Poverty in all Its Forms Everywhere." *United
Nations.* https://sustainabledevelopment.un.org/sdg1.

"What is Fair Trade?" *Fair Trade Campaigns.* https://fairtradecampaigns.org/about/faq/.

"What is the Current Poverty Rate in the United States?" *Center for Poverty
Research, UC Davis*, October 15, 2018. https://poverty.ucdavis.edu/faq/
what-current-poverty-rate-united-states.

"Why Fair Trade." *Fair Trade Certified.* https://www.fairtradecertified.org/
why-fair-trade.

Williams, Simone. "What is the Definition of a Third-World Country?" *The Borgen
Project*, March 12, 2018. https://borgenproject.org/definition-
of-a-third-world-country/.

CYCLE 10: ROOT ROT – THE TIPPING POINT

Baer, Drake. "19 'Local and Natural' Brands That Are Owned by Giant Corporations."
Business Insider, August 27, 2014. https://www.businessinsider.com/
natural-brands-owned-by-large-corporations-2014-8.

Catalyst, Women CEOs of the S&P 500 (August 13, 2019). https://www.catalyst.org/
research/women-ceos-of-the-sp-500/.

"Coke Buys Odwalla." *CNN Money*, October 30, 2001. https://money.cnn.
com/2001/10/30/deals/coke_odwalla/.

Collings, Richard. "Annie's Stock Jumps on Acquisition by General Mills." *The Street*,
September 9, 2014. https://www.thestreet.com/story/12872364/1/annies-stock-
jumps-on-acquisition-by-general-mills.html.

"Energy Use and Energy Efficiency Opportunities in Restaurants." *EnergyStar.* https://
www.energystar.gov/ia/business/small_business/restaurant_factsheet.pdf.

Hyman, Mark. "Are You a Food Addict." *Dr. Hyman.* https://drhyman.com/
blog/2015/04/24/are-you-a-food-addict/.

Kress, R. "Numbers Show Women-Led Companies Outperform Competitors." *Ivy Exec.*
https://www.ivyexec.com/career-advice/2017/women-led-companies-
outperform-competitors/.

Leonard, Jayne. "Junk Food and Diabetes: Tips for Eating Out." *Medical News* Today,
April 5, 2019. https://www.medicalnewstoday.com/articles/317122.php.

McNeal-Leary, Tonya. "Companies with Lots of Women Are Actually More Successful."
Forbes, June 23, 2016. https://www.forbes.com/sites/tonyamcnealweary/2016/06/23/
companies-with-lots-of-women-are-actually-more-successful/#1360b0f76e36.

Mudie, S., E.A. Essah, A. Grandison, R. Felgate, "Electricity use in the commercial
kitchen." *International Journal of Low-Carbon Technologies*, Volume 11, Issue 1,
March 2016, Pages 66–74, https://academic.oup.com/ijlct/article/11/1/66/2363520.

Tartakovsky, Margarita. "Wearing Your Weight as Armor." *PsychCentral*, March 16,
2019. https://psychcentral.com/blog/wearing-your-weight-as-armor/.

"The State of the Gender Pay Gap 2019." *Payscale.* https://www.payscale.com/data/
gender-pay-gap.

"This Infographic Shows How Only 10 Companies Own All the World's Food Brands." *Someecards*, January 18, 2019. https://www.someecards.com/news/food/this-infographic-shows-how-only-10-companies-own-all-the-worlds-food-brands/.

Sieh, Marty. "Foodservice Finds Sustainability Reduces Costs by 30 Percent." *Food Safety Magazine*, September 10, 2018. https://www.foodsafetymagazine.com/signature-series/foodservice-finds-sustainability-reduces-costs-by-30-percent/.

DIGGING DEEPER IV

Aldred, Jessica. "Timeline: Al Gore." *The Guardian*, October 12, 2007. https://www.theguardian.com/environment/2007/oct/12/climatechange1.

"Award Ceremony Speech." *The Nobel Prize*. https://www.nobelprize.org/prizes/peace/1993/ceremony-speech/.

"Dolly the Sheep." *Science Daily*. https://www.sciencedaily.com/terms/dolly_the_sheep.htm.

Dunlop, Stewart. "A Personal Review of An Inconvenient Truth Documentary." *DocumentaryTube*, 2015. http://www.documentarytube.com/articles/a-personal-review-of-an-inconvenient-truth-documentary.

Eversley, Melanie. "Oklahoma City Area Targeted by Tornado was Hit in '99." *USA Today*, May 20, 2013. https://www.usatoday.com/story/news/nation/2013/05/20/oklahoma-city-tornado-1999/2343937/.

"Food Addiction." *WebMD*, August 3, 2018. https://www.webmd.com/mental-health/eating-disorders/binge-eating-disorder/mental-health-food-addiction#1.

Hoerle, Scotte. "Spotlight On: Ruth Bader Ginsburg." *Rocky Mountain Arts Association*, January 21, 2019. https://www.rmarts.org/dwc/spotlight-on-ruth-bader-ginsburg/.

"How Farm Subsidies Encourage the Big to Get Bigger." *National Sustainable Agriculture Coalition*. December 21, 2017. http://sustainableagriculture.net/blog/farm-subsidies-encourage-big-get-bigger/.

Langford, Sam. "Break the Internet: Remembering That Time Y2K Threatened to Kill Us All." *Junkee.com*, February 5, 2019. https://junkee.com/y2k-bug-1999-hoax/192228.

"Nelson Mandela: Biographical." *The Nobel Prize*. https://www.nobelprize.org/prizes/peace/1993/mandela/biographical/.

Olsen, Natalie. "Junk Food and Diabetes: Tips for Eating Out." *Medical News Today*, April 5, 2019. https://www.medicalnewstoday.com/articles/317122.php.

"The Cold War: Causes, Major Events, and How it Ended." *History on the Net*. https://www.historyonthenet.com/cold-war-causes-major-events-ended.

Wells, Jeff. "12 Natural and Organic Brands Owned by Big Food." *Mental Floss*, January 13, 2016. http://mentalfloss.com/article/72624/12-natural-and-organic-brands-owned-big-food.

EVOLUTION V: MATURITY
CYCLE 11: RESTORATION

"195 American Firstlady quotes." *Successories*. https://www.successories.com/iquote/category/144/american-firstlady-quotes/1.

"A Super Brief and Basic Explanation of Epigenetics for Total Beginners." *What is Epigenetics*, July 30, 2018. https://www.whatisepigenetics.com/what-is-epigenetics/.

"Books." *Bruce Lipton*. https://www.brucelipton.com/books.

Brady. Adam. "Nature Therapy: How Nature Can Help Heal and Expand Your Awareness." *The Chopra Center.* https://chopra.com/articles/nature-therapy-how-nature-can-help-heal-and-expand-your-awareness.

"Compulsive Behaviors." *Psychology Today.* https://www.psychologytoday.com/us/basics/compulsive-behaviors.

Dickerson, Kelly. "Mount Everest Isn't the Earth's Tallest Mountain." *Business Insider,* June 3, 2015. https://www.businessinsider.com/earths-tallest-mountain-is-hawaii-2015-6.

Fernando, Nimali. "Gardening with Kids: How It Affects Your Child's Brain, Body and Soul." *PBS for Parents,* March 16, 2016. https://www.pbs.org/parents/thrive/gardening-with-kids-how-it-affects-your-childs-brain-body-and-soul.

Gates, Donna. *Body Ecology Diet: Recovering Your Health and Rebuilding Your Immunity.* Hay House Inc, 2011.

Groves, Alex and Cesar Gamboa. "The Tucker Wildlife Sanctuary presents 'Wolves: Myths and Legends.'" *Daily Titan,* October 6, 2014. https://dailytitan.com/2014/10/the-tucker-wildlife-sanctuary-presents-wolves-myths-and-legends/.

"Help with Addiction and Substance Use Disorders." *American Psychiatric Association.* https://www.psychiatry.org/patients-families/addiction.

Jane. "20 Inspiring Quotes from Lao Tzu." *Habits for Wellbeing.* https://www.habitsforwellbeing.com/20-inspiring-quotes-from-lao-tzu/.

Kowalski, Kyle. "A Deep Look at 'A New Earth' by Eckhart Tolle." *SLOWW,* December 13, 2018. https://www.sloww.co/eckhart-tolle-a-new-earth-101/.

"Loving-Kindness Meditation." *The Center for Contemplative Mind in Society.* http://www.contemplativemind.org/practices/tree/loving-kindness.

McLeod, Saul. "Id, Ego, and Superego." *Simple Psychology,* 2016. https://www.simplypsychology.org/psyche.html.

"Meet Dr. Daniel Amen." http://danielamenmd.com/about/.

Nemko, Marty. "On An Albert Ellis Quote: How Much Free Will Do We Really Have?" *Psychology Today,* August 19, 2016. https://www.psychologytoday.com/us/blog/how-do-life/201608/albert-ellis-quote.

"Nessa Carey." http://www.nessacarey.co.uk/.

"Nutrition & the Epigenome." *Learn Genetics.* https://learn.genetics.utah.edu/content/epigenetics/nutrition/.

Parris, Jennifer. "10 Surprising Work-from-Home Jobs for Moms." *Working Mother,* June 7, 2019. https://www.workingmother.com/10-surprising-work-from-home-jobs-for-moms.

Rodenhizer, Samuel. "'Be Patient with Yourself. Self-Growth is Tender; It's Holy Ground.' (STEPHEN COVEY)." *Quotation Celebration,* March 19, 2018. https://quotationcelebration.wordpress.com/2018/03/19/be-patient-with-yourself-self-growth-is-tender-its-holy-ground-stephen-covey/.

Siegal, Daniel. "Dr. Dan Siegel on Neuroplasticity: An Excerpt from Mind." *PsychAlive.* https://www.psychalive.org/dr-daniel-siegel-neuroplasticity/.

Sorgen, Carol. "Do You Need a Nature Prescription?" *WebMD.* https://www.webmd.com/balance/features/nature-therapy-ecotherapy#1.

"The Brain-Gut Connection." *John's Hopkins Medicine.* https://www.hopkinsmedicine.org/health/wellness-and-prevention/the-brain-gut-connection.

"The Human Microbiome Project." *Baylor College of Medicine.* https://www.bcm.edu/departments/molecular-virology-and-microbiology/research/the-human-microbiome-project.

"The Human Microbiome Project." *Baylor College of Medicine.* https://www.
bcm.edu/departments/molecular-virology-and-microbiology/research/
the-human-microbiome-project.

"The Neuroscience of Addiction and Recovery." *The Best Brain Possible,*
February 18, 2018. https://www.thebestbrainpossible.com/
neuroplasticity-addiction-recovery-brain/.

"What is Addiction?" *Center on Addiction.* https://www.centeronaddiction.org/
addiction.

Williams, Terry Tempest. *When Women Were Birds: Fifty-Four Variations on Voice.* New
York: Sarah Crichton Books, 2012.

"Your Mind Is a Garden That Only You Can Tend To." *Musevault:
Wordpress,* March 7, 2012. https://musevault.wordpress.com/2012/03/07/
your-mind-is-a-garden-that-only-you-can-tend-to/.

CYCLE 12: REGENERATION

"Cities for Climate Protection Campaign." *United Nations Sustainable Development.*
https://sustainabledevelopment.un.org/partnership/?p=1498.

"Climate Change Quotes." *Earth Future.* http://www.earthfuture.com/stormyweather/
articles/quotes.asp.

"Eco Quotes." *Feminist.com.* https://www.feminist.com/resources/quotes/quotes_eco.
html.

"Fermented Foods: How to 'Culture' Your Way to Optimal Health." *Mercola.* https://
articles.mercola.com/fermented-foods.aspx.

Gunders, Dana. "Wasted: How America Is Losing Up to 40 Percent of Its Food from
Farm to Fork to Landfill." *Natural Resources Defense Council,* August 2012. https://
www.nrdc.org/resources/wasted-how-america-losing-
40-percent-its-food-farm-fork-landfill.

"Hawai'i State Legislature: Bill Status and Documents." *Hawai'i State Legislature.* 2012.
http://www.capitol.hawaii.gov/.

"HB2703 HD2." *Hawai'i State Legislature.* 2012. https://www.capitol.hawaii.gov/ses-
sion2012/Bills/HB2703_HD2_.pdf.

"Increase Food Security and Food Self-Sufficiency Strategy." http://hawaiicountyag.
com/images/pdf/INCREASED%20FOOD%20SECURITY%20AND%20
FOOD%20SELF%20SUFFICIENCY%20STRATEGY.pdf.

"Key Facts on Food Loss and Waste You Should Know!" *Food and Agriculture
Organization of the United Nations.* http://www.fao.org/save-food/resources/
keyfindings/en/.

Mercola, Joseph. "Fermented Foods: How to 'Culture' Your Way to Optimal Health."
Dr. Mercola. https://articles.mercola.com/fermented-foods.aspx.

"North Kohala Community Development Plan." *Hawai'i County Planning Department.*
https://www.hawaiicountycdp.info/north-kohala-cdp.

Office of Planning. "Increased Food Security and Food Self-Sufficiency Strategy."
Department of Agriculture, October 2012. http://hawaiicountyag.com/images/pdf/
INCREASED%20FOOD%20SECURITY%20AND%20FOOD%20SELF%20
SUFFICIENCY%20STRATEGY.pdf.

Rosenthal, Joshua. *Integrative Nutrition: Feed Your Hunger for Health and Happiness.*
Integrative Nutrition Publishing, 2007.

Sundaram, Jomo Kwame. "The World Produces Enough Food to Feed
Everyone. So Why Do People Go Hungry?" *World Economic*

Forum, July 11, 2016. https://www.weforum.org/agenda/2016/07/
the-world-produces-enough-food-to-feed-everyone-so-why-do-people-go-hungry.

"The Story of Stuff." YouTube Video. 21:16. "The Story of Stuff Project," April 22, 2009. https://www.youtube.com/watch?v=9GorqroigqM.

"The World Produces Enough Food to Feed Everyone. So Why Do People Go Hungry?" *World Economic Forum*. https://www.weforum.org/agenda/2016/07/
the-world-produces-enough-food-to-feed-everyone-so-why-do-people-go-hungry.

"Total Number of Farmers Markets in the United States from 1994 to 2014." *Statista*, August 14, 2014. https://www.statista.com/statistics/253243/
total-number-of-farmers-markets-in-the-united-states/.

"Wangarĩ Muta Maathai." *Wangari Maathai Community School*. https://wangari-
maathaischool.org/wangari-maathai/.

Wheatley, Margaret J. "It's an Interconnected World." *Margaret J. Wheatly*, April 2002. https://margaretwheatley.com/articles/interconnected.html.

DIGGING DEEPER V

Kearns, Jeff, Hannah Dormido and Alyssa McDonald. "China's War on Pollution Will Change the World." *Bloomberg*, March 9, 2018. https://www.bloomberg.com/
graphics/2018-china-pollution/.

Amadeo, Kimberly. "ARRA, Its Details, With Pros and Cons." *The Balance*, July 30, 2019. https://www.thebalance.com/arra-details-3306299.

Aris, Aziz, and Samuel Leblanc. 2011. "Maternal and Fetal Exposure to Pesticides Associated to Genetically Modified Foods in Eastern Townships of Quebec, Canada." *Reproductive Toxicology* 31 (4): 528–33.

Associated Press in Washington. "Air Pollution in China is Killing 4,000 People Every Day, a New Study Finds." *The Guardian*, August 14, 2015. https://www.theguardian.com/world/2015/aug/14/
air-pollution-in-china-is-killing-4000-people-every-day-a-new-study-finds.

Berry, Wendell. *The Art of the Commonplace: The Agrarian Essays of Wendell Berry*. New York: Counterpoint, 2003. Accessed August 15, 2019.

Blinder, Alan S., and Mark Zandi. "The Financial Crisis: Lessons for the Next One." *Center on Budget and Policy Priorities*, October 15, 2015. https://www.cbpp.org/
research/economy/the-financial-crisis-lessons-for-the-next-one.

Borenstein, Seth. "Global Warming Seen as More Concrete, Urgent Problem Since Kyoto." *PBS*, November 19, 2015. https://www.pbs.org/newshour/world/
global-warming-seen-as-more-concrete-urgent-problem-since-kyoto.

Borger, Julianne. "Bush Kills Global Warming Treaty." *The Guardian*, March 29, 2001. https://www.theguardian.com/environment/2001/mar/29/globalwarming.usnews.

Chapman, John. "The Real Reasons Bush Went to War." *The Guardian*, July 27, 2004. https://www.theguardian.com/world/2004/jul/28/iraq.usa.

Dunwell, Matt. "Bill Mollison Obituary." *The Guardian*, October 10, 2016. https://
www.theguardian.com/environment/2016/oct/10/bill-mollison-obituary.

"Enron Corporation - Company Profile, Information, Business Description, History, Background Information on Enron Corporation." *Reference for Business*. https://
www.referenceforbusiness.com/history2/57/Enron-Corporation.html.

Ghadban, Najib. "The War on Iraq: Justifications and Motives." *Aljazeera*, August 10, 2003. https://www.aljazeera.com/archive/2003/08/2008410151856461833.html.

Higgs, Micaela Marini. "America's New Recycling Crisis, Explained by an Expert." *Vox*, April 2, 2019. https://www.vox.com/the-goods/2019/4/2/18290956/
recycling-crisis-china-plastic-operation-national-sword.

Holstein, E.H., R.W. Thier, A.S. Munson, and K.E. Gibson. "The Spruce Beetle." *United States Department of Agriculture. Forest Insect and Disease Leaflet 127*, November 1999. https://www.fs.usda.gov/Internet/FSE_DOCUMENTS/fsb-dev2_043099.pdf.

Joyce, Christopher. "Where Will Your Plastic Trash Go Now That China Doesn't Want It?" *NPR*, March 13, 2019. https://www.npr.org/sections/goatsand-soda/2019/03/13/702501726/where-will-your-plastic-trash-go-now-that-china-doesnt-want-it.

Kelley, Ernest J. *God-Life*. Xulon Press, 2009.

Lau, Eric. "Developing Honesty and Integrity." *MyStarJob*, July 11, 2015. http://mystar-job.com/articles/story.aspx?file=/2015/7/11/mystarjob_careerguide/3650344&sec=mystarjob_careerguide.

"Network." *Rotten Tomatoes*. https://www.rottentomatoes.com/m/network/.

Osborne, Hillary. "Stern Report: The Key Points." *The Guardian*, October 30, 2006. https://www.theguardian.com/politics/2006/oct/30/economy.uk.

"Prestige oil tanker disaster crew acquitted in Spain." *BBC*, November 13, 2013. https://www.bbc.com/news/world-europe-24930976.

Rich, Robert. "The Great Recession: December 2007–June 2009." *Federal Reserve History*. https://www.federalreservehistory.org/essays/great_recession_of_200709.

"The Recession That Is Already Here, and What to Do About It." *NewFireGiving*, February 6, 2018. https://www.newfiregiving.com/the-recession-that-is-already-here-and-what-to-do-about-it/.

Vidal, John. "The Environment in the Decade of Climate Change." *The Guardian*, October 16, 2009. https://www.theguardian.com/environment/2009/oct/17/environment-decade-climate-change-vidal.

"War-Terror." *The Price of Oil*. http://priceofoil.org/thepriceofoil/war-terror/.

"What is the Kyoto Protocol?" *United Nations: Climate Change*. https://unfccc.int/kyoto_protocol.

"What's Bugging Alaska's Forests? Spruce Beetle Facts and Figures." *Alaska Department of Natural Resource: Division of Forestry*. http://forestry.alaska.gov/insects/sprucebeetle.

Woolsley, GL. "GMO Timeline: A History of Genetically Modified Foods." *Rosebud*, December 3, 2013. http://www.rosebudmag.com/truth-squad/gmo-timeline-a-history-of-genetically-modified-foods.

EVOLUTION VI: OLD GROWTH
CYCLE 13: AWAKENED

"Bioneers: Purpose." *Bioneers: Revolution from the Heart of Nature*. https://bioneers.org/about/purpose/.

"Hānai." *Hawaiian Dictionary*. http://wehewehe.org/gsdl2.85/cgi-bin/hdict?e=q-11000-00---off-0hdict--00-1----0-10-0---0---0direct-10-ED--4-------0-1lp0--11-en-Zz-1---Zz-1-home-hanai--00-3-1-00-0--4----0-0-11-10-0utfZz-8-00&a=d&d=D2868.

Kaushik. "Bristlecone Pines – The Oldest Trees on Earth." Amusing Planet, June 2, 2013. https://www.amusingplanet.com/2013/07/bristlecone-pines-oldest-trees-on-earth.html.

"Rep. Tulsi Gabbard Celebrates Earth Day and Action to Improve and Protect Coastal Reefs in Hawai`i." *Congresswoman Tulsi Gabbard*, April 22, 2015. https://gabbard.house.gov/news/press-releases/rep-tulsi-gabbard-celebrates-earth-day-and-action-improve-and-protect-coastal.

"Stephan Dinan." *Evolutionary Leaders.* https://www.evolutionaryleaders.net/leaders/sdinan.

DIGGING DEEPER VI

Akwasane Notes. *Basic Call to Consciousness.* (Summertown, TN: Book Publishing Company, 1995).

"APA Stress in America™ Survey: US at 'Lowest Point We Can Remember;' Future of Nation Most Commonly Reported Source of Stress." *American Psychological Association,* November 1, 2017. https://www.apa.org/news/press/releases/2017/11/lowest-point.

"Climate and Health Showdown in the Courts: State Attorneys General Prepare to Fight." *NYU School of Law State Energy and Environmental Impact Center,* March 2019. https://www.law.nyu.edu/sites/default/files/climate-and-health-showdown-in-the-courts.pdf.

"Ecuador Adopts Rights of Nature in Constitution." *Global Alliance for the Rights of Nature.* https://therightsofnature.org/ecuador-rights/.

"Fact Check: President Trump's Speech on Intention to Withdraw from the Paris Agreement, 1 June 2017." *Climate Analytics.* https://climateanalytics.org/media/fact_check_trump_pa_withdrawal_announcement.pdf.

Francois, Willie D. "Trump's USDA Threatens Food Security for Hard-Working Americans." *The Hill,* February 12, 2019. https://thehill.com/opinion/civil-rights/429508-trumps-usda-threatens-food-security-for-hard-working-americans.

Hawken, Paul. *Project Drawdown: The Most Comprehensive Plan Ever Proposed to Reverse Global Warming.* Penguin Books: April 18, 2017.

"Humanizing Trees: The Fascinating Research of Suzanne Simard." *Plant Solutions.* https://plantsolutions.com/humanizing-trees-fascinating-research-suzanne-simard/.

Irfan, Umair. "Restoring Forests May be One of Our Most Powerful Weapons in Fighting Climate Change." *Vox,* July 5, 2019. https://www.vox.com/2019/7/4/20681331/climate-change-solutions-trees-deforestation-reforestation.

Lyons, Oren. Interview with Bill Moyers. *Oren Lyons the Faithkeeper.* Bill Moyers. July 3, 1991. https://billmoyers.com/content/oren-lyons-the-faithkeeper/.

Makower, Joel. "'Drawdown' and Global Warming's Hopeful New Math." *GreenBiz,* April 17, 2017. https://www.greenbiz.com/article/drawdown-and-global-warmings-hopeful-new-math.

McKie, Robin. "Portrait of a Planet on the Verge of Climate Catastrophe." *The Guardian,* December 2, 2018. https://www.theguardian.com/environment/2018/dec/02/world-verge-climate-catastophe.

Orr, David W. *"Ecological Literacry: Educating Our Children for a Sustainable World"* October 1st 2005 https://www.ecoliteracy.org/book/ecological-literacy-educating-our-children-sustainable-world

Popocih, Nadja, Livia Albeck-Ripka and Kendra Pierre-Louis. "84 Environmental Rules Being Rolled Back Under Trump." *New York Times,* June 7, 2019. https://www.nytimes.com/interactive/2019/climate/trump-environment-rollbacks.html.

"Prof. Suzanne Simard Talks About 'Mother Trees.'" *Faculty of Forestry.* https://forestry.ubc.ca/2011/05/prof-suzanne-simard-talks-about-mother-trees/.

Rufo, Christopher. "An Addiction Crisis Disguised as a Housing Crisis: Opioids are Fueling Homelessness on the West Coast." *City Journal,* June 14, 2019. https://www.city-journal.org/opiods-homelessness-west-coast.

Simard, Suzanne. "How Trees Talk to Each Other." Filmed June 2016 in Alberta, Canada. TED Video, 18:11. https://www.ted.com/talks/suzanne_simard_how_trees_talk_to_each_other.

Sleeth, Nancy. *Go Green, Save Green: A Simple Guide to Saving Time, Money, and God's Green Earth*. Nashville, TN: Daniel Literary Group, 2009.

Stevens, Fisher, Leonardo DiCaprio, Trevor Davidoski, Jennifer Davisson Killoran, Brett Ratner, James Packer, Mark Monroe, et al. *Before the Flood*. 2017.

Taylor, Lenore. "Enough Scandalous Time-Wasting on Climate Change. Let's Get Back to the Facts." *The Guardian*, March 12, 2019. https://www.theguardian.com/environment/2019/mar/13/enough-scandalous-time-wasting-on-climate-change-lets-get-back-to-the-facts.

"The Truth About Big Oil and Climate Change." *The Economist*, February 9, 2019. https://www.economist.com/leaders/2019/02/09/the-truth-about-big-oil-and-climate-change.

Vince, Gaia. "The Heat is On Over the Climate Crisis. Only Radical Measures Will Work." *The Guardian*, May 18, 2019. https://www.theguardian.com/environment/2019/may/18/climate-crisis-heat-is-on-global-heating-four-degrees-2100-change-way-we-live.

Wallace-Wells, David. "It is Absolutely Time to Panic About Climate Change." *Vox*, February 24, 2019. https://www.vox.com/energy-and-environment/2019/2/22/18188562/climate-change-david-wallace-wells-the-uninhabitable-earth.

"Wangari Matthai: Nobel Peace Prize and Environmental Activist." *Tottenhamtrees*. https://www.tottenhamtrees.org/wangari-maathai.html.

Women in the World Staff. "'I Want You to Panic': Climate Activist Greta Thunberg, 16, Lays it on the Line for World Leaders." *Women in the World*, January 29, 2019. https://womenintheworld.com/2019/01/29/i-want-you-to-panic-climate-activist-greta-thunberg-16-lays-it-on-the-line-for-world-leaders/.

"World 'Nearing Critical Point of No Return' on Climate Change, Delegate Warns, as Second Committee Debates Sustainable Development." *United Nations Meetings Coverage*, October 15, 2018. https://www.un.org/press/en/2018/gaef3500.doc.htm.

Yam, Kimberly. "This Video Will Turn Even the Biggest Cynic into A Tree-Hugger." *Huffpost*, April 22, 2015. https://www.huffpost.com/entry/prince-ea-video_n_7118988.

Aloha Beautiful Souls,
I look forward to connecting and co-creating with you.
We are the Soulution.

www.donnamaltz.com
https://www.facebook.com/dmaloha
https://twitter.com/Soil2Soulutions
https://www.instagram.com/soiltosoulsolutions/
https://www.linkedin.com/in/donna-maltz-soil-to-soul-entrepreneur-b6b47b8/
https://www.goodreads.com/user/show/40944963-donna-maltz

If you enjoyed this book, please share, leave a review
or wherever, to help others find it. MAHALO!

If you have a child or know someone who does,
please check out my other book
Yummy Recipes ~ Wilderness Wonders for Kids and Adults.
https://donnamaltz.com/book-2/

Profits from my books go to protect our Mother Earth.

Many Blessings and Big Love, Mama Donna

CPSIA information can be obtained
at www.ICGtesting.com
Printed in the USA
LVHW042258280422
717483LV00005B/700